HOSPITALITY
MANAGEMENT
LIBRARY

Human Resources

David Wheelhouse

Disclaimer

The author, David Wheelhouse, is solely responsible for the contents of this publication. All views expressed herein are solely those of the author and do not necessarily reflect the views of the Educational Institute of the American Hotel & Motel Association (the Institute) or the American Hotel & Motel Association (AH&MA). Nothing contained in this publication shall constitute an endorsement by the Institute or AH&MA of any information, opinion, procedure, or product mentioned, and the Institute and AH&MA disclaim any liability with respect to the use of any such information, procedure, or product, or reliance thereon.

Neither AH&MA nor the Institute makes or recommends industry standards. Nothing in this publication shall be construed as a recommendation by the Institute or AH&MA to be adopted by, or binding upon, any member of the hospitality industry.

©Copyright 1989
By the EDUCATIONAL INSTITUTE of the
AMERICAN HOTEL & MOTEL ASSOCIATION
1407 South Harrison Road
P.O. Box 1240
East Lansing, Michigan 48826

The Educational Institute of the American
Hotel & Motel Association is a nonprofit
educational foundation.

Printed in the United States of America
   3 4 5 6 7 8 9 10 93 92 91 90

Library of Congress Cataloging-in-Publication Data
Wheelhouse, David R.
   Managing human resources in the hospitality industry.

   Bibliography: p. 445
   Includes index.
   1. Hotels, taverns, etc.—Personnel management—
Handbooks, manuals, etc.   I. American Hotel & Motel
Association. Educational Institute.   II. Title.
TX911.3.P4W44 1989 647.94'068'3 89–11661
ISBN 0–86612–045–9

Editors: Timothy J. Eaton
            Kent F. Premo

Contents

Preface

Managing Human Resources in the Hospitality Industry is a handbook and guide for hospitality managers—managers who make human resources decisions on a daily, if not hourly, basis. While written primarily with the operating manager in mind, the book serves many other audiences as well—hospitality management students, individuals just beginning their careers in human resources management or who have just been promoted into the human resources function, and human resources managers, to name a few. Top management, too, should find it very helpful in shaping the human resources strategies that will determine the productivity of the worker and the quality of service. On a broader scale, even though the book's examples and illustrations are chiefly oriented toward hospitality organizations, the book is useful for managers in every service setting.

In the world of hospitality, guidelines for determining food costs and marketing budgets are commonplace, yet guidelines for managing human resources expenses, such as training and turnover, are often non-existent. These areas offer great potential for savings and return on investment. This book provides a framework for establishing such guidelines. It also provides a common language for communicating important human resources matters between all levels of management.

Lately, hospitality organizations have been placing greater emphasis on human resources management. They are investing more money into this management function and depending on human resources departments more and more. The size and budget associated with human resources departments have grown steadily in recent years, as has their scope of responsibility, accountability, and influence. This expanded role is mirrored by the growing preference of businesses for the broader term "human resources" over "personnel." Still, readers should feel free to regard all references to the terms "human resources" and "personnel" as interchangeable. In fact, as an aspect of the management of people, "personnel" is alive and well and quite respectable. Personnel forms, personnel files, and personnel processing are vital to the operation of any business.

Increasingly, hospitality organizations have found they can't operate or manage effectively without a human resources department—even smaller operations where such departments were thought to be unnecessary just a few years ago. Thus, the book sometimes assumes that a personnel or human resources department is in place within the organization. However, we recognize that the hospitality industry comprises establishments of all types and sizes, and that many aren't large enough to justify the creation of a separate office or position. In these operations it's usually the general manager who handles the human resources function, as well as marketing and other key management areas. Whatever the arrangement of the organization, one person must be responsible for management and coordination of all aspects of the human resources function.

The body of legislation that deals with the worker and the work environment is growing and changing rapidly; therefore, particular emphasis is given to the background and the intent, or spirit, of the laws, so as to lay a solid foundation on which to base plans and decisions. Intelligent decisions can only be made if there's a clear understanding of the principle involved. Philosophy, legal considerations, and principle serve as background for the practical how-to steps and examples that relate to day-to-day activities.

No one book—or any collection of books, for that matter—can tell managers all they need to know. A book can only tell what to do and how to do it. Knowing when and where is a matter of judgment. Decisions are made on the floor as managers respond to real-life situations. A human resources or personnel department can furnish support, education, and assistance, but the management of human resources is the job of *managers*.

I wish to thank the following reviewers for their significant contributions to this text: Ann Atkinson, Vice President of Training, Management & Organization Development, Days Inn of America, Inc., Atlanta, Georgia; Steve Bittove, Director of Human Resources, The Westin Hotel, Detroit, Michigan; Bill Clifford, CHA, Senior Vice President of Human Resources, MHM, Inc., Dallas, Texas; Mike Cothran, CHA, Director of Education and Training, Quality Inns, Silver Spring, Maryland; Frank Danehy, Vice President/Director of Training, Franchise Division, The Sheraton Corporation, Boston; Jim Hart, CHA, Vice President Human Resources, Mississippi Management, Inc., Jackson, Mississippi; Nick Horney, Ph.D., Corporate Director of Training, Stouffer Hotel Company, Solon, Ohio; Carole Kohn, Vice President, Human Resources, Lincoln Hotels, Dallas, Texas; Mike Mallott, Manager, Systems Implementation, Hampton Inn Hotel Division, Memphis, Tennessee; and Bob Moister, Director, Holiday Inn University, Olive Branch, Mississippi.

1 The Changing Role of Human Resources Management

Probably no other area of management has undergone more dramatic changes in recent years than that of human resources. These changes have been driven by powerful forces sweeping through society, business, and government.

One factor causing these changes has been the tremendous growth of the service sector. This explosive increase has created an even greater demand among hospitality companies for skilled workers. Not only must hospitality managers be able to recruit and hire competent employees, they also must be able to retain them despite strong competition from other employers.

In addition, the body of legislation relating to employment is growing at a startling rate. Such legislation makes interviewing and hiring employees both a technical and legal challenge for those with human resources responsibilities. Besides creating difficulties in the staffing process, legislation is also making it harder to dismiss employees who are performing below standards.

Add to these challenges the unique problems facing the hospitality industry. More and more hospitality properties are specializing in order to capture an ever-elusive market. The industry is plagued by high turnover, all too often reaching an annual percentage rate in the hundreds.

In order to meet these many challenges, hospitality employers must realize the vital importance of managing human resources in the service environment. This chapter addresses the major differences between management in manufacturing industries and management in service industries. In addition, it looks in greater detail at the unique situations faced by hospitality organizations. In this manner, we can build the foundation for a human resources strategy which recognizes the difficulties faced by hospitality managers while offering practical solutions for everyday problems.

Forces in the Labor Market

Managers everywhere, regardless of the nature of their business, are becoming acutely aware of changes affecting their labor supply. As the profile of the population changes, so does the nature of the work force available for staffing all types of businesses. Hospitality managers must compete for good workers not only with other hospitality managers, but also with every other sector of the business community.

To understand the challenges facing managers, we should look at some of the major forces shaping the labor market. These include the changing values of workers, the growing amount of legislation concerning the workplace, the shrinking labor market, and the changing demographics of the labor market. By understanding these forces, managers can better prepare themselves for the tasks of staffing and managing an organization.

Changing Values of Workers

In the early half of this century, simply having and keeping a job were a worker's primary concerns. Many workers were immigrants with a work ethic deeply rooted in the class system. They expected to be told what to do by those they perceived literally to be their "superiors." The manager's authority was absolute. The working class was poor, humble, and obedient, and they sacrificed to make things better for their children. The family, religion, and ethnic and neighborhood groups were at the center of their lives.

As years passed, however, the United States experienced great social, economic, political, and technological evolution. Social reforms and laws, organized labor, higher educational levels, and a better standard of living have all contributed to creating vastly different circumstances.

Work has taken on a greater significance as family and ethnic units break up and religious and community influences decline. For many, the job is now the central life role. Today's workers want:

- Jobs that are interesting, challenging, and fulfilling
- The opportunity to think for themselves, rather than just carrying out instructions
- The chance to see the results of their work and to be recognized and respected for it
- A say in how the company is run
- More latitude from their bosses
- Open lines of communications with their managers
- A chance to develop their skills

In short, workers are becoming less willing to perform boring jobs and are challenging the traditional management role which relied on the use of power and authority.

At the same time, workers expect their jobs to be harmonious with other personal considerations, such as health, leisure activities, family needs, and lifelong goals. As an outgrowth of this, many chain operations are finding it difficult and expensive to convince employees (particularly those from two-income families) to relocate.

Legislation

Legislators respond to social and economic changes by enacting new laws. In recent years, an enormous number of laws have been enacted to protect and control the working environment. In fact, possibly no other single factor has had more influence on the rapid growth of human resources departments than this growing body of legislation.

Exhibit 1.1 Employment Growth in the Hospitality Industry

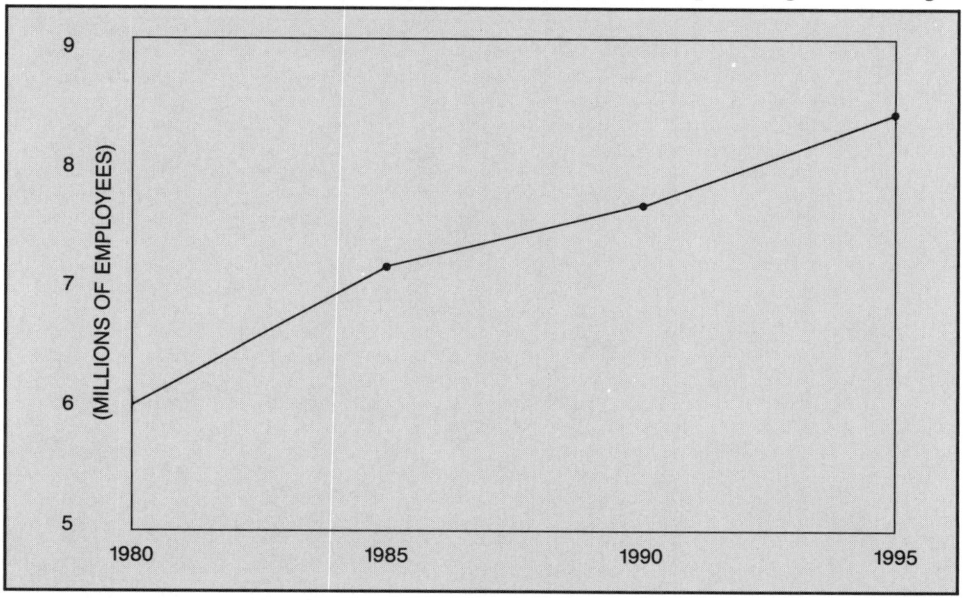

Sources: U.S. Bureau of the Census and J. Richard Sousane, "Hotels and Motels," U.S. Department of Commerce, *U.S. Industrial Outlook 1988* (Washington: Government Printing Office, 1988), pp. 64-1–64-4.

Shrinking Labor Market

The rate of growth of the labor market between 1986 and 2000 is expected to be only half that of the period between 1972 and 1986.[1] This slowdown is largely due to a decline in the number of young people who will be entering the work force. "Baby boomers" (the post-war generation born between 1946 and 1964) fueled our expanding labor market in earlier years. As they've grown older, however, this generation has moved from seeking entry-level jobs to occupying positions of skill and authority.

The decline in entry-level job seekers is particularly significant to the hospitality industry, which has traditionally relied on young workers and first-time job holders as the mainstay of its labor supply. In food service, for instance, about half of all workers are under the age of 25.[2] Exhibit 1.1 charts employment growth in the hospitality industry. Exhibit 1.2 reveals the enormous decline in the population of 16- to 24-year-olds over the same time frame. With the current shortage of young workers, the hospitality industry needs to look at alternative sources of labor.

Changing Demographics of the Labor Market

Besides the shrinking labor market, other demographic changes are likely to have major effects on the labor market. The U.S. Bureau of Labor Statistics has projected the breakdown of growth in the labor force between 1986 and 2000.[3] It predicts that 90% of the growth will come from minorities and females. It also projects the following for that period:

[1]Ronald E. Kutscher, "Overview and Implications of the Projections to 2000," *Monthly Labor Review*, Sept. 1987, p. 3.
[2]National Restaurant Association, "Food Service and the Labor Shortage," *NRA Current Issues Report*, Jan. 1986, p. 3.
[3]Kutscher, "Projections," pp. 3–4.

Exhibit 1.2 Decline in Population of 16- to 24-Year-Olds

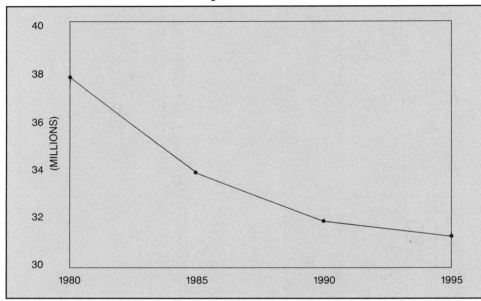

Source: U.S. Bureau of the Census.

- The number of blacks in the labor force will grow by 29%; approximately 17% of the growth in the labor force will be among blacks.

- The number of Hispanics in the labor force will grow by 74%; approximately 29% of the growth in the labor force will be among Hispanics.

- The number of Asians, Native Americans, Alaskan Natives, and Pacific Islanders in the labor force will grow by 70%; approximately 11% of the growth in the labor force will be among these groups.

- Women will account for 64% of the growth in, and will constitute more than 47% of, the labor force.

Since women are expected to make up a larger part of the work force, many employers are considering new benefits and programs directly targeted at attracting women. Programs such as child care, flexible hours, job sharing, and special parental leaves help women reconcile their multiple roles as parent, homemaker, and worker.

The work force is also aging rapidly. The number of workers between 35 and 46 will increase by 42% between 1985 and 1995.[4]

Today, our work force has more people from a variety of cultural, economic, and educational backgrounds. People of other nationalities and ethnic backgrounds may present special challenges in the form of different languages, social customs, and standards. Economically, culturally, and

---

[4]John Naisbitt and Patricia Aburdene, *Re-Inventing the Corporation* (New York: Warner Books, 1985), p. 14.

educationally disadvantaged workers are entering the work force in greater numbers, supported by government and private programs. Employers may have to provide training in the most basic skills, such as reading and social behavior, before job training can begin. Literacy training is becoming a major budget item for many employers.

A manager now needs to be flexible enough to deal both with workers who have limited schooling and social skills and with workers who are better educated than their supervisors.

Management in the Service Environment

Responding to these changes in the business environment is a significant challenge for every manager. The manager involved in a service-producing business faces unique additional challenges. The explosive growth of the service sector is creating more jobs than the labor market can fill. The U.S. Bureau of Labor Statistics projects 21 million new jobs for the period from 1986 to the year 2000, and the service sector will account for most of that growth.[5]

This rapid growth reflects a shift in our nation's economy from an industrial base to a service base (see Exhibit 1.3). The traditional approach to the management of human resources comes from the manufacturing environment. However, the successful approach to human resources management for service differs vastly from the manufacturing approach because of the enormous differences between these two industries. This means current managers often must learn different management skills and even give up beliefs and techniques that were once successful for them.

To understand the contrast between management approaches for manufacturing and those for service, it's helpful first to understand something of the development of a management philosophy oriented toward manufacturing: **scientific management**.

Scientific Management

Frederick Winslow Taylor was a pioneer in the formal study of work and how it's done. Perhaps the first "efficiency expert," he developed detailed time studies, job descriptions, and definitive manuals. His principles of scientific management, introduced in the early 1900s and sometimes called **Taylorism**, became the backbone of philosophies about managing people. His approach was to increase productivity by reducing each job to its simplest skill level and having each worker perform one task repeatedly. By measuring the time it took to perform any task, productivity standards could be set and checked.

As long as industrialism thrived and the immigrant work ethic predominated in the work force, scientific management was successful. Decisions were based on intensive studies and reports that required rigid work and production controls. Success was measured in terms of unit cost and output. Quality was measured in terms of inspection to standards, scrap piles, returned merchandise, warranted repairs, and other elements that were easy to measure.

Personnel policies and programs followed and supported this direction. They depended on detailed job and task analyses, repetitive work models,

[5]Kutscher, "Projections," p. 5.

Exhibit 1.3 Employment Growth of Manufacturing and Service Industries

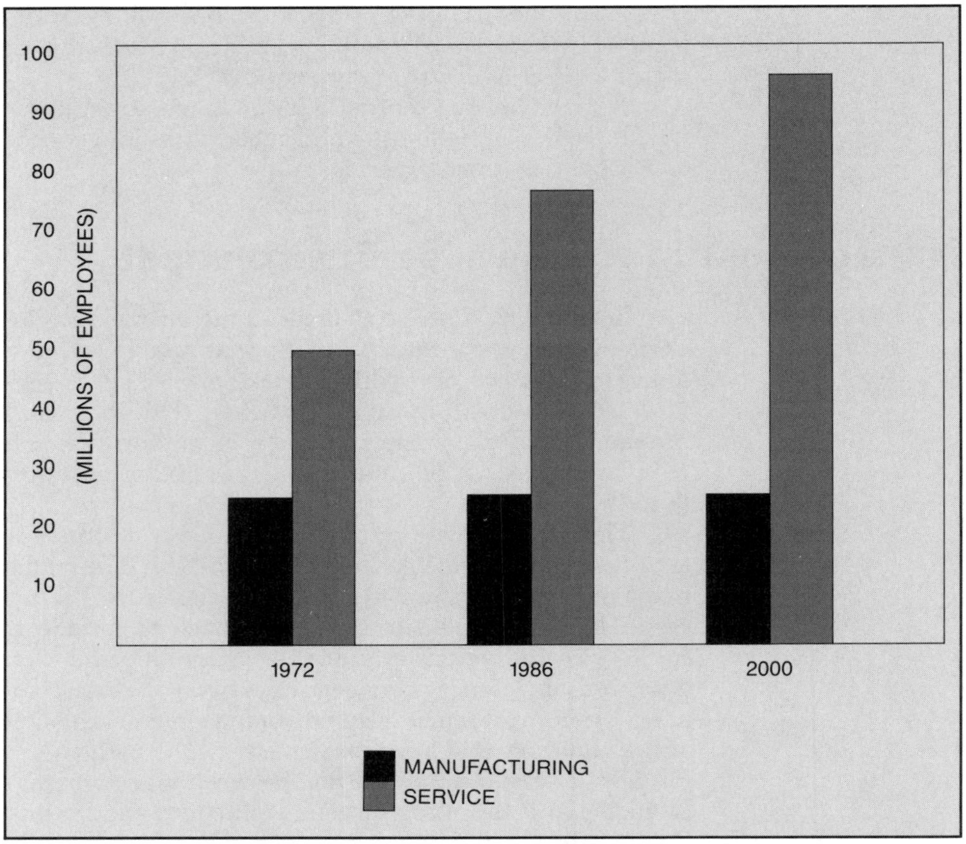

Source: Ronald E. Kutscher, "Overview and Implications of the Projections to 2000," *Monthly Labor Review*, September 1987, p. 5.

ranking, classifying, and comparison analyses. Job descriptions were extensive, narrowly defined, and highly restrictive—more suited to robots than to people. Enthusiasm, pride, attitude, and commitment were not considered key factors in the drive to increase productivity and quality.

How Service Differs from Manufacturing

Manufacturing companies have a strong financial orientation. From a manufacturing standpoint, money is the most important capital, a means of expansion and growth. From a service standpoint, *people* are the most important capital. They represent not only a company's major investment, but also its chief asset. Employees and their professional growth are more important than financial capital in determining the extent of company growth.

People are the biggest competitive edge that a service company has. No matter how much money the company invests or how well a facility is built, the employees will ultimately determine success. Quality, productivity, and consistency are determined by factors like sensitivity, responsiveness, helpfulness, friendliness, good instincts, courtesy, teamwork, risk-taking, initiative, flair, self-confidence, innovation, and creativity. The approach to human resources management must be designed to create an environment that will allow these factors to grow and develop.

Service is a "product" that, in many ways, is intangible and unmeasurable. For instance, one receptionist can help twenty people and drive ten of them away, while another can serve twenty so that all return again and again. According to scientific management principles, both receptionists meet the production quota, but only one represents success in service. If an employee's attitude is poor, guests cannot express their dissatisfaction by returning a product for exchange. Most don't even complain—they just don't come back.

Management by Measurement

Of course, hospitality operations do use measures and set standards of performance. Whether intended or not, what a company chooses to measure controls its direction, sets its priorities, and determines its values.

The routine in manufacturing allows managers to measure precisely all the elements of production and then manage by measurement. This is particularly true in centralized companies where the decisions are made by upper and middle managers who spend most of their time measuring, writing reports, and sending statistics up to top managers who analyze the operation. If more information is needed, special reports are ordered. How fast and ably managers handle reports is heavily emphasized on their salary reviews.

Management by exception, management by objectives, and other management techniques were designed for this environment of measurement. When these methods are applied to the service environment, however, they are less effective and often detrimental for many reasons. Measuring service is a far more complex process than measuring manufacturing quotas. A service manager has to evaluate three areas—financial success, guest satisfaction, and employee satisfaction—and all three must be given equal weight. Many key elements of these areas are difficult to measure. The factors that do get measured are often the less important ones. Measuring them can overemphasize their importance and even put priorities in the wrong order.

For example, if buspersons know that the only productivity standard by which their performance will be measured is how many tables they set, that will become their first priority. The result could be the creation of a manufacturing environment in a service outlet, with workers concentrating more on setting tables than on making guests happy.

In a similar way, the attention and priorities of managers may also be poorly directed. While the importance of controlling payroll costs clearly must never be overlooked, the coffee shop manager whose performance is evaluated largely on labor costs may wait until cover count increases substantially before hiring additional staff. Consequently, new employees are likely to start on a day when the restaurant is at its busiest and there is no time for training. Customers, employees, and the manager will probably all suffer, because no emphasis is placed on measuring guest satisfaction along with the number of people served.

The frequency of measurement may also poorly direct the attention and priorities of managers. As stated above, key elements of the service environment are often difficult to measure. If evaluated at all, they may not be measured as often as less important elements which are more easily measured. However, managers generally come to see the frequency of measurement as a clear indication of what upper management thinks is important. If labor cost is measured daily and guest satisfaction only monthly, labor cost will be seen to be more important.

In a service business, people are an important part of the product. (Courtesy of Bob Evans Farms, Columbus, Ohio)

In addition, how information is controlled and used (and by whom) will affect the organization's priorities and shape its environment. For example, controlling food cost, which is important in any food service business, should be the chef's responsibility. Far too often, however, the chef becomes overly involved in providing information for upper management to use in analyzing food cost and deciding how to control it. Time that the chef should spend working on the floor, managing employees, and controlling food cost directly is instead spent filling out reports and justifying variances. This emphasis often gives the appearance that the chef works for the controller, and that the controller is ultimately responsible for food cost.

Rather than telling the chef what information it wants, upper management should spend more time finding out what information the chef needs to control food cost. A key aspect of the controller's job is to support operating managers like the chef by providing them with the information they need to make informed decisions. This information should be in a format that is simple, concise, and readily understood by the average line manager.

Structure vs. Flexibility The scientific approach to human resources management may communicate other values that can detract from service. As we've seen, scientific management emphasizes structure, standardization, and the use of extremely detailed job descriptions and procedure manuals. If the work structure and training manuals involve doing things in only one very precise way, employees may be afraid to deviate from what's covered in the manual or job description. They may lose flexibility, responsiveness, initiative, and resourcefulness. When a problem arises that's not covered, confused employees—rather than helping the guest—may say, "Nobody told me," and just do nothing. This kind of response can be devastating in the service environment, where exceptions are the rule and every guest encounter must be handled personally.

Even something as seemingly harmless as having employees conform to a standardized speech, such as "Thank you, have a nice day," can take the "personal" out of personal service and make employees sound phony. Guests can tell, for instance, whether food servers are recommending the house special because they sincerely liked it or just because they were told to promote it.

Providing service often involves peaks and valleys of business that cannot be accommodated by structured jobs. Think of the daily, weekly, and seasonal peaks and valleys experienced with meals, occupied rooms, or resort operations. In a service setting, there is nothing to accumulate and store on a shelf during the valleys to bring out and sell during the peaks.

During periods of slow business, there is less demand for guest service. The guest-contact people have to be given other work to do or be put out of their jobs. Given the current labor shortage, no one can afford to cut hours and lose talented employees because business is sometimes slow. On the other hand, during peak periods certain employees may need to be moved into other positions temporarily to meet guests' needs.

Hence, in many jobs, flexibility is far more important than detail and structure. If managers (or worse, guests) hear employees saying, "It's not my job," the organization is probably too structured for a service company. Matters are complicated, however, when union contracts are involved. The classic approach of some labor unions, rooted in the manufacturing approach, is to impose restrictive terminology that prevents people from working outside their job descriptions.

Service managers supervise, teach, and organize right on the floor with their workers. Managers need to be in touch, and many unique situations require immediate and individual responses. In addition, each manager's technical skills are the very essence of the service which that entire department provides. According to the specifications of a union contract or federal wage and hour laws, however, salaried employees (that is, administrative, professional, or executive employees who are exempt from overtime and minimum wage provisions) may be restricted from doing the work of hourly (non-exempt) employees. Because of such restrictions, an exempt chef may not be allowed to cook, or a restaurant manager may not be allowed to fill in for a cashier on break. In practice, this is highly unrealistic and unproductive.

Other common union practices, such as using fixed-rate pay systems and basing all work-related decisions on seniority, also serve to discourage rather than support the very elements that the service industry requires to survive. Factors like attitude and personality are not accepted as appropriate criteria in any decision affecting a person's work status. Compounding this situation, the bulk of all federal, state, and local government regulations discourage the use of subjective considerations as a basis for paying one employee more than another, deciding whether an employee gets promoted or fired—even choosing which applicant gets hired. If the use of such subjective criteria can be proven to be a pretext for discrimination, the law forbids their use altogether.

Subjective appraisal of attributes like friendliness and courtesy is necessary if managers are to maintain the quality of service that guests expect. Knowing what to do to make a guest happy is both a skill and an art and, like any other art form, hard to define. True, it's possible to list some observable

Service managers, such as this executive housekeeper, are almost always actively involved in operations.

and measurable standards for cleaning a hotel room, but the list cannot include all the intangibles and unpredicted situations, like knowing what to do for one guest who speaks only a foreign language or another who has a headache.

Currently, the ranks of union membership are shrinking. Between 1986 and 2000, the number of manufacturing jobs in the United States is projected to decrease by 800,000.[6] With the shift in growth toward the service sector, the hospitality industry is likely to become one of the next big targets of unionization efforts. The tendency of unions is to try to put into place the traditional philosophies and standards that served union workers well in manufacturing. By the same token, the volumes of recently enacted employment laws are still rooted in principles of scientific management. Maintaining high standards of service, which is already a challenge, will become even more difficult unless government and union policies affecting human resources become more responsive to the true nature and needs of the service environment.

Service and Change

In manufacturing, planning and capital investment are for the long term. By contrast, service tends to be more dynamic, with success often depending on the ability to respond rapidly to change. The service sector is also highly subject to fads, changing tastes and social values, and economic trends. A service company must spot coming changes well in advance, then

[6]Kutscher, "Projections," p. 5.

quickly redirect the efforts of the entire organization. If the company is too slow or analytical, it will lose the market. Emphasis has to be more on short-term paybacks and less on long-range planning; capital investment decisions and business strategies must consider the need to adapt quickly and frequently to an ever-changing business environment.

The service business's approach to managing its human resources must support this need for responsiveness. Policies, procedures, and job definitions have to be simple and flexible. Businesses dealing with constant change cannot operate on the basis of highly detailed programs and procedures; they can hardly keep their telephone directories current, much less policy and training manuals. That's why many service companies are far less structured than manufacturing companies of similar size.

Management in the Hospitality Environment

We've been considering the differences between the manufacturing and service sectors and, in particular, the changing role of human resources management for service. Nowhere are these differences and changes more clearly represented than in the hospitality industry. The growth and change in this industry has been phenomenal. Many experts predict that, by the year 2000, travel and tourism will be the largest industry in the world.[7]

The nature of the industry itself has changed radically. Managers need to understand these changes in order to perceive more clearly the current directions in which the industry is moving. In this way, human resources managers will be able to deal with this industry's particular set of problems and challenges.

The Changing Face of the Hospitality Business

Even before the 1920s, and well into the 1930s and 1940s, the first-class, centrally located hotel became a prominent landmark in every major city. During that era, many of today's most experienced professionals got their start, receiving their training from other professionals, learning their skills as they worked, and working their way up from apprentice to master.

Even a business as dominated by the dictates of tradition as ours, however, could not avoid the inevitability of change. The American enchantment with the automobile brought a revolution to lodging, and the 1950s and 1960s saw the countryside's highways dotted with motor courts, roadside inns, and motels. These were usually small establishments, often family-owned and operated, offering convenience and economy for traveling families.

During the 1970s, however, many of those establishments started to reach the end of their design life, just as many of the nation's highways began to deteriorate. Roadside motels declined in popularity. The increased cost of operating a car contributed to the disillusionment of the average American about the charms of traveling by car. Also, as many people began to have more money but less time for travel, air travel and airport hotels became more attractive.

The 1970s also brought other influences. The reliance of so many businesses on up-to-date and new information (the so-called "information

---

[7]Jerome J. Vallen and James R. Abbey, *The Art and Science of Hospitality Management* (East Lansing, Mich.: Educational Institute of the American Hotel & Motel Association, 1987), p. 6.

In the 1920s, '30s, and '40s, the first-class downtown hotel was a prominent landmark in many U.S. cities. (Courtesy of the Amway Corporation, Ada, Michigan)

boom") resulted in a need for more convention meetings and, thus, convention hotels. The rebirth of the inner city led to renovations and new construction of hotels in many downtown areas. Chains and huge corporations continued to purchase and replace independent operations in the hospitality industry.

The 1980s brought a special refinement to the re-emergence of the luxury hotel, along with the phenomenon of **market segmentation**—that is, offering highly specialized facilities to a limited clientele. Examples of such facilities include tennis resorts, conference centers, all-suite hotels, and health spas. As a result, many more specialty operations arose, each providing a unique set of services directed at a narrow segment of the market. Exhibit 1.4 depicts Marriott Corporation's market segmentation.

The history of the hotel industry in the United States in some ways parallels the current situation in human resources. Many of the old masters who helped open and run those original classics are nearing or past retirement age. That means the industry is left with fewer skilled managers. Since we have depended so heavily on these masters to pass along their technical skills to the newcomers, we're now faced with the challenge of losing some of our best teachers as well.

Exhibit 1.4   Marriott Corporation Market Segmentation

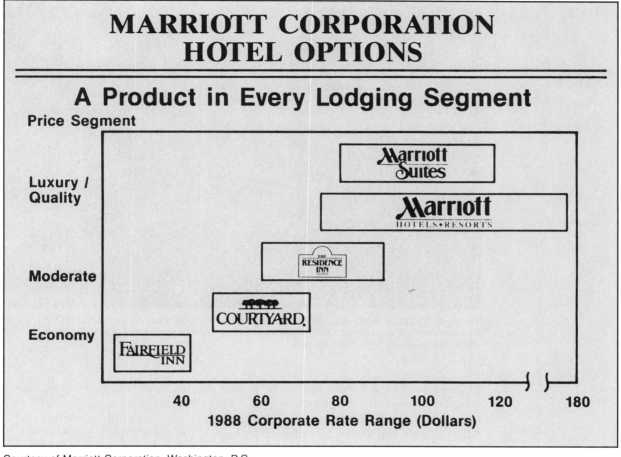

Courtesy of Marriott Corporation, Washington, D.C.

As noted earlier, many of the family-operated roadside motels have declined. While this appears to leave us with experienced hospitality managers, these individuals often have the wrong skills to operate in the high-tech, service-intensive environment found in modern facilities.

Over the years, hotel operators have seen trends come and go. Lately, it seems that each trend has taken a shorter time to develop. The initial growth of the large hotels took place over many decades, while the motel era exhausted itself in about half the time. By the early 1980s, it seemed that a business hardly had time to gear up for the demands of the latest consumer fancy before a new fad was sweeping the country. Since each new development is aimed at a small, specialized market, it reaches its **market saturation point** quickly.

With further market segmentation, increasingly specialized job requirements place severe constraints on **worker elasticity** (the ability of the worker to move among different jobs or among different work areas, units, or facilities). Once trained, an employee is often able to perform only in a limited capacity. No longer can a general manager of a hotel without food facilities be readily transferred to one with food service; nor can the manager of a free-standing restaurant move easily into a position of food and beverage

The Hyatt Regency Wiakoloa, a $360 million 62-acre "Fantasy Resort" completed in 1988, helps demonstrate just how much the hospitality industry has changed and grown. (Courtesy of Hyatt Hotels Corporation, Rosemont, Illinois)

management in a hotel. The same is true for the convention hotel manager who tries to move to a resort, or the motel operator who wants to shift to a large hotel. Today's trainees become tomorrow's **structurally unemployed**— that is, their job skills do not match those required by the available jobs.

The overall impact is that experience becomes less relevant. Nearly everyone you hire has to be retrained for your hotel or restaurant.

Labor Shortages and Rising Costs

All segments of the service sector have experienced spectacular growth. Hospitality organizations are competing with health care facilities, retail establishments, financial institutions, construction firms, and personal services for the same labor force, driving up wages and benefit costs. The impact of this competition will be particularly severe for the hospitality industry. In this industry, self-service and automation cannot be implemented to the extent that they can in other service settings, such as pumping gas or making simple bank transactions.

In addition, some of our most talented managers are being lured away, not by competing U.S. industries, but by other countries. This is fueled in part by the rapid development of third world nations. At the same time, advancements in other nations and recent world economic trends are making it more difficult to persuade skilled foreign workers that employment in the United States is the most attractive option available.

Other Industry Labor Problems

For generations, the hospitality industry has relied heavily on promotion from within. Many managers still working today learned their technical skills and management practices from older managers. While the technical skills may still be relevant, many of the management practices are now outdated.

Some of these practices are an outgrowth or adaptation of the principles of scientific management which, as noted earlier, are not suited to the hospitality industry. These practices have survived in our industry not because they were ever particularly appropriate to a service environment, but rather because the abundance of cheap unskilled labor in the past tended to minimize the consequences of their use. However, cheap unskilled labor is no longer abundant. Nonetheless, the outdated management practices still get routinely passed along to younger managers. The prevalence of these outmoded practices has contributed to industry problems such as high turnover, a poor image, and manager burnout.

High Turnover. Anyone who has experience with hotel or restaurant operations knows that the annual industry rate of turnover has been excessive. The hospitality industry has rates of turnover hitting annual percentages in the hundreds.[8] Compare this to other types of industries, in which annual rates of 25 to 30% are considered too high.[9]

Industry leaders have begun to realize the catastrophic effects of high turnover on productivity and quality of service, and are placing increased emphasis on correcting its causes. Turnover is still far too high, however, and progress must be pursued more vigorously. Chapter 3 will look in greater detail at the turnover problem facing our industry and at ways of reducing its impact.

Poor Image. In the past, the hospitality industry was characterized by low pay, inadequate benefits, and unpleasant working conditions. A reputation for long hours, split shifts, layoffs, bad management, and insufficient training made it difficult for hospitality businesses to compete with other employers for a share of the labor pool. Unfortunately, many people wrongly believe these conditions are still the norm in hotel and restaurant businesses. Thus, our image is another major issue that must be addressed if we're going to be competitive with other businesses in attracting candidates.

Little has been done in the United States to cultivate a positive perception of our business as a good place to work. For years, the Europeans have considered it an honor to have a career in hospitality. Europeans often choose many hours of training and apprenticeship to achieve the status and prestige associated with our industry. The average American, however, thinks of even a master chef as nothing more than a "cook" and food service as a job only worth doing until a better position can be found.

This failure to communicate accurately the advantages of our industry is particularly evident among minority groups. Many minority workers can remember their own parents working in servile roles so their children could get an education and have a better life. With such emotional associations, it isn't easy to convince those offspring that returning to the service environment is their best career move. Given the tremendous growth rate of minorities in the labor force, this will become increasingly significant.

Hospitality schools face some of the same problems with prestige as our industry. Within the university environment, there is often an attitude that a

---

[8]Toni Lydecker, "How to Stop the Revolving Door," *Restaurants and Institutions,* January 22, 1988, p. 31.

[9]Thomas E. Hall, "How to Estimate Employee Turnover Costs," *Personnel,* July-August 1981, p. 43.

This poster is part of a campaign developed by fifteen hospitality industry associations to improve the hospitality industry's image. ("Ours Is A Special World" and "America's Hospitality Industry" are service marks of the National Restaurant Association and used by related hospitality associations.)

hotel/restaurant program isn't "academic" enough and should be left to the trade schools. Consequently, many hotel schools have difficulty getting funding and support. Even when hospitality programs do get started, management courses are still taught in the business school with philosophies and textbooks that are oriented toward manufacturing rather than service. Furthermore, the hospitality schools' desire for top-caliber teachers often faces at least two obstacles: the academic community's compensation practices are not always competitive, and its sometimes unrealistic educational requirements tend to undervalue industry experience.

Manager Burnout. However, improving these areas will not be enough unless we confront some very real problems facing our managers. More and more managers are succumbing to the pressures of the job and leaving the industry for employment elsewhere. The reasons they give most often are the inability to cope with the job stress and upward mobility that's too rapid.

The serious shortage of skilled managers means the best and brightest employees may be promoted too quickly to positions for which they have not been adequately trained. Too much responsibility may be given to inexperienced employees, resulting in reduced morale and lower productivity. The subsequent stress and burnout causes frustrated young managers to drop out and seek work in other fields with fewer aggravations.

Changing Consumer Demands

Today's consumers are more sophisticated and better informed. They have more choices and are strongly motivated by quality, whether it's in durable goods like cars, consumables like food, or services. Guests are demanding higher levels of service and personal attention, and are becoming less tolerant of poor service. This puts greater pressure on hospitality employees to perform in a highly competent manner, all the time maintaining a good service attitude.

Managing the Changes

Hospitality managers of today and the future are going to have to perform under far greater economic and social pressures than any previous generation. They will have to improve quality, consistency, and productivity in order to deliver the total guest experience. At the same time, they will have to deal with rapidly rising labor costs, shrinking labor markets, a vastly different type of worker, more restrictive government legislation, explosive industry growth, constant change, and a work ethic that will require them to manage without relying on the use of power and authority. All of these challenges point to the necessity of a better strategy for managing human resources designed for a new standard of service.

Key Terms

market saturation point
market segmentation
scientific management
structural unemployment

Taylorism
turnover
worker elasticity

Discussion Questions

1. Why is human resources management so much more important to a service company today than it was 50 years ago?

2. How are worker attitudes and values changing? How must managers adapt to these changes?

3. How is the shrinking labor market affecting the level of service in America?

4. What special management skills are needed to respond effectively to the challenges presented by the changing demographics of the labor market?

5. Are people more important in a service-based company than they are in a manufacturing company? Why or why not?

6. What would happen if you tried to apply the principles of scientific management to managing the human resources of a business which strongly emphasizes personal service?

7. Why is it so hard to attract people to the hospitality industry? What should be done about it?

2 Developing a Human Resources Strategy

If you were to ask a number of people about the jobs they've had, almost everyone would have a favorite. It may not have been the one that paid the most, or even the place that had the best equipment. They've also had jobs they didn't like, although they can't always say why: "Things just didn't click," or "The chemistry wasn't right."

Why is it that one business with outdated facilities, cramped quarters, and limited supplies can consistently outsell and offer better service than a competitor with a new plant and all the latest technology? The answer often lies in the human elements of the workplace environment. These elements have a profound effect on a worker's commitment to teamwork, quality, productivity, consistency, and, most important, his or her willingness to help other people. Ultimately, therefore, the level of service will be controlled by the worker's environment.

This human environment—often called the **organizational** or **corporate culture**—is especially important to a company's success because of its impact on management plans. The company's **marketing plan** identifies who the company's customers are and defines its marketing objectives. The **business plan** then outlines how to accomplish the marketing objectives in terms of finance, materials, timetables, measurement systems, and so forth. The organizational culture must support the marketing and business plans, or neither will work successfully.

An example will make this clear. A service company's marketing direction and advertising program are designed to create guest expectations. If its organizational culture doesn't support its advertising, the company won't be able to deliver what guests expect. For instance, when Burger King used an ad campaign that said, "We do it your way," they had to make sure that the mission was clearly communicated to all levels of the organization and that every employee was committed to achieving the same objective. This meant that each unit manager had to be willing to risk lowering production rates and that employees had to be willing to change their routines and even do extra work. Without such willingness, the customers wouldn't have received what the marketing people were selling.

The **human resources strategy** is a long-term, systematic approach to the development and maintenance of all the elements that affect the organizational culture of a workplace, so that all the elements support one another and the goals of the company. In the past, managers didn't think about improving operating effectiveness and profitability through direct involvement in the development of the human resources strategy. Today, effective managers know they need to master its development and integrate it with the marketing and business plans. Otherwise, they won't be able to achieve the level of service demanded by guests or the profitability demanded by the company. Before you can develop this strategy, you must understand how the organizational culture is developed.

Organizational Culture

The organizational culture determines how employees perceive the company. It is the learned attitudes and behaviors that determine how work is done in the company. It's manifested in shared customs, traditions, beliefs, and norms. It's this culture that makes each organization unique, gives its membership a sense of identity, and ultimately may determine its success or failure.

This is especially true in the hospitality industry. When employees find themselves face-to-face with guest needs and compelled to make quick decisions—in those situations Albrecht and Zemke call "moments of truth"[1]—it's the organizational culture that will dictate how they'll respond. Take, for example, an engineering worker who has been told that the company doesn't approve of overtime. If he or she gets a call five minutes before the end of the shift to handle a guestroom repair that will take at least 20 minutes, how does that employee decide what to do if the boss is gone? The decision will probably be further complicated by personal considerations, such as missing a ride home or being late for dinner. Does the employee clock out on time and leave a work order for the next day or take a risk by violating company policy to do the work at once? This decision will be based on both the employee's level of commitment and what the organizational culture tells the employee is important to the company.

An organizational culture will evolve whether a company controls its evolution or not. It takes time, but once in place, it's very difficult to change.

Merely running a short campaign with slogans, pins, and posters won't create a culture. The culture must be rooted in the very foundation of the company itself. It's driven by a vision, shared by all, of the company's beliefs, values, and goals. The human resources strategy must be designed to reinforce these beliefs, values, and goals continually.

As today's workers demand more control over their environment and a voice in how the company is managed, and as companies decentralize more, it will be the organizational culture that holds the whole operation together.

Developing the organizational culture begins with the company's statement of philosophy.

The Statement of Philosophy

Many companies state their philosophy and values in a formal statement of purpose. They may refer to it as their goal, mission statement, company objective, or statement of philosophy. A company's **statement of philosophy** sets a clear direction for the integral development of the marketing, business, and human resources plans. It says, this is what we are, what we do, and what we believe in. It's a reflection of the company's passions and visions and

---

[1]Karl Albrecht and Ron Zemke, *Service America!* (Homewood, Illinois: Dow Jones-Irwin, 1985), p. 31.

In "moments of truth," guests often turn to employees with urgent or unusual needs which call on the employees to make quick decisions.

an expression of their beliefs. It gives people something to strive for (see Exhibit 2.1).

In earlier generations, the great companies became great largely because of the strength and determination of their owners. Everyone knew what the company stood for, because everyone knew what its owner stood for. That person had an unshakable commitment to a mission. It might have been quality, service, reliability, or some other clear objective, but it was passionate, unswerving, and it built the company. In many large corporations today, that unshakable commitment and passionate intensity are often missing. The directors and stockholders shift priorities on the basis of the last quarter's financial report. Today it's, "Put flowers on all the tables in the restaurant— this is a quality operation." Tomorrow it's, "Take them off, we can't afford flowers."

The mission can't change with the quarterly statement. A company must decide what it thinks is important and make a commitment to it. Without this commitment being clearly established and then communicated to all levels, a company won't achieve consistency when its employees face their moments of truth.

This commitment starts at the top and should be a driving force not only for the owners, directors, and stockholders, but also for the general manager and every other manager. If these people all have different goals or different interpretations of the company's goals, the company won't achieve its potential or continuity. This is because each department will develop its own culture with its own set of goals and values which may in fact be different from the company's.

It takes time to develop a statement of philosophy. It should embody a worthy objective, because people want to be part of something important. It

Exhibit 2.1   Sample Statement of Philosophy

Hilton's Corporate Mission

To be recognized as the world's best first-class hotel organization, to constantly strive to improve, allowing us to prosper as a business for the benefit of our guest, our employees, and our shareholders.

Fundamental to the success of our mission are:

PEOPLE
Our most important asset. Involvement, teamwork, and commitment are the values that govern our work.

PRODUCT
Our programs, services, and facilities. They must be designed and operated to consistently provide superior quality that satisfies the needs and desires of our guests.

PROFIT
The ultimate measure of our success - the gauge for how well and how efficiently we serve our guests. Profits are required for us to survive and grow.

With this mission come certain guiding principles:

QUALITY COMES FIRST
The quality of our product and service must create guest satisfaction, that's our No. 1 priority.

VALUE
Our guests deserve quality products at a fair price. That is how to build business.

CONTINUOUS IMPROVEMENT
Never standing on past accomplishments, but always striving - through innovation - to improve our product and service, to increase our efficiency, and profitability.

TEAMWORK
At Hilton, we are a family, working together, to get things done.

INTEGRITY
We will never compromise our code of conduct - we will be socially responsible - we are committed to Hilton's high standards of fairness and integrity.

Courtesy of Hilton Hotels Corporation, Beverly Hills, California.

should evoke passion in others and touch the heart of every member of the organization. The more it does this, the more effective it will be. At the same time, it must be believable, realistic, and easily communicated to all levels within the organization. It should be written in simple, down-to-earth terms that generate enthusiasm.

The service industry is the most dynamic of all industries, because its success or failure depends on the ability to anticipate and respond to rapid change. In a service organization, a philosophy is very important because it's the solid footing that enables all employees to keep their direction. It allows a company to shift its objectives in order to change with the market without losing sight of what it is and how it operates. It also provides a sense of security for employees so that they're more comfortable dealing with change.

Values   Deciding what a company's philosophy is includes determining the values or standards by which the company will operate. The values reinforce the company's beliefs and goals. A fast-food chain might emphasize speed, cleanliness, and dollar-value, while a gourmet restaurant might stress anticipation of guests' needs and creativity. The values that a company emphasizes make the difference between it and its competitors.

In manufacturing, you may hear about values like the dependability of an appliance or the durability of a suitcase. In a service business, qualities such as teamwork, risk-taking, initiative, showmanship, responsiveness, attention to detail, cleanliness, innovation, speed, and creativity are the kinds of values that determine the levels of service, quality, and productivity.

Once the philosophy and values have been determined, all of the other elements of the organizational environment must be adjusted to support and reinforce them. For example, if you're operating in a dynamic, changing marketplace, your culture would probably encourage responsiveness to change as a value by reducing the number of policies and procedures and paying more for performance than seniority.

If personal service is important, and you want to put the guest first, employees will have to be allowed to go outside their job descriptions and do something extra or unexpected in the pursuit of making a guest happy. If the organizational culture dictates that the manager's first reaction should be to find out who's to blame when something goes wrong, employees will focus on doing just what they're told. They may lose sight of the mission of giving personal service.

If creativity is a value you need to emphasize, you'll probably also have to allow your people to challenge the way things are done, think frivolously, and joke about problems.

Friendliness may also be important to you. If so, encourage employees to smile with recognition programs that reward friendliness and with training programs that emphasize talking to guests and using the guest's name. Furnish nametags to managers as well as line employees, and have people call one another by their first names.

A philosophy will be meaningless and values will have little integrity if they're not validated by the manner in which the company, both officially and unofficially, communicates what's important in its day-to-day operations. You couldn't say that cleanliness is important, for instance, and expect workers to keep lobbies clean if the locker rooms and support areas of the facility aren't maintained. Nor could you ask for high food quality for guests

THE MARRIOTT
MANAGEMENT
PHILOSOPHY

A living tradition of values and beliefs

ABOUT THIS PUBLICATION
The material printed in blue is a collection of quotations from J. Willard Marriott which—although practical rather than philosophical—illustrates principles that are the foundation of the company. This material was assembled primarily from memos he wrote to J. W. Marriott, Jr., after he turned over the company's day-to-day operations to him in 1964. Drawing from this personal correspondence between father and son, this publication explains the company's traditional values and beliefs and how they apply to Marriott managers today.

The Marriott Corporation communicates its philosophy and values with a booklet for managers. (Courtesy of Marriott Corporation, Washington, D.C.)

and feed the employees meals that are less than first-rate. Similarly, if corporate leaders choose to place extremely tight budget restraints on the individual units in an effort to keep the company "lean," support must start at the top. Such a chain might find little employee commitment to the austerity program if the corporate office building has marble walls and fountains and if visiting corporate executives wine and dine like royalty at the expense of the unit being visited.

A business dealing with constant change can't rely on highly complex policies and procedures. Flexibility, spontaneity, and the ability to "think on your feet" are all necessities. If you always quote policy as the basis for making decisions, or try to train new employees with extremely comprehensive and detailed programs, you're sending a message that following procedures is high on your list of values—whether you mean to or not. Companies with the strong philosophy and value orientation of a well-established organizational culture can operate with fewer policies and manuals and still maintain the desired levels of quality, productivity, and consistency.

Creating a Strategy for Service

The human resources strategy that effectively supports and maintains the organizational culture must address several aspects of the company's development:

- The role the organization's structure plays in the culture: how authority and responsibility are distributed and delegated, and who makes decisions

- The manager's role in the culture: the style of management and the approach taken to team building and goal setting

- How values are put into practice: what is emphasized, measured, and rewarded, and how personnel policies and procedures reinforce the culture

The Role of Organizational Structure in Shaping the Culture

How well a company's philosophy is reflected in the actual organizational structure will determine the level of service the company will be able to give. A look at some principles of organizational structure may help clarify how the service philosophy is reinforced through the manner in which these principles are used. They include line and staff functions, advisory and functional authority, unity of command and span of control, and decentralization.

Line and Staff Functions. In a very small company, the owner or manager will probably be a jack-of-all-trades responsible for every element of the operation. As companies grow, the operating, or **line**, managers face more demands and acquire more responsibilities. As these demands and responsibilities grow, **staff** personnel are added. The primary responsibility of the operating departments is to carry on the functions that directly fulfill the company's goals. The major role of the staff departments is to support, advise, and assist the operating departments. Exhibit 2.2 depicts this relationship on an organization chart.

Hospitality managers spend a great deal of time on the floor managing, listening, and talking to guests. They often make direct use of their technical skills by working alongside line employees. In addition, they devote a substantial amount of their time to teaching those skills to their workers. For

Exhibit 2.2   The Relationship of Line and Staff Departments

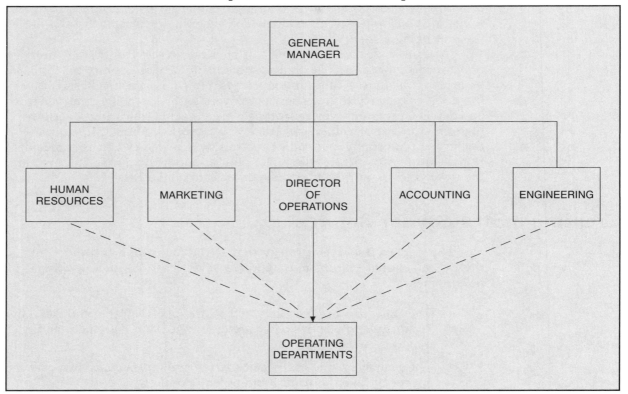

example, chefs must know not only how to cook and spend time on the line making adjustments when recipes don't turn out right. They must also show others how to cook and make adjustments.

Therefore, a hospitality company usually structures itself to provide a great deal of organizational support for the operating manager through the hiring of staff experts. Examples of staff departments would include human resources, accounting, marketing, and engineering.

Advisory and Functional Authority. Staff departments have what's known as **advisory authority**. This means they don't have any authority over operating employees and aren't directly involved in the responsibilities of an operating department. If a staff department becomes involved in running an operating department, each crisis that occurs in the operating department becomes a priority for the staff department. This detracts from the staff department's ability to perform its basic function of providing support for *all* operating departments.

Thus, the human resources department supports the development of an employee cafeteria that's comfortable and pleasant, but it doesn't operate the cafeteria. The role of purchasing might be to get the best price for food supplies, but not to decide what food to serve.

The relationship between operating and staff personnel should be clearly defined. This helps to eliminate the potential conflict that can arise when operating departments have the responsibility and accountability for ultimate production, but the staff departments tie their hands or direct their priorities. For example, if the chef specifies a certain blend of coffee, does the purchasing agent have the authority to change the specifications if that blend is too expensive?

Functional authority gives a staff department operational authority over a specific function. For instance, the human resources department might have a safety director with functional authority to deal directly with line supervisors on matters of employee safety. Again, the boundaries of such authority must be clear to avoid conflict.

Another example of functional authority is the **project team**, a kind of ad hoc committee created as needed for a special purpose and dissolved when the project is completed. Each project has a team leader who's in charge and pulls team members together to accomplish a job. This leader may have authority over someone who was in charge of a previous project. A quality assurance team is such a project team.

The extent to which staff departments exercise authority over operating departments determines how control-oriented the organizational culture becomes. The manufacturing environment is commonly typified by strong staff functions, while the service industry tends to be more operations-driven.

Unity of Command and Span of Control. Unity of command is a commonly-accepted organizational principle which states that each employee should be accountable to only one boss. When functional authority is assigned, or if there's a conflict between line and staff requirements, employees should know who has the ultimate authority. If two people are doing a job, the one who's accountable and responsible for the results should be in charge.

Span of control refers to the number of people that one person can manage effectively. It is influenced by many factors. In general, the closer a manager is to the top of the organization, the lower is the number of people that can be supervised. Other considerations include:

- The amount of supervision workers require
- The physical proximity of the people being supervised
- The complexity of the work
- The cost or impact of an error
- The number of hours and days of the week a business is open
- The frequency with which problems and exceptions are likely to occur
- Other responsibilities of the manager
- The amount of experience of the manager and other workers
- The extent of staff and other support, such as assistant managers
- The turnover rate

It's typical for a hospitality company's organization chart to be fairly "flat," that is, to have fewer levels of management than other kinds of businesses. Because there are fewer managers, the span of control is broader and

Exhibit 2.3   Flat Organization and Broad Span of Control

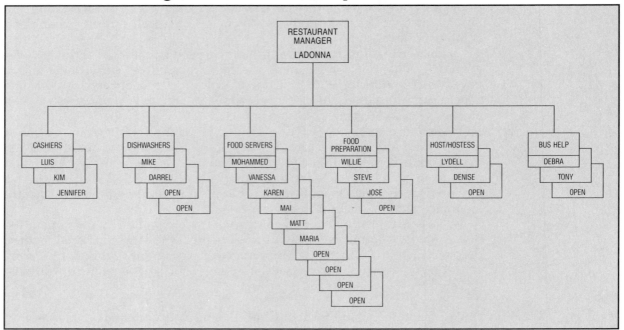

unity of command is not as well-defined. Line employees have more responsibility, must exercise more autonomy, and perform more of the management tasks, such as opening and closing duties. Exhibit 2.3 depicts the broad span of control typical of a flat organization chart.

Delegation of Authority. Decentralization is the delegation of decision-making authority to the lowest possible level in an organization. In contrast, a centralized organization has one central core of staff members make decisions for all levels and departments. A company isn't usually totally centralized or decentralized. Depending on its organizational problems, it may shift from one to the other. A company losing money or one with many new managers may wish to centralize authority until the problems have been resolved or the new managers trained. It may then begin to decentralize and delegate.

Where speed, responsiveness to change, or employee involvement are important, a company may prefer more decentralization. In a centralized operation, more levels of management are required, making it harder to achieve common objectives. More levels also mean more interpretations of objectives, more distortions of communications, and more time required to make decisions.

A manufactured product, such as a car or radio, can consistently serve many different geographic areas without modifications. However, a hospitality business must be responsive to the immediate area it services. It must often adjust to the specialized requirements and tastes of the community. This is challenging enough in single properties and regional chains. Without decentralizing, large multi-regional chains may be slow in changing to meet the needs of their individual properties.

Exhibit 2.4   Bulls-Eye Organization Chart

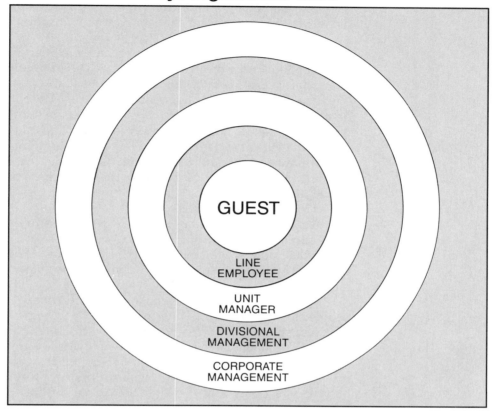

GUEST

LINE
EMPLOYEE

UNIT
MANAGER

DIVISIONAL
MANAGEMENT

CORPORATE
MANAGEMENT

The Manager's Role in Shaping the Culture

What the human resources strategy dictates about how employees are directed or managed strongly influences the organizational culture. Personal service isn't achieved by giving orders—employees have to derive a service attitude from the prevailing culture. They then must make a personal commitment to service.

In a service company, it might be helpful for the manager to view his or her role as if the organization chart were a bull's-eye (see Exhibit 2.4). In the center would be the guest. Surrounding the guest would be the employees, who should have the freedom to interact with and respond to the needs of the guest. On the outer rings would be managers, who are there to support the employees—to keep them supplied, obtain the necessary equipment, get paychecks out on time, help them solve their problems, teach and develop them, and reinforce the values and goals of the company.

Every employee will bring the cultural influences of previous jobs to your organization. In Chapter 4, we'll talk about the importance of expressing your philosophy and values to job applicants, since they must be able to accept them before going to work for you. This is especially true with management employees. Because of the impact of managers on the development and maintenance of a company's culture, careful attention must be given to their selection, orientation, and training. Each manager must know what the philosophy and values are, believe in them, and support them enthusiastically in order to communicate them to the service staff. The managerial candidate who doesn't accept the company's philosophy shouldn't be hired.

Management Style. Employers communicating their goals and values need to exercise control over the management style used. If a company says it stands for one set of values, its managers must not be allowed to operate with different ones. For instance, having a recruiting motto of "The company that cares" in an organization where managers clearly don't care about their employees would be worse than making no effort at all to communicate values.

Management styles change to reflect changing social values. While **autocratic management**—in which a manager rules with power—might have worked for Attila the Hun, today **participative management**—in which employees participate in setting objectives and goals—better reflects society's expectations and standards.

A manager's style may also vary with the situation. If three of an airplane's four engines go out, the pilot wouldn't take a poll of the flight crew before determining whether to keep flying or land. The maturity of the work force and how secure employees feel in their jobs may also influence management style.

In addition, most managers don't have the time or resources to supervise people closely. Therefore, their role must be to help create—through leadership, coaching, support, and example—the environment that encourages employees to manage themselves. If employees are going to take responsibility for their own actions, they must know what's expected and how they're measured. They must be given regular supportive feedback so they can judge how they're doing and feel that they're an integral part of making things happen.

Giving service comes down to the one-on-one relationship established between the employee and the guest. Each guest is a human being, with different needs, expectations, and values. Service people must be able to recognize these differences and respond accordingly. To do so, they need a secure environment. If they're preoccupied or worried about making a mistake or losing their jobs, they won't take any risks.

Managers are role models. What they do communicates values more strongly than what they say. The general manager who, when on rounds, never takes note of the employees' grooming standards or the wilted flowers on the tables can't expect employees to take a genuine interest in quality or attention to details. Similarly, a manager who frequently doesn't arrive on time or doesn't keep his or her shoes shined will find it difficult to get employees to do so.

Instead of forcing performance standards on workers, managers are going to have to learn how to negotiate to obtain the employee's commitment to the company's standards. To be effective in this role, the manager must have a relationship with employees that's based on trust, understanding, and acceptance.

Whatever the type of business, management style, or company mission, the main role of managers is still to manage employees to carry out the company's business plan. The manager must be able to get every worker to meet the company's standards and follow its procedures. To achieve this in today's environment, the manager must be an expert at team building in order to get every worker in the department or work unit to share the same goals and

A conflict arises when a company's stated values are not reinforced by the manager's actions.

values. All must be involved in working together to achieve them. In effect, the work unit has to develop a culture which reflects and supports the organizational culture. This group culture is the foundation for building a team.

Understanding Group Culture to Build a Team. Merriam-Webster defines teamwork as "work done by several associates with each doing a part but all subordinating personal prominence to the efficiency of the whole." If the team is effective, it will be able consistently to achieve results that are higher than the combined total of individual efforts would be. This increased effectiveness through joint action, sometimes referred to as "synergism," is what makes the team the best avenue for achieving high productivity. To build an effective team, a manager must understand some things about group development and behavior.

Employees tend to place themselves in loosely structured work groups, sometimes called cliques, usually composed of five to seven members.[2] Work group formation is mainly the result of proximity and common interests and objectives. If the department is large enough and they have some choices,

---

[2]Bernard Berelson and Gary A. Steiner, *Human Behavior: An Inventory of Scientific Findings* (New York: Harcourt, Brace & World, Inc., 1964), p. 358.

people will try to associate with others they like, and by whom they're liked. They'll migrate to the group that shares similar attitudes, opinions, and feelings because they'll feel more comfortable. If there are two or more such groups, they're likely to join the one with which they have the most contact.

The needs for friendship, personal contact, and a sense of belonging to a group shouldn't be underestimated. Few employees will be able to stay on the job without becoming part of a group.

Each group will have its own **norms**—the common attitudes, opinions, and feelings that determine their actions. They'll develop and share uniform values, standards, and rules of acceptable behavior that will dictate how work will be done. Often, they'll also have inside jokes and a special vocabulary.

Interaction of members tends to strengthen the group. Change also affects its strength and cohesiveness, as well as the morale of its members. On the one hand, a group that's stable and has little turnover is likely to be tightly-knit. In fact, when one member leaves, others often follow suit soon afterwards. On the other hand, the addition of several new members at once may threaten the group, causing a tightening of the original group. The result could be difficulty in assimilating new employees, and their exclusion could lead to higher turnover among them.

The stronger and more cohesive the group is, the likelier its members are to be influenced by its norms, and the more pressure will be put on members to operate within accepted norms. Because this peer pressure is much stronger on line employees than it is on management or professional employees, line employees may see their relationships with their peers as more important than their relationships with their managers. Anyone who attempts to resist the group's standards and work to individual standards will be excluded from the group.[3]

The people who are most susceptible to group pressures and norms are those who feel least accepted or secure, have low self-esteem or inadequate job skills, have previously experienced failure on the job, or have had a negative experience as a result of deviation from group norms. Regardless of whether these people privately accept the norms, they'll generally give the appearance of agreement. In most groups, some ranking occurs by status. Compliance to norms tends to increase among those with lower status or prestige. They may feel they have more to lose by deviation, or they may be more vulnerable to criticism, embarrassment, or rejection.

The most effective and productive teams are those groups that have aligned their own goals with those of the company. As a manager, you'll need the cooperation of the majority of the groups within the department to function with any success. Obtaining their cooperation requires effective and open communication. In the absence of adequate and accurate information, group members will exercise their own interpretations, and undesirable norms may emerge. If the company and the managers are unclear or inconsistent about the mission and values, group members will develop their own shared objectives which may not support those of the company.

Every group also has informal leaders, whose influence will increase as the strength of the group increases. You must be able to identify existing

---

[3]Robert R. Blake and Jane Srygley Mouton, *Productivity: The Human Side* (New York: AMACOM, 1981), p. 44.

leaders and either win their cooperation or neutralize their effectiveness. You may even be able to influence their selection.

Often, someone who's very vocal and something of an agitator may seem to the manager to be the group's leader. In fact, such an employee is usually a less-secure member of the group trying to attract attention and win acceptance. Spotting the actual leader may be more difficult, so the manager has to watch for more subtle signs.

Group members polarize around the group's informal leader, and even imitate his or her behavior and body language. They sit where he or she does in the cafeteria, and when the leader leaves, the others also leave. Group members go to the leader with their questions or for confirmation of rumors, and it's his or her opinions and work standards that are soon adopted by everyone. Even exact words and phrases first heard from the group leader will soon be picked up and used by others.

The person who emerges as leader generally represents the group's norms, and is also well-informed and knows the job. As the manager, you can help to influence the group's choice of leaders and norms by providing the people who best represent company standards with information and training. However, if leaders become too much more skilled or achieve too much more status, the group may begin to exclude them.

The bond that holds the department together is mutual respect. Develop a sense of belonging and a climate that reduces defensiveness by providing recognition, encouragement, and reward. Encourage creativity, flexibility, and sensitivity to others in the group. Train employees for participation in decision making, problem solving, and goal setting, as well as in job skills.

The importance of group membership is a fact of life in the workplace. Many managers have learned to move slowly until they've identified group members and leaders and their norms.

When the group norms aren't consistent with the company's mission and values, modification must also be handled through the group rather than through individuals. Just asking employees to accept a change is unlikely to have much effect.

The manager who uses power or authority to break up a group, prevent its formation, or undermine prevailing norms fails more often than not. The manager's actions may actually strengthen the group's bonds by providing a common cause. The group may become resentful or even vengeful. Morale and productivity may both fall significantly. Similarly, firing a popular leader because of the group's norms could create a martyr whose significance you can never overcome.

If you can't win leaders over, transfer them to another shift or department, wait until they go on vacation to make changes, or back others within the group to challenge their leadership. Show open support for these new contenders. Provide them with facts on upcoming changes and let them disseminate the information to others.

If a clique must be broken up, transfer some of its members to another, larger group of workers that has a strong positive work standard or combine the two groups. Then, promote interaction and open communication among them. Show strong support for the informal leader who represents the standards you want to reinforce.

You need to use group influence to modify a group norm. The group pressure will then influence individual behavior to change. Present the problem frankly and factually to all members of the affected group. Then, ask

The manager must be an expert at team building in order to get every worker in the department to share the same goals and values.

them together to identify the cause of the problem and the solution, including specific changes to operations and work methods. Be prepared to provide evidence of the problem by citing particular instances, because participants are likely to react at first by denying responsibility and placing blame elsewhere. Some members may also react with anger. They should be given time to express it, since you won't make progress until you clear the air. Listen quietly and say something like, "I understand why you feel that way; so let's work together to solve the problem. I'm sure we'll all be happier."

If possible, get people who are well-respected to introduce the idea that group standards may need to be changed, using a "what if" rather than an accusatory approach. Also, try to get someone else to back them up, or support them yourself. If the person presenting a new idea is meeting with resistance, try saying, "Tom might have a good idea, here. Let's give him a chance to explain it." Since people may be more honest if their identity isn't revealed, consider using a secret ballot to get the group's consensus. Keep in mind that, even when workers do agree to adopt a new norm, it will take a while for it to become entrenched. Be prepared for some regression to the more familiar, easier ways.

The willingness of people to join together and share common objectives can help you build teams, as long as individual skills and differences are also recognized and appreciated. Encourage people to think independently and challenge undesirable norms by promoting individuality and initiative as values.

Goal Setting. Goal setting is another technique at which managers must become more skilled, since it's one of the best ways to manage and motivate a team. While objectives or mission statements are broad, goals focus on the short term and are much more specific.

While setting individual goals is used in the performance appraisal process, the emphasis has to be on aligning individual goals with group goals, and ultimately with the company's goals. For instance, a training director might set individual goals of developing a cook training program and training 20 cooks each year. However, these goals can't be met if the chef is short of help and can't send anyone to the training program, or doesn't feel it's needed. Even if the chef does accept the training director's goals, that chef could leave and be replaced by another who has different priorities. In any case, the training director's goals will not be met because not all of the people needed for their successful accomplishment were committed to them. Thus, when goals are set for a group, every affected employee should be involved. All must know what their contribution toward achieving the goals will be, and that the contribution of each is important.

Even if jobs are narrow and highly repetitive, you can encourage a strong sense of achievement and responsibility through identification with the goals of the whole company as well as those of the department or team. For example, show the trash hauler guest letters that praise the cleanliness of the facility. Copies of such letters could be sent to him or her along with a note from the general manager expressing appreciation and stressing the importance of the job. People from offices, telecommunications, stewarding, and other support areas could be invited occasionally to view an elaborate buffet preparation or a new guestroom before guests arrive.

All must agree that each goal is important. Goals should be specific, realistic, and measurable. Establish a time frame for completion and provide employees with regular feedback on how they're doing. To ensure that goals are understood and interpreted consistently by all, express them in simple terms and write them down. Review them regularly and be able to adapt them as necessary.

Once a goal is realized, it must be replaced to provide a continued direction and sense of purpose. When a new facility is being opened, morale, enthusiasm, productivity, teamwork, and effort are all high in spite of long hours and high stress, because there's a common, clearly-defined goal to get the place open. Once the mission is accomplished, however, another goal must take its place or the company's direction will falter. Morale and performance will begin to drop, and poor service will result. In many new operations, the work force goes through a noticeable decline in productivity and morale after the opening because of the absence of a replacement goal. The higher the morale was for the first goal, the more significant the decline is likely to be with the absence of a replacement goal.

Putting Values into Practice

We have seen that all elements of the human resources strategy must support the values by which the company intends to operate. The company's values are put into practice in several ways, including the choice of measurements that will be used to gauge success, the allocation of wages and benefits, and the kinds of performance that will be recognized, rewarded, and talked about. All of these determinations, in turn, will be carried out through the personnel policies and procedures.

Measurement. Regardless of what a company says its philosophy is, what it measures is one of the biggest communicators of what its values really are. If food costs, labor costs, and inventory turnover are all it measures, talks about, and uses to evaluate performance, people will adapt to that and the

An organization must decide whether its first priority is maintaining inventory and accounting records or serving the needs of the guest.

company culture will be control-oriented. As noted in Chapter 1, the frequency of measurement also has a profound impact on the organizational culture in communicating the true values of the company.

An organization must decide whether its systems are there for the convenience of the guest or the accounting office. Are bartenders, front desk agents, and cashiers part of guest service or are they really data-entry clerks? Is the first priority of the company maintaining the accounting records or helping guests? If your employees believe their first priority is keeping proper inventory and accounting records, in reality "service" isn't your philosophy. If you want service, you have to place equal or greater emphasis on measuring service. This may mean evaluating guest satisfaction by measuring repeat business, heeding guest reactions, comments, and suggestions, and even conducting guest surveys.

Further, how you treat your employees will also communicate how you think guests should be treated. If you want guest satisfaction, you also have to measure employee satisfaction, since their behavior is part of the product. Employees must be happy and content themselves before they can make guests happy. When people feel good about themselves and are comfortable with their skills, they're more willing and able to perform in public. The happier they are, the likelier they are to go out of their way to help a guest or co-worker. If your human resources strategy is working, you won't need a customer service training program to teach workers to smile. On the other hand, employees in uncomfortable situations will generally tend to be ruder to guests and one another. Employee turnover, absenteeism, attitude surveys, and accident rates are all indicators for measuring employee satisfaction.

When managers know that employers consider achieving guest and employee satisfaction to be as important as achieving financial results, they're likelier to give proper emphasis to service and the importance of their employees in achieving successful service. When that happens, employees know that management means it when it says, "Our employees are our greatest asset."

Compensation. Compensation policies will also communicate the values of a company. If a company wants to emphasize service, employees who are on the service line should be adequately compensated. If front desk agents, cashiers, and telephone operators earn minimum wage, while clerks in accounting, the storeroom, or the mail room are paid substantially more, this communicates that service isn't the company's top priority.

Recognition and Reward. Values can be reinforced by recognition programs. When employees perform consistently according to your values, they should be recognized and rewarded—turned into heroes who become role models. Others who see them being rewarded will know what's important to the company and what it takes to get ahead, and they'll want to follow suit. It's only when everyone understands what the goals and values are and can see that the company really does operate by them that they can begin to identify with and commit to them.

Storytelling. One of the most effective ways of reinforcing values is to talk about the people who best represent them. Every organizational culture is characterized by traditions and legends of which all employees quickly become aware. The process, sometimes known as **storytelling**,[4] has a powerful influence on the behavior and attitudes of workers, because it summarizes the beliefs and values of the company.

A favorite example of many in the hospitality industry is a story Disney employees tell about Walt Disney taking his children to an amusement park. After observing the level of maintenance there, he's said to have vowed that if he ever had an amusement park, he'd never want to have chipped paint on the horses on his carousel. Clearly, that determination is understood and upheld by employees in the Disney organization today.

Another example can be found in a true story told at the Amway Grand Plaza Hotel, in Grand Rapids, Michigan. During the opening days, in one of the hotel's fine restaurants, a child asked for a peanut butter sandwich. Not a jar of peanut butter was to be found, but a food server ran across the street to a convenience store during a snowstorm to get some. Not only was the employee not disciplined for leaving the job, she won an award for putting the needs of the guest first; and years later, employees still hear about the "peanut butter story" and the choice she made for personal service.

The Personnel Program. The personnel program is the practical application of your mission and values, the translation of a philosophy statement into a working operation. *No area of management communicates and controls your values more forcefully than the development and day-to-day administration of your personnel policies and procedures.* These are the rules and how-tos that determine what you require and permit, who you hire, how you

---

[4]Terrence E. Deal and Allan A. Kennedy, *Corporate Cultures: The Rites and Rituals of Corporate Life* (Reading, Mass.: Addison-Wesley Publishing Company, 1982), p. 87.

An elegant gilded sunburst hangs in our Rendezvous Lounge. This rare one-of-a-kind wood sculpture was hand-carved by Italian craftsmen in 1740. It was commissioned by the Moroscini family for their castle, which was the center of the social world in Genoa, Italy. For 150 years, the sunburst graced the wall of their main ballroom. Tragically, the castle was destroyed by fire, and the sunburst was left among the ruins until one of the servants rescued it and stored it in an attic. Eventually it was sold at a public auction.

In 1979, the restoration of the Pantlind lobby began. As work progressed and the beauty of the Pantlind again emerged, it was obvious the lobby needed something to pull it all together. When Amway Corporation became aware of the sunburst, it purchased the sculpture and commissioned local craftsmen to reconstruct it piece by piece. Some of the pieces were nearly perfect, others were twisted and needed repair. Some were large; others quite small. But all were important in the restoration of the sunburst. When it all came together, it was finished in gold as you see it today. The sunburst had found a new home at last.

Although the history of the sunburst is fascinating, it is the present significance that gives it real meaning. No two pieces are exactly alike. And yet, as they are all joined together, they form a breathtaking display of balance and beauty. All the pieces are essential. There is no one piece more important than another. If one piece were missing— no matter how small—the beauty of the sunburst would be lost.

That is why we chose it as our symbol. Just like the sunburst, it is the collection of all of us that makes the Amway Grand Plaza Hotel a rare one-of-a-kind experience . . . different from any other hotel in the world.

The "sunburst" story appears in the employee handbook to communicate the values of the Amway Grand Plaza Hotel.
(Courtesy of the Amway Grand Plaza Hotel, Grand Rapids, Michigan)

train, what you praise and pay for, and why you discipline or terminate someone.

It is to this end that your human resources strategy should direct and dictate all of your personnel programs. You can't buy a set of ready-made programs or borrow them from another employer and expect them all to support your culture. Your own human resources strategy should control every program and event you implement. As you will see in the chapters that follow, how you use this strategy to manage—in recruiting, interviewing, evaluating, hiring, training, rewarding, promoting, firing—will communicate and reinforce your organizational culture.

Key Terms

advisory authority
autocratic management
business plan
corporate culture
decentralization
functional authority
human resources strategy
line department
marketing plan

norms
organizational culture
participative management
project team
span of control
staff department
statement of philosophy
storytelling
unity of command

Discussion Questions

1. Why is the organizational culture so important in a hospitality business?

2. What do you think would happen if a staff department exercised too much functional authority in a hospitality business?

3. Why is a manager's style of management so important in shaping the organizational culture?

4. Why is it important for a manager to control the values of the work group?

5. How can a manager minimize the effectiveness of an informal leader who is having a negative effect on the values of the work group?

6. Why would a personnel program set up for a successful manufacturing company be unlikely to work well for a hospitality business?

3 Staffing: Managing Turnover and Selection

Managers are ultimately responsible for ensuring that their operations are properly staffed. The key to effective staffing is to select and keep the best people. As we've seen in Chapter 1, finding qualified people is becoming more and more difficult in today's labor market. Managers are realizing the importance of retaining good employees and are, therefore, placing greater emphasis on turnover control.

How managers handle their responsibilities during the selection process has an enormous influence on turnover rates and related costs. Conversely, understanding how to evaluate and estimate turnover can be a highly effective staffing tool. Before we consider (in this and the next two chapters) how to fill vacancies using recruitment, interviewing, and evaluation techniques, we need to examine the relationship between selection and turnover.

Understanding Employee Turnover

Employee **turnover** occurs when the work unit loses a worker who must be replaced. In this case, the work unit refers to the group of workers for which turnover is being evaluated. A work unit could be a particular work shift, a department or group of workers within the department, an independent place of business, one property within a chain, or an entire corporation.

Analyzing the Causes of Turnover

There are many reasons employees leave jobs, and the reasons probably vary from one position to another. From a managerial standpoint, major causes usually fall into one of the following categories:

1. Mishandled selection process

2. Mishandled hiring process

3. Employee dissatisfaction with job opportunities or compensation

4. Poor management

The selection process offers the best opportunity for controlling turnover. In fact, the other three factors usually result from mishandling the selection process. Poor hiring procedures and mismanagement can generally

Turnover represents an enormous expense to an employer in terms of lost revenue.

be traced to upper management's inappropriate choices of people to handle the mid-level managerial responsibilities. The more authority that an opening has, the more crucial the selection process becomes in controlling turnover.

Indeed, an employee's future job satisfaction depends to a great extent on the skills the manager uses during the selection process. In matching the job to the candidate, the manager must communicate information about compensation, company philosophy, and job requirements. If employees leave because they are dissatisfied with their jobs, want higher wages, or are entering different industries, you may need to re-evaluate the steps of your selection process by asking the following questions:

- Was the job properly defined?

- Did you have adequate and accurate information about every applicant?

- Did final candidates receive enough accurate information about the company and the job?

Losing people isn't the only way poor selection can affect turnover. The poor choices who do not leave can disrupt an operation, lowering the morale of and even driving away your good workers. Aside from entry-level positions, many positions are filled by promotion from within; making a wrong choice initially leaves you with fewer options later.

Exhibit 3.1   Direct Costs of Turnover

Search and selection costs:

- advertising
- recruiting
- agency fees
- screening and testing
- candidate and recruiter travel
- relocation
- the wages and overhead costs (including office space and supplies) of all personnel involved in these steps

Hiring and training costs:

- preparation of offer letters, hiring agreements, or employment contracts, including preparers' time and any legal costs
- preparation, development, and printing of publications such as processing forms, the employee handbook, and benefits booklets
- wages and overhead associated with training and orientation, including the preparation, development, and maintenance of all training programs

Separation costs:

- overtime
- severance pay
- wages and overhead related to termination recordkeeping, processing, and any other special services, such as exit interviews or review boards
- lost production of the position and associated equipment while the vacancy remains unfilled
- additional FICA and unemployment insurance payments
- legal costs for any employment litigation arising as a result of a termination

Assessing the Costs of Turnover

Regardless of the cause, unnecessary turnover represents an enormous expense that operating executives and owners are no longer willing to tolerate. Current reports estimate the cost to replace the average hourly hotel employee to be as high as $1,500.[1] This cost can quickly rise into the five-figure range when the position involves highly specialized or managerial skills.[2] In 1987, estimates set the average cost of relocation alone at $36,000.[3]

Cost figures are most commonly developed on the basis of direct costs and indirect costs. The direct costs are easily calculated, and may be the only figures a company uses to estimate turnover costs. Direct costs include search and selection costs, hiring and training costs, and separation costs. Exhibit 3.1 lists a number of expenses under each of these three categories. Separation costs are perhaps the most expensive of the direct costs, estimated to be as much as three-and-a-half times the combined costs of employment and training.[4]

Indirect costs are harder to assess accurately. By some estimates, they

[1]Robert Bové, "In Practice," *Training and Development Journal*, April 1987, p. 14.
[2]Walter L. Polsky and Loretta D. Foxman, "Career Counselor," *Personnel Journal*, Nov. 1986, p. 38.
[3]Allan Halcrow, "Portfolio," *Personnel Journal*, Feb. 1988, p. 18.
[4]Dean B. Peskin, *The Doomsday Job: The Behavioral Anatomy of Turnover* (New York: AMACOM, 1973), p. 69.

may run nearly twice as much as the direct costs.[5] Indirect costs are the intangibles for which specific figures are not available, but whose toll is usually apparent to all. Indirect costs of employee turnover include production losses; breakage, waste, and accidents; loss of morale and work unit cohesion; and lost customers.

Production Losses. New workers are less efficient and productive than experienced workers. In addition, they interfere with the smooth operation of the work unit. They require more time and attention from managers and experienced employees, whose productivity is then also reduced.

Breakage, Waste, and Accidents. The incidence of these problems is higher among less experienced workers. This increases the cost of equipment and supplies, adds to workers' compensation insurance expenses, and raises the potential for liability lawsuits by employees and guests.

Loss of Morale and Work Unit Cohesion. Turnover increases the difficulty of building an effective team. It affects the attitude and commitment of remaining workers, who know they'll have to carry an extra share of the workload until a new worker is found and trained.

Managers often note that the departure of one employee is soon followed by the resignations of others. The likelihood of further turnover may be even greater if the vacated position was supervisory, since a new manager usually makes many changes in areas such as procedures, rules, goals, management style, and even personnel. These changes may create feelings of dissatisfaction and insecurity among workers, leaving them more susceptible to possible unionization attempts or hiring offers from competitors.

Lost Customers. The most expensive loss caused by unmanaged turnover is the loss of customers. Such losses may be incurred when an inadequate and inexperienced staff provides poor service. This can and usually does result in a permanent loss of business.

Calculating Turnover Rate

Controlling turnover and its related costs is every manager's responsibility. A major aspect of that control requires understanding and anticipating the turnover rate. Excessive turnover is a direct reflection on the manager, so calculating a department's turnover rate is one good way of evaluating the manager's effectiveness. Some companies even consider the turnover rate of a manager's department when conducting salary and performance reviews for the manager.

Turnover rate can be determined for any period of time and for any group of workers. One simple method of calculating turnover rate is to divide the number of terminations for the period by the average number of employees for the same period. Since the rate is usually expressed as a percentage, the result of this division is multiplied by 100.

The average number of employees can be easily calculated as follows:

1. Take the number of people on payroll at the beginning of the time period.

[5]William W. Holloway, "Coping with Employee Turnover in the Age of High Technology," *Personnel Administrator*, May 1985, p. 109.

2. Add this number to the number of people on payroll at the end of the same period.

3. Divide by two.

For instance, last year a small fast-food establishment had 90 terminations, with an average of 30 employees on payroll. Given this information, its annual rate of turnover may be calculated as follows:

$$\text{Annual rate of turnover} = \frac{\text{Number of terminations}}{\text{Average number on payroll}} \times 100\%$$

$$\text{Annual rate of turnover} = \frac{90}{30} \times 100\%$$

$$\text{Annual rate of turnover} = 3 \times 100\%$$

$$\text{Annual rate of turnover} = 300\%$$

Obviously, 300% is a high rate of turnover. The result of this determination would clearly point to the need for turnover control and justify closer scrutiny to determine the underlying causes.

In many cases, companies learn more by analyzing monthly or seasonal turnover rates than by determining annual percentages. Large operations usually try to pinpoint problem areas by determining turnover rates by department, shift, work group, or even position. Exhibit 3.2 presents a labor turnover analysis form which is used to chart turnover by department. Once the turnover problem is pinpointed, the manager is better able to isolate, examine, and handle its specific causes, whether poor supervision, employee cliques, workload distribution, hours, or morale problems.

It's critically important to analyze actual turnover, including the reasons people are leaving. One department may appear to be hiring a lot of people due to vacated openings. If the openings are caused by promotions, however, the department head should probably get an award instead of criticism. Events such as retirement and death are beyond anyone's control and should not be seen negatively when evaluating a manager.

When analyzing turnover rates, you'll often notice a large, stable group of employees and just a few positions that keep turning over again and again. These are the positions which will provide the greatest test of your management skills. This is the turnover you must control, or it will control you.

Given that the costs of each new hire are so high and that most turnover results from hiring the wrong people, managers urgently need to improve their selection techniques. In today's competitive environment, a manager's success or failure may hinge on his or her ability to recruit and keep the best people. Clearly, managers will be spending more time in the staffing area and will require professional selection skills.

Forecasting Labor Needs

Selection begins with the ability to anticipate and plan for your labor needs before they reach an emergency stage. Anticipating job vacancies will give you the necessary **lead time** to select the right replacement for an employee with

Exhibit 3.2 Labor Turnover Analysis

DEPARTMENTS	VOLUNTARY					INVOLUNTARY						SERVICE							ACTUAL NUMBER ON PAYROLL	NUMBER OF SEPARATIONS		
	PERSONAL	OPPOR-TUNITY	DISSAT-ISFIED	OTHER	TOTAL	PERFOR-MANCE	CONDUCT	STAFF REDUCTION	NON-UNION RETIRE	OTHER	TOTAL	UNDER 30 DAYS	1-6 MONTHS	7-12 MONTHS	1-2 YEARS	3-5 YEARS	OVER 5 YEARS	TOTAL		THIS MONTH	YEAR TO DATE	LAST YEAR TO DATE
FRONT OFFICE																						
RESERVATIONS																						
HOUSEKEEPING																						
GUEST SERVICES																						
PABX																						
HEALTH CLUB																						
F & B ADMIN.																						
CATERING																						
BANQUETS																						
CULINARY																						
STEWARD																						
BEVERAGE																						
ROOM SERVICE																						
VIP's																						
CAFE REN.																						
CHATZ																						
DEE JAY'S																						
LA FONTAINE																						
GALLERIA BAR																						
CASHIERS																						
INNER CIRCLE																						
... RELATIONS																						
PROPERTY MAINTENANCE																						
LAUNDRY																						
ENGINEERING																						
VALET																						
TOTAL																						

ANNUAL TURNOVER GOAL   % HIRES: MO./YEAR

HOTEL: TURNOVER % THIS MONTH:

TURNOVER % YEAR TO DATE:

Courtesy of Westin Hotels, Seattle, Washington.

minimum disruption to your department. A **labor needs forecast form** (see Exhibit 3.3) can help you anticipate and keep up with your labor needs.

For example, assume that when a position opens up in your department, it takes about a week to fill out the paperwork to requisition a new employee, get approval, and begin recruiting efforts. Another week of screening, in-depth interviewing, and reference checking is required before the right person can be hired. Often the selected applicant must work out a two-week notice elsewhere. At least one week of orientation and training is necessary before the new employee can be considered anywhere near an adequate performance level. At this rate, a position could easily take five weeks to fill.

The period of time required to fill a position and bring the new employee to the minimum expected performance level is known as **downtime**. As the

Exhibit 3.3   Labor Needs Forecast Form

Department: Coffee Shop

<table>
<tr>
<th rowspan="3">POSITIONS</th>
<th rowspan="3">Number Full Staff</th>
<th rowspan="3">Current Number</th>
<th rowspan="3">Staff Openings</th>
<th rowspan="3">Anticipated Turnover During Buildup*</th>
<th rowspan="3">Total to be Hired</th>
<th rowspan="3">Training Time</th>
<th rowspan="3">Number Trained at one Time</th>
<th rowspan="3">Recruiting Time</th>
<th colspan="8">LEAD TIME — Hiring / Training Schedule ** — Week Beginning **</th>
<th rowspan="3">Date Needed Full Staff</th>
</tr>
<tr>
<th>7/10</th><th>7/17</th><th>7/24</th><th>7/31</th><th>8/7</th><th>8/14</th><th>8/21</th><th>8/28</th>
</tr>
<tr></tr>
<tr>
<td>Server</td><td>10</td><td>6</td><td>4</td><td>1</td><td>5</td><td>2 wks</td><td>2</td><td>3 wks</td>
<td></td><td></td><td>2</td><td>2</td><td></td><td></td><td>1</td><td></td><td>9/4</td>
</tr>
<tr>
<td>Bus Help</td><td>3</td><td>2</td><td>1</td><td>2</td><td>3</td><td>1 wk</td><td>2</td><td></td>
<td></td><td></td><td></td><td></td><td>2</td><td></td><td>1</td><td></td><td>9/4</td>
</tr>
<tr>
<td>Cashier</td><td>3</td><td>3</td><td>0</td><td>0</td><td>0</td><td></td><td></td><td></td>
<td></td><td></td><td></td><td></td><td></td><td></td><td></td><td></td><td></td>
</tr>
<tr>
<td>Food Prep.</td><td>4</td><td>3</td><td>1</td><td>1</td><td>2</td><td>4 wks</td><td>1</td><td></td>
<td>1</td><td></td><td></td><td></td><td>1</td><td></td><td></td><td></td><td>9/4</td>
</tr>
<tr>
<td>Host / Hostess</td><td>3</td><td>2</td><td>1</td><td>0</td><td>1</td><td>3 wks</td><td>1</td><td></td>
<td></td><td></td><td></td><td></td><td>1</td><td></td><td></td><td></td><td>9/4</td>
</tr>
<tr>
<td>Dishwasher</td><td>4</td><td>2</td><td>2</td><td>3</td><td>5</td><td>2 days</td><td>2</td><td></td>
<td></td><td></td><td>2</td><td>2</td><td></td><td></td><td>1</td><td></td><td></td>
</tr>
<tr>
<td>Totals</td><td>27</td><td>18</td><td>9</td><td>7</td><td>16</td><td></td><td></td><td></td>
<td>1</td><td>2</td><td>3</td><td>3</td><td>3</td><td>3</td><td></td><td></td><td></td>
</tr>
</table>

* Consider Terminations, Transfers, Promotions and other Turnover Factors.
** Consider Total Training Time Available in one week along with Business Levels, Vacations/Holidays, Timing of other Departments or Area Recruiting Practices.

Signature _____   Date _____

labor market shrinks, the downtime involved in filling any given position is likely to increase. The average length of time it takes to fill a management position may be considerably longer. The higher the level of skill and authority of the position, the longer it will take to fill.

If you don't have adequate lead time to fill a position, you'll be forced to hire the first person who walks through the door. If you're unable to hire the best available candidate because of time constraints, you cannot possibly hope to meet your guests' expectations, maintain your productivity standards, or control your turnover and its resulting costs.

Reducing downtime by accurately anticipating needs thus becomes an important element of the staffing process. Forecasting labor needs is as important as forecasting sales. For years, managers have figured in lead time when requisitioning supplies like linen, food, and equipment. They are just now beginning to realize its importance in staffing.

As a matter of fact, the employment requisition is very similar to a purchase order, except that the item being ordered is the most complex and expensive on earth. Each full-time person hired will cost at least $10,000 in wages and benefits every year, and frequently a great deal more. It takes time to find the best value for your investment.

Require Proper Notice

To help reduce your downtime, be absolutely certain every employee in your department understands the company's notice and rehire policies, which should appear in the employee handbook. It's typical for companies to require that employees serve at least two weeks' notice before leaving a job. Although it's a difficult requirement to enforce, many companies advise employees in the employee handbook that failure to give proper notice may be mentioned in the references they receive and may affect certain benefits. For example, some employers don't pay for accrued vacation time or days off earned through perfect attendance to employees who quit without giving notice. It's also common to prohibit the rehire of employees who fail to give adequate notice.

You should have a good enough relationship with your employees that they tell you as far in advance as possible that they're leaving. When they do give proper notice, allow them to work out their notice without harassment. Also, let them know you appreciate having the warning, perhaps with a statement such as the following:

> Thanks for letting me know. Keeping our department running smoothly is important, and I appreciate having the notice. As long as your performance doesn't slip, you can stay the full two weeks; and I'm sure it won't. I always could count on you. In fact, I'd like to make these last two weeks your best time here so that all your fellow workers have a good memory of you, you can get the best possible reference, and we can see that you receive all the benefits you have coming to you.

If you penalize employees who give adequate notice by discharging them early, eventually no employee will give notice before quitting, and your department's production will ultimately suffer. In addition, if you fire someone who has given notice without being able to show just cause, most states will see it as a termination which requires your company to pay unemployment compensation.

Enforce the company's policies and take a hard line on giving proper notice. For every position that's left vacant, the remaining employees have an extra load to carry. Don't hesitate to let them know when their work increases because of a former employee who left without giving notice.

Spot the Signs of Potential Turnover

The most successful staffing obviously results when a company experiences no turnover. If you can identify and work with those who are thinking about leaving, you may be able to head off some turnover. Keep in touch with the grapevine. Other employees know well in advance who is troubled enough to leave, and this information should be funneled to you.

Once you've identified a distressed employee, talk to that person immediately and try to head off any chance of resignation. If the person has personal problems, help work them out if you can. You must extend this assistance before the employee has actually made a conscious decision to leave. Otherwise, it's unlikely that the positive commitment can be regained.

Not all turnover, however, can or should be avoided. It may not be advisable to try salvaging someone who has already abandoned the job in terms of attitude and commitment. To do so is difficult at best and can be damaging to the performance and morale of the department. In some cases, it may be best to help the resignation of such employees along. Have a frank and honest discussion about the situation to help the person see that he or she would be better off somewhere else. If necessary, discreetly give the person some time off to search for another job or offer a favorable exit package. Even if you already have a few openings, keeping a non-productive person around may be more harmful to your operation than creating another vacancy.

Other factors that signal a possible vacancy are increased absenteeism and lateness, a decrease in productivity and work performance, a negative attitude, a tendency of the employee to avoid you, and an increase in disciplinary problems. Certainly by the time an employee is on a "final warning" status, you should be preparing for a potential opening.

Anticipate Business Cycles and Future Needs

Keep in mind your long-term staffing needs. Maintaining records of employee turnover will help you keep track of trends and predict problem times. Know your peak hiring months and advise applicants who inquire at other times when they might call back. It's important to acquaint the local labor market with your staffing cycle.

When business is slow, people who leave are not normally replaced. When the busy season arrives, all departments usually begin to prepare their job requisitions at the same time. Since the person or department that handles recruitment (often called the human resources or personnel department) isn't staffed to handle such peaks, longer delays are inevitable.

About half of all turnover occurs within the first 30 days, so you may have to plan on hiring more people than the number of actual job openings in order to fill the openings permanently. To know exactly how many more, you must be well-acquainted with your department's turnover history.

Your forecast should allow for additional normal turnover which will occur during the period of time for which you're increasing staff, including transfers out of your department. Some vacancies can be predicted well in advance, such as those created by employees returning to school or retiring. Other vacancies can only be estimated based on your familiarity with your department's turnover history.

You should also consider how many people you can train at one time and how long training will take. Stagger your hiring accordingly.

Keep in mind that your competitors are usually on the same business cycle as you. If you start your staffing program a week or two earlier than your competition, you can gain a competitive edge in the recruiting drive.

Working with Your Recruiting Coordinator

At many properties, a single person or department is responsible for coordinating staff recruitment upon notification of an opening, even if you anticipate filling it internally through a promotion or transfer. This recruiting coordinator may manage advertising, agency referrals, work programs, acceptance of applications, applicant screening, and extension of offers. If your property is part of a large corporation, a national or regional headquarters office may recruit candidates; if your property is a small, independent facility, the general manager will probably oversee this function. In any case, the department manager usually initiates the request to begin an applicant search and provides the necessary information, cooperation, and support along the way.

Define Your Needs

The **job profile** (see Exhibit 3.4) is a description of your job opening. It is intended to aid you and the recruiter in matching the right person to the job. Before compiling the job profile, particularly the personal traits, you need a solid understanding of the environment in which the employee will be working. You must also be familiar with the company's values and goals.

A job profile should be as brief as possible, but must contain everything you and the recruiting coordinator need to know to find the right candidate, including:

- All the key information about the job, such as hours and wages

- A **job task list**, with key duties of the job listed in order of importance

- **Primary job requirements**, which list the minimum requirements of the job, such as heavy lifting, language proficiency, special licenses, and typing or arithmetic skills

- **Secondary job requirements**, which list characteristics you would like a candidate to have, such as pleasant telephone voice, good handwriting, and preferred education

- A list of personal traits that would make one applicant preferable over another

Don't make the primary requirements too restrictive. The tougher they are, the more limited your labor market. For example, you could put in a request for a sales secretary and require that the person work flexible shifts, any day of the week; have three years' sales experience; type 60 words per minute, with prior word processing experience; and present an attractive business appearance, nice wardrobe, and pleasant telephone voice. In today's labor market, you could wait the rest of your life for someone to meet those specifications. The human resources department doesn't manufacture people; they can only send you the best available candidates from among those who apply.

Exhibit 3.4   Job Profile

JOB PROFILE

JOB TITLE_____DEPT._____

REPORTS TO_____STARTING RATE_____

Full-   Part-   On   ADDITIONAL INCOME
time_____   time_____   Call_____   (Tips, OT, etc.)_____

HOURS: FROM_____TO_____AVERAGE HOURS/WEEK_____

DAYS OFF_____

KEY DUTIES, LISTED BY PRIORITY:

_____

_____

_____

_____

PRIMARY REQUIREMENTS:

_____

_____

_____

_____

SECONDARY REQUIREMENTS:

_____

_____

_____

_____

STRONG PERSONAL TRAITS REQUIRED:

_____

_____

_____

In addition, if you set tough specifications and then, at the last minute, hire someone who doesn't meet them, you may have to justify your hiring decisions to the Labor Board, Equal Employment Opportunity Commission (EEOC), or other government agencies. Also, good candidates may have been turned away early in the search.

Use an Employment Requisition

To control the hiring process, larger companies use an **employment requisition** (see Exhibit 3.5). Remember that the requisition is essentially your purchase order, and never underestimate its importance. If the requisition

Exhibit 3.5   Employment Requisition

EMPLOYMENT REQUISITION

Job
Title_____Department_____Starting
Date_____

Replacement?_____If yes, who_____Termination
Date_____

Addition?_____If yes, reason_____

Permanent?_____If no, until what date_____

Full-time?_____If no, hours per week_____

Starting   Hours*   am   am   Days*
Salary_____From_____pm To_____pm Off_____

Primary Requirements_____

_____

Secondary Requirements_____

_____

Authorizations:
                                 Department   Division
Date_____Head_____Head_____

Personnel_____General Manager_____

To be completed by Human Resources Department:

Date Filled_____By Whom_____

(* It is understood that hours and days off may change with work schedules.)

procedure isn't followed or the information is incomplete or inaccurate, you can waste countless hours interviewing people who don't meet your needs.

Based on the lead time you've established, send the employment requisition to the recruiter when you want to start recruiting actively, and not before. If you don't anticipate the need to fill the position for six months because you're in the slow season, wait to send the requisition.

You should complete a requisition for each job opening. Personally see that any necessary approvals are obtained.

**Make Sure the
Recruiter
Understands
the Job**

Hand carry every requisition to the recruiter, and discuss the opening. This serves two purposes. First, it eliminates the days of delay that can result from mailing the requisition. Second, it gives the recruiter the opportunity to learn of any special needs and to ask additional questions about the specifications. Furnishing a copy of the job profile could also be helpful.

A recruiter who is unfamiliar with the job might want to talk to some of your better employees in order to identify the correct employee profile for that job. Similarly, the recruiter can obtain first-hand knowledge by spending time in your department to see how it operates.

Conduct a Follow-Up
Keep a copy of all active requisitions and check on their progress regularly. It's best to contact the recruiter just before the Sunday help-wanted ads are arranged. Keep in mind that the recruiter usually has many openings to fill, and must balance your priorities with those of the entire company.

Notify the recruiter at once if the requirements of your job opening change. For example, if a night-shift employee transfers to your open day-shift position, the recruiter must know that the hours of the open position have changed. Once the opening is filled, the name of the person hired should be added to the requisition and the requisition placed in the newly hired employee's personnel jacket. This record of applicant flow is necessary in the event of any EEOC claims.

Internal Recruiting

Managers can use a number of effective recruiting techniques to reduce downtime without ever going outside the company. Internal recruiting offers the greatest consistency, improves morale, and provides a fast and relatively inexpensive source of skilled applicants. A well-publicized policy of promotion from within can be a strong employee motivator.

Cross-Training
Employees should be taught to fill the requirements of more than one position whenever union contract permits. Make sure that each potential new employee understands that **cross-training** is included in the job duties before you make an offer.

Succession Planning
Increasingly, managers are faced with the need for trained back-ups in each department, especially for hard-to-fill, highly skilled, or specialized positions. This may even mean restructuring an entire department to have assistants in place and ready to step into key positions should the need arise.

In **succession planning**, a manager identifies a key position and an employee in the department who might eventually be able to fill that position. If management determines that further training is necessary, a plan should be prepared outlining where and when it takes place, and who should be responsible for managing the process.

Identifying and Recording Unused Skills
The annual review provides an excellent opportunity to ask employees what additional skills they have which are not currently being used. If their skills and interests lie in another department, notify that department's head or the human resources department. Managers must realize that, in order to keep good employees in the company, they will occasionally lose them to other departments. If employees are unable to move where they can best apply their skills, they may choose to leave the company for better opportunities.

Check on the progress of employee succession plans. Make sure employees take advantage of tuition reimbursement or other programs which enable them to obtain the needed skills.

Paying for Performance
It's extremely demoralizing for someone who works very hard and cross-trains for additional skills to get the same pay increase as everyone else. As employees begin to develop other skills, they become more valuable to your department and should be paid accordingly. As the competition for good workers intensifies, the possibility of losing your most talented

employees increases, particularly if they are not receiving adequate compensation.

Posting Job Openings

An effective **job posting** program can reduce turnover and provide good applicants interested in your job opening. Some of your employees may be interested in transferring or moving up to the position. The recruiter posts the position as soon as he or she receives the requisition. Such postings should be maintained for a specified period of time *before* you hire an outside applicant; three days may be sufficient. Exhibit 3.6 is a sample job posting.

The posting location should be a highly visible area, such as the employee break room. Use a central bulletin board to post all company openings except those you expect to fill from within your own department. Even posting non-skilled or entry-level positions can be useful. Although the employees themselves may not apply, quite often they will refer their friends.

Always try to understand and respond to the needs of your employees. If employees apply for positions but aren't qualified, you may encourage and assist them in developing the needed skills. That way, they will be ready the next time such an opening occurs.

It's imperative that employees who apply for a posted opening receive treatment equal to or better than that received by outside applicants. Follow up with employees interested in the position. If someone else gets the job, explain the real reason—don't give a phony excuse. If your own employees apply and don't understand why they are turned down, they may get discouraged, their productivity might slip, they may consider leaving, and, in extreme cases, they could even undermine the department or the new employee.

Keeping a Call-Back List

Recruiting is a never-ending process. To assist future recruiting efforts (both internal and external), keep a record, or **call-back list**, of all employees and outside applicants with special skills who express an interest in positions in your department. In addition, you may want to keep the names of former employees who can be called back during temporary emergencies. Many fine employees leave for reasons other than dissatisfaction, and may make excellent back-ups should the need arise.

External Recruiting

As we've learned, internal recruiting offers an organization many advantages; however, your system should not be so inflexible as to exclude outside applicants. New people bring in fresh ideas and help your existing staff stay current, avoid stagnation, and reduce complacency.

Rather than relying totally on promotion from within, a company's staffing policies should allow for some regular external recruitment, especially at the management level. A worthwhile goal for the average independent operation would be to fill about 10% of management openings at all levels with people who come from outside the company.

Your Image as an Employer

Crucial to the success of your outside recruiting efforts is a good image for you personally, for your department, and for your company. Employees want to work for a company that's well respected in the community. What

Exhibit 3.6   Sample In-House Job Posting

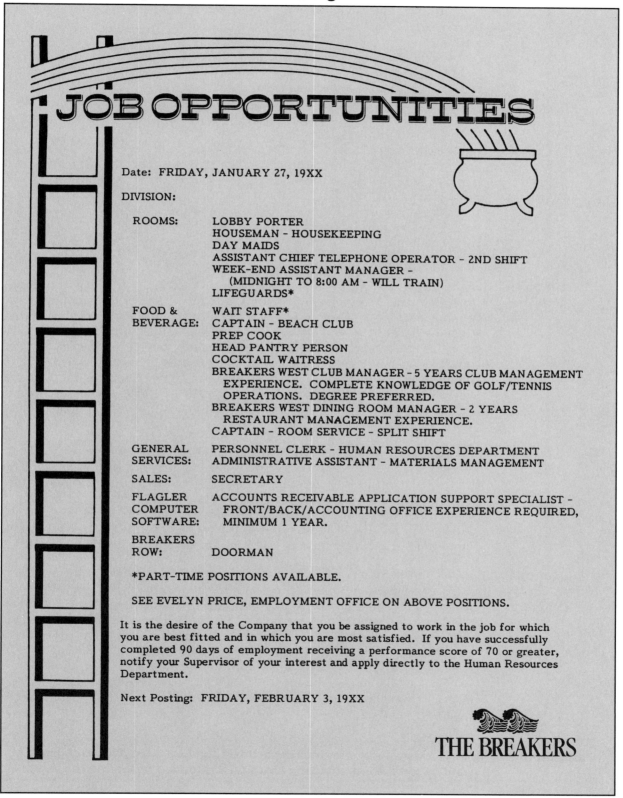

JOB OPPORTUNITIES

Date: FRIDAY, JANUARY 27, 19XX

DIVISION:

ROOMS:	LOBBY PORTER
	HOUSEMAN – HOUSEKEEPING
	DAY MAIDS
	ASSISTANT CHIEF TELEPHONE OPERATOR – 2ND SHIFT
	WEEK-END ASSISTANT MANAGER –
	(MIDNIGHT TO 8:00 AM – WILL TRAIN)
	LIFEGUARDS*

FOOD &	WAIT STAFF*
BEVERAGE:	CAPTAIN – BEACH CLUB
	PREP COOK
	HEAD PANTRY PERSON
	COCKTAIL WAITRESS
	BREAKERS WEST CLUB MANAGER – 5 YEARS CLUB MANAGEMENT
	EXPERIENCE. COMPLETE KNOWLEDGE OF GOLF/TENNIS
	OPERATIONS. DEGREE PREFERRED.
	BREAKERS WEST DINING ROOM MANAGER – 2 YEARS
	RESTAURANT MANAGEMENT EXPERIENCE.
	CAPTAIN – ROOM SERVICE – SPLIT SHIFT

GENERAL	PERSONNEL CLERK – HUMAN RESOURCES DEPARTMENT
SERVICES:	ADMINISTRATIVE ASSISTANT – MATERIALS MANAGEMENT

SALES:	SECRETARY

FLAGLER	ACCOUNTS RECEIVABLE APPLICATION SUPPORT SPECIALIST –
COMPUTER	FRONT/BACK/ACCOUNTING OFFICE EXPERIENCE REQUIRED,
SOFTWARE:	MINIMUM 1 YEAR.

BREAKERS	
ROW:	DOORMAN

*PART-TIME POSITIONS AVAILABLE.

SEE EVELYN PRICE, EMPLOYMENT OFFICE ON ABOVE POSITIONS.

It is the desire of the Company that you be assigned to work in the job for which you are best fitted and in which you are most satisfied. If you have successfully completed 90 days of employment receiving a performance score of 70 or greater, notify your Supervisor of your interest and apply directly to the Human Resources Department.

Next Posting: FRIDAY, FEBRUARY 3, 19XX

THE BREAKERS

Courtesy of The Breakers, Palm Beach, Florida.

are job seekers saying about your company? Are unsuccessful applicants being treated well? What's your reputation with local suppliers? It isn't just your customers who are talking about your company, but the community as a whole.

The reputation of being a bad place to work can be devastating. A poor image for your department or operation greatly reduces the caliber and number of applicants. A department with high turnover is likely to generate bad public relations. Word gets around. Most of your staff have probably worked for one of your major competitors at some time. They still know people at those other places and they stay in touch.

On the other hand, a good reputation can have applicants knocking at your door. Use the same professionalism that the sales department uses to market the property as "a good place to stay" to sell your department as "a good place to work."

Improve your sales pitch. Today's applicants have many choices. You must know and discuss your company's benefits and be able sell their value. Know the pluses and minuses of your company and those of your competition.

Community Activities

Industry professionals should lecture at local high schools and colleges, support Junior Achievement programs, and attend career days and job fairs. Become a member of the advisory boards of schools that train hospitality students. Offer tours of your facility to organizations that supply referrals. Consider speaking to professional organizations, business associations, and civic groups. Join the Lions Club or the Kiwanis Club, and participate in community activities with high civic interest, such as the Toys for Tots and United Way campaigns. Companies may even consider paying employees' membership costs to join organizations that make a positive contribution to the community.

Positive Press

Look for newsworthy items and suggest press releases to publicize them. Recognize the service or sales person who goes "beyond the call of duty" to service your business, then send out a press release to the local newspaper and various trade magazines, and notify the person's employer. Develop a good citizenship award to recognize employees for doing work in the community. The success of these types of programs depends on your input and commitment to them, but they yield rewards in the positive image created.

Educational Work Programs

Practically every high school offers a distributive education program, and most colleges have **internship programs** (sometimes called **externship programs**). These programs allow students time off to work and obtain actual job experience, often while they earn school credit. Participating in such programs is an excellent way to find good temporary help while you evaluate the student's potential to become a permanent employee. Most students would like to return to work for the companies where they've interned.

Naturally, you must be sure that the intern has a positive experience and returns to the school with a good report of your company. This leads to more and better candidates from which to choose the next time.

Unscheduled Interviews

In a tight labor market, a company must be prepared to act as soon as a good applicant comes in the door because it may not get another chance to talk to the person. If a company representative can't talk to them right away,

This Ronald McDonald House in Michigan is part of an international program to provide temporary housing for families of seriously ill children who must come from out of town to receive medical treatment. Through their support of the Ronald McDonald House program, the McDonald's Corporation and its employees make a valuable contribution to the community. (Courtesy of West Michigan Ronald McDonald House, Grand Rapids, Michigan)

the better candidates won't wait a few days for an interview—they'll continue to look until they find a job, perhaps the same day.

When a good applicant makes an unscheduled visit, if the appropriate personnel are unable to speak with him or her immediately, they should not send the person away until they have expressed a serious interest and set up a specific time for an interview in the near future. A statement such as the following could help to dissuade the person from continuing to look elsewhere:

> I'm sure the manager would be very interested in talking to you. You seem to have the skills he's looking for, and he'd like to fill the job opening as soon as possible. Can you come back at two o'clock this afternoon?

For entry-level and unskilled jobs, reviewing applications that have been on file for a month or two is usually unproductive. Good people will have found jobs already, and those still looking are less likely to be desirable candidates. If you do go back to the files, call the most recent applicant first,

Hospitality educators take a tour of the Amway Grand Plaza Hotel, Grand Rapids, Michigan.

rather than trying to contact people in the same order in which they applied. For a skilled applicant, such as a pastry chef, you may wish to keep the application in a call-back file for years.

Networking   Finding the best candidate often depends on your ability to develop and use a network of your own personal contacts. A network may include your friends, business associates, and counterparts at other companies. In addition, there are many sources within the community which can be developed.

For example, teachers and placement counselors at local trade schools, high schools, and colleges are often excellent sources for referrals. When interviewing students, have them identify their favorite teachers, and then develop a relationship with these individuals. They greatly influence their students and often stay in touch with better graduates. If your company finds that a school is especially helpful, management should consider donating used equipment, contributing funds to establish scholarships, and offering its teachers summer employment.

The people who supply or service your hotel or restaurant may also have useful information. The companies that sell and service your cash registers, telephone systems, computer systems, and other equipment are familiar with other local operations. They often know who else in town has good people with the necessary skills.

Most large cities have trade associations you can join. Contact your local chapter of the Educational Institute of the American Hotel & Motel Association, Hotel Sales and Marketing Association International, or the front office managers, controllers, or chefs associations. Get involved.

After you have located your network sources, identify the key contacts and deal with a specific person, such as a teacher, minister, or counselor. (Record your contacts when recruiting or networking on a form such as the **recruiting source log** shown in Exhibit 3.7.) Establish a relationship and keep

Exhibit 3.7   Recruiting Source Log

RECRUITING SOURCE LOG

Organization_____ Phone_____

Address_____ Best time to
contact_____

Key Contacts_____

_____

Personal Data (Interests, birthday, mutual friends, prior jobs, etc.)_____

_____

_____

Referral specialties, if any (cooks, handicapped, elderly, etc.)

_____

Date Contacted	Type of Contact (job listing, site visit, etc.)	Notified When Position Filled	Results of Contact

---

in touch. Visit them at their jobs. Provide them with printed materials about the company, including employee programs. Invite them for lunch or dinner and a tour of your facility. Send them regular copies of the employee newsletter, Christmas cards, and relevant press releases or clippings. While networking is every manager's responsibility, remember to have all applicants referred to the recruiting coordinator.

If you have requested their help in filling an opening, by all means call them back when you do fill the job. Communication is important in maintaining your network.

The Corporate Office

If your property is part of a chain, the corporation or another unit in the chain may be able to assist, particularly in key management areas. Many corporations keep records and maintain files of promotable employees.

Temporary Agencies

Temporary agencies were once regarded primarily as a labor source for vacation relief or extra help on special projects, particularly in the clerical areas. Today, temporary agencies can supply personnel for almost any position in the company, including chefs and upper-level managers. In many cases, they can hire and train people to meet your specific needs. Some can furnish a supervised crew, including uniforms and tools.

The hourly rate these agencies charge will probably be higher than the usual rate you pay employees, but this may be offset by a number of other savings. Temporary firms can usually supply help very quickly, which may reduce your overtime expense, as well as recruitment and hiring costs. Using temporary labor may reduce costs in areas like medical benefits, paid time off, Social Security, and workers' compensation insurance. When business slows down, temporary help can be released without the cost of paying unemployment compensation or the worry of defending wrongful dismissal lawsuits. In addition, the temporary agency's employees have been screened. They are probably full-time and receive benefits and training, and are likelier to regard their work as permanent and worth making a commitment to.

Altogether, these savings may be particularly significant to a smaller employer. Often, smaller employers are unable to carry extra people during slow periods or reassign them to another work area. Even some larger companies are finding advantages in developing long-term relationships with reliable temporary agencies which are able to provide a supervised crew of workers on demand.

On the other hand, many employers feel that they cannot get the desired levels of consistency and commitment from temporary employees. Others express doubts about paying premium wages for people who learn the work only to leave. Using such agency employees is not without its problems. In an emergency, however, reliable temporary help can provide the time you need to find good permanent help. As with any other recruiting source, careful selection and management can help eliminate many concerns.

Before selecting an agency, someone from management or the human resources department should visit the firm and evaluate the operation. Exhibit 3.8 is a checklist of possible questions for prospective agencies. If your representative doesn't receive satisfactory answers to these questions, he or she may want to keep looking. Once your company has selected an agency, it should send someone to visit the agency's facilities once or twice a year.

Try to give the temporary workers the same treatment you give regular employees. Show them the location of the break areas and restrooms, get to know them, and treat them as an important part of your operation. It may be best to have temporary workers perform simple jobs under the best supervisors until you can assess their skills. Schedule conventional hours at first, until you're sure they are dependable. Don't schedule new temporary workers for a 6 a.m. opening shift if you're not sure they'll arrive on time.

Finally, tell the agency representatives about any problem areas, as well as areas of the program which are working well for you.

Leased Employees

When workers are needed on a more permanent basis, leasing employees may be more feasible than using a temporary agency. In a leasing arrangement, the leasing agency hires the employees and leases them to the hospitality business, billing the employer on a regular basis for the costs of the employees.

Some employers are even entering into agreements with leasing companies in which the latter hires all of the former's current workers and leases them back to the employer. The employees are happy because the leasing company can provide better job security and more benefits than most small, independent hospitality employers can afford. The manager is also happy

Exhibit 3.8 Checklist for Evaluating Temporary Agencies

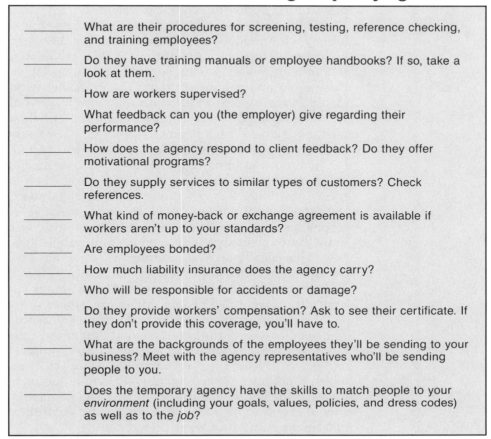

_____ What are their procedures for screening, testing, reference checking, and training employees?

_____ Do they have training manuals or employee handbooks? If so, take a look at them.

_____ How are workers supervised?

_____ What feedback can you (the employer) give regarding their performance?

_____ How does the agency respond to client feedback? Do they offer motivational programs?

_____ Do they supply services to similar types of customers? Check references.

_____ What kind of money-back or exchange agreement is available if workers aren't up to your standards?

_____ Are employees bonded?

_____ How much liability insurance does the agency carry?

_____ Who will be responsible for accidents or damage?

_____ Do they provide workers' compensation? Ask to see their certificate. If they don't provide this coverage, you'll have to.

_____ What are the backgrounds of the employees they'll be sending to your business? Meet with the agency representatives who'll be sending people to you.

_____ Does the temporary agency have the skills to match people to your *environment* (including your goals, values, policies, and dress codes) as well as to the *job*?

because the leasing company can provide services and benefits at a lower cost. In addition, the leasing company offers many of the same advantages as a temporary agency. The leasing agency handles such responsibilities as recruitment and screening, payroll administration, and government compliance. Thus, the manager can spend more time managing.

Private Employment Agencies

A company's recruiter usually coordinates efforts in such areas as employment agency contacts and help-wanted advertising. However, there are a few relevant points that every manager should know.

In general, there are two types of searches done by private employment agencies: the contingency search and the retained search. Some firms do both types of searches, while others do only one. In a **contingency search**, the agency refers applicants for salaried and skilled hourly positions for a fee. If you hire one of their applicants, you pay a fee; if you don't, there is no charge. Since the fee is usually based on a percentage of the employee's salary, those employers who pay the highest wages or provide the most volume usually get the best choice of applicants. Fees are often negotiable in spite of the agency's stated policy. Such agencies will often provide a **guarantee period**. Under this guarantee, if you hire through an agency a person who leaves you within a specified length of time, the agency agrees to replace the employee for free or refund the fee. Be sure to discuss longer guarantee periods and discounts for prompt payment.

Since contingency searches only make money if there is a placement, the agency will usually work harder if you give them—at least temporarily—an exclusive or semi-exclusive listing. If they are unable to develop applicants within a couple of weeks, you may consider listing with another agency. Advise the original agency that you are listing with another firm but will gladly interview any additional candidates they would like to send.

The **retained search** is used chiefly for middle to upper-level management positions. With a retained search, you pay a portion of the agency's fee in advance, another portion within a specified period (usually 90 days), and the final portion upon filling the job. You usually commit to paying this fee regardless of whether the job is filled, or even if it's filled from another source. Exhibit 3.9 is an outline of the retained search process.

The agency working on a retained search is likelier to seek out and screen qualified candidates not actively in the job market. They are also more thorough at screening and matching people to your company and position. This usually takes extra time; in fact, it may be 90 days or more before the first applicants start to arrive. These agencies maintain that, because of their thoroughness, you don't need to see as many candidates or waste your time with unqualified people. Many times, they're right.

Choosing a firm to conduct retained searches should be done with care. The people making the choice should obtain the names of other clients and talk to them to find out what type of written contract is furnished, how they will bill you, what type of guarantee they provide, and when you will begin to see candidates. They should get to know the representative who will be working for you. Since your company will be paying for their services, you should expect to be able to exercise greater control over their activities than you might with other types of agencies.

Private employment agencies may have advertising budgets and very economical help-wanted rates in local newspapers. Consider letting them include your positions in their help-wanted ads.

Other Agencies and Strategies

Exhibit 3.10 presents a list of recruitment strategies. In addition to the various agencies mentioned in Exhibit 3.10, public and religious agencies offering excellent sources for applicants include:

- State employment services
- Agencies for single parents
- Shelters for abused women
- Veterans' groups
- The YMCA and YWCA
- The Salvation Army
- Orphanages

Once your recruiting coordinator has identified the agencies which work best for you, he or she should identify a key contact to add to the network of referral sources. Of course, if your company lists openings with any agency, it should follow up with a letter when the position is filled.

Exhibit 3.9 Outline of the Retained Search Process

BOWMAN & ASSOCIATES
MANAGEMENT SERVICES

DEVELOPMENT & EXECUTION OF THE EXECUTIVE SEARCH PROCESS

- **CLIENT MEETING**

  - Staffing need analysis & organizational chart review

  - Job description development; compensation/benefits; evaluation of corporate culture

  - Determine geographic range of search effort

  - Establish search schedule and targeted hire/start date

  - Issue to client the letter of engagement & fee agreement

- **RESEARCH PHASE** (Time required: 3 to 6 weeks)

  - Determine all of client's direct and related competitors

  - Develop the names and exact titles of all persons who now hold or have recently held targeted responsibilities

  - Submit this information to client for review as to direction of the search process, and for feedback as to anyone with whom the client may be familiar

  - Typical resultant data base: 75 to 125 candidates

- **CONTACT/RECRUITING PHASE** (Time required: 3 to 6 weeks)

  - Contact all listed executives to determine level of interest, if any, and do preliminary screening. as to professional, compensatory, and geographic issues.

  - Of interested candidates not screened out, gather complete professional background and, as appropriate, personal information

  - Submit results to date for client review and discussion

  - Typical resultant data base: 15 to 25 candidates

- **FINAL SCREENING** (Time required: 2 to 5 weeks)

  - Further screening to include personal interviews and confidential reference checking, as appropriate

  - Analysis of cultural compatability of final candidates

  - Presentation of candidates' credentials to client, and arrangement of client/candidate meetings

  - Typical resultant data base: 2 to 5 candidates

- **CANDIDATE SELECTION** (Time required: 2 to 6 weeks)

  - Compile any candidate information requested and perform any additional reference checking.

  - Assist with the formulation, presentation, and negotiation of compensation/relocation package to selected candidate

  - Following acceptance, counsel candidate on "counteroffer" and other transitory issues

  - Assist client and candidate as necessary through first day of employment.

1660
SOUTH
AMPHLETT BLVD.
SUITE 245
SAN MATEO, CA
94402
(415) 573-0188

Courtesy of Bowman & Associates, San Mateo, California.

Exhibit 3.10 Recruitment Strategies

RECRUITMENT STRATEGIES

1. **Youth**
   Schools, Vo-Techs, Colleges
   — Meet with counselors
   — Speak to classes
   — Sponsor work study programs
   — Participate in career days
   — Invite classes to tour hotel

2. **Minorities**
   — Meet with representatives from minority community agencies and invite for lunch and tour of hotel
   — Advertise in minority newspapers
   — Visit schools in minority neighborhoods
   — Notices at churches in minority communities
   — Visit youth centers and place notices there

3. **Disabled Persons**
   — State Rehabilitation Agencies
   — National Alliance of Business
   — Private Industry Councils
   — National Association of Retarded Citizens
   — Goodwill Industries
   — Other local agencies

4. **Women**
   — Local organizations which assist women in transition
   — Community colleges, universities
   — Bulletin board notices in supermarkets, libraries, YWCAs, exercise centers
   — Flyers in parking lots
   — Displaced Homemakers organizations
   — Craft centers
   — Child care centers

5. **Older Workers**
   — AARP Senior Employment Services
   — Senior Citizen Centers
   — Synagogues and churches
   — Retirement communities and apartment complexes
   — Newspaper ads worded to attract
   — Retired military

6. **Individuals in Career Transition**
   — Newspaper ads
   — University evening programs
   — Referrals
   — Teachers
   — Unemployed actors
   — Laid off workers from other industries
   — Speak at community functions, i.e., Rotary, Toastmasters

7. **Lawfully Authorized Immigrants**
   — Ads in foreign language newspapers
   — Churches
   — English as a Second Language classes
   — Citizenship classes
   — Refugee resettlement centers
   — Employee referrals

Courtesy of Radisson Hotel Corporation, Minneapolis, Minnesota.

Tax Credits   Some government programs direct tax incentives to private employers who provide job opportunities to certain categories of workers. One current federal program is the **Targeted Jobs Tax Credits Program**. Any worker you hire under this program *must* be certified as a member of a targeted category by a local office of your state employment security agency *before* you extend a hiring offer. If a member of a targeted group applies for a job, you may direct that person to the state employment office with a request for certification. The targeted categories include:

- Vocational rehabilitation referrals
- Economically disadvantaged youths from 18 to 24 years of age, inclusive
- Economically disadvantaged Vietnam-era veterans
- Supplemental Security Income (SSI) and general assistance recipients
- Youths participating in a cooperative education program (with certification provided by the school administering the program)
- Economically disadvantaged ex-convicts
- Eligible work incentive employees
- Qualified summer youth employees

For a company to claim the targeted job tax credit on the wages paid to the employee, the person must not have worked for the company before and may not be a relative or dependent of the company's owner. If a certified applicant or employee does not work out, you are under no special constraints to hire or keep the person.

Employee Referral Programs   Since word-of-mouth is one of the best forms of advertising, some organizations have formal referral programs to encourage their employees to help recruit. Such programs generally involve rewarding employees who refer applicants to the organization. By bringing in more applicants, the program can help lower the cost per hire. In addition, such programs frequently help improve morale and reduce employee turnover.

Satisfied employees can be your most effective salespeople. They often know other people with similar skills and interests. For example, your maintenance engineers may know and have worked with other good maintenance people. As a general rule, good employees refer other good employees, while poor workers generally provide poor referrals.

To set up a program, management should begin with detailed guidelines that clearly establish the size of the rewards, conditions which must be met to earn rewards, and methods of crediting referrals. Most organizations don't seek referrals for all job classifications, just those jobs that are hard to fill or require unusual skills.

The program can be conducted over the short term (a few months at the beginning of your hiring season) or can be part of an ongoing process. It should have a campaign theme supported by posters, pay envelope inserts, and articles in the company newsletter. An occasional mailing sent directly to employees' homes can effectively involve their families. To make them better salespeople, provide employees with a list of all the reasons your company is a good place to work.

Recognize all who participate. For example, anyone who refers a person might be eligible for a grand prize drawing. Once the referred applicant has had a legitimate interview, offer some form of immediate reward for the referring employee, such as a T-shirt or golf cap. If the applicant is hired and remains on the payroll for a designated period of time, provide a more meaningful reward to the person who made the referral. This reward should be significant enough to motivate employees to go through the effort of making referrals.

Advertising

To many, recruitment advertising means having a clerk call in a few Sunday help-wanted ads each week to local or nearby newspapers. However, the scope and style of recruitment advertising have changed. With competition for employees often as intense as the competition for customers, a company should invest its recruiting campaign with the same professionalism and financing that it devotes to its sales advertising. Indeed, from the standpoints of slogans, typeface, and feeling, your ads should tie in with your marketing themes.

Your company's advertising has to persuade people to come to you and apply for a job, which may be especially difficult if they are already working. Advertising has to grab their attention, then provide enough information about your company and the job to make them want to find out more.

Advertising must be impressive enough to attract high caliber applicants, yet this can be extremely expensive. For instance, placing a modest-sized ad for a managerial position in a large newspaper could easily push costs over a thousand dollars. An effective advertising program does not stop at newspaper ads. It also includes the use of magazines, radio, television, billboards, posters in markets and shopping centers, and direct mailings.

With such high costs involved, top managers must give careful attention to the advertising budget and to the selection of those coordinating its application. Some companies hire private agencies specializing in recruitment advertising. Others, after assessing the costs, more readily accept the expenses of private employment agencies and search firms. Still, many people judge advertising to be the best choice or at least one of several tools used. Therefore, managers should look at how the money spent on advertising can best produce the intended results.

No matter which form your company's advertising takes, it will very likely be seen or heard by employees, customers, suppliers, and stockholders. Many newspaper readers look at recruitment ads regularly, regardless of whether they are looking for a job. Everything your ad says should have a positive effect on your image and suggest that your company is a good place to work.

Many companies are now recruiting among their customers. A table tent, placemat, or just a sign in the front window can bring in applicants, particularly to outlying locations. However, point-of-sale advertising must be done extremely well, or it can harm a company's image. A sign on your marquee that reads "Help Wanted—All Positions Open" may suggest labor problems or inadequate service because of short-staffing. Changing the sign to read "Increasing Staff Due to Increasing Business—Apply Within" presents a better image.

An example of effective help-wanted advertising. (Courtesy of Hampton Inns, Inc., Memphis, Tennessee)

This billboard is an example of how recruitment advertising may tie in with a company's marketing theme—in this case, Burger King's "Have it your way" campaign. (Courtesy of B.B.D. Enterprises, Burger King, Grand Rapids, Michigan)

Consider whom you are trying to attract, then go after that very specific market. If you would like to attract people who enjoy cooking, try advertising in the foods section of your newspaper rather than in the help-wanted ads. You can find special magazines and journals for almost every field of work or interest; although it normally takes longer to get responses from magazine ads, they can furnish a wealth of new contacts. For instance, if you want someone with a maintenance background, place an ad in the *Army-Navy Times* to attract former military personnel or take out an ad in the newsletter of a local technical institute.

Advertising can be worded so that it will be either restrictive or general in its appeal. If you are interested in finding applicants with a particular skill, you may wish to list all the specific qualifications so as to minimize the number of unqualified people applying. On the other hand, if you are interested in what skills the labor market has to offer, use an ad that's very general.

Avoid words that suggest discrimination, such as "young," "age fifty or over," "junior secretary," and "recent grad." Don't use job titles which indicate sex, such as busboy, pantry girl, waitress, and hostess. Instead, list these positions as busperson, pantry help, food server, and host/hostess. Have a tag line at the end reading, "An Equal Opportunity Employer, M/F." To encourage people to come to you first, you may wish to advertise flexible interviewing hours and immediate openings.

Sunday is usually the best day for newspaper advertising, attracting applicants well into the week. Morning papers usually attract different types of readers than evening papers do. One newspaper may reach more of the outlying areas, while another may have a larger circulation. Your own experience with respondents will help you determine which papers get the best results for you.

Ads generally are arranged alphabetically, usually with the largest ad first. However, a large ad may not necessarily be best. It can discourage

This table tent photo used by McDonald's is an example of effective point-of-sale recruitment, directed at the labor force of people over 55. The McDonald's Corporation has developed the highly successful McMasters™ program to recruit, train, and retain workers aged 55 and over. (Courtesy of McDonald's Corporation, Oak Brook, Illinois)

people who doubt their qualifications and can encourage over-qualified applicants. As long as your ad is listed in the right category, it will probably be read regardless of its wording or size. Run different ads for each category of position, unless you are planning to put four or more positions in one large ad.

Blind ads use a box number instead of a company name for response. They generally receive much lower response, but may be required to avoid public awareness of certain openings. For example, if you run an ad for a night watchman and identify your operation's name, you might get robbed the next evening.

The same ad should not be run more than two or three Sundays, since it will get no more exposure and can begin to create negative images. If you haven't filled the job, rework the entire ad and then resubmit it.

If you have an affiliate hotel or restaurant in your area, check with your counterparts there. They may want to share advertising with you. In any case, you should advise them of your advertising, so that if applicants go to the wrong unit they can be referred to you.

To help you run ads in other cities, many advertising agencies deal specifically with help-wanted ads. While you pay for the ads, the newspaper usually pays the cost of the agency's service by means of a percentage based on the size of the ad. The agency can help you write the ad, call it in, and send you a copy for your recruiting files.

If you use more than one form of advertising, keep track of how well each performs.

Making Jobs Easier to Fill

To find qualified people and maintain a high standard of service, employers are attempting to expand their labor market by making jobs more attractive and accommodating the personal needs of employees. Some popular programs include transportation assistance, child care assistance, and alternative scheduling plans.

Transportation Assistance

Employers may subsidize or assist employees by helping with transportation arrangements. This approach offers some clear advantages:

- The employer does not have to provide as much space for employee parking.

- Employees assured a means of getting to work are less likely to be late or absent.

- Employees may have higher morale and more energy if they haven't had to fight traffic.

- Employees who share rides get to spend time together outside of work—often with those not in their immediate work areas.

- It may reduce or eliminate some of the employees' expenses and aggravations of owning and maintaining vehicles.

- Shared transportation conserves energy, reduces pollution, and assists traffic flow.

Companies in areas with mass transportation systems may encourage their use by providing employees with free or discounted transit passes. Keep in mind that mass transportation systems are often limited; transportation may not be available during all business hours and may not extend to all of the areas where employees live.

Organizing ride-sharing programs is a very popular alternative to mass transit. The extent of employer involvement varies from simply sponsoring the organizational efforts to subsidizing the vehicle and driver. A small company might introduce the idea of ride-sharing by developing a simple carpooling plan. A larger company, or one with a strong ride-sharing program in place, might provide and operate a company van.

Helping employees meet their child care needs pays off in higher morale, less absenteeism and lateness, and lower turnover. Opryland Hotel operates its own state-licensed child care facility on-site. Child care is available from 5 a.m. to midnight, seven days a week, including holidays. (Courtesy of Opryland Hotel, Nashville, Tennessee.)

Some third-party services are emerging to help coordinate ride-sharing efforts for entire communities or for area companies setting up their own programs. In many cases, public funding ensures that these services involve no additional charges for the users.

Child Care Assistance

Families with two wage-earners and single working parents are becoming the rule rather than the exception. Every employer needs to consider the increasing interest in child care. The federal government and some states provide tax incentives to encourage companies to assist their workers' child care needs. Even more government support is likely.

Providing specific child care facilities is still too costly for all but the largest employers. Most companies are forced to consider alternatives. Other options include paying child care allowances, granting maternity and paternity leave, offering child care referral programs, and alternative scheduling.

Alternative Scheduling

Alternative scheduling is any arrangement of work hours or staffing which varies from the traditional workweek of five 8-hour days per worker. Some common approaches are part-time hours, flexible work hours, compressed work schedules, and job sharing.

Naturally, any program of alternative scheduling requires careful consideration. Does the program meet the workers' needs? Does it meet the employer's needs? How will the program affect worker productivity and morale? How do government and union requirements affect the program?

Part-Time Employees. Part-time employees are non-regular employees who work fewer hours than the company's established standard workweek. Part-time employees are an increasingly important source of labor. Many potential workers (particularly young people, parents with small children, and retirees) are unwilling or unable to work full-time. Employing workers on a part-time basis can give employers the flexibility to respond more readily to fluctuating customer demands. It may also help reduce overtime costs and the high cost of benefits, thus reducing unit labor costs.

Flexible Work Hours. A flexible work hours program, often called **flextime**, permits employees to vary their times of starting and ending work. During a shift, certain designated hours (core time) require the presence of all workers. The remainder of the shift is flextime, during which employees may set their own arrival and departure times. Arrangements vary widely as to whether overages or shortages can be carried over to other workdays within the workweek or to other workweeks; consideration must be given to union contracts and wage and hour restrictions when hours are carried over from day to day or week to week.

For example, a sales manager of a hotel could specify core time hours between 9:30 a.m. and 3 p.m. and set flexible starting hours of 6:30 to 9:30 a.m. and flexible ending hours of 3 to 6 p.m. Assume that the workday requires eight hours of work and a half-hour lunch period, with all modifications made within the same workday. Given these facts, an employee's ending time would always be eight-and-a-half hours after his or her starting time.

One employee could begin at 6:30 a.m. and be finished at 3 p.m., while another could choose to start at 9:30 a.m. and leave at 6 p.m. A third person might prefer to work from 8 a.m. to 4:30 p.m. If the hotel is located in the Central Time Zone, the sales department is accessible to potential customers in other time zones for a longer period of time each day. The department can cover eleven-and-a-half hours without overtime pay, and employees are happier in the process.

Working with flextime schedules requires more time and attention from supervisors. Care must be exercised to prevent disruptions each time another worker comes on duty or leaves. Some extra planning is required to assure that every hour of the workday is covered. If the department doesn't already operate around the clock, another supervisory position may even have to be added to payroll. However, the benefits of a flextime program—more recruiting power, increased employee morale and performance, and overall job satisfaction—may make the extra investment worthwhile.

Compressed Work Schedules. A compressed work schedule is an adaptation of typical full-time work hours. It enables an employee to work the equivalent of a standard workweek in less than the traditional five days; one common adaptation is four 10-hour days. Unlike plans involving flextime, compressed work schedule hours are fixed; however, many employees prefer an additional day off to flexible starting and ending times. Its chief advantages include increased recruiting benefits, reduced absenteeism, and improved morale.

A survey of companies using the compressed work schedule of four 10-hour days revealed no declines in performance associated with the longer workday. In fact, a positive impact was noted on quantity and quality of work, employee reliability, and job satisfaction. However, the study gave some indications of increased levels of stress among supervisors.[6]

Job Sharing. Job sharing (also called **job pairing** or **job splitting**) is an arrangement in which two or more part-time employees share all of the responsibilities of one full-time job. The workers involved usually work different hours of the day or different days of the week, although some overlap of work times is preferable to facilitate communications. Each worker may perform all aspects of the job, or duties may be divided among participants.

When selecting people to share a job, consider such questions as:

- Who is responsible for seeing that certain tasks get done?

- How is performance evaluated for purposes of bonuses, promotions, and raises?

- Are the participants definitely compatible?

- Do the participants have similar work standards?

To some extent, job sharing is likely to increase labor costs and add to the supervisor's burden, but the benefits may be worth it. Job sharing often increases your ability to recruit qualified personnel. In addition, job sharing may help to reduce turnover, absenteeism, and burnout. Job continuity is improved; when one partner leaves, the other person remains to train a new partner. Someone who knows the job is available to fill in during vacations or other absences, and both people may be available during periods of peak business.

Legal Considerations

Violations of employment law can be extremely costly. Therefore, some cautions and guidelines should be considered and followed carefully.

Every employer which employs more than 100 people must fill out an **EEO.1 Report** annually (see Exhibit 11.6 in Chapter 11). This report summarizes the number of males, females, minorities, and other protected categories employed by your establishment, listed by specific job groups.

In the event of a discrimination claim, the EEOC may compare the percentages shown on the employer's EEO.1 Report to the percentages occurring in the labor market in which recruiting is conducted. The employer with a labor force composition that closely parallels the ratios of that labor market is said to have achieved **parity**. According to guidelines in the administrative procedures of the EEOC, employers should achieve 80% or more of parity. For this reason, it's advisable for any employer that doesn't achieve at least 80% of parity to document that extra efforts were made to achieve parity. Otherwise, that employer may have a more difficult time defending against the claim that discrimination—whether intentional or not—took place.

---

[6]Commerce Clearing House, "1987 ASPA/CCH Survey," *CCH Human Resources Management Service*, June 26, 1987, p. 5.

This provides another reason for you to be cautious about relying solely on employee referrals or walk-in traffic for applicants. Using these sources too heavily tends to perpetuate the same ratio of employees that you have currently.

It's important to keep adequate records on all recruiting activities. All help-wanted advertisements *must* be saved for one year, or until any EEOC charges have been resolved. The human resources department or someone designated by management should maintain a log which lists the names of referral sources, contact persons, telephone numbers, and activity. These records meet the requirements of the EEOC and assist your defense in the event of claims. They also provide accurate facts should disputes arise over such items as agency fees.

Giving an application to any person who requests it—whether or not there is an actual opening—is strongly suggested, particularly if the person is a member of a protected group, such as women, minorities, and those over the age of 40. All applications must be stored in a central location and kept for a minimum of six months, and if the applicant is over 40, for one year. Since you cannot ask an applicant's age, it's probably best to keep all applications for one year. If there is an EEOC charge pending, all applications must be kept until that charge is resolved.

Key Terms

blind ad
call-back list
compressed work schedule
contingency search
cross-training
downtime
EEO.1 Report
employment requisition
externship program
flextime
guarantee period
internship program
job posting
job profile

job sharing
job task list
labor needs forecast form
lead time
networking
parity
primary job requirements
recruiting coordinator
recruiting source log
retained search
secondary job requirements
succession planning
turnover

Discussion Questions

1. What can a manager do to control turnover?

2. What can a manager do to minimize the cost and impact of unavoidable turnover?

3. Select a specific position for a hospitality business. What are its primary and secondary job requirements?

4. What steps should a manager take to fill a vacancy before deciding to recruit outside the company?

5. What does networking mean to a manager? How might it be developed and maintained effectively?

6. How can a company meet its labor needs by meeting its workers' needs?

4 Employment Interviewing

Managers don't usually fail because they lack the technical skills to manage. Rather, they fail because they haven't learned how to select the right people and match them to the environment of the work unit.

Selecting people for the hospitality industry requires more care than hiring for most other industries. The very skills that make a service employee an outstanding performer—such as risk-taking, creativity, and friendliness—are many times just a state of mind. Detecting such skills in potential employees is difficult, especially since the interview environment may sometimes inhibit good applicants from displaying the traits the interviewer hopes to find.

Interviews: Approaches and Objectives

Many screening techniques have been developed to assist managers in making employment decisions. The **patterned interview**, for example, asks every applicant the same questions in the same order. This approach ensures that all important areas are covered with every applicant. It also minimizes the impact of possible interviewer bias by treating everyone equally. One type of patterned interview is the **computer interactive interview**, in which applicants are "interviewed" by a computer. The applicants read the questions on the viewing screen and enter their answers into the computer. In addition to monitoring the responses, the computer measures the response time taken to answer each question—information that may indicate which questions an applicant was uncomfortable with.

Another highly structured format is the **behavioral interview**. This type of interview identifies key behavioral characteristics that can help determine success on a particular job. It then uses specific questions designed to seek out these characteristics in applicants.

Some companies swear by these advanced interviewing techniques. Others consider them too time-consuming and expensive to set up and administer. All would agree that they are not personal enough to be the sole basis for a final selection.

Regardless of the interviewing format, the manager should still base the final selection on personal contact. The traditional **personal interview** is more spontaneous and less structured than the interview formats just mentioned. It remains the commonest method of selecting people. To date, there

Exhibit 4.1   An Interviewer's Five Primary Objectives

> 1. Establish a basis for a working relationship.
> 2. Get enough accurate information to make a decision.
> 3. Provide enough information to facilitate the applicant's decision.
> 4. Sell the company and the job to your preferred applicant.
> 5. Create a feeling of goodwill between the company and the applicant.

is no other selection tool that is as economical or as flexible, considering the amount of time invested. Exhibit 4.1 lists the five primary objectives of an interviewer.

The techniques of employment interviewing are not hard to learn. An interview is really just another form of conversation, involving a consistent and definable set of procedures. With practice, these procedures can make you an effective interviewer rather quickly.

As a manager, you probably spend more time with your employees than you do with your family. You sometimes have to call employees in the middle of the night and ask them to work on their days off. You supervise, teach, and discipline them. You work closely with them to achieve the company's goals, often under pressure. For your department to succeed in all these efforts, you must have a solid working relationship with your employees.

As you meet and interview each new applicant, you will be laying the groundwork for a working relationship. Project yourself sincerely. The applicant can then perceive accurately who you are and begin to form realistic expectations of what it would be like to work for you. Ask yourself whether this applicant is a person with whom you could develop a rapport. If not, it's best to keep looking.

The interview process has several distinct stages. We will discuss preparing for the interview, beginning the interview, conducting the interview, and closing the interview.

Preparing for the Interview

The initial interview strongly affects the applicant's first impressions of what it would be like to work for your company. These impressions are as important for the applicants as first impressions are for our guests. A direct relationship should exist between what applicants are led to expect and what they get. Once employees are on the job, their overall attitudes and productivity are influenced by whether their initial expectations are met or not. For this reason, the first impression must be carefully managed to reflect as precisely as possible what the employee will actually experience.

To prepare for the interview, you must first determine who will conduct the interview. Next, you must plan where the interview will take place. Finally, you must have sufficient time to preview the candidate's application before beginning the interview.

Select an Interviewer   The human resources department usually screens applicants to eliminate those who don't meet the primary requirements of a position. However, the responsibility for the main interview and the final hiring decision rests with the department head. This person is ultimately responsible for the department's success and must suffer the consequences of mistakes made by the department's employees.

While the department head is generally the main interviewer, heads of large departments may delegate the task to an assistant. The interview may also include the person in charge of training the new employee. This is likely to elicit a greater commitment from the trainer to make sure that the new person succeeds.

Interviewers and their assistants must have a thorough understanding of the job and the environment in which the employee will work. In addition, an interviewer should be:

- A good judge of people

- Understanding and accepting of the differences in people

- A good listener and communicator

- A good role model for the department

- A good salesperson

- Optimistic and enthusiastic about the job, the department, and the company

- Objective

Proper selection and training of the interviewer is one of the most important steps in the hiring process.

Choose the Interview Site

The atmosphere of the interview should be relaxed, business-like, and private, with few (if any) distractions or interruptions. If you have an electronic pager, turn it over to someone who can handle your telephone calls and any problems that may arise.

The classic office setting may not be the best place for an interview. An interviewer sitting behind a desk can be intimidating to someone who isn't accustomed to working in an office. Also, interviewing in an office might create artificial expectations about the work environment. Since part of your purpose is to acquaint the applicant with the job, the site chosen should be relevant to the job, if possible. If the applicant is interviewing for a restaurant job, for instance, then consider conducting the interview where the job will be performed, or as near to that area as feasible. If the actual workplace is too distracting, as in the case of a dishwashing position, preferred applicants should at least be given a tour of the area before the interview is over.

Preview the Application

If the applicant has been screened by an interviewer in the human resources department, find out what areas have already been covered so that you don't ask the same questions. You can save time and compare notes later.

As a courtesy to the applicant, read the application over *before* you conduct the interview. Note areas which you wish to explore during the interview (see Exhibit 4.2), but don't write on the application itself. Instead, use a separate sheet of paper, such as the **interview summary form** (see Exhibit 4.3), to note areas you wish to pursue and, later, to record your observations.

Check the handwriting and neatness of the application. Look for gaps in

Exhibit 4.2   Previewing an Application: General Observations

- Is the application neat and clean—or messy, with erasures and misspellings?
- Did the applicant follow instructions?
- Is the handwriting acceptable for the job in question? Writing that goes above and below the lines may indicate poor dexterity or vision or limited education.
- Are there any omissions? These may indicate that the applicant has something to hide. They should be explored carefully.
- Does the signature match the handwriting? People who read and write poorly, or not at all, sometimes obtain an application, take it home, and have someone else fill it out for them.
- How long was the person employed in each previous job? If the length of employment gets shorter with each job, the applicant may have an intensifying problem.
- Do job responsibilities or pay rates indicate a career that is going up, staying at the same level, or going down?
- Do job choices indicate strong preferences for certain types of work?

the employment history. Later, during the interview, make sure that the applicant fully explains any large spans of time between jobs.

Sometimes, what an application doesn't include can be as significant as what it does. Look for any omissions, erasures, and areas left blank. For example, be sure to follow up during the interview if an applicant fails to answer the question, "Have you ever been convicted of a felony?"

An application can also help determine whether a person is advancing in his or her field or is on the way down. Signs of frequent career-jumping or job-hopping may indicate that the person has difficulty fitting in or lacks self-direction. Look for normal salary progressions. For hourly positions, try to account for the most recent 25% of the applicant's life. For managerial positions, you may wish to go back even farther.

The interviewer should see an application as an accounting of a person's work history. Understanding the reasons for the choices that people have made in the past provides one of the best guidelines for predicting how they'll respond in the future.

Exhibit 4.4 presents a sample completed application. To the trained eye, this application contains much which calls for further investigation. Several of these points are numbered on the exhibit; the numbers correspond to the following list. Examine the application to see what questions you would ask the applicant. Then look at the following list.

1. If you don't recognize the employer or street address, find out what city it's in. If it's not in Chicago (this applicant's current address), what brought him to Chicago? In addition, if your company conducts police record checks, get the names of other cities in which he has lived as an adult. Record checks should also be obtained from those cities.

2. All of his job choices are different, which could mean he lacks direction and isn't sure what he likes.

3. Dates indicate a gap in employment between this job and the previous one. What was he doing during that period?

Exhibit 4.3 Interview Summary Form

INTERVIEW SUMMARY FORM

APPLICANT'S
NAME_____

DISTINGUISHING CHARACTERISTICS

_____

SOURCE_____

WHEN AVAILABLE_____

TELEPHONE (_____)_____

WHOSE NUMBER/
WHEN TO CALL_____

Call Back Record	Date	Times	
Second Interview Scheduled	Date	Time	Who

POSITION/DEPT. RECOMMENDATION

FILE CODE

SPECIFIC RECOMMENDATIONS

CHECK REFERENCES_____ DATE COMPLETED_____

COMMENTS_____

_____

_____

_____

_____

_____

_____

_____

_____

_____

_____

INTERVIEWER'S SIGNATURE   DATE

Exhibit 4.4   Sample Completed Application

HYATT 🟦 HOTELS CORPORATION

AN EQUAL OPPORTUNITY EMPLOYER

NAME OF HOTEL *Hyatt Regency Chicago*

APPLICATION DATE *9/5/89*

NAME *John Doe*

SOCIAL SECURITY NUMBER *500 - 12 - 4891*

STREET ADDRESS *125 Lyon*

CITY *Chicago* STATE *Ill.* ZIP *60606*

PHONE-HOME *555 -1896* PHONE-WORK

POSITION DESIRED *Managment Trainee*

SALARY/WAGE DESIRED *open*   DATE AVAILABLE FOR WORK *ASAP*

FULL TIME ☑   PART TIME ☐

TEMPORARY ☐ IF SO, SPECIFY PERIOD   LIST DAYS AND HRS PREFERRED *any*

ARE THERE ANY DAYS OR SHIFTS YOU WILL NOT BE ABLE TO WORK? PLEASE SPECIFY: *no*

ARE YOU WILLING TO WORK OVERTIME AS REQUESTED?   YES ☑   NO ☐   NOT APPLICABLE ☐

AGE. ARE YOU AT LEAST 18 YEARS OLD? YES ☐ NO ☐   ARE YOU AT LEAST 21 YEARS OLD? YES ☑ NO ☐

IN ORDER TO PERMIT A CHECK OF YOUR WORK AND EDUCATION RECORDS, SHOULD WE BE MADE AWARE OF ANY CHANGE IN NAME OR ASSUMED NAME THAT YOU PREVIOUSLY USED? YES ☐   NO ☐   IF YES, IDENTIFY NAME(S) AND RELEVANT DATES

IF YOU HAVE WORKED FOR HYATT BEFORE, STATE WHERE, WHEN, FINAL POSITION, AND REASON FOR LEAVING

WORK EXPERIENCE

List your previous experience beginning with your most recent position. If additional space is needed, attach a supplemental sheet.

1 EMPLOYER *Joe's Diner*
ADDRESS (Street, City, State & Zip) *555 Outter Belt Dr.* PHONE *555-1222*
STARTING POSITION *Cook*   STARTING SALARY *4.50*
LAST POSITION   FINAL SALARY
DATES EMPLOYED FROM *1/89* TO *3/89*   IMMEDIATE SUPERVISOR *Mike Davis*
DUTIES *night maneger - lowered food cost more than 20%*
REASON FOR LEAVING *Place closed*

2 EMPLOYER *Brocks Shoe Store*
ADDRESS (Street, City, State & Zip) *Woodland Maul Shoppin Cr.* PHONE
STARTING POSITION *Sales Person*   STARTING SALARY *4.50*
LAST POSITION *Mgt. Trainee*   FINAL SALARY *4.50*
DATES EMPLOYED FROM *1/88* TO *10/88*   IMMEDIATE SUPERVISOR
DUTIES *out sold everyone + got promoted*
REASON FOR LEAVING *need more money*

3 EMPLOYER *Three Crowns*
ADDRESS (Street, City, State & Zip) *514 Michigan Ave.* PHONE *555-6262*
STARTING POSITION *Bartender*   STARTING SALARY *4.65*
LAST POSITION   FINAL SALARY
DATES EMPLOYED FROM *1/87* TO *11/87*   IMMEDIATE SUPERVISOR *Jack Smith*
DUTIES *implemented bev. control that saved over thousands per yr.*
REASON FOR LEAVING *Layed off*

4 EMPLOYER *Waterwork Resturant*
ADDRESS (Street, City, State & Zip) *215 State St.* PHONE *555-7878*
STARTING POSITION *Mgt. Trainee*   STARTING SALARY *5.25*
LAST POSITION   FINAL SALARY *5.25*
DATES EMPLOYED FROM *11/85* TO *12/86*   IMMEDIATE SUPERVISOR *Joyce Johnson*
DUTIES *Trained everyone + increase sales over 50% on my shift*
REASON FOR LEAVING *better opportunity*

○ Please circle the name of any employer or supervisor whom you do not want contacted at this time.

EDUCATION AND TRAINING

SCHOOL	NAME, STREET, CITY, STATE AND ZIP CODE FOR EACH SCHOOL	NUMBER OF YEARS COMPLETED	GRADUATED	MAJOR
HIGH SCHOOL	*Harry Truman, Independence Mo*	*4*	*yes*	*General*
COLLEGE	*Kansas State U. Manhattan KS*	*4*	*yes*	*Business*
ADDITIONAL TRAINING	*Tri-State Culinary Institute*	*1*	*no*	*cooking*

WHICH LANGUAGES OTHER THAN ENGLISH DO YOU SPEAK FLUENTLY? *spanish*

IF JOB RELATED, INDICATE THE KINDS OF WORK WHICH YOU HAVE DONE

☐ TYPING (___ WPM)   ☐ WORD PROCESSING EQUIPMENT (TYPES)

☐ SHORTHAND (___ WPM)   ☐ COMPUTERS (TYPES)   ☐ OTHER

Exhibit 4.4 *(continued)*

ADDITIONAL EMPLOYMENT HISTORY INQUIRIES

(13) HAVE YOU EVER BEEN DISMISSED OR FORCED TO RESIGN FROM ANY EMPLOYMENT?
☒ YES ☒ NO   IF YES, PLEASE EXPLAIN. _____

(14) EXCEPT FOR VACATIONS AND HOLIDAYS, HOW MANY DAYS WERE YOU ABSENT DURING THE PAST TWELVE MONTHS?
☐ 0 - 6 DAYS   ☐ 6 - 12 DAYS   ☐ 12 - 20 DAYS   ☐ 21 + DAYS
COMMENTS. _____

PERMISSION TO WORK

(15) IF EMPLOYMENT IS OFFERED, CAN YOU PRODUCE IDENTIFICATION SUCH AS A U.S. PASSPORT, A DRIVER'S LICENSE OR PHOTOGRAPHIC IDENTIFICATION CARD ISSUED BY THE STATE?
☒ YES ☐ NO
IF EMPLOYMENT IS OFFERED, CAN YOU SUBMIT A BIRTH CERTIFICATE, SOCIAL SECURITY CARD, CERTIFICATE OF U.S. CITIZENSHIP OR VERIFICATION OF YOUR LEGAL RIGHT TO WORK IN THE U.S.? ☒ YES ☐ NO

FELONY CONVICTION RECORD

(14) HAVE YOU BEEN CONVICTED OF A FELONY WITHIN THE LAST 5 YEARS? ☐ YES ☐ NO   IF YES, STATE DETAILS AND DATES.

PHYSICAL LIMITATIONS-EMERGENCY NOTIFICATION DESIGNATION

DO YOU HAVE ANY PHYSICAL CONDITION OR HANDICAP WHICH MAY LIMIT YOUR ABILITY TO PERFORM THE JOB FOR WHICH YOU ARE APPLYING? ☐ YES ☒ NO
IF YES, WHAT CAN BE DONE TO ACCOMMODATE YOUR LIMITATION?

PERSON TO NOTIFY IN CASE OF EMERGENCY. NAME *Mary Doe*   PHONE NO. *(616) 555-1645*
STREET ADDRESS *33 Library*   CITY *Grand Rapids, MI*   STATE & ZIP *49503*

MILITARY SERVICE

(16) HAVE YOU EVER SERVED IN THE UNITED STATES ARMED FORCES? ☒ YES ☐ NO
WHICH BRANCH? _____
INDICATE ANY SPECIAL JOB RELATED TRAINING RECEIVED. _____

CAREER OBJECTIVES

(17) WHY ARE YOU INTERESTED IN WORKING FOR HYATT, AND WHAT ARE YOUR CAREER OBJECTIVES?
friend told me it was great place to work

Obtain challenging position with room for advancement with a progressive company

REFERRAL SOURCE, CHECK ONE

WALK-IN APPLICANT   ☐ COMMUNITY ORGANIZATION ☐
EMPLOYMENT AGENCY   ☐ NAME
NAME   EMPLOYEE REFERRAL ☐
SCHOOL/COLLEGE   ☐ NAME
NAME   NEWSPAPER AD ☒
OTHER

APPLICANT'S STATEMENT

I hereby affirm that the information provided on this application (and accompanying resume, if any) is true and complete to the best of my knowledge. I also agree that any falsified information or significant omissions may disqualify me from further consideration for employment and may be considered justification for dismissal if discovered at a later date.

I authorize a thorough investigation of my past employment and activities, agree to cooperate in such investigation, and release from all liability or responsibility all persons and corporations requesting or supplying information. I further authorize any physician or hospital to release any information which may be necessary to determine my ability to perform the job for which I am being considered or any future job in the event I am hired.

I hereby agree to submit to any lawful drug, polygraph, integrity, or skills testing that may be required as a condition of employment or continued employment and understand that unless otherwise prohibited by law, refusal to submit to such testing during the course of my employment may result in disciplinary action, up to and including discharge. I further agree to submit to search of my person or of any locker or work area that may be assigned to me, and I hereby waive all claims for damages on account of such examination.

I understand that my employment is terminate-at-will, and that this application is not, and is not intended to be, a contract for continued employment.

SIGNATURE *John Doe*   DATE *9/5/89*

R6-87

Form reprinted by permission of Hyatt Hotels Corporation, Chicago, Illinois.

4. Lengths of employment—14 months, 11 months, 10 months, and 8 months—indicate the time span is getting shorter with each job, suggesting a number of possibilities. For instance, he may be quitting each job because he can't accept direction or responsibility. He may have been fired because of poor work habits. Or he might have a personal problem that's getting worse, such as substance abuse.

5. His descriptions of job responsibilities are often vague and suggest the possibility of misrepresentation. Watch for words like "implemented," "developed," and "managed," which are often used to avoid being specific or to exaggerate one's accomplishments and responsibilities. Phrases such as "more than 20%" or "over 50%" and "trained everybody" also suggest exaggeration and should be pursued for more details.

6. The reason given for leaving is that the "place closed." Find out what happened. If it was poorly run, he may have developed poor work habits and lower standards.

7. The telephone number and name of supervisor aren't given, although he was able to supply this information for other jobs. Perhaps he is making it difficult for your company to check on his work record at that job because he was fired.

8. He says he left for more money, but the next job didn't pay any more. Try to find out what his real reason for leaving was.

9. He indicates he was laid off. In a tight labor market, employers usually lay off poor workers first unless company policy dictates that layoffs be based on seniority. Note also that this layoff would have come during the holiday season, an unlikely time for a bar to lay someone off. Find out if others were also laid off.

10. He spent 14 months on this job with no pay increase. Find out about the employer's pay policies.

11. The next job doesn't really appear to have been a better opportunity. Find out why he thought it would be, or why he really left the Waterworks Restaurant.

12. Spelling errors suggest the level of education may actually be lower than what is claimed.

13. This erasure suggests that he may have changed his mind and decided to conceal some instance of dismissal from a past job.

14. These questions weren't answered. Any omission should serve as a warning to an interviewer that the applicant may be trying to conceal information.

15. He consistently fails to get the x right in the box. This could indicate that he has a possible problem with eye-hand coordination, that he needs glasses, or that he lacks attention to detail.

16. This answer is incomplete, perhaps because he doesn't follow instructions well, rushes through his work, or doesn't take the application process seriously.

17. Get the name of the friend who suggested your company. This kind of recommendation is generally made by an employee or ex-employee. Good employees usually refer other good people, while poor employees are likely to refer other poor workers.

Beginning the Interview

As an interviewer, you must develop your own style; otherwise, you won't seem natural. Be yourself and show your personality. This helps the applicant to do the same. The interview should take place in a non-threatening environment. Establishing a warm but business-like relationship will speed up interviews by enabling applicants to relax, open up, and talk about themselves and their experiences.

While it's a good idea to review the application just before an interview, it's a bad idea to interview directly from the application form. You'll lose spontaneity and miss opportunities for exploring additional areas mentioned by the applicant. Since the application is a matter of record, its facts can be easily verified later by checking references.

Greet the Applicant

Courtesy produces courtesy in return. Think of this meeting as your first opportunity to train a potential employee. Treat all applicants with the same hospitality that you would expect them to extend to guests.

Don't keep the applicant waiting. Walk up to the person, smile, make eye-contact, and shake hands. Establish the basis for a first-name relationship, then use the applicant's name several times during the interview. Be consistent in your approach to every applicant. It will help you judge how fast each warms up.

Observe Physical Appearance

Take time to look the person over carefully. Pay close attention to the appropriateness of dress, the cleanliness of the clothing, and the condition of the shoes. Note the general standards of grooming, particularly those concerning fingernails and hair. Observe posture and physical stamina. Note any jerkiness, quickness of gestures, or any other behavior that seems out of place. The person should exhibit good manners; for instance, waiting for your invitation before sitting and asking permission before smoking.

Look at the eyes. Bloodshot eyes may be due to drinking, but could simply indicate problems with contact lenses. Dilated pupils might indicate drug use or illness. A normal blinking rate is 32 times per minute;[1] a slower rate could mean the applicant is not very alert or could be the result of drug use, while a faster rate may mean health problems.

Obviously, any person interested enough to apply for a job is concerned with making a good impression. If someone comes to an interview with dirty clothes and messy hair, this may be the best standard you can expect from the applicant. If you hire this person, you may have to invest a great deal of time to change those personal standards later.

Start the Conversation

You should start talking first. Make small talk to help both you and the applicant relax. If the person lists fishing as a hobby, or has a belt buckle with a fish on it, talk about fishing. Ask people who have just moved from

---

[1]Vance Packard, *The Hidden Persuaders* (New York: D. McKay, 1957), p. 107.

A Schedule to Fit Your Schedule

Freshman or senior, a part-time job at McDonald's® is in a class by itself. Flexible hours and scheduling allows you to work just a few hours a week—weekends only if you like—leaving you with plenty of time for school and activities.

Money for Now...And Later

Earn extra spending money, save for college or both. Just a few hours a week can add up quickly and gives you money toward that class ring or savings for future tuition.

Whatever your goals are, a part-time job at McDonald's can be a step in the right direction.

Just Around the Corner

Your neighborhood McDonald's is probably just around the corner. You won't spend a lot of time getting to and from work.

Life Skills

A part-time job at McDonald's will be enjoyable and a challenge. A challenge that will give you skills like managing time...managing your money...dealing with people...accepting responsibility...teamwork and decision-making. In addition to learning these lifetime skills, you'll be getting a paycheck.

And more...

McDonald's offers you meals, flexible scheduling, free uniforms and a competitive starting wage no matter what your year in school. We also offer activities, the chance to meet people and have some fun!

Getting Started

It's easy. Talk to your parents, teacher or guidance counselor. Talk to the manager of your neighborhood McDonald's. Or fill out the form attached to this brochure and drop it off at your local McDonald's.

Keep on earning while you're learning—stay in school.

© 1988 McDonald's Corporation

DATA SHEET

Name ___

Street Address ___

Suite or Apt. No. ___ City ___ State ___

Zip ___ Phone ( ) ___

Date Completed ___

Are you 18 or older? ☐ Yes ☐ No

If not, age: ___

Ever work for McDonald's before? If yes, date and location ___

Availability — Total Hours Available per week

Hours Available	M	T	W	T	F	S	S
From							
To							

How far do you live from store? ___

Do you have transportation? ___

School ___ Grade ___

Teacher/Counselor ___

This kind of short application form is easy for applicants to complete and adequate for the interviewer's initial screening interview. (Courtesy of McDonald's Corporation, Oak Brook, Illinois)

another city how they like the area. Ask easy questions that stimulate a positive response or get them talking about something they like.

Once the ice is broken and the person relaxes, set out the parameters of the interview. Whether you're going to conduct a 5-minute screening interview or a lengthy in-depth interview, say so initially and spell out the areas you're going to cover. This will allow you to stay on schedule and help you control the interview.

Conducting the Interview

Keep the interview in a conversational tone and speak on the other person's level, but don't talk down to the person. Although you should control the content and direction of the interview, let the applicant set the pace. If the individual is shy or slow, you'll have to be more patient.

Never tell applicants specifically what you're looking for at the beginning of the interview, or they may alter their answers. Don't show excessive approval, or the person may begin to slant comments just to win your approval.

Give spontaneous responses if they are called for. If an applicant talks about a death in the family, be sympathetic. If someone has done something worthy of recognition, compliment the person. Listen sincerely and with interest. Don't interrupt.

When making the transition from small talk to the body of the interview, the opening questions should refer to the applicant's job expectations. For example, ask "What type of work are you looking for?" or "What made you decide to apply here?"

Observe the applicant's body language. A sudden shift in body position, an unusual pitch of the voice, fidgeting with the hands, or evasive eye movements could indicate you're in an area of discomfort. Watching a person's eyes and facial expressions can give you a great deal of insight into feelings and behavior.

Encourage response through your own facial expressions and body gestures; nod your head, lean forward in the chair, and smile. At this point, the applicant should be doing about 80% of the talking.

Listen carefully to the person's responses. If you ask a question and the applicant hesitates before answering, pursue the subject. For example, you may ask someone, "Is there any day of the week you prefer not to work?" The longer it takes for a response, the more difficult you can assume working on a given day would be. Follow up with, "Which days would give you the biggest problem?"

Be alert for areas skimmed over by the applicant. People won't want to talk about their bad experiences. If the applicant gives a vague answer or shifts topics, it could indicate that something is being covered up.

As the interviewer, you are in authority but shouldn't be authoritarian. You are expected to lead the conversation. Never apologize for a question or ask, "Do you mind if I ask this?"

In answering an applicant's questions about the job or the company, the interviewer should always be honest and straightforward. The fastest way to lose credibility in the applicant's eyes is to beat around the bush or try to hide something.

If you're asked a personal question, such as "Are you married?" or "Where did you go to school?" don't be afraid to answer briefly and tactfully. When an applicant asks a question that seems inappropriate or too personal, such as, "How do you keep your kids from using drugs?" it usually indicates that the applicant has a problem of his or her own, which you may want to pursue. If you have sound advice and you're asked for it, give it. Then, promptly and tactfully steer the conversation back to the format of having the other person doing most of the talking—again, by being sympathetic and interested.

Avoid any disagreements or confrontations. Play down unfavorable information about former employers, using remarks like, "Everyone runs into someone like that sooner or later. Tell me more about that incident." (Of course, it's never appropriate for the interviewer or the applicant to disparage a competitor.) Use your sense of humor to break up tension.

Writing should be kept to a minimum during the interview. Instead, take most of your notes immediately after the interview. Initially, make a casual reference, such as, "You don't mind if I make a few notes as we go along, do you?" While you should record names and dates, you shouldn't give the applicant the impression that you are transcribing comments word for word.

Confine your questions to one major area at a time. Start with work experience and cover it completely before going on to education, personal information, and other topics. With younger applicants, it's appropriate to cover the person's early years, since they are important in shaping expectations and values. A first job or first supervisor will have a great deal of influence on one's standards and expectations. Ask such applicants to tell you who has influenced them the most (for example, their parents) and what they are like.

If your organization has no human resources department and you are the initial interviewer, early in the interview you should attempt to verify whether the applicant meets the primary requirements stated on the job profile (see Exhibit 3.4 in Chapter 3). You should also mention that anyone hired must be able to prove the legal right to work in this country. Mention any other qualifications that require validation upon hiring, such as minimum age for working around alcohol. Then make sure that the job meets the applicant's needs in terms of compensation (pay and benefits), working conditions (hours, shift, and days off), and the type of work desired.

Many of these areas can be quickly covered with a few simple questions or by reading the application. If there is a severe mismatch, end the interview. Keep in mind that someone who is desperate for a paycheck may say anything to get the job, even though the job may not match the person's needs. If hired, this person will probably continue looking for work elsewhere, leaving when something better comes along.

Employees usually fail not because they can't do the job, but because they don't *want* to do the job. Unfortunately, assessing an applicant's willingness to work requires more skill and a great deal more time than assessing basic qualifications. Hence, you should spend the bulk of the interview trying to determine the applicant's values, work standards, expectations, motivations, and outlook on other people and life in general.

You should form opinions and collect data to confirm or modify those opinions. You don't need to cover every item on the application from beginning to end. Interviewing is like drilling for oil—probe into different areas until you find a productive topic, then dig deeper. Keep digging until the answers prove or disprove your opinions. Don't move on until you're satisfied that the subject has been completely covered. If you have any concerns, put them directly to the applicant about three-quarters of the way through the interview. This will allow you enough time to conclude the interview and still wind up on a positive note.

As you begin to draw conclusions, compare them to the applicant's self-evaluation. This evaluation of weaknesses and strengths should match your own assessment of the applicant. If not, continue to interview or have someone else interview the person. You may even wish to have the applicant return another time. People who can't assess themselves accurately are generally poor risks for service jobs because they are unlikely to understand the needs and motives of others. Do not contemplate making an offer unless you're reasonably sure you have a reliable feeling about the person's values, motivation, and attitudes.

Closing the Interview

Before concluding their interviews, ask applicants whether they have anything to add. This gives them the opportunity to ask questions, sell themselves, or provide any additional information you hadn't discussed. The questions they ask will provide additional insight into their needs and interests.

If you have found a good applicant, don't cut the interview short to save time. No one values a job obtained too easily, so represent your company as very selective. Spend the time to sell the company and the job, including the company benefits. Now is the best time to talk about the goals of the company and your specific department. Discuss your pride in the company's products and services. People want to be part of a successful team.

There's no such thing as an unimportant job, or you wouldn't have it on your payroll. Tell the applicant how important the job is to you personally. For instance, if you're interviewing for a third-shift kitchen cleaner, point out the consequences of poor performance in this position: when the restaurant opens in the morning, the cooks aren't set up to work, so the food servers will fall behind; service could be off for hundreds of guests.

Say what's expected and why. If the person doesn't accept what you're saying, don't consider making an offer.

If you are seriously considering a candidate, explain the job precisely and completely. If you fail to mention swing shifts, short workweeks, working on Sunday, or other undesirable aspects of the job now, it will come back to haunt you later. Don't oversell the job, but don't make it sound worse than it is, either. Many managers feel that their employees have no right to complain later if they were warned about the worst before they took their jobs. This idea is not valid, however, because the person who needs a job will consent to anything, without necessarily accepting it.

Don't promise things that won't happen. If you cannot inform the applicant on the spot that he or she is getting the job, give information about when to expect an answer or a second interview. On first interviews or screening interviews, it's appropriate just to say that a decision will be made within a few days. You may say, "If you don't hear from us by then, you can assume we've hired someone else." It isn't necessary to get back to every applicant. It is important, however, to get back promptly to those applicants who made a special effort, spent a great deal of time or money in the interview process, or made more than one trip.

If the applicant isn't going to get the job, say so. Don't string someone along. No one really expects to get every job he or she applies for. An applicant may accept a rejection more gracefully if you offer comments like, "We've been so pleased with the great turnout from our ad; we've had so many qualified applicants," or "We're also considering promoting from within."

However you soften the blow, it's important to end the interview cleanly, with authority and without hesitation. Take a deep breath and tell the person why he or she isn't being considered any further. Don't give the applicant a chance for a rebuttal. After you've brought the conversation to a close, stand up. If you've been sitting at a desk or table, walk out from behind it. This physical gesture may be necessary to end some interviews. Make sure you shake hands and thank the applicant for showing an interest and taking the time to apply.

No matter who gets the job, everyone should leave thinking your company would be a good place to work.

Techniques for Questioning

The commonest questioning technique is a two-step process which involves first asking for specifics: who, what, when, or where. Follow each specific question with a second, broader question on the same subject that asks why or how. For example, begin by asking "Who was your best supervisor?" Then follow the reply with, "Why did you pick that person?"

Ask for a list of things rather than an individual response, such as "What were the courses you liked best?" or "What are your three strongest assets?" This will allow the applicant to be more spontaneous when responding. After hearing the list, you can ask which single asset is the strongest.

Use direct questions—those that usually require yes or no answers—to verify facts and cover a lot of material quickly.

The applicant will normally have a standard answer for every expected question. Your mission is to get more than the standard answer. One way is to ask indirect or open-ended questions like, "Can you tell me what a typical day was like on your last job?" Another good technique is asking the applicant to make comparisons. Instead of asking what it was like to work at a certain company, try, "How did working for your latest employer differ from working for your previous employer?"

Listen to the responses and reasons. Do they make logical sense? If not, pursue the answer. For example, an applicant may describe leaving a job to accept a better position. You might suspect a cover-up, however, if the application indicates the subsequent position paid less and started three months later. Ask something like, "How was your new job better?" or "What didn't you like about the previous job?" Quitting a job is a very difficult thing to do; either the person was very unhappy about something, had other compelling reasons, or leaving wasn't by choice.

If you don't get a complete answer, encourage the person to continue by restating the answer as a question: "So you didn't really like working for them, did you?" Other responses, like "Yes," "Go on," and "I see," could also encourage someone to keep talking. Another method is simply not to ask another question when the applicant stops talking. Your silence will be a clear indicator that you expect to hear more.

On the other hand, if you ask a question and don't get a satisfactory response, it may be because the applicant doesn't understand what you're looking for. In some instances, it may be appropriate to clarify the question by suggesting some sample answers from which to choose. For example, "Was the chief reason for leaving your last job the hours, the salary, or transportation problems?"

When dealing with sensitive areas, like police records or reference checking, it's better to state your position before asking the question: "We do police checks on every applicant. I noticed you didn't answer the question asking whether you have ever been convicted. What is your response?"

Don't ask questions that suggest an answer, such as, "You don't mind working on Sundays, do you?" Instead ask, "Are there any days you're not available for work?" or "Do you have any preferred days off?" Along the same lines, the question, "How many days a year of absenteeism do you think are normal?" will get more information for you than, "How often were you absent from your last job?"

On the other hand, sometimes an interviewer wants to pose a question that makes an assumption in order to find out how the interviewee reacts to the assumption. For instance, you might ask a food server, "Why do you think people don't tip well anymore?" A less desirable candidate might have more negative things to say about guests, such as, "People just don't care anymore," or "Money is so tight these days." The better candidate might be the one who disagrees with you and says, "I don't find that to be true. People still appreciate good service." The latter response indicates a more positive outlook. In addition, it suggests that the candidate is independent and self-confident enough to correct you. Certainly, a positive outlook and the ability to think independently are characteristics you'd look for in a hospitality employee. The same type of approach is illustrated in asking a managerial candidate, "Why do you think employees today are so hard to motivate?"

Making comments in place of questions helps maintain a conversational tone; for example, "I'll bet that was a busy place," or "Working third shift can really require adjustments."

What to Ask   Exhibit 4.5 gives sample questions to help you develop your own list of questions. With the exception of the questions for managers at the end of the exhibit, the sample questions are divided into the same categories that you'll find on the interview evaluation form presented in the next chapter (Exhibit 5.1). The categories are:

- Relevant job background
- Education/intelligence
- Physical factors
- Personal traits
- Questions for managers

Depending on the response, any one question might give you insight into a variety of traits or abilities. Your skill at interpreting the responses will get better with experience.

Keep your questions relevant to the job and appropriate. You would not ask a managerial candidate the same things you would ask a line employee. Inquiring about someone's early years or first job may be inappropriate if the applicant is 65 years old.

What Not to Ask   There are several categories of questions which should be avoided altogether, since they may be interpreted as a possible violation of the applicant's rights. These categories often vary from state to state and may change from year to year. Therefore, those involved in the selection process must be acquainted with the current laws affecting their jurisdiction. See Exhibit 4.6 for a sample guide detailing lawful and unlawful questions.

The general topics to be avoided in the interview are those that will produce information which should not enter into the decision process. Topics to avoid include birthplace, age, religion or creed, race or color, height, weight, marital status, sex, national origin, citizenship, memberships in lodges and religious or ethnic clubs, and arrest records. In most states, however, you can ask about conviction records or whether any felony charges are pending against the applicant.

Exhibit 4.5   Sample Interview Questions

Relevant Job Background
- What were your gross and take-home wages?
- Did you regularly work 40 hours a week? How much overtime did you get?
- What benefits did you have? How much did you pay for them?
- What salary are you looking for? What is the lowest amount you can accept?
- Which days of the week work out best for you?
- Have you ever worked weekends before? Where? How often?
- Which shift do you enjoy working the most? Which shift can't you work?
- Do you regularly have to be somewhere besides work at a certain time?
- How many hours a week would you like to work?
- Are you a morning person or a night person?
- How will you get to work at that hour?
- Is your transportation reliable?
- Who is taking care of your children? What happens when they get sick? (Make sure you ask *both* men and women.)
- How many days a year do you think is normal for a person to be absent or late?
- What position did you hold when you started that job? When you left?
- What was your starting salary there? What were you making when you left? How did you get increases?
- How many people gave you orders there?
- What were the most important duties of your job?
- What three things do you want to avoid on your next job?
- What do you expect from a supervisor?
- Why did you choose this line of work?

Education and Intelligence
- What subjects did you like best/least?
- Do you think your grades are a good indicator of your overall abilities?
- What accounted for your good grades?
- Have you ever thought about continuing your schooling?
- Why did you choose that school/major?
- Is it a good school? Why or why not?
- If you had to do it all over again, would you make the same decisions? Why or why not?
- What is the most important thing you've learned in the past six months?
- Do you like to read? What do you like to read?

Physical Factors
- What do you like to do in your spare time?
- When was the last time you saw a doctor? What was the reason?
- How many times were you absent or late on your last job? Do you think that's normal? What were the reasons?
- On your last job, were they tough on absenteeism and lateness? Do you think their policy was fair? Did they ever talk to you about it?
- What do you consider a good night's sleep?

Personal Traits
The following are more suitable for younger people without much work background.
- What does your family think of your working as a cook?
- How old were you when you got your first job?
- What was the first job you ever had?
- What was your first boss like?
- How did you get your first job? Your most recent job?

Exhibit 4.5 (continued)

The following are general questions about personal traits. Change the job title to meet your needs.

- Who has the greater responsibility—a desk agent or a reservations agent?
- Do you feel that food servers are too competitive among themselves?
- Do you find that a lot of guests are leaving smaller tips these days?
- How would you handle a guest who never tips?
- Have you ever had to deal with a guest who is angry or complaining about everything? How did you calm the person down?
- Were you ever chewed out or criticized unjustly?
- What do you consider to be the main reasons cooks quit their jobs?
- What do you consider to be the most important responsibilities for a good desk agent? Why?
- Why is the housekeeper's job so important?
- Suppose your supervisor insisted you do a certain thing in a certain way, when you definitely know there's a better way. What would you do?
- Have you ever had a supervisor "play favorites"? What did you do about it?
- Which company did you like working for the most/least? Why?
- What would you change if you managed that department? Did you try to change it?
- What was your biggest accomplishment or contribution at that job?
- Would you go back and work there again? Why or why not?
- Who was the best/worst supervisor you ever had?
- What can you do for us that other applicants can't do?
- What made you stay at that job for so long?
- Did your last company have a good product?
- How much notice did you give when you left your last job? Why?
- Have you ever had to "stick your neck out" and make a decision on your own? How long did it take you to decide, and what did you consider before you decided?
- How would your former boss and fellow employees describe you?
- What areas did your last performance review say you needed to improve on?
- What was the most important thing you learned on that job?
- What are your three strongest assets?
- What are the three areas in which you would most like to improve yourself?
- Are you happy with your present status and income? Do you think it's in line with your peers?
- What one thing have you done of which you are the proudest?
- Where would you like to be five years from now? Ten years from now? What are you doing to make it happen?
- What's the funniest thing that ever happened to you?

Questions for Managers
- When you left, who replaced you?
- What type of training program did you have for your employees?
- What have you done in the last twelve months to improve your department and/or customer base?
- What do you think are the most important attributes of a manager?
- Who were your biggest competitors? What were their strengths/weaknesses?
- Did you ever have to take an unpopular stand?
- How would your employees describe you as a supervisor?
- Why do you think people today are hard to motivate?
- How many people did you have to fire on your last job? For what reasons?

Exhibit 4.6   Pre-Employment Inquiry Guide

SUBJECT	LAWFUL PRE-EMPLOYMENT INQUIRIES	UNLAWFUL PRE-EMPLOYMENT INQUIRIES
NAME:	Applicant's full name. Have you ever worked for this company under a different name? Is any additional information relative to a different name necessary to check work record? If yes, explain.	Original name of an applicant whose name has been changed by court order or otherwise. Applicant's maiden name.
ADDRESS OR DURATION OF RESIDENCE:	How long a resident of this state or city?	
BIRTHPLACE:		Birthplace of applicant. Birthplace of applicant's parents, spouse or other close relatives. Requirement that applicant submit birth certificate, naturalization or baptismal record.
AGE:	*Are you 18 years old or older?	How old are you? What is your date of birth?
RELIGION OR CREED:		Inquiry into an applicant's religious denomination, religious affiliations, church, parish, pastor, or religious holidays observed. An applicant may not be told "This is a Catholic (Protestant or Jewish) organization."
RACE OR COLOR:		Complexion or color of skin.
PHOTOGRAPH:		Requirement that an applicant for employment affix a photograph to an employment application form. Request an applicant, at his or her option, to submit a photograph. Requirement for photograph after interview but before hiring.
HEIGHT:		Inquiry regarding applicant's height.
WEIGHT:		Inquiry regarding applicant's weight.
MARITAL STATUS:		Requirement that an applicant provide any information regarding marital status or children. Are you single or married? Do you have any children? Is your spouse employed? What is your spouse's name?
SEX:		Mr., Miss or Mrs. or an inquiry regarding sex. Inquiry as to the ability to reproduce or advocacy of any form of birth control.
HEALTH:	Do you have any impairments, physical, mental, or medical which would interfere with your ability to do the job for which you have applied? Inquiry into contagious or communicable diseases which may endanger others. If there are any positions for which you should not be considered or job duties you cannot perform because of a physical or mental handicap, please explain.	Inquiries regarding an individual's physical or mental condition which are not directly related to the requirements of a specific job and which are used as a factor in making employment decisions in a way which is contrary to the provisions or purposes of the Michigan Handicappers' Civil Rights Act. Requirement that women be given pelvic examinations.
CITIZENSHIP:	Are you a citizen of the United States? If not a citizen of the United States, does applicant intend to become a citizen of the United States? If you are not a United States citizen, have you the legal right to remain permanently in the United States? Do you intend to remain permanently in the United States?	Of what country are you a citizen? Whether an applicant is naturalized or a native-born citizen; the date when the applicant acquired citizenship. Requirement that an applicant produce naturalization papers or first papers. Whether applicant's parents or spouse are naturalized or native born citizens of the United States; the date when such parent or spouse acquired citizenship.
NATIONAL ORIGIN:	Inquiry into languages applicant speaks and writes fluently.	Inquiry into applicant's (a) lineage; (b) ancestry; (c) national origin; (d) descent; (e) parentage, or nationality. Nationality of applicant's parents or spouse. What is your mother tongue? Inquiry into how applicant acquired ability to read, write or speak a foreign language.
EDUCATION:	Inquiry into the academic vocational or professional education of an applicant and the public and private schools attended.	
EXPERIENCE:	Inquiry into work experience. Inquiry into countries applicant has visited.	
ARRESTS:	Have you ever been convicted of a crime? If so, when, where and nature of offense? Are there any felony charges pending against you?	Inquiry regarding arrests.
RELATIVES:	Names of applicant's relatives, other than a spouse, already employed by this company.	Address of any relative of applicant, other than address (within the United States) of applicant's father and mother, husband or wife and minor dependent children.
NOTICE IN CASE OF EMERGENCY:	Name and address of person to be notified in case of accident or emergency.	Name and address of nearest relative to be notified in case of accident or emergency.
MILITARY EXPERIENCE:	Inquiry into an applicant's military experience in the Armed Forces of the United States or in a State Militia. Inquiry into applicant's service in particular branch of United States Army, Navy, etc.	Inquiry into an applicant's general military experience.
ORGANIZATIONS:	Inquiry into the organizations of which an applicant is a member excluding organizations, the name or character of which indicates the race, color, religion, national origin or ancestry of its members.	List all clubs, societies and lodges to which you belong.
REFERENCES:	Who suggested that you apply for a position here?	

*This question may be asked only for the purpose of determining whether applicants are of legal age for employment.

Source: Michigan Department of Civil Rights.

It's also illegal to ask specific questions of one sex and not the other. For instance, it's discriminatory to ask only female applicants whether they have small children at home or what arrangements are made when their children are sick. If this question is job-related, then you must ask it of both male and female applicants.

There are some types of information you need but which can be obtained only after the hiring decision has been made, usually at the time the person is filling out the hiring paperwork. Examples of such information are proof of age and proof of legal right to work in this country.

Care must also be used when asking questions about an applicant's health. Specific inquiries about a person's physical or mental condition should be avoided unless directly related to the job in question. However, it is acceptable to ask, "Do you have any impairments—physical, mental, or medical—which would interfere with your ability to do the job for which you have applied?" or "Do you have any health conditions or contagious diseases which would prevent you from doing the job for which you have applied?"

The most important thing to remember is that there must be a good business reason in asking a particular question. General inquiries concerning a woman's maiden name may disclose her national origin, commonly regarded as information you don't need in making an employment decision. If you intend to check references of a female applicant who was recently married, however, it would be acceptable to ask what name she used when she worked for previous employers.

Asking applicants to include photographs with their resumes (or even suggesting that it's acceptable) may be unlawful. On the other hand, if the applicant has a picture attached to the resume, you don't have to remove it.

Questions about transportation seem to be in a gray area. The employer has a legitimate reason for determining whether the transportation to work is reliable. It would probably be considered discriminatory to ask, "Do you own a car?" but acceptable to inquire, "How long will it take you to get to work?"

Refusing to hire a woman because she's pregnant is an obvious instance of sex discrimination. However, you can ask her for a doctor's report confirming her physical ability to work and indicating the length of time before leave is required, provided that there is a similar policy for all potentially disabled employees.

There are no hard and fast rules concerning the use of confidential material obtained during an interview. Often an applicant is willing to discuss personal problems with an interviewer but trusts that you won't make this information public. Beyond observing the rules of common decency and courtesy, the best rule of thumb is to provide such information only on a need-to-know basis.

Key Terms

behavioral interview
computer interactive interview
interview evaluation form

interview summary form
patterned interview
personal interview

Discussion Questions

1. As an interviewer, why is it important for you to project yourself sincerely?

2. What is the significance of the relationship between what applicants are led to expect and what they get?

3. Who should be included in the interviewing process? Why?

4. What are some of the things a manager should do in order to prepare for an interview?

5. What is the purpose behind questions that ask about the applicant's preferences in hobbies, work, and school?

6. What problems might be associated with overselling or underselling the job and the company?

7. Why would you ask a food server, "Who is more important—a cook or a food server?" What types of responses might you get?

5 Evaluating Applicants

It's difficult to separate the evaluation phase from the recruiting and interviewing steps. All three are interdependent elements of the selection process. You use evaluation skills when you assess your job needs, fill out the job profile and employment requisition, judge applicants in the interview process, review test scores, and perform reference checks. All of these steps are necessary *before* a hiring decision can be made.

Your final step before hiring an applicant is to choose from among the available candidates. This choice involves weighing your observations about each of them against your knowledge of the job opening. Your use of evaluation tools and techniques is essential to this vital human resources function.

Knowing when to make the hiring decision is an art. It's impossible to achieve the best results if you hire mediocre candidates, especially since many laws are making it very difficult to get rid of bad hiring choices. On the other hand, you must know when to stop looking. In today's labor market, you may not find perfection. Knowing when to stop looking and start hiring depends in large part on your ability to evaluate job candidates.

Evaluating the Interview

The **weighted interview evaluation form** (Exhibit 5.1) is a list of key traits for employees in the hospitality industry.[1] You should use the form to help you evaluate an applicant's strengths and weaknesses and determine whether the applicant meets the demands of the job. The interview evaluation form is composed of four main categories:

- Relevant job background
- Education/intelligence

---

[1]The form is called *weighted* because the values skip from one to three. If someone has outstanding ability in a needed skill area, the evaluator wants it to show up clearly in the totals. Such a trait, with a plus-three value, would outweigh or at least counteract a couple of less important areas scoring minus-one. This approach keeps minor shortcomings from ruling out some applicants who have the relevant skills for the job in question.

Exhibit 5.1   Weighted Interview Evaluation Form

	Poor Match		Acceptable	Strong Match	
WEIGHTED INTERVIEW EVALUATION FORM Applicant Name ___ Position Evaluated ___ Date ___	−3	−1	0	+1	+3
RELEVANT JOB BACKGROUND					
General background					
Work experience					
Similar companies					
Interest in job					
Salary requirements					
Attendance					
Leadership experience					
EDUCATION/INTELLIGENCE					
Formal schooling					
Intellectual ability					
Additional training					
Social skills					
Verbal and listening skills					
Writing skills					
PHYSICAL FACTORS					
General health					
Physical ability					
Cleanliness, dress, and posture					
Energy level					
PERSONAL TRAITS					
First impression					
Interpersonal skills					
Personality					
Teamwork					
Motivation					
Outlook, humor, and optimism					
Values					
Creativity					
Stress tolerance					
Performing skills					
Service attitude					
Independence					
Planning and organizing					
Problem solving					
Maturity					
Decisiveness					
Self-knowledge					
Flexibility					
Work standards					
Sub-totals					
TOTAL POINTS ___					

- Physical factors
- Personal traits

The following sections discuss each of these categories in detail.

Relevant Job Background

General Background. The hospitality industry is a world of constant stress, changes, and demands. To deal successfully with these challenges, hospitality employees must be well-suited to this unique environment and secure in their jobs. Your task as an interviewer is to fit round pegs into round holes. Start by looking at an applicant's general background.

You'll typically find that, depending on their aptitudes and interests, people fall into three broad categories: people who work best with people, people who work best with things, and people who work best with data.

The first category includes people who enjoy working and being with others. These people like helping, teaching, and serving other people. People in this category are the best choices for guest service positions.

The second category consists of people who like working with things. These people can be readily identified by their interest in activities which require working with their hands; for instance, handling materials, operating equipment, or preparing food items. Many of them may prefer working in the engineering department rather than in guest contact jobs.

The third category consists of people who like working with data. This work includes coordinating, analyzing, counting, copying, and comparing data. These people generally seem happiest in areas like accounting, information collection and dispersal, and computing.

Consider the types of jobs, clubs, hobbies, volunteer work, and elective schooling the person has chosen. People who have consistently chosen jobs in highly structured organizational cultures, such as government and insurance companies, usually have a hard time adjusting to the lack of structure in the hospitality industry.

Ask whether the person has ever worked weekends or jobs that required different shifts. If you're looking for a third-shift employee, you'd probably be well advised to hire someone who's already worked that shift and likes it. If people have worked outdoors and have outdoor hobbies, they may find that working indoors is too confining, particularly if they're young. On the other hand, if the work history indicates the applicant has always worked outdoors, but subsequent interviewing indicates that health reasons have forced the person to work inside, you may not have to be concerned.

Work Experience. Obviously, an applicant must meet the job's requirements and possess the proper licenses or necessary skills. However, what should you do if an applicant exceeds the requirements?

A great deal of controversy has been generated over whether to consider someone who is over-qualified. The concern is that over-qualified workers may not take their resumes off the market and will leave as soon as they find positions more closely suited to their qualifications. In the meantime, they may lack interest in their work, find it less than challenging, work in an unproductive manner, and even create morale problems in the department.

However, you must consider each person's situation individually. Every person has different motivations and will respond uniquely to a given situation. Furthermore, there may be lower risk if you're in a fast-growth organization going through rapid expansion and offering advancement opportunities.

A person's past job choices are among the best predictors of future job success.

Similar Companies. Look at other companies where the applicant has worked to determine how closely the cultures and types of businesses match your own. Three years' cooking experience at a fast-food restaurant won't be the same as three years at a formal restaurant. A hospital has a far different culture from a hotel. You may also find that a person who enjoys working in cafeterias or breakfast service would rather stay in those environments than move to fine dining service.

Interest in the Job. It's not sufficient to find someone with the required years of cooking experience if, in fact, the person doesn't want to be a cook anymore. People eventually quit jobs that don't meet their needs. Other factors like salary, hours of operation, location, and days off also may not meet the applicant's needs. A good applicant is going to express obvious interest in the opportunity you offer.

Salary Requirements. Salary is one of the most important issues to address in the interviewing and evaluation process. The standard rule for many years has been not to hire someone at a pay rate less than that of his or her previous job, unless: (1) you offer an offsetting fringe benefit package, or (2) the person has the potential to reach the former rate within a reasonable period of time.

The premise of this rule is that people will not be happy nor give the required extra effort when working for less money. Employees dissatisfied over low wages may be less productive, speak ill of the company, spread dissension among fellow employees, or suggest that a union be considered.

Today, salary isn't as important a motivator as it used to be, particularly when an applicant's spouse also has a job. Benefits, flextime, and job fulfillment all have greater meaning. Through interviewing, you may find that the applicant has children in school and has just bought a house, so taking a cut in pay would be very difficult. On the other hand, you may find that an applicant has just retired and paid off the house, is on a pension, and has a spouse who just went back to work. The main consideration becomes what importance the applicant places on the pay rate for the job you're offering.

After the questioning, an applicant may still indicate an interest in the job in spite of having conveyed to you some feelings of value and worth higher than you're willing to pay. This person had better convince you that benefits, location, and other factors offset the wage or salary difference. Otherwise, the person will probably stay in the job only until he or she can find one that is more satisfactory.

Managers often need to be able to convert wage figures quickly when determining whether a job's pay rate is in line with an applicant's requirements. One useful tool for this purpose is a wage conversion table such as the one shown in Exhibit 5.2.

Attendance. To deliver quality service consistently, you must be able to count on employees working their scheduled hours. Try to find out about an applicant's record of absenteeism and tardiness. Get background information on shifts worked, days off, and preferred schedule.

Leadership Experience. If the job being offered has supervisory responsibilities, prior supervisory experience is an obvious plus and should be noted. In the interview, attempt to identify the person's leadership abilities and experience and then score accordingly.

Education/ Intelligence

Formal Schooling. If the job requires a college degree, verify that the person has the degree. Because more and more applicants are providing inaccurate information, companies are writing for complete transcripts.

Remember that you must set your requirements for the job that the applicant will be doing, not for later possible promotions. If you require a high school diploma of those applying for a busperson job, you may have to prove that the job hasn't been successfully completed by anyone lacking that level of education.

Once you've established the level of education, look at other achievements, such as grades, awards, scholarships, and extra activities. Make sure the type of education and areas of specialization suit the job for which the person is applying.

Intellectual Ability. Today's business world is becoming increasingly sophisticated. Generally speaking, the ability to perform in an upper-management capacity is related to intellectual ability. However, instead of relying exclusively on a person's level of education or grades, try to assess his or her ability to learn and style of learning. Some people learn best by reading, and others only by doing. Some are quick learners, and others are slow learners.

Exhibit 5.2   Wage Conversion Table

WAGE CONVERSION TABLE

(Approximate figures based on an 8-hour workday and 40-hour workweek)

Hourly Rate	Daily Rate	Weekly Rate	Monthly Rate	Annual Rate
$ 2.50	$ 20.00	$ 100.00	$ 433.33	$ 5,200.00
2.75	22.00	110.00	476.67	5,720.00
3.00	24.00	120.00	520.00	6,240.00
3.25	26.00	130.00	563.33	6,760.00
3.50	28.00	140.00	606.67	7,280.00
3.75	30.00	150.00	650.00	7,800.00
4.00	32.00	160.00	693.33	8,320.00
4.25	34.00	170.00	736.67	8,840.00
4.50	36.00	180.00	780.00	9,360.00
4.75	38.00	190.00	823.33	9,880.00
5.00	40.00	200.00	866.67	10,400.00
5.25	42.00	210.00	910.00	10,920.00
5.50	44.00	220.00	953.33	11,440.00
5.75	46.00	230.00	996.66	11,960.00
6.00	48.00	240.00	1,040.00	12,480.00
6.25	50.00	250.00	1,083.33	13,000.00
6.50	52.00	260.00	1,126.66	13,520.00
6.75	54.00	270.00	1,170.00	14,040.00
7.00	56.00	280.00	1,213.33	14,560.00
7.25	58.00	290.00	1,256.66	15,080.00
7.50	60.00	300.00	1,300.00	15,600.00
7.75	62.00	310.00	1,343.33	16,120.00
8.00	64.00	320.00	1,386.66	16,640.00
8.25	66.00	330.00	1,430.00	17,160.00
8.50	68.00	340.00	1,473.33	17,680.00
8.75	70.00	350.00	1,516.66	18,200.00
9.00	72.00	360.00	1,560.00	18,720.00
9.25	74.00	370.00	1,603.33	19,240.00
9.50	76.00	380.00	1,646.66	19,760.00
9.75	78.00	390.00	1,690.00	20,280.00
10.00	80.00	400.00	1,733.33	20,800.00

CONVERSION SCALE

+ .01	.08	.40	1.73	20.80
.02	.16	.80	3.47	41.60
.03	.24	1.20	5.20	62.40
.04	.32	1.60	6.94	83.20
.05	.40	2.00	8.67	104.00
.10	.80	4.00	17.33	208.00

You may be better off with a slow learner who remembers than a quick learner who forgets.

Intelligent people are generally observant; they will look around the interview area and notice things. Vocabulary should correspond with schooling. Responses—even questions—will be sharp and to the point, not rambling. Ask applicants to give you a personal history, including education, family, jobs, and main accomplishments. Do they wander, exhibit poor recall, or lose concentration?

A logical person will tend to keep things in order, even in conversation. Watch for the use of phrases like, "In the first place" and "First of all," then determine whether the statement that follows does indeed belong first.

Make the distinction between intellectual ability and common sense. A person may be smart but not logical or practical. The hospitality industry relies heavily on sound instincts and common sense.

Additional Training. Make sure you allow applicants time to talk about any other training, on or off the job, that they may have received. With the rising interest in adult education programs, much valuable training is now being gained after formal schooling has been completed. Many companies have fine educational programs for both technical and managerial development. In fact, industry today is investing as much in workplace training as the entire school system of America is spending on formal education.[2]

Social Skills. Courtesy, tact, discretion, and the ability to choose the appropriate behavior for the situation are indispensable qualities in the service environment. Observe the person's manners during the interview.

Verbal and Listening Skills. Effective, "on-your-feet" spoken communication is extremely important in the hospitality business. Some of the qualities of a good communicator include:

- Appropriate vocabulary

- Clear speech that's easily understood

- A pleasant tone of voice

- The ability to articulate ideas and feelings

- Skill at carrying on a conversation

- An understanding of what needs to be passed on to others so that they can be advised and informed

- The ability to listen intently and to retain accurately what's said

For different jobs, of course, you'll have to emphasize different qualities. A telephone operator should have a good voice and be able to speak clearly. For face-to-face communications, however, these qualities may be less important than listening and articulation.

Writing Skills. Many jobs require handwritten records such as guest checks. Other jobs require writing documents like letters, memorandums, reports, and special instructions. The application can give you a general idea of neatness, penmanship, eye/hand coordination, correct grammar, vocabulary, and spelling. Even if a typed or printed resume is submitted, have the applicant quickly fill out an application.

---

[2]Anthony P. Carnevale, "The Learning Enterprise," *Training and Development Journal,* January 1986, p. 18.

Physical Factors

General Health. Hospitality is a high-stress industry and requires good general health, so concern about an applicant's health is appropriate. Many companies give pre-employment physical examinations to avoid placing people with health problems like foot or back trouble in jobs which may significantly aggravate those problems.

Even without the pre-employment physical, you can still ask general questions about health if they relate to the job and a person's history of absenteeism. An observant interviewer can also learn a lot by making a visual assessment. Does the applicant look healthy? Are the eyes clear or bloodshot, glassy, or dull? How is the complexion? Does the posture suggest poor health? Do you notice a limp which might indicate foot problems? Does the applicant have a persistent cough?

Physical Ability. If the job has specific physical requirements, you must be sure the applicant knows and meets them. How much standing is involved? How much weight must be lifted? Does the applicant have the finger dexterity to work in the kitchen or to type on a computer keyboard? Can the person adjust from working behind the kitchen ranges to entering the walk-in coolers?

Cleanliness, Dress, and Posture. On guest surveys, guests list cleanliness as one of their top considerations when deciding whether to return to a hotel or restaurant. Applicants lacking high personal standards of cleanliness may not be able to work up to guests' expectations or the standards of the job.

Styles of clothing may vary among different cultures, races, and age groups. The real concern should be whether the clothes are appropriate to the wearer; they should be clean, neat, well-fitting, and pressed. Worn-down heels, dirt under the fingernails, unpolished shoes, and even a dirty collar will be noticed by a good interviewer.

Check the person's posture. Bad posture often conveys to the guest an attitude of boredom or lack of interest. The ability to project a positive image is important, especially for jobs in highly visible areas such as the dining room or the lobby.

Energy Level. Most of the work in the hospitality industry comes in peaks and valleys. Workers must have the endurance and staying power to handle the peaks and respond quickly to any situation that arises.

If the job requires speed and responsiveness, you can watch how quickly the applicant walks into your office, and note the speed of hand movements and other gestures. Energetic people will often tell you that the jobs they liked were the ones that kept them busy.

Personal Traits

First Impression. In guest contact positions such as door attendant, desk agent, and bellperson, the employee needs to make a positive first impression on each guest. An applicant for such a position should make a good first impression on you.

Does the applicant smile easily, warm up quickly, and establish a rapport? You should be able to sense an easy, warm, and open feeling. Look for eye contact, natural gestures, good body language, and upright posture. Listen for a pleasant voice and a conversational tone.

First impressions are important for many jobs in the hospitality industry.

Interpersonal Skills. People skillful in dealing with others are enthusiastic and friendly. They treat everyone with the same courtesy regardless of race, education, or level of authority. They deal effectively and patiently with all types of people. People with good interpersonal skills recognize that customers are not simply occupants or covers—they are guests.

Personality. Is the applicant outgoing or introverted, warm or cold, friendly or aloof, calm or nervous? The most successful employee will probably be one who's happy, emotionally stable, and even-tempered.

Teamwork. The ability to work with other employees, supervisors, and guests cannot be emphasized too strongly. Team players can place the goals of the department and the company ahead of their own interests. They can take direction, follow orders, and work under authority. They listen to the ideas and suggestions of others, rather than being opinionated and "hard-headed." They're cooperative rather than competitive, and know how to behave in a positive manner to gain cooperation. They're sensitive to the needs and feelings of others and can resolve conflicts with a supervisor or another employee without flare-ups. They encourage goodwill, smooth over problems, go out of their way to help, and share credit with others.

Motivation. Don't hire someone you can't motivate. Motivation is indicated by qualities like a sense of direction and realistic goals, as well as hopes and dreams. The motivated employee enjoys a challenge, has fun while working, and motivates other employees. This person is probably enthusiastic, ambitious, and assertive.

You should also try to determine what motivates a person—security, recognition, achievement, money, or something else. If you decide to make a job offer, the motivators may be your key selling points.

Outlook, Humor, and Optimism. Regardless of the position, those applicants with a positive outlook on life and the ability to laugh at themselves will bring something special to a job. Look for the person who compliments others easily, expects good things to happen, and sees the brighter side of each situation. Other preferred characteristics include self-esteem and confidence. People with a positive outlook don't let one bad situation influence the next opportunity, and they don't worry about things they can't control.

Values. The values of the applicant must match those of the organization. At a minimum, these values will include knowing the difference between right and wrong, treating people fairly, and possessing high ethical standards, integrity, loyalty, sincerity, and honesty.

Creativity. Some positions require more creativity, originality, imagination, and artistic ability than others. For these jobs, you should look for people with creative hobbies, varied interests, possibly even musical talent. Creative people are willing to try the new or unusual, and may offer a number of solutions to a problem. They may display some childlike qualities, such as playfulness and a tendency to react with feelings rather than logic.

Stress Tolerance. Hospitality businesses are characterized by last-minute changes, confrontations, peaks and valleys of business, crises, uncertainty, and difficult or demanding customers. The ability to deal with stressful situations without losing control, becoming hostile, or decreasing work performance is a 24-hour-a-day challenge. Look for people who remain calm under pressure, seem to tolerate frustration fairly well, and can deal with and even enjoy a crisis. A person frequently in trouble for arguing or fighting may be a high risk in the hospitality industry.

Performing Skills. There's certainly a place in the hotel and restaurant business for the person with poise, presence, flair, and showmanship. Look for those who could maneuver gracefully in a crowded dining room, have expressive facial and body movements, and are comfortable getting up in front of strangers. Often, they'll enjoy entertaining at home or performing in theater groups. Also look for interests in singing, dancing, playing musical instruments, or actively participating in sports.

Service Attitude. Customers today are paying well for our services and have a right to expect value for their money. It is important that those who work in the hospitality business understand the difference between being servants and having a service attitude. Being able to care about others and make them happy is a rare gift and something of which a person can be proud.

For Executive Pastry Chef Gilles Renusson of the Amway Grand Plaza Hotel, creativity and artistic ability are an integral part of the job.

Look for people who like helping, caring for, and guiding others. They don't take guests' complaints or anger personally, and are sympathetic, patient, and tolerant of others' shortcomings. They are curious about others. They like children, often help other people with their personal problems, and may do volunteer work. They can put themselves in the other person's shoes, instinctively anticipate and understand the needs and feelings of others, and remember their preferences. They believe that the guest is always right.

Independence. The employee who can work without constant supervision will be more resourceful than employees who lack this ability. This type of person is a self-starter, maybe even a risk-taker, with initiative and perseverance.

Planning and Organizing. Planning and organizing may be among the main requirements for a particular job. In this case, look for applicants who can set priorities, and can then follow through by planning, organizing, and scheduling their own work. These people can manage their time effectively and can understand the short- and long-term effects of a plan.

Problem Solving. Effective problem solving generally requires both common sense and creativity. It is associated with asking the right questions,

Being able to care about others and make them happy is a skill a service employee can be proud of. (Courtesy of Walt Disney World, Lake Buena Vista, Florida)

gathering facts, identifying actual causes, drawing logical and unbiased conclusions, and considering all the options rather than just the obvious ones.

Maturity. Maturity includes emotional stability, self-control, dependability, and a sense of responsibility. A mature person is able to accept the consequences of personal behavior, can admit mistakes or say, "I don't know," and can leave personal problems at home.

Often, immature people are those who become upset about things over which they have no control, handle disappointments poorly, or look for someone else to blame. They may exaggerate or frequently use exclamatory words like "radical," "awesome," or the latest slang. Other signs to watch for include restlessness, nervousness, impatience, or inflexibility.

Decisiveness. Many times, incidents arise suddenly that must be dealt with at once. Workers must be able to make decisions in a timely manner, based only on the facts at hand.

Self-Knowledge. To understand others, people must know and understand themselves. They should have a realistic perception of their own strengths and weaknesses, and should have an ability to see themselves through the eyes of others. This is a particularly important trait for managers.

Flexibility. Versatility and adaptability to unforeseen circumstances are desirable traits for employees in hospitality businesses. Most employees operate in

Hospitality workers face many unexpected situations that require flexibility and decisiveness.

an unstructured environment. They must be able to change direction without warning and with no loss of performance.

Work Standards. Evaluate the applicant's attitudes toward work. Look for consistency, pride in jobs well done, perseverance on tough assignments, and attention to detail. High work standards include the desire to get the job done right the first time without wasting time or materials.

Testing and Reference Checking

The evaluation of applicants is often criticized as being too subjective, and this criticism can result in charges of discrimination in hiring practices. Thus, many companies are seeking more objective forms of evaluation, such as testing and background checking. It's vital that the responsibility for these functions be placed in the hands of a company specialist, someone either in the human resources department or designated by the general manager.

Our legal system leans heavily toward the protection of the individual's rights. The possibility of lawsuits involving libel, slander, invasion of privacy, and discrimination makes every employer extremely cautious about how testing and background checking are used.

On the other hand, the consequences of failing to evaluate a candidate thoroughly may be just as serious as improperly using evaluation tools. Consider, for example, a hotel that offers baby-sitting services to its guests. If management fails to check the backgrounds of employees used as sitters, someone with a history of abusing children could be hired. Such an error and the resulting liability could destroy a business. In a 1984 case in Arizona, a jury awarded $6 million in damages to the husband of a woman who was murdered by a motel employee. The motel was held liable because it hired the murderer without performing a background check which, the plaintiff claimed, would have revealed that the applicant had a long history of violence and arrests for aggravated assault and attempted rape. Instead, he was hired and put to work sweeping immediately following his interview.

Testing

Testing is a widely accepted practice in the evaluation process. Skills testing is routine for a variety of positions. In addition to skills testing, some companies screen job applicants by means of psychological and honesty tests, polygraph tests, pre-employment physical examinations, and drug tests.

Testing by itself won't protect an employer from accusations of subjectivity, inconsistency, and discrimination. Any test used must have direct and established relevance to the requirements of the job. It's normally acceptable to give a typing test for a secretarial position or a math test for food servers. Such tests, however, must be administered consistently to every candidate who reaches that point in the screening process. Even so, if the test disqualifies applicants from protected categories more often than non-protected applicants, it may still be deemed discriminatory.

To prove that a test does, indeed, evaluate qualities needed for the job, it must be validated by an often difficult and expensive process. The test in question must be administered to a large group of employees who do the job for which you're testing. **Validation** establishes that high test results are associated with high performance and that the test isn't weighted against any member of a protected minority, either intentionally or unintentionally. Even then, the results are not always clear-cut.

Developing a testing program and validating tests is a job best left to trained professionals. Government standards and proper procedures for determining validity are extremely complex. In other words, managers can't just develop a list of their favorite questions and start testing applicants.

Good packaged tests and validation services are available. If you're considering purchasing such materials or services, ask to see the company's research and validation studies. They should be conducted on exactly the same types of jobs and workers you're testing. Persons participating in test validation should have similar language, cultural, and reading levels as those you'll be testing. Find out what type of training the testing service provides to your employees who will be administering the tests. Obtain the names of companies similar to yours which have used the materials, and then check those references.

Health tests and pre-employment physical examinations are expensive and time-consuming. The employer must decide whether the information gained is worth the expense. If these tools are used, they must be a part of normal procedure for everyone. They should not be arbitrarily administered just because someone appears to have health problems ("I think this person is too heavy—we'd better have him take a physical"). Screening out the applicant due to the results of a physical exam must be based on job requirements.

Honesty tests, polygraph tests, and testing for the presence of drugs are particularly sensitive issues. Laws and attitudes about these areas are

Exhibit 5.3   Sample Application Form Release

> I authorize a thorough investigation of my past employment and activities, agree to cooperate in such investigation, and release from all liability or responsibility all persons and corporations requesting or supplying information. I further authorize any physician or hospital to release any information which may be necessary to determine my ability to perform the job for which I am being considered or any future job in the event I am hired.

Courtesy of Hyatt Hotels Corporation, Chicago, Illinois.

changing rapidly. It's best to consult a lawyer before deciding to adopt one of these programs.

Before adopting any new test, consider the problem you're having and determine how much that problem is costing. Weigh the cost of the problem against the cost of the test. Consider the costs of the materials, time, and space needed to administer and score the test. Also consider that a poor test may unnecessarily reduce the field of qualified job applicants. In addition, testing may cause a delay in the hiring process, a delay which could hurt guest services. After all these costs and drawbacks have been carefully evaluated, you're in a better position to decide whether implementing the test is a sound business decision.

The results of all tests should remain confidential. The employer generally does not have to furnish them to applicants.

Background and Reference Checking

The background and reference sections of a job application are areas of much misrepresentation. If the job you're filling requires a particular college degree, certification, or level of education, make sure applicants are able to back up their statements with a diploma, transcript, or other documentation. You'll need to get the applicant's written permission before you write or call for a transcript. You can also ask the applicant to make the request directly.

Checking personal references has limited value, but some general insights may be gained. Look at the names given, their positions in the community, relationships to the applicant, and how long they've been acquainted. People are unlikely to submit the names of others who might say something negative about them. Occasionally, however, a brazen applicant will list names of people he or she has never met.

You must check work records to verify that people are who they say they are and that they have represented themselves correctly. Check credit references only if it's job-related, as in the case of someone who will be handling money.

Your risk in collecting reference information is small unless you pass along false information to anyone or confidential information to those who don't have a need to know. If a job offer isn't made because of a bad reference, any legal action would be against the company giving the reference, not the company requesting it. To reduce any possible liability, however, a company should have applicants sign a release (usually at the bottom of the application) that gives it permission to contact references while holding references blameless for anything they may say. Exhibit 5.3 presents the release found at the end of the application form discussed in Chapter 4. Exhibit 5.4

Exhibit 5.4   Sample Mailed Employment Verification

```
┌──────────────────────────────────────────────────┐
│              EMPLOYMENT VERIFICATION               │
│                                                    │
│  I hereby authorize Amway Grand Plaza Hotel to     │
│  verify my employment history with your company.   │
│                                                    │
│  _____  │
│                    SIGNATURE                       │
│                                                    │
│  _____  │
│                    PRINT NAME                      │
│                                                    │
│  _____  │
│               SOCIAL SECURITY NUMBER               │
│                                                    │
│  Employed From _____ to _____    │
│                                                    │
│  Job Title: _____   │
│  How would you rate this employee? _____   │
│  _____  │
│  _____  │
│                                                    │
│  Why did this person leave your company?           │
│  _____  │
│  _____  │
│                                                    │
│  Would you rehire? [ ] Yes [ ] Questionable [ ] No │
│                                                    │
│  If questionable or no, please explain _____   │
│  _____  │
│  _____  │
│                                                    │
│  Additional comments _____   │
│  _____  │
│                                                    │
│  SIGNED _____   │
│  TITLE _____ DATE _____    │
└──────────────────────────────────────────────────┘
```

Courtesy of Amway Grand Plaza Hotel, Grand Rapids, Michigan.

presents a combined release and information request form which, after being signed by the applicant, is mailed to a previous employer. A form used when checking references by telephone is shown in Exhibit 5.5.

Check references before hiring someone and don't make any definite offers until you have checked the references. You shouldn't tell an applicant that he or she will get the job if his or her references are acceptable. Companies are not bound to reveal why hiring decisions are made. The earlier the reference check, the more gracefully you can get out of an uncomfortable situation.

When you begin reference checking, you're likely to find that most companies now direct such requests to their human resources department. The information provided may be restricted to job title, dates of employment,

Exhibit 5.5 Sample Telephone Reference Form

OPRYLAND HOTEL
TELEPHONE EMPLOYMENT VERIFICATION

Date_____

Applicant's Name_____

Company_____

Dates Employed: From:_____   To:_____

Position _____

Reason for Leaving _____

Would you Rehire? _____

Person Verifying _____

Telephone number of company _____

Comments _____

_____

FORM 3755D   OPRYLAND HOTEL

Courtesy of Opryland Hotel, Nashville, Tennessee.

and salary verification. Former employers rarely reveal whether the person is even eligible for rehire because it increases their potential liability in case the person charges libel, slander, or defamation of character.

Due to the potential for lawsuits, companies providing references are reluctant to disclose information or offer opinions which cannot be proven. For example, a statement like, "The person was fired for suspected drug abuse," could be construed as damaging the subject's reputation and might leave the speaker extremely vulnerable to legal retaliation. If a former employer provides outsiders with information from a confidential record (such as a security report or a medical file), the disclosed information becomes a matter of public record. The ex-employee may then be able to see the complete document or even an entire confidential file.

Try to speak directly with the person's former department head, but be realistic in your expectations. The ex-supervisor will be operating under severe constraints imposed by legal considerations. The reference cannot provide unsolicited comments or statements that are unrelated to the job. Former employers are still free, however, to respond to direct questions and to offer opinions to someone with a legitimate need to know. They can say, for instance, that an applicant had attendance problems or quit without giving notice if it's true and there are records to back it up.

Keep in mind that, without a doubt, you will be called upon as a reference. To protect itself and its managers, a company may consider having newly hired employees sign a release (sometimes placed on the application form) giving the company permission to respond to later inquiries about them and waiving any right they might have to written notice of such disclosure. Even so, of course, you must use caution in making such responses. For additional information on reference checking, see Chapter 11.

Police Record Checks

Companies check police records to ensure that potential employees aren't risky choices. Before refusing to hire an employee because of a police record, however, be sure the nature of the conviction is relevant to the job.

For instance, housekeepers must be free of suspicion because they have easy access to guestrooms, the ability to move about the building unquestioned, and a limited amount of supervision. In recruiting housekeepers, you may be justified in refusing to hire any persons who have been convicted of theft or shoplifting.

Similarly, a person who has a record of driving convictions may not be qualified to be a valet parker. However, the same person may be employable as a cashier.

Common Errors of Evaluation

Errors in evaluation are both commonplace and serious. Many errors are created when an interviewer lacks judgment and allows personal prejudices to enter the evaluation process. A serious error can result in hiring the wrong person for the job or turning away a good candidate without justification.

As an interviewer, you should know your own personal biases and not let them interfere with your decisions. Don't base decisions on handshakes or how the applicant looked you in the eye. If you feel you may be personally biased either for or against an applicant, get someone else involved in the interviewing process. Be especially careful to avoid the following common errors.

The Halo Effect

The **halo effect** refers to the situation in which the interviewer assumes that *all* of an applicant's traits are good because of one or two outstanding traits. To avoid this trap, the interviewer needs to evaluate each trait separately and objectively.

Projection

Sometimes, interviewers will look for people who have personal traits similar to their own through a process known as **projection**. People with different motives and personalities can still get the job done. If an organization were to hire only people who think alike, it would soon become stale and unimaginative.

Over-simplification

Interviewers may incorrectly assume that because a person reacted one way in a given instance, he or she will probably react that way in all instances. Look for repeated behaviors and patterns by asking additional questions.

Stereotyping

Assigning characteristics to all of the members of a group is the worst form of prejudice. Assuming that all chefs are temperamental, that women are absent more than men, and that handicapped people are accident-prone is unfair and incorrect. (In fact, statistics have clearly shown that handicapped people have fewer workers' compensation claims, and women generally have better attendance records.)

Impulsive Conclusions   A common error in evaluating applicants is to draw conclusions too quickly and without supporting evidence. Don't assume, for instance, that just because an applicant was president of a college fraternity, he's a leader. By interviewing, you may find the applicant obtained the position through seniority, default, or influence.

Expectations   It is a mistake to form an opinion before meeting an applicant. Just because one of your best employees recommends an applicant, don't automatically assume that he or she would make an excellent employee. Back up your expectations with facts gained through the interview process.

Physical Appearance   There is an unfortunate tendency to assess people on the basis of physical appearance. For some reason, tall people and attractive people are evaluated as being more successful. Good looks have nothing to do with a person's actual ability on the job.

Writing Up an Evaluation

In most cases, the perfect candidate doesn't exist, so you must determine which of the available applicants is likeliest to succeed in the job you have open. A systematic approach in rating helps minimize the risks of overlooking important areas and letting your personal feelings influence your decision. The rating form should include those factors that are most important to the success of the job.

Evaluate an applicant for a specific job. If a person were to be interviewed for another job, quite often the ratings would be different. Some companies have different forms for different types of jobs, such as management, food service, and office work.

A fairly simple applicant evaluation form (such as that shown in Exhibit 5.6) will often be sufficient. Sometimes, however, a more complex form such as the weighted interview evaluation form (discussed earlier and shown in Exhibit 5.1) may be needed. This form is like a shopping list of traits. To use it, the interviewer places a check in any of five different columns according to the following criteria:

- Check the center column if the applicant meets an acceptable level of skill in a given area or if the skill is not needed.

- Check the plus-one column if the applicant has better than acceptable skills.

- Check the minus-one column if the applicant has less than acceptable skills.

- Check the plus-three column if the applicant has a very clear and observable strength in a relevant area.

- Check the minus-three column if the applicant has a very clear and observable weakness in a relevant area.

According to this system, the person with the highest point total will usually make the best employee. A shortcoming in one area will seldom eliminate a candidate. Every person has strengths and weaknesses. If the

Exhibit 5.6   Application Evaluation Form

Walt Disney World ®

APPLICANT'S NAME:	SOCIAL SECURITY NUMBER	HIRE DATE

POSITION INTERVIEWED FOR:

DATE INTERVIEWED:

REFERRED TO:

INSTRUCTIONS

Applicants may not be discriminated against because of race, color, religion, age, sex or national origin. Your comments should be restricted to the applicant's bona fide occupational qualifications for employment, transfer, or promotion.

EVALUATION OF APPLICANT

☐ MAKE OFFER   ☐ NO INTEREST   ☐ CONSIDER WITH OTHERS   ☐ FUTURE INTEREST

INTERVIEWED BY: _____ SIGNATURE _____ EXT. _____ DATE _____

To properly maintain our records, we are required to have evaluations that show that each individual was given fair consideration and what factors determined the choice of a more qualified candidate. Legal requirements necessitate the thorough completion of these evaluations.

RETURN THIS FORM IMMEDIATELY TO _____ **EXT.** _____

30271 0388

Courtesy of Walt Disney World, Lake Buena Vista, Florida.

form is a series of checks down the middle column, the interviewer simply didn't do the job properly. Use the checklist as a basis for an evaluation and make your recommendation in a positive manner. List all the good points about the applicant first.

If you still have any negative or uneasy feelings after you have completed your evaluation, testing, and reference checks, there are a couple of things you can do. You can set up a second interview; often the applicant's attitude is entirely different during the second meeting. Alternatively, you can have the person meet with another interviewer and, in so doing, get a different evaluation.

Finally, if you're still unsure, go with your intuition. Many times managers have said, "I knew there was something wrong with the applicant, but I just couldn't put my finger on it." If that's the case and you're satisfied that your intuition is not the result of prejudices, you're better off taking the applicant out of consideration.

Key Terms

halo effect
interview evaluation form
validation
weighted evaluation form

Discussion Questions

1. What qualifications do you think are important for a front desk agent and for an accounting bookkeeper? Why would certain traits receive more weight for one job than for the other?

2. What problems might occur if you hire someone whose salary history indicates a pay range higher than that of the job for which you're hiring?

3. What elements would you consider before deciding to require pre-employment physicals?

4. How should you respond to a request for reference information on a former employee of yours?

5. What are some of the sources of information you might want to use in checking references on an applicant?

6. What are some specific examples of the common errors of evaluation?

6 Hiring

After completing efforts to recruit, interview, check the references of, evaluate, and select a candidate, the new employee's manager may be tempted to sit back and contemplate a job well done. Actually, the job isn't finished. The final phase of the selection process is the **hiring period**, which starts when an offer is extended and lasts through the new employee's initial adjustments to the job.

Because the need for workers is so pressing, many managers fail to give the critical steps of the hiring period adequate attention, or may even overlook some of them altogether. As with the mishandling of other aspects of the selection process, the result is often a significant increase in turnover among the newly hired.

The hiring period starts when the employer makes an offer to a prospective employee. It involves all of the arrangements necessary to prepare the new person and current employees for a successful working relationship, including the initial processing of personnel records. The hiring period is culminated by the job orientation, which is the period of time beginning when the employee starts work and ending when the employee has learned most of the basic skills and knowledge required for the job.

This chapter covers all of the major steps of the hiring period and concludes by discussing the hiring of management employees, which requires a slightly different set of procedures from those used for hiring line employees. Responsibility for seeing any new worker through these steps rests with the person's department manager. Some stages are often delegated to another employee, but the manager should still understand each phase of the process in order to provide the appropriate information and support.

Making and Closing Offers

Extending an offer to a potential employee is the crucial first step in the hiring process. Because of the skill needed to do this effectively while complying with complex labor laws, most companies extend all of their offers through the human resources department or some other person designated by management. This tends to enhance the professionalism of the process and also saves managers time. In addition, when only one or two people extend all offers, the company has more control over how the job is represented and what promises are made. This is important, since employee misunderstanding of the job offer is a leading cause of employment lawsuits. A strong point of the company's defense in such cases is the consistency and experience of the person who makes the offer. Someone responsible for making all job offers for a company is unlikely to be confused about the terms of the hiring arrangement.

Extending the Offer

Timing is a very important element of making offers successfully. Based on the information given to the applicant, he or she has some idea of when to expect to hear from you. This is probably earlier than your own timetable because of the person's anxiety. The longer you wait past the applicant's timetable to make an offer, the less successful you'll be. This occurs because the applicant will have begun to talk himself or herself out of wanting the job.

A carefully worded offer can give the potential employee a good name to live up to and set the stage for a commitment to the company's goals. The human resources representative extending an offer might use a statement like, "Of all the people the manager has interviewed, she feels that you can do the best job in helping her meet the goals of her department."

The human resources representative should cover all the key elements of an offer, which are listed in Exhibit 6.1.

It may not be advisable to have the new employee start the first day at the beginning of a shift. Department heads usually have so many opening duties they don't have time to handle new employees properly. A delay of an hour or even half a day may be appropriate on the first day, but be sure to clarify that purpose in arranging this one-time delay.

Negotiating the Offer

If your research was thorough during the selection process, by now you should be well acquainted with the applicant's background and expectations. Authorize the human resources representative to extend an offer only if you're reasonably sure of its acceptance, and only after you have all the facts to put together a complete offer package. Before authorizing an offer, you should have covered areas that might arise as obstacles to negotiations—things like relocation problems, salary needs, starting dates, and special benefits. If you first extend job offers and then have to haggle with candidates over items you've overlooked but that they consider important, you'll probably have to concede to their demands on every point and will certainly lose control of the negotiations. Such bargaining tends to place employer and potential employee at odds with each other and can damage the relationship you're trying to build. It also suggests to candidates that the company isn't concerned about their best interests.

If you're unsure of whether the candidate will accept, ask the human resources representative to try to make the offer in person rather than by telephone or letter. He or she should review all the positive elements of the job and any unusual benefits, find out whether there are any questions, and ask for a decision or determine when an answer can be expected.

Establishing a starting date offers the perfect opportunity to let the person know that your company doesn't like employees leaving without proper notice. For instance, the human resources representative may emphasize this by saying, "I'm sure your current boss doesn't like it when people leave without giving notice any more than we do. However, we really need you as soon as possible. What's the earliest date you think you can start?" It's inconsistent to expect proper notice at your company if you're not prepared to let a newly hired employee give proper notice before leaving a current job.

Exhibit 6.1   The Key Elements of a Job Offer

- position title
- person to report to
- salary
- shift
- starting date
- starting time
- ending time
- days off
- equipment needed
- clothing required
- meal arrangements
- parking
- when to come for processing of personnel forms

Concluding the Offer

Once the candidate has accepted the offer, the individual should be assured that he or she has made the right decision and that the new manager will also be very pleased.

The person making the offer shouldn't promise things that aren't true or can't be documented. Statements like, "This job is permanent," or "You can stay here as long as you do a good job for us," can be interpreted as oral contracts. Later, such statements can be used against you in employment lawsuits. Even telling someone, "You'll receive complete training," could lead to a lawsuit if you release an employee for poor performance who then charges that you never provided the promised training.

Instead, new employees should be told that the organization doesn't expect them to know everything, but that their managers believe that, with their abilities, they will be able to do their jobs. This establishes a standard of expecting things to be done properly, expresses confidence, and helps eliminate some of the fears that go along with starting new jobs.

The new hire should be told that the manager will begin to take steps immediately to prepare for his or her arrival. These steps may include notifying all the other applicants and making an announcement to the department's staff. The person making the offer should obtain the new employee's uniform size and the name he or she wants to use on name tags or business cards. (If a nickname is preferred, use it.) The more plans the new employee feels the company has made, the harder it will be for the person to back out of his or her commitment before starting (for instance, due to a **counter-offer**).

Making Offers to Managers

After presenting an offer for a management position, the human resources representative should send a follow-up offer letter. Again, choose the wording with great care. Statements like, "We're looking forward to a long and happy relationship with you," or "As long as you do a good job around here you have nothing to worry about," can be interpreted as offering a job for life. Exhibit 6.2 shows a sample offer letter.

Exhibit 6.2   Sample Offer Letter

Regent Court Hotel

June 2, 19XX

Mr. John Doe
1234 Elm Street
Miami, FL 33138

Dear John:

I am delighted to confirm the verbal offer extended to you
to join the team of the Regent Court Hotel.

We believe that you have an exciting and bright future and
that your particular experience and background will serve
you and the Regent Court well as we work toward our goal of
setting a new standard of excellence in the hospitality
industry.

Listed below are the specific details of your employment.

1.   Your title will be Executive Housekeeper. You will
     report directly to Jane Smith, Rooms Division Manager.

2.   Your starting date will be July 5, 19XX. Please report
     to the Human Resources Department at 10:00 a.m. Your
     starting salary will be at the rate of $3,000 per month,
     equalizing to $36,000 annually. Salary reviews are
     conducted annually. Paydays are on the 15th and last
     day of each month.

3.   The Hotel will support all reasonable costs up to a
     maximum of 13,000 gross pounds associated with the
     packing, transportation and storage, in transit, up to
     90 days, along with the delivery and unpacking of your
     personal and household effects. In addition, the
     company will cover the insurance on your household
     effects at the rate of up to $2.50 per pound.

4.   To assist you in finding suitable housing, arrangements
     have been made for you to stay at the Regent Court
     Hotel for up to four weeks. The Hotel will provide
     your room, food (not liquor), laundry and reasonable
     telephone usage.

5.   You will also be reimbursed at the rate of 24 cents per
     mile, plus any additional charges for overnight lodging,
     meals, or tolls, while you are relocating from Miami to
     Grand Rapids.

6.   You will also be entitled to free parking, duty meals,
     and valet service for business wear.

Regent Court Hotel
1234 Main Street/Grand Rapids, MI 49503

Exhibit 6.2 *(continued)*

RC
Regent Court Hotel

7. Currently the benefits that you will be entitled to include hospitalization, dental insurance, life insurance, vision insurance, travel accident insurance, and short-term disability, and will be effective on your first day of employment.

8. The Hotel will pay the full employment agency fee of $10,800 from Search, Inc. If you terminate your employment in less than six months from the date of hire, you will be responsible for reimbursing the Regent Court Hotel 100% of the agency fee; more than six months, 50%; after one year no reimbursement will be required.

I trust you will find this letter comprehensive and consistent with our discussions. If you have any questions or concerns regarding the above, please advise me at your earliest convenience. Please sign the carbon copy where it indicates your acceptance and return it to my attention. The original is for your records.

Again, John, I would like to say that we are proud to have you as a part of our team and look forward to a mutually rewarding association.

Sincerely,

REGENT COURT HOTEL

Ed Brown

Ed Brown
Director of Human Resources

EB/abd

cc: General Manager
       Director of Operations
       Rooms Division Manager

ACCEPTED: _____

DATE: _____

If a managerial candidate is good, his or her present employer will probably make a counter-offer. As the labor market continues to tighten, this will happen more and more. To minimize the impact of counter-offers, the person making the offer should openly discuss the probability with the person. The person may even be told that people have been known to remain with a company on the basis of a counter-offer, only to discover that the promises made are not kept. The human resources representative should mention that counter-offers are not unusual, but that accepting your company's offer was the right decision. The human resources department can also help the new employee write a carefully-worded resignation letter that might minimize the possibility of counter-offers.

A welcome letter sent promptly to the spouse (see Exhibit 6.3) can encourage family support for the change. Your organization should consider offering assistance to the spouse in locating new employment, particularly if a long-distance move is involved. Possibilities include helping with the preparation of resumes, providing leads, and furnishing letters of introduction explaining why the spouse is looking for a job.

The human resources department should send the family a copy of your local Sunday newspaper each week until the new manager arrives. This allows you to stay in touch, helps the family get acquainted with the area, and builds anticipation about the move.

Above all, the human resources representative should maintain regular contact by telephone to reinforce the decision and provide assistance through a difficult time.

Using Employment Contracts

More and more employers are making use of **employment contracts**, particularly for managerial employees. These contracts represent an effort to cope with the increase in litigation related to **breach of contract** and wrongful dismissal charges by former employees.

An employment contract may spell out the hiring arrangements and the circumstances under which the employee could be terminated. It may provide details about the specific remedy available, such as severance pay, should the person be fired under other circumstances. The contract could also spell out the in-house procedures for handling disputes and resolving problems. It might require that all steps of this process be exhausted before the employee can take legal action.

Keep in mind that such contracts are binding on the employer as well as the employee. The format for the employment contract should be carefully developed with the assistance of a labor attorney.

Preparing Other Employees

As a manager, you can head off potential problems and ensure faster start-up time for the new employee by properly preparing your existing staff. The smaller your department or the higher the level of responsibility of the new person, the greater the importance of this step.

Tell fellow employees that a new employee has been hired. Inform them of the person's name, previous jobs, and starting date. Often, other employees will have worked at some of the same places as the new hire; friendships and positive expectations can begin to form.

If the hire involves an addition to staff, explain the reasons to current employees. This is particularly recommended for staff additions involving tipped positions, which can be perceived as reducing the tips, hours worked, and thus the income of current employees. If this situation is handled improperly, the successful hiring of the new employee could be threatened by a discontented staff.

Exhibit 6.3   Sample Welcome Letter to Spouse

$\mathcal{RC}$

Regent Court Hotel

June 9, 19XX

Mrs. Jane Doe
1234 Elm Street
Miami, FL 33138

Dear Jane:

I thought I would drop you a line to tell you how pleased we
are to have your husband join our staff at the Regent Court
Hotel. I am confident that with John's fine background and
abilities he will prove to be a valuable asset to us.

The Executive Housekeeper is an important position in our
operations, one that I feel will be a real challenge to him,
as well as giving him the opportunity to grow and advance in
his profession.

Ed Brown, our Director of Human Resources, has been
gathering additional information for you to help you get
acquainted with the Regent Court Hotel and the Grand Rapids
area. As you get closer to a moving date, I'm sure you will
find him to be very helpful. He will also make arrangements
for you and your children to come down to the hotel for a
tour. In addition, if there is anything I can personally
do, please don't hesitate to call. I look forward to
meeting you in person.

Warmest regards,

REGENT COURT HOTEL

Mary Johnson

Mary Johnson
General Manager

MJ/abd

Regent Court Hotel
1234 Main Street/Grand Rapids, MI 49503

In some cases, you may need to manage starting dates. One case arises when a department is made up predominantly of one class of people, and a new employee belongs to a different class. Some managers find it better to start two new employees of a different class at the same time. In an area of all male workers, for example, you may wish to arrange starting dates and shift times so that two women could begin working at the same time.

If your department has strong cliques, meet with the informal leaders and ask for their cooperation. Review the goals of your department with them, and make them accountable for seeing that new employees are accepted.

Explain who the new person will report to and what responsibilities he or she will have. If the new employee will have any authority, explain the extent of this authority and emphasize that the person has your full support. Express confidence in the new employee and stress the importance of getting the new person settled in as quickly as possible. Ask current employees for their help.

Make a special point of notifying the person who'll be responsible for the job orientation of the new employee.

Processing

Initial processing of personnel records should be handled by the human resources department or the person designated to handle this function. Many companies handle processing and preparation of personnel forms before the first day of work and treat it as unpaid time. Opinions vary on whether to pay for this time, but currently payment is not required by law in most states. Check with legal counsel on this issue.

As a department head, you may not need to be present for this phase of the hiring period. However, you should know how processing ties in with your departmental responsibilities.

Processing new employees before they actually start working permits them to be better prepared for the first day of work. They can be given materials to read ahead of time. It's also a good idea that uniforms be fitted and name tags ordered at this time. These items are needed on the first day of the job—not two weeks later.

Build a Relationship

The tone of the processing period should express warmth, caring, and professionalism. If it's too light or casual, new employees may conclude the company is lax in its policies and procedures. People who arrive late for processing should be told that that's not the way management expects things to be done.

The human resources department should help the employee accurately perceive what to expect on the job. For instance, if recent management changes have resulted in some confusion in the new employee's department, he or she should be told so right up front.

This processing period is an excellent time for the human resources department to cement a solid relationship with the new staff member. The human resources department and the employee's department head should convey the image that this is the place for employees to go with problems when they don't think anyone in the department can assist. Companies are better off dealing with problems within the company rather than having employees go directly to the Equal Employment Opportunity Commission, federal or state Department of Labor, the union organizer, or other outsiders.

New employees should be introduced to all of the human resources department staff and urged to stop back in to relate their progress. Better yet, someone from that department could visit new employees on the job after a few days.

Processing is also a good time to convey what's expected of the employee in the way of service, and to talk about the goals of the company. These goals can be reinforced by means of a letter sent to the new employee's home. Exhibit 6.4 is a sample welcome letter.

Cover Necessary Information

During processing, the human resources department should cover points common to all departments. These points may include timecards, pay procedures, house rules, instructions on reporting for the first workday, and uniforms. Careful coordination between the human resources department and the new employee's department on coverage of these points will minimize duplication and confusion.

Care should be taken not to cover too much material. The attention span and retention of most new employees may be quite limited. At this point, everything is new and confusing to them. Handouts are useful and will reduce the amount of time needed for processing. The human resources department should cover only those key areas that have immediate priority. Other information can be covered by means of the employee handbook, the policy manual, and, at a later date, the general company orientation. At this point, telling new employees where to find information is often as important as actually telling them the information. The use of a checklist can ensure that all points are covered. Exhibit 6.5 is a sample **personnel processing checklist**.

Information should be presented in a logical order. For instance, when the timecard is issued, employees can be told that they should be in uniform at the start of the shift and before punching in. Other topics relevant to hours and pay include:

- Whether employees are paid for meal breaks
- How much time is allowed for meals and breaks
- How overtime is calculated
- How tips are reported
- What the policy is on leaving the premises during the shift
- Which day of the week employees are paid
- When the first paycheck can be expected
- What deductions to expect

House rules refer to a set of behavioral standards for all employees; one instance of violation may result in immediate termination. If an employee is fired for violation of the house rules, the company must be able to prove that the person was given a copy. Therefore, the human resources representative should always obtain a signed receipt for the house rules, as well as for the

Exhibit 6.4   Sample Welcome Letter to New Employee

Amway Grand Plaza Hotel · Pearl at Monroe. Grand Rapids. Michigan 49503-2666 USA · 616-774-2000

Executive Office

July 5, 19XX

Mr. John Doe
1234 Elm Street
Grand Rapids, MI 49506

Dear John:

Welcome! You have joined the team of one of the most exciting
and dynamic hotel complexes in the United States--the Amway Grand
Plaza Hotel. The group of people you will be working with are
the best in the world.

The founders of the Amway Grand Plaza Hotel, Jay VanAndel and
Rich DeVos, are committed to some basic values of life which we
have enclosed. Please read them very carefully. You have been
hired because we believe you have the ability and the desire to
maintain these values.

It is our goal to set a new standard of excellence in the
hospitality industry. We look to our new employees, like
yourself, to assist us in achieving this goal by getting involved
and bringing in fresh and exciting ideas.

You will be learning more about the Hotel in the days ahead. The
orientation program is an important part of that learning process.
It will be valuable to you and should not be missed.

We hope you will enjoy your work and take pride in your
contribution to the Amway Grand Plaza Hotel and the fine
reputation that your fellow employees worked so hard to achieve.

We also hope that in the coming months, we will all grow together
in our Commitment to Excellence at the Amway Grand Plaza Hotel.

Sincerely,

Barb VanAndel-Gaby
Resident Manager

BG/sg
Enclosure

Courtesy of Amway Grand Plaza Hotel, Grand Rapids, Michigan.

Exhibit 6.5   Personnel Processing Checklist

Check

_____ Application
_____ Requisition
_____ Test Results
_____ Positive I.D.
_____ Immigration Form I-9
_____ Social Security Number and Name

_____ Hiring Form
_____ Reference Checks
_____ Terminated Files
_____ Proof of Age (if needed)
_____ Work Permit (if student or minor)

Forms

_____ Federal/State/City Tax
_____ EEO Declaration
_____ Bonding Application (Cashiers)
_____ Conflict of Interest (Managers)

_____ Insurance Cards
_____ Uniform Control Card
_____ Hiring Agreement
_____ Police Checks

Issue

_____ Locker #_____
_____ Name Tag
_____ Meal Card
_____ Take-Home Training Manuals
_____ Parking Information
_____ Dress Code Standards
_____ Foot Care Brochure
_____ Employee Handbook
_____ General Company Orientation
         Date

_____ Identification Card
_____ Employee/Guest Safety and
         Security Data
_____ Company Organization Chart
_____ Sales Brochure
_____ Timecard
_____ Tip Credit Notification
_____ Benefit Data
_____ Directory of Guest Services

employee handbook and any other items issued. He or she should also make sure the employees read and understand what they are signing.

A **probationary period** is a trial period, usually one to three months, representing a condition of employment. New employees hired on probation should be advised that they'll be observed during this period to determine whether they meet job requirements. They should understand that if they don't meet expectations, the job offer may be revoked. When explaining the probationary period, the human resources representative should be sure to clarify that it's possible to be terminated at any time *during or after* the probationary period. Completing a probationary period does not protect an employee from being fired later.

A definite time and place should be established for reporting on the first day. Also, the new employee should be told to whom to report. It may be a good idea to provide all of this information in writing.

Assign Uniforms

Being a good performer requires a high degree of self-confidence. Employees can't feel confident, particularly in front of the public, if they don't feel good about their appearance. Although uniforms represent a major expense to the company, they're also an important factor in job performance. Companies that provide uniforms at all should do it right.

All staff members should have their own uniforms assigned and specifically fitted to them. Walking around in someone else's poorly fitted clothes doesn't make anyone feel good. Well-fitted uniforms and proper name tags are particularly important to new employees when meeting peers on the first day. No one wants to appear different.

The uniform design can be either unisex or tailored according to the sex

Exhibit 6.6 Sample Uniform Control Card

	WARDROBE RECORD	☐ Full Time ☐ Part Time ☐ On Call

NAME_____ POSITION_____

DEPT. _____ AUTHORIZED SIGNATURE _____

PLEASE REPORT ANY MISSING BUTTONS, STAINS OR TEARS FOR SPECIAL HANDLING. You must turn in a soiled uniform in order to pick up a clean one.

Required uniform accessories, provided by the employee, are:

Shoes _____ Socks _____
Skirt _____ Other _____
Pants _____ Other _____
Belt _____ Other _____

RECORD OF ISSUE

QUANTITY	TYPE	SIZE	DATE

I understand that the items indicated above will be altered (if necessary) and issued to me without deposit.

I further understand that if I should leave the company or change positions, I must turn in every item listed above. I also authorize the company to deduct from my final paycheck the cost of replacing lost items or repairing items damaged from other than normal wear.

_____ _____ _____ _____
UNIFORM ATTENDANT'S SIGNATURE   DATE   EMPLOYEE'S SIGNATURE   DATE

Form 5/14 12/84

Courtesy of Amway Grand Plaza Hotel, Grand Rapids, Michigan.

of the wearer. Female employees should not be asked to wear clothing made for men. The style should be appropriate for both young and old; a paper cap and flight-crew jumpsuit may not be suitable for a retiree.

Most employees are issued three uniforms: one to wear, one in the laundry, and one in the uniform room for exchange. Cooks and others who soil uniforms more quickly may need up to six sets, particularly if the laundry is only open five days a week.

At the time uniforms are being fitted and issued, the employee should be told:

- How to pick up uniforms
- Whether the company or the employee pays for them
- Whether a deposit is required
- How uniforms are to be maintained
- How to report damage such as rips, lost buttons, and bad stains

The employee should also get a list of personal items that will be needed to complete the uniform, including the type and color of shoes, belts, and socks or stockings. Exhibit 6.6 shows a wardrobe record which can be used to list employee-provided accessories and to serve as a receipt for company-provided uniforms.

Exhibit 6.7   Types of Orientation

Type:	Job Orientation	General Company Orientation
When:	begins at once	usually occurs two weeks to a month after the job begins
Purpose:	to help new employees begin to function productively as quickly as possible	to elicit employee commitment

Orientation Programs

Almost every company has an employee orientation program. The purpose of the program, how it's conducted, and even what it's called may vary from one employer to another. However, there are commonly two overall objectives:

1.   To help new employees begin to function productively in the work environment as quickly as possible

2.   To elicit employee identification with and commitment to the company and its philosophy

These two objectives are best achieved not only through different means but also at different times. This can best be handled by means of two separate orientation efforts: job orientation and general company orientation (see Exhibit 6.7).

Job orientation begins when the worker begins. It's the responsibility of the employee's department manager and is directed at teaching the individual the principles of the job. Job orientation is discussed later in this chapter.

The **general company orientation** is a formal program designed to introduce the company's mission and values to a group of employees. It does this in a manner which suggests that each individual's needs and goals can best be met through the accomplishment of the company's goals. This program is conducted by the human resources department or the person designated to handle processing of personnel forms. Since it isn't (or shouldn't be) part of the hiring period for most employers, how to plan for and conduct the general company orientation will be discussed in Chapter 7. However, since some companies mistakenly believe that general orientation should always be part of the first day hiring activities, we will discuss here why it is not appropriate at this time. Every manager should understand the impact that timing can have on the effectiveness of the program.

The general company orientation is most successful when it occurs two weeks to a month after the job begins. Some companies, particularly those which do a large amount of seasonal hiring, prefer to introduce the general company orientation on the first day on the job, since they need very little long-term commitment from employees. In most other cases, however, the program will be more effective if employees attend only after they have worked for some time.

There are a number of reasons it shouldn't be presented during the first days on the job. The timing of the general company orientation should be based largely on three factors:

1. Impact on employee attitude and commitment
2. Readiness of employees for information provided
3. Economic considerations

Impact on Employee Attitude and Commitment

New employees often begin a job full of enthusiasm and high hopes, anticipating that the job, the customers, and the managers will all be perfect. The progress and tone of the initial processing and job orientation must be geared toward helping new employees keep their expectations realistic.

The general company orientation should emphasize the positive aspects of the company and elicit an enthusiastic response from employees. To achieve this goal, it's usually designed to be something of a show. It may include inspiring speeches by top managers and often involves a tour of the most lavish guest areas on the property. It may include an entertaining film of the company in action. Such a film can show the best employees performing at some of the most impressive events they've ever handled.

If the company sounds all of its "bells and whistles" on a person's first day, already exaggerated expectations can be blown completely out of proportion. Few companies run as smoothly or offer as much excitement as this type of orientation suggests. If employees experience an extremely upbeat orientation in the first few days, they can get the false impression that everything is perfect. They'll soon feel let down when the job fails to live up to their inflated expectations. Negative experiences will make the orientation message seem false and lead to discouragement, suspicion, lowered morale, and, in the end, higher turnover.

After three or four weeks, employees have had time to experience some disillusionment and come to terms with the basic elements of the job—both good and bad. At this point, the general company orientation provides the perfect opportunity for some positive reinforcement. Just when some people may be beginning to have some second thoughts about their new jobs, the program can provide an emotional boost. As they're reminded of the positive aspects of the company, pride and loyalty can be instilled through shared visions and goals.

Readiness of Employees for Information Provided

A new employee has much to learn during the first few weeks of the job. Many companies prefer to focus this time on what the employee needs to get started with the work. A new employee's initial concerns center on getting along with co-workers and the supervisor, learning the job, and remembering basic details like timeclocks, working hours, meal breaks, and payday. New employees aren't interested in (nor can they begin to absorb) the finer points of company benefits and opportunities, many of which won't even be relevant for weeks or months. If medical insurance goes into effect after 90 days, for instance, there's no reason to tell new employees how to file a claim on the first day of work.

After employees find they can do the job and are comfortable with the company, they're ready to make a commitment and can begin to think about the future. At this point, they'll be more interested in detailed information about benefits, programs like tuition reimbursement and internal promotion, and positions for which they'll be eligible in the future.

Exactly how long employees should work before attending a general company orientation program depends on your property's turnover and the types of workers hired most. If your property's turnover patterns reveal a high number of people leaving after the same length of time, management and the human resources department should consider scheduling programs to catch workers before they reach that point.

The timing of general company orientation may also depend on the level of responsibility associated with the job. In general, the higher the level of responsibility, the sooner employees will be ready to learn more about their benefits and opportunities, and what the company's goals and philosophy mean to them. Employees in entry-level or unskilled positions may need three or four weeks to gain a degree of comfort within their jobs. More skilled workers may be ready for the general company orientation in a week or two. New managers may be briefed about profit sharing, career pathing, and dental coverage within days of joining a company.

Economic Considerations

At many companies, new employees start almost daily. The majority of the people who leave in the first two or three weeks leave because they find they can't adjust to the job. They may not like the work, the working conditions, or hours. They may have personal problems, such as babysitting or transportation, which can't be resolved through other channels. A general company orientation won't help these people stay, and in this case represents a non-productive use of time and money.

The general company orientation is expensive. In addition to the costs of producing the program and handouts like benefits booklets, the company must pay those who attend and those who conduct the program. Thus, it's more economical to conduct the program only occasionally, when the number of new employees who can attend justifies the expense. It can be scheduled on a slow business day when workers are not busy, meeting rooms and equipment are more readily available, and top managers are free to participate.

Job Orientation

Job orientation is the final step of the hiring period. It involves two steps: first day activities and initial job training. First-day activities help the employee become acquainted with basic elements of the job, the workplace, and co-workers. Initial job training takes place on the first and subsequent days and imparts the basic skills and knowledge required for the job.

There's no clear time frame to indicate when this final step of the hiring period is over. Job orientation is more likely to evolve into a transition period of on-the-job training during which the new worker gradually grows more skilled and self-reliant.

The First Day on the Job

The first day on the job can be confusing to new employees. To help new employees make a smooth transition, consider using a checklist for each key area to be covered on the first day. This will help ensure faster start-up time, higher productivity, and greater consistency. It will also suggest to the new employee that your operation is well-organized and run according to plan. Exhibit 6.8 is a sample first-day checklist of areas to be covered.

Exhibit 6.8 First-Day Checklist

EMPLOYEE'S NAME		FIRST DAY ON JOB	
EMPLOYEE'S POSITION		ORIENTATION SUPERVISOR	

ITEM	DISCUSSION COMPLETED (Supervisor's initials)
I. WORDS OF WELCOME	
A. Welcome the new employee to Hilton, your hotel and department.	___
B. Chat with the employee to reduce tension	___
C. Build the employee's confidence. Convince him of success on the job.	___
D. Make the new employee feel important. Explain the importance of the job.	___
II. TOUR OF THE ENTIRE WORK AREA	___
III. INTRODUCTION TO COWORKERS AND MANAGEMENT	
A. Introduce some of the coworkers during the tour. Try to show the friendly atmosphere of the department.	___
B. Introduce the new employee to the person who will be responsible to do the training on the job if you will not be doing the training yourself.	___
C. Introduce the new employee to his immediate supervisor, if it's someone other than yourself or the trainer.	___
D. Make sure the new employee understands whom he reports to during the training/probation period.	___
E. Identify who he can go to for help when he cannot find his Supervisor.	___

EMPLOYEE'S NAME		FIRST DAY ON JOB	

ITEM	DISCUSSION COMPLETED
IV. EXPLANATION OF OVERALL DEPARTMENT ORGANIZATION AND ITS RELATIONSHIP TO OTHER DEPARTMENTS	
A. Identify where in the hotel his work area is located	___
B. Explain what his department does	___
C. Explain how his work fits in with the work of his department in the hotel.	___
V. DISCUSSION OF JOB CONTENT AND REVIEW OF THE JOB DESCRIPTION	
A. Explain the basic duties and responsibilities of the job. Again emphasize the importance of the job in relation to the department and hotel.	___
B. Discuss job performance standards with the new employee. Explain what they are during and after the training period.	___
C. Indicate what uniforms or clothing is required.	___
D. Indicate what equipment will be used.	___
E. Review all safety practices and safe work methods.	___
VI. DEPARTMENTAL POLICIES AND PROCEDURES	
A. Explain pertinent departmental policies and their administration.	___
B. Explain general housekeeping duties and responsibilities.	___

Exhibit 6.8 (continued)

EMPLOYEE'S NAME _____   FIRST DAY ON JOB _____

ITEM	DISCUSSION COMPLETED
VII. WORKING CONDITIONS	
A. Explain where in the hotel his work area is located.	____
B. Explain when he does his work	____
1. Starting time - time cards or sheet	____
2. Quitting time - time cards or sheet	____
3. Break periods and location	____
4. Meal period and cafeteria	____
5. Rest rooms	____
6. Personal use of telephones	____
7. Overtime policy and requirements	____
8. Payday and method of payment	____
9. Uniforms	____
10. Locker rooms	____
11. Employee entrance	____
12. Employee use of elevators	____
a. Service	
b. Guest	
13. Other	____
VIII. DEPARTMENTAL TRAINING PROGRAM	
A. Describe the training program to the new employee again, building confidence in the probability of success. Explain the importance of the training.	____
B. Let the new employee know how long he is considered to be in training and the duration and conditions of any probationary period.	____

EMPLOYEE'S NAME _____   FIRST DAY ON JOB _____

ITEM	DISCUSSION COMPLETED
IX. PROBLEM SOLVING PROCEDURE OR GRIEVANCE PROCEDURE	
A. Explain hotel standards for:	
1. Performance of duties	____
2. Attendance and punctuality	____
3. Behavior	____
4. General Appearance	____
5. Wearing of uniform and name badge	____
X. GENERAL INFORMATION	
A. As appropriate, explain:	
1. Available parking facilities	____
2. Available transportation (Car Pools)	____
3. Who and how to call if a problem develops and employee is going to be absent or late.	____
B. Review any policy questions from the new employee	____
XI. SEQUENCE OF REPORTING TO WORK	
1. Employees' entrance	____
2. Time clocks	____
3. Back door security system	____
4. Uniform Room	____
5. Locker Room	____
6. Getting to the work area	____
7. Sign-in/Signout in the department	____
8. Explain daily work routine	____
XII. BEGINNING ON-THE-JOB TRAINING	____

Courtesy of Hilton Hotels Corporation, Beverly Hills, California.

Inconsistency in the departmental processing is confusing to everyone and particularly risky in high turnover areas. If only half of the people in your department are told about a policy or procedure, no one will follow it.

The Manager's Role

It's advisable that the new employee report to the manager or the person in the department who did the interviewing. A familiar face to greet the employee helps relieve some of the first-day jitters. If the new employee has to come through the security department or an employee entrance, make sure the staff there are prepared to handle the encounter properly.

When you greet the new employee, be sure to smile, make eye-contact, and shake hands. Establish a preferred-name basis for both of you. Extend a welcome and mention that other staff members are looking forward to meeting the new person. To show your personal interest, ask whether there were any problems parking or clocking in. All this helps put the new employee at ease.

The human resources department can do those things that are common to all employees. However, as the manager, you must decide how much of the departmental processing to do personally and how much to delegate to assistants. Many items can be turned over to a trainer, but you should cover the following areas: overview, guest relations and security, work schedule, paycheck procedures, appearance standards, and work standards.

Overview. Give the new staff member a summary of what the first day will entail to help eliminate any initial fears. For instance, say, "After we've had a chance to talk for a few minutes, I'm having one of my best employees work with you the first day. She's very good and can tell you what's expected. She'll also show you around and take you to lunch. I have a lot of confidence in her because she knows the job very well."

It's much harder to raise expectations and standards after the employee has been on the job awhile, so set the standards high from the beginning. You might say, "I'd like to spend a few minutes to cover some very important areas because I want to make sure you get started on the right foot. I really want you to succeed."

Cover the goals for the department and establish a clear direction as to what's to be accomplished. Detail the actual job duties and the standards by which job performance is measured. Consider reviewing the organization chart with the new person. Point out who's in charge of each area, to whom the person directly reports, and the new employee's relationship to other employees. Cooperation with other departments and teamwork are high priorities and should also be emphasized.

Guest Relations and Security. Guest relations and security are every employee's job. Even employees in support positions not in direct contact with guests must be sensitive to the guest's needs. Emphasize the importance of the company's personal service philosophy. Explain that smiling, using the guest's name, and never saying no or giving excuses to a guest are among the ways you expect all employees to treat guests.

All employees should be aware of the need for good security procedures. Point out that employees need to be very careful when handling guest keys. Explain that an employee should never mention a guest's name and room number together where they can be overheard by others. Insist that employees immediately report any situation that appears out of the ordinary. Among situations to be reported are:

- Guests whose behavior suggests drunkenness, illness, or mental health problems
- Damaged or missing furnishings
- Strangers in unauthorized areas
- Guest complaints
- Any indication of the possession of illegal paraphernalia

Work Schedule. Cover the hours to be worked, outlining how specific meal and break periods are taken. Explain the expected days off, whether they are rotated or fixed, and how to handle requests for a day off before the schedule is posted. Indicate where the schedule will be posted and emphasize that punching in or signing in should be done accurately. Review timecard procedures. Mention whether it's your policy for employees to report to their supervisors before starting work, taking a break, going to lunch, or leaving for home.

If absenteeism and lateness are problem areas, spell out your exact policy and procedures specifically and thoroughly. Be explicit about what you will and will not accept. This can be done in a positive manner. For example: "Being on time means being in uniform and ready to begin work at the start of the shift. Most of our employees have found it works best for them to be here five minutes early so that they can be ready for work on time."

Paycheck Procedures. Review where and when to pick up paychecks. For tipped employees, explain procedures for reporting tips to the company and the government. You may point out that paychecks aren't issued until several days after the pay period because accounting needs time to prepare the payroll. This is worth noting since new employees may have the misperception that the company "holds back" a week's pay.

Appearance Standards. Emphasize the importance of having a complete uniform. Where appropriate, mention that shoes must be polished. Review personal appearance standards, including makeup, jewelry, length of hair, and hairnets. Explain why personal cleanliness is important for employees. Stress that you expect all employees to clean up after themselves not only where they work, but also in locker rooms and break areas.

Work Standards. Explain the quality and quantity of work that you expect. Review, discuss, and document specific standards so employees know and accept how they'll be measured. Explain any quotas you may have, such as a given number of rooms per housekeeper, check-ins per bellperson, or food covers per food server. Emphasize quality and the necessity of learning the procedures correctly, pointing out that speed will come with experience. If these standards are provided in writing, obtain a signed receipt for the list.

Encourage new employees to ask questions, indicating that questions show interest and a desire to do a good job—qualities you like to see. Tell them that you know a good new employee by the number of questions he or she asks. Identify whom to go to with questions or problems.

Completion of the First Day

If you aren't handling the training yourself, as a final step in the first-day procedures, you should introduce the new staff member to the person who'll take over the balance of the hiring process: the trainer. Explain the trainer's position and authority. In the trainer's presence, praise the trainer as particularly competent and state that you are proud of his or her past accomplishments in training new employees. This gives the trainer a good name to live up to. Give the trainer a brief background on the new person, and turn over the first-day checklist so that all remaining points can be covered. Check on the new employee several times during the day to see how the training is progressing.

Ask the new employee to stop and see you before going home at the end of the first day. This gives the employee an opportunity to ask any questions that may have come up during the day. You want to end this day on a positive note, so it's not a good idea to bring up problems now, since the new employee is probably already feeling somewhat inadequate. Simply assure the person that the job done the first day was satisfactory.

Don't neglect new employees after the first day. As a manager, you should make an extra effort to communicate with new employees during the first few weeks.

Job Training

Given the proper guidance, every new employee will quickly learn the rules, standards, and procedures of the department. It's particularly important that they be taught by the right people. New employees left on their own at this time are very susceptible to the negative influences of disgruntled employees.

The trainer should be one of your company's better employees—someone well-respected by you and by fellow employees. In addition, the trainer should be a good communicator, an employee committed to the goals of the department, and a positive role model. This is especially significant if there are strong cliques operating within your department. The trainer should represent all the standards you want the new employee to learn, including personal appearance standards such as wearing a clean, well-pressed uniform, shined shoes, and name tag in place. Training skills and the selection of the trainer will be discussed in greater detail in Chapter 7.

The trainer should put new employees at ease in much the same fashion as the manager. Beginning this part of the orientation with a tour provides an opportunity for the trainer to find out more about each new employee: his or her family, hobbies, interests, previous jobs, and concerns about the job. This makes the new employee feel comfortable while helping the trainer determine how to approach individual training.

The tour itself should include the work area, time clocks, the place where schedules are posted, supply areas, location of the first-aid kit, bulletin boards, restrooms, and break and smoking areas. A tour of related departments could be accompanied by an explanation of the work flow and the need for teamwork. During the tour, the trainer should introduce fellow employees with whom the new employee will be working and other department heads with whom contact is likely.

New employees should be shown how their jobs fit into the operation. If they'll be washing dishes for a restaurant, for example, they can be taken into the restaurant to see how their hard work pays off in the form of attractive service settings. If their main job will be serving bread and pastries, they should visit the bake shop to see how the bread is made and who makes it.

A tour of the entire facility will come later with the general company orientation. At this time, the trainer should just cover those areas the employee will need to know to get the job done. For example, food servers may be asked to get cigarettes for guests, and should know the location of the vending machines.

During the tour, the employee may be issued items of a permanent nature, such as a house bank, keys, or electronic pagers. The employee can meet the appropriate staff members responsible for overseeing custody of such company property and for ensuring its security. For each item issued, the person should sign a receipt.

Once the tour is completed, the trainer and new employee should return to the work area for a review of the key policies and procedures for the department. The trainer should also review any equipment needed for the job. After that, skills training can begin.

A few minutes before the meal period begins, the trainer should take the new employee to the break area. Extra time is taken on the first day so that everything can be explained. If it's a policy to check with the manager before going to lunch, the trainer should do so. If there is an employee cafeteria, the trainer should go through the line explaining how the system works. For instance, the trainer may explain:

- Which menu items are offered to employees on a complimentary or discount basis

- The policy on coffee and soft drinks

- How long breaks are

- How to record the time taken for breaks

- Whether employees can leave the premises

- How the cost of meals is handled

As other workers arrive and join the table, the trainer should introduce them by first names and see that the conversation is kept informal and appropriate. The meal period should end punctually. The trainer and the new employee should then return to the work area to resume training.

At the end of the day, the new employee should be taken back to the manager for a progress report.

Managerial Resistance to Orientation

After reviewing the amount of work involved in getting new employees started, many managers resist the idea of providing adequate orientation. Many feel they cannot spare the time. In reality, however, they already spend the time. One way or another, the inadequately-prepared employees and managers who don't quit out of frustration eventually learn to "get by." Often, what they learn and whom they learn it from may cost managers and the company more in time and money spent correcting problems than if the employees had been started properly.

Starting Management Employees

Every new manager brings unique ideas, values, and aspirations to an organization. This influx of "new blood" contributes to a company's development and progress. To ensure continuity of service or product,

Extra time is taken during first-day job orientation so that everything can be explained.

however, the manager must perform according to the company's established values, standards, and beliefs. Top management and the human resources staff must plan carefully to ensure that new managers can begin immediately to identify with and commit themselves to the company's philosophy and objectives.

Preparation for the New Manager

The general manager should send out a memorandum to all department heads advising them that a new manager has been hired. The memo should ask for their cooperation and assistance. It should also include the following information about the new manager:

- Name
- Job title
- Starting date
- Experience
- Former employer
- Some personal background

One way to introduce the new manager to all employees is to post a memo such as that in Exhibit 6.9.

The **new management preparation checklist** (see Exhibit 6.10) can help to minimize the new manager's start-up time.

Processing

Management employees should be processed in the same manner as all other employees. Even if not all of the information applies to them specifically, they'll get a good understanding of the information and benefits provided to employees working under them.

Exhibit 6.9 New Employee Announcement

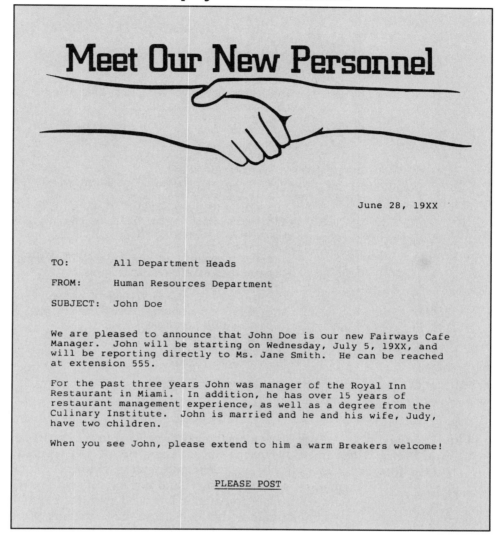

Meet Our New Personnel

June 28, 19XX

TO: All Department Heads

FROM: Human Resources Department

SUBJECT: John Doe

We are pleased to announce that John Doe is our new Fairways Cafe Manager. John will be starting on Wednesday, July 5, 19XX, and will be reporting directly to Ms. Jane Smith. He can be reached at extension 555.

For the past three years John was manager of the Royal Inn Restaurant in Miami. In addition, he has over 15 years of restaurant management experience, as well as a degree from the Culinary Institute. John is married and he and his wife, Judy, have two children.

When you see John, please extend to him a warm Breakers welcome!

<u>PLEASE POST</u>

Courtesy of The Breakers, Palm Beach, Florida.

In addition, the human resources representative should review any special benefits, sometimes called **perquisites** or **perks**. A perk is a privilege or benefit provided to an employee in addition to the regular compensation package provided to all employees.

Processing is also a good opportunity to review management policies. Details regarding these policies are not always the same for salaried employees and hourly employees. For instance, the company may use different pay guidelines. Additional policies may also be needed, such as those concerning conflict of interest or use of company facilities. Therefore, it's important to have a separate handbook directed at salaried employees. Each manager should receive and sign for a copy of the salaried employee handbook, which defines terms and conditions of employment, rules, and benefits for salaried employees.

Exhibit 6.10   New Management Preparation Checklist

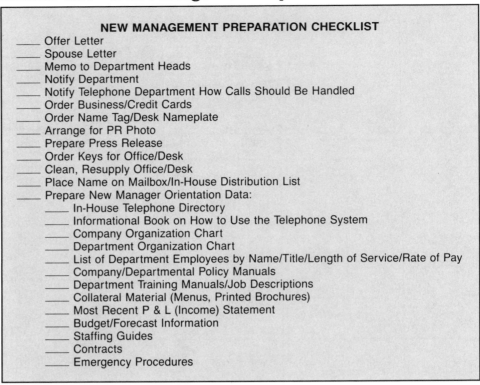

NEW MANAGEMENT PREPARATION CHECKLIST

____ Offer Letter
____ Spouse Letter
____ Memo to Department Heads
____ Notify Department
____ Notify Telephone Department How Calls Should Be Handled
____ Order Business/Credit Cards
____ Order Name Tag/Desk Nameplate
____ Arrange for PR Photo
____ Prepare Press Release
____ Order Keys for Office/Desk
____ Clean, Resupply Office/Desk
____ Place Name on Mailbox/In-House Distribution List
____ Prepare New Manager Orientation Data:
    ____ In-House Telephone Directory
    ____ Informational Book on How to Use the Telephone System
    ____ Company Organization Chart
    ____ Department Organization Chart
    ____ List of Department Employees by Name/Title/Length of Service/Rate of Pay
    ____ Company/Departmental Policy Manuals
    ____ Department Training Manuals/Job Descriptions
    ____ Collateral Material (Menus, Printed Brochures)
    ____ Most Recent P & L (Income) Statement
    ____ Budget/Forecast Information
    ____ Staffing Guides
    ____ Contracts
    ____ Emergency Procedures

The First Day and Week on the Job

As soon as a new manager walks into the department, employees begin to test and challenge the person. Guest complaints, everyday problems, and exceptions to policy begin to demand attention. Before a new manager can start *being* a manager—making decisions and dealing successfully with these types of situations—adequate preparation is needed in the form of training and orientation.

Unfortunately, the high demand for managers means that newly hired managers are often put to work as soon as they arrive. Upper management may have new managers skip training altogether just to get them on the job as quickly as possible. The result is that far too many managers receive less training than the employees they supervise.

Starting such inadequately prepared managers so soon is generally counterproductive. When new managers are put on the floor immediately, they usually are able to perform only routine, non-management functions which are probably already being handled better by experienced assistants. Not only does their presence fail to significantly improve departmental productivity, their inability to perform their managerial duties—to make good decisions quickly or provide the right answers—can cause employees to question their competence.

A better approach for upper management is to act as if the new person's former employer had required a lengthier advance notice. Management would have found a way to cover the need for the manager under those circumstances. The company should plan according to this assumption and ensure that the new manager receives sufficient training. The new manager should spend an initial week or two preparing to perform more effectively. Better preparation means greater success, fewer problems, and higher productivity and achievement in a month's time.

This job orientation should be thorough, well planned, and structured in a logical order. Exhibit 6.11 is a new restaurant manager's job orientation list outlining this period. Upper management should allow plenty of time and reserve a place for the new person to read all the training and orientation information. The new manager should meet assistants and key employees (usually informal leaders and people who have been with the department a long time). The new manager should have easy access to his or her immediate superior. He or she should spend some time in the department during its peak hours to observe operations.

Upper management should assign another manager—preferably not a superior—to each new manager. This assigned manager can help answer questions about the informal organization and assist in getting the new manager settled in the community as well as in the job. Just going to dinner together once in a while and sharing ideas can be of great value.

During the job orientation period, the new manager should be encouraged to listen, look, and ask questions. The person can be advised to make notes of all impressions. New eyes catch a lot of things, and there's never enough time to deal with all of them during the first several months. These early impressions can be forgotten if not written down for future reference.

At the end of the period, the new manager should be able to come up with an action plan which discusses department goals, including how and when they'll be accomplished. This can form the basis for discussion with his or her immediate supervisor, and eventually helps them agree upon the priorities of the department.

At the time the new manager actually takes over responsibilities from the current manager, there should be a general meeting of all employees. The new manager's supervisor should be present to show support. The official "changing of the guard" should be performed with some ceremony. Shortly after the new manager takes over, he or she should make a presentation at a meeting, send some memos, or make some other visible and productive change to further establish that he or she is in charge.

The orientation needs of a new manager will vary with each person and each type of job. The point is that top management has to think about the process and structure it individually for each new manager.

Key Terms

breach of contract
counter-offer
employment contract
general company orientation
hiring period
house rules
job orientation

new management preparation checklist
new manager's job orientation list
perks
perquisites
personnel processing checklist
probationary period

Discussion Questions

1. What elements should be included and what should be avoided in an offer letter for a supervisory position?

Exhibit 6.11   New Restaurant Manager's Job Orientation List

NEW RESTAURANT MANAGER'S JOB ORIENTATION LIST

Job Title	Areas to be Covered
General Manager	1. Welcome 2. Hotel Goals and Values 3. Divisional Expectations
Director of Human Resources	1. Processing 2. Organization Chart 3. Explanation of Benefits and Special Perks 4. Scheduling Orientation 5. Policies and Procedures 6. Union Contracts 7. Current Labor Problems
Food and Beverage Director	1. Department Goals 2. Menus 3. Staffing 4. Forecasts 5. Profit and Loss 6. Entertainment Contracts 7. Daily Patterns/Volumes 8. Hours 9. Capital Expenditures 10. Projects 11. Business Plan 12. Health Inspections 13. Special Customer List 14. Keys/Mail/Office Procedures 15. Committees/Meeting Schedule 16. Reports Due—When and Where 17. Hours to Work (Best Days Off) 18. Standards of Measurement (Payroll, Food Costs, Revenues, Quality, Guest Comments) 19. Current Priorities and Problems 20. Areas of Authority/Responsibility for Making Changes
Director of Marketing	1. Organization of Department 2. How Sales Forecast is Compiled 3. Marketing Plan 4. Calendar of Promotions 5. Ad Campaigns
Executive Chef	1. Overview of Kitchen Structure, Philosophy, Standards 2. Meeting with Restaurant Chef to Review Recipes and Menus 3. Review of Kitchen Staffing 4. Plate Presentations
Executive Steward	1. Cleaning Responsibilities 2. Inventories of Glass, Silver, China 3. Cleaning of Glass, Silver, China
Beverage Manager	1. Liquor Laws 2. Brands and Prices 3. Drink Presentations 4. Hours of Operation 5. Intoxicated Guest Procedures 6. Wine List 7. Pricing Structure

Exhibit 6.11 *(continued)*

Job Title	Areas to be Covered
Food and Beverage Controller	1. Check Control 2. Lost Check Procedure 3. Figuring Beverage Costs 4. Figuring Food Costs 5. Figuring Labor Costs 6. Discounts, Coupons, Packages, Gift Certificates 7. Authorized Signature List for Charges
Controller	1. Issue Bank 2. Discrepancy Reports, including Overage and Shortage 3. Payroll Procedures (Timecards, Check Deductions and Distributions, and Tip-Reporting Problems) 4. Credit and Cash-Only Guest Lists, Credit Card Policies 5. Cash Register Systems (Complete Orientation)
Director of Purchasing	1. Purchase Orders and Requisitions 2. Purveyor Relations 3. Hours of Operations, Other Purchasing Policies and Procedures, including After-Hour Requisitioning 4. Receiving, Storage, and Inventory Procedures
Rooms Division Director	1. Overview and Explanation of Rooms Division 2. How Rooms Forecast Is Made 3. Procedures for Concierge, Bellstand, Front Desk (Including Check-In and Check-Out Times), Guest Folios, VIP Procedures, Guest Parking 4. Invitation to a Rooms Division Meeting
Executive Procedures	1. Uniform Issue and Control Housekeeper 2. Uniform Inventories and Pars 3. Procedures for Obtaining Napkins, Tablecloths, Linens 4. Lost and Found Procedures 5. Housekeeping Cleaning Responsibilities in the Restaurant 6. Rag Procedure
Telephone Operator	1. Introductions to All Operators 2. Telephone System Orientation 3. New Manager's Home Telephone Number 4. Information Operators Need 5. Telephone Service in Department, Restrictions, Charges, Problems
Director of Security	1. Fire and Emergency Procedures 2. Procedures for Guest Illness and Accident 3. Burglar Alarms, Robbery Procedures, and all other Security Policies 4. Package Pass Procedures
Chief Engineer	1. Work Order Systems 2. Restaurant Heating, Lighting, and Sound Controls 3. In-House Music System
Front Office Manager	1. Restaurant Charge Posting 2. Cash-Only List 3. Direct Billing

2. What steps should a department head take to prepare the workers in his or her department for a new assistant manager?

3. Why is it usually unwise to conduct the general company orientation during an employee's first few days on the job?

4. Why is it so important to help new employees keep their expectations realistic?

5. What are some of the key areas a department head should cover with a new employee on the latter's first day on the job?

6. Why is top management so tempted to put new managers on the job right away? What's wrong with that idea?

7 Training

Today's managers, supervisors, and employees need more knowledge and skill than ever before to perform effectively in the fast-paced world of business. Experts predict that, during the rest of this century, "over half of the job content of all positions will change, and at least a third of existing types of jobs will disappear."[1] Nowhere is this kind of change more apparent than in the hospitality industry. Under these pressures and those of the decreasing labor market, hospitality companies will grow only as quickly as they can train and develop people. Since an increasing amount of each manager's time will be spent in this role, managers need a better understanding of the training function.[2]

Top management executives of hospitality companies are beginning to recognize the importance of training and are making training a priority within their organizations. The success of any organization's training program depends upon this direction and support from top management. The support must be strong enough to overcome any resistance to change that managers, supervisors, or employees may have about new policies, procedures, or work methods. Resistance may also result when people believe any of several unfortunate myths about training (see Exhibit 7.1).

Top management executives are now pushing for effective training, budgeting for it, and asking for progress reports. Large companies are developing professional training departments, while other companies are basing the performance and salary reviews of individual managers at least in part on each manager's ability to train and develop people. Hospitality companies that are serious about training may spend as much as 30% of their training budget on research, which includes follow-up and evaluation of the training program.

As training receives top management's support, training budgets and methods of evaluating training costs are becoming more realistic and sophisticated. In the past, many hospitality companies did not even have a training budget. Today, companies are beginning to develop separate training budgets

[1]David J. McLaughlin, "The Turning Point in Human Resources Management," *A Strategic Report: Linking Employee Attitudes & Corporate Culture to Corporate Growth Profitability* (Philadelphia: Hay Management Consultants, 1984) p. 172.
[2]For an extensive examination of this topic, see Lewis C. Forrest, Jr., *Training for the Hospitality Industry*, second edition (East Lansing, Mich.: Educational Institute of the American Hotel & Motel Association, 1989).

Exhibit 7.1   Training Myths

- Positions turn over so fast, it doesn't pay to train.
- Experienced employees don't need training.
- What do we have a human resources department for?
- Training is a waste of time.
- Training is simple. Anybody can do it.
- Employees always resist training.

Source: Educational Institute of the American Hotel & Motel Association.

for each department. When training expenses are charged to departments and individual managers bear the responsibility for their departments' training costs, they demand value for the dollars spent and are more inclined to closely supervise the training function.

Responsibility for Training

The responsibility for training and developing people rests squarely on the shoulders of the manager. This does not mean that a department manager must assume the duties and responsibilities of a trainer. The actual training activities may be delegated to supervisors or even to talented employees.

Training Directors
In large hospitality operations, department managers may be supported by a **training director** who works in the human resources department. This person is responsible for the overall administration and control of the training function and budget. The major duties of a training director may include:

1. Assisting department managers in the development of their own training programs—Generally, this involves helping department managers develop and organize their training programs, and training the individuals designated as department trainers.

2. Conducting general training programs—These programs usually focus more on the overall goals of the organization than on specific operational procedures. Activities in this area may include conducting the company's general orientation program as well as several specific supervisory and management development programs, such as workshops in correct delegating procedures, time management, assertiveness training, and so forth.

3. Coordinating elements of the overall training function—Responsibilities in this area may include implementing the company's tuition reimbursement policy; coordinating the use of outside training resources, such as seminars; directing the course of the company's career pathing, succession planning, and cross-training activities; and administering supervisory and management development programs.

4. Researching, monitoring, and evaluating training activities—The focus of this duty is to ensure that the right training programs are selected and that the company gets value for the money spent on training programs.

Currently, the position of training director is one of the fastest growing in America.

Department Trainers

Training activities that focus on operational procedures and skills are generally conducted either by department managers or individuals designated as **department trainers**. There are no hard and fast rules about whether the manager should conduct skills training or delegate it to department supervisors or talented employees. The general principle that should guide the decision is consistency. If some employees are taught one way and others are taught a different way or not at all, the result is confusion in the work area. The greatest consistency comes from using the same trainer as much as possible and effectively communicating the performance standards of the job.

Performance standards are the observable, measurable benchmarks by which you decide when the job is well done. These standards should not restrict initiative. Rather, they should enable employees to know when they're doing their jobs right. For example, if giving fast service is important, one of the standards for restaurant cashiers may specify: "A complete transaction should be rung up within one minute—if more than four people are waiting to pay their checks, call for help." About 20 clearly defined standards per job may be enough to determine if an employee is performing the job well. It is the manager's responsibility to ensure that performance standards within the department are compatible with the overall goals of the organization.

Since the manager often knows the jobs in the department best, he or she is usually the first choice as department trainer. For training to be properly received, a department manager must create the right climate through an effective approach and attitude toward training. As a trainer, you actually act in three capacities: as a master craftsman passing your skills on to an apprentice, as a coach, and as a role model for every employee you train.

Training involves much more than merely lecturing or passing along information. Your mission is to share your experience and develop the talents of the employee. Establish an atmosphere of trust by displaying a sincere interest in the trainee as an individual and clearly expressing your desire to help him or her succeed.

A good trainer sees the job through another's eyes. When people experience difficulties in performing new tasks, they may become discouraged and develop a self-defeating attitude. On the other hand, as they achieve success in learning new skills, their self-esteem grows. Effective training sessions permit trainees to develop pride in their abilities.

Although the department manager may be the first choice as department trainer, the management style of some department heads may intimidate employees. In these cases, employees may not learn effectively because they are afraid of making mistakes. Furthermore, since the role of the trainer is that of a working coach, the manager's image of authority within the department can become blurred, resulting in some confusion on the employee's part.

As evidence of top management's commitment to training, Holiday Inn University implemented its Road Scholars program. Under the program, a fleet of HIU vans and expert trainers bring guest service, marketing, and reservations training to more than 1400 Holiday Inns across the United States. (Courtesy of Holiday Inns, Inc., Memphis, Tennessee)

Common sense should prevail. Obviously, if the manager doesn't have the time or qualities to become a good trainer, it's preferable to turn the skills training function over to someone else. Also, managers of large departments may be unable to handle all of the training activities without assistance. Regardless of the size of the department or the company, however, the manager cannot avoid the responsibility of the training function. The accountability for seeing that every employee is trained cannot be delegated.

When selecting a department trainer, you should consider that a good trainer may not always be the supervisor or employee who had the least difficulty learning the job. In fact, the best trainer may be an employee who had more difficulty than most in learning the skills of the job. Employees who become effective trainers are generally those who are:

- Good judges of people
- Objective
- Aware, understanding, and accepting of the differences in people
- Good at listening and communicating

- Good role models for the department

- Optimistic and enthusiastic about the job, the department, and the company

Good trainers also take pride in their own work and give attention to detail, accuracy, and neatness. They are logical, patient, good planners, and are tactful, cooperative, helpful, sincere, and honest. They often have a sense of humor and make friends easily. In addition, they are not selfish or competitive, and they don't play favorites. Obviously, finding good trainers isn't easy. But, once found, they may prove to be your most valuable employees.

Individuals selected as department trainers must be taught how to train, given adequate feedback, and rewarded. Give your trainers more contact with you than you give to the average employee. Monitor performance more often and show support for their efforts. Make sure they know what's happening in the company and what policy and procedure changes are anticipated. Managers should ensure that department trainers attend the company orientation program yearly. In addition, have them attend an occasional management meeting. If there are other department trainers, get them together every three to six months to discuss their problems and review and polish their training skills. To keep their skills current, department trainers should also have regular access to appropriate reading materials such as magazines which focus on training. Whenever warranted, they should have opportunities to attend relevant seminars and to pursue other appropriate educational activities. They should be recognized through a pay increase, title change, or other means of recognizing their special status.

No matter who conducts actual training activities, the department manager is responsible for defining and communicating the department's goals and values. Even when routine skills training is delegated to a supervisor or a lead employee, the department manager must continue to monitor and evaluate the progress of trainees, show a sincere interest in their efforts, and communicate to them that quality and consistency are important.

The Goal of Skills Training

The goal of a skills training program should be 100% compliance of employees to the performance standards of their jobs. There is no other way for a hospitality company to meet guest expectations consistently. All employees must understand that 100% compliance means error-free work and that management expects this of them all of the time.

Each employee must believe that he or she is capable of 100% compliance to the performance standards of the job. It is easy to point out that, in everyday life, people do many things completely correctly all of the time. If they are committed to performing their jobs well, they should find that it's just as easy to achieve error-free work on the job. Morale is often high in organizations with demanding standards, because employees feel a personal sense of pride in meeting such standards.

Since only total compliance is acceptable, don't use terms like "poor," "fair," "average," "good," or "excellent" to rate employee performance during training. While 90% compliance may seem "good," in reality it means that guests are not getting some of the services or other elements that they expect and are paying for. Employee performance resulting in dissatisfied guests should hardly be rated good.

As a manager, you need to stress to each employee that providing

Total compliance to standards is a goal for every employee. McDonald's Corporation has over 800 Field Operations Consultants, as pictured here, whose job includes ensuring 100% compliance to company standards. (Courtesy of McDonald's Corporation, Oak Brook, Illinois)

quality service is everyone's personal responsibility and that this is why performance standards are written for each position. You can point out to employees that complying with standards is the first step in learning and growing within your organization, and that you won't be happy until they're the best they can be.

When employees want to grow, managers should help them. Have additional books available, and provide short training sessions regularly. Tell them that their participation is considered at the time of salary reviews.

You'll probably never reach 100% compliance with all of your employees, but you must never be content with anything less. Remember, regardless of the size of the company or the amount of support provided by the human resources function or department, the ultimate accountability for the performance of a department still rests with the department manager.

Needs Analysis

Before you undertake any training activities, analyze your needs. Give priority to the basic orientation and training of your existing employees in order to establish a unified work force with a consistent set of standards. Once their needs have been addressed, they'll become part of the stable environment into which new people and procedures can be merged. Don't attempt to introduce specialized programs for limited numbers of people before you've laid the groundwork with your main work force.

Training has been called the "aspirin of industry" because of the tendency to prescribe it for every problem, but it may not always be what you need. Many times, employees already know how to do the work, but don't do it properly or have poor productivity as a result of lack of motivation, equipment shortcomings, poor job design, physical limitations, or other areas unrelated to training.

Since it isn't possible, logistically or financially, to train every employee at the same time, choices have to be made. Besides, companies can't afford to develop a training program for every job and every single procedure, nor do they have the time. To ensure the best use of your training time and money, consider your company's priorities for the year (such as sales or service), then allocate time and money accordingly. Start where you have room for the most improvement, with emphasis on the areas of greatest guest contact, most frequent sources of guest complaints, and largest number of employees that have to be trained to bring improvement in those areas. Evaluate the cost and savings or benefits of each training program to determine if there is an adequate return on investment.

Consider the amount of time you have in which to accomplish the training, and the amount of money you can allocate to it. Look at the number of people that can be trained at one time, when and how often you need to train employees, and whether it will be a one-time program or conducted regularly. The larger the number of employees in the same job and/or the higher its turnover, the more quickly you can expect a return on your training costs.

After you identify the areas in which training is needed, determine what specific job or skill is lacking. If you have a problem with cashiers, for example, your needs analysis may indicate that the only problem is cash shortages, resulting primarily from mistakes in cash handling and secondarily from incorrect ringing of codes on the register. You may only need a training program on one element of the job, such as cash handling procedures, and a **job aid** such as a code reference booklet next to the cash register or a plastic overlay for the register keyboard—not a full-blown training program. (A job aid is a brief, at-hand reminder of the key steps of a procedure—for example, a reminder sign on the side of a mixer showing how to use the safety guard or a simple pocket-size handout card of key procedures—which explains information helpful to employees. Exhibit 7.2 is a job aid showing how to stock a room attendant's cart.)

Set a clear objective that defines what the program can be expected to accomplish and how results will be measured. Decide who should teach it, whether they'll need training first, and what training method will be used. (Training methods are discussed later in this chapter.)

Buying or Developing a Program

After the training need has been identified, another major decision involves whether to buy a program or to develop one. This decision is increasingly complicated by the number and variety of programs on the market. As new programs enter the market, some will probably be little more than gimmicks or fads, and many won't have had their effectiveness tested.

Companies sometimes rush to implement a currently popular program regardless of whether it fits their organizational climate, and often without even waiting to find out whether it was effective at other companies. An

Exhibit 7.2   Job Aid for a Room Attendant

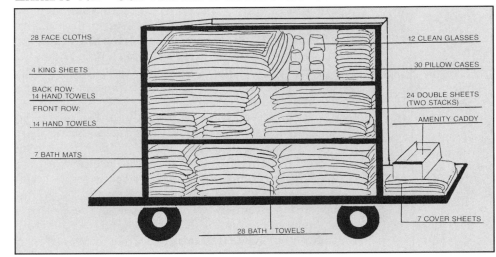

28 FACE CLOTHS

4 KING SHEETS

BACK ROW:
14 HAND TOWELS

FRONT ROW:

14 HAND TOWELS

7 BATH MATS

28 BATH TOWELS

12 CLEAN GLASSES

30 PILLOW CASES

24 DOUBLE SHEETS
(TWO STACKS)

AMENITY CADDY

7 COVER SHEETS

employer can, in fact, do much damage by teaching some of the new concepts on the market today if the company doesn't practice them. You'll seldom succeed in incorporating training programs—or any human resources program, for that matter—into your organization without careful consideration of your specific needs and the environment in which you'll be training.

Generally speaking, off-the-shelf programs can't provide detailed training that applies to every aspect of a specific job at a specific property. Rather, they explain or illustrate the important tasks and responsibilities which are common to a given position in most properties. They often stress the concepts behind the tasks or responsibilities and then encourage the trainee to apply the concepts to other elements of his or her job.

Managers should be careful when selecting off-the-shelf programs, because some are too general to be of any real value. However, the best off-the-shelf programs can be very helpful. If financial considerations make it impossible for you to design and create all of your training programs, you may get satisfactory results by supplementing a purchased program with material specific to your property. Exhibit 7.3 summarizes several points you should consider when deciding whether to use an off-the-shelf program.

With programs that teach management skills, caution should be exercised to ensure that content and examples are job-related. For example, one commonly used training film to teach supervisory skills depicts a sales manager setting goals with an industrial sales representative by discussing the optimum number of sales calls that can be made in one day. It's much harder for a chef or restaurant manager to measure performance and productivity, and different kinds of skills are required in discussing performance and setting goals with an employee whose chief duty is service. A film or other training tool that provides only unrelated, manufacturing-oriented settings and examples might prove to be more confusing than enlightening.[3]

---

[3]The Educational Institute produces dozens of videotapes specifically created for the hospitality industry. These tapes cover several topics and range from general conceptual introductions to quite specific procedural demonstrations. For more information, contact the Educational Institute, P.O. Box 1240, East Lansing, Michigan, 48826.

Exhibit 7.3 How to Choose an Off-the-Shelf Training Program

- For whom is it designed? Find out the type of industry, type of trainee, level of education, and so forth.
- What are the main areas of expertise of the production company? For instance, do you need sales motivation films or management development seminars?
- What is the background of the program's developers? Would a degree in video production or food service management be more useful to you?
- What other companies use it? Are they similar to yours? Can you call them for references?
- Are the principles being communicated by the program consistent with your company's philosophy and values?
- Are pre- and post-testing provided to ensure that trainees learn something?
- What kind of feedback do trainees get during the program?
- How closely related to your jobs are the demonstrations, examples, and models?
- Is the content too general, or are specific how-to skills presented? For instance, does the program just say that a front desk representative should up-sell, or does it show how to up-sell?
- Is the material well organized and logically presented?
- Is the material interesting?
- Is the production current or dated?
- Is the language appropriate for your trainees?
- How much time does it take to use the program?
- Do expected results justify the cost?
- Is satisfaction guaranteed?

If such programs are used, their effectiveness can be improved if they're accompanied by live examples that are directly related. Remember, the more that training answers a current need with actual job-related examples, the more effective it will be.

Implementation and Types of Training

If upper management and line managers have been involved in the development of a training program, its implementation will be far easier. They'll see it as their program. When they have not had input, managers and supervisors should at least be given data that will allow them to answer questions about the program.

Perhaps the most important principle of training adults is that they only learn when they want to. The trainer has to give them a reason to learn something new. They must understand the reason and how it benefits them, and the benefit has to be realistic, legitimate, attainable, and appropriate to the amount of change you expect from them. Without this step, any program will fail.

All of your current employees should go through a new training program first. Once you've established an acceptable performance level for your current staff, new employees will quickly adjust to that level, since they'll perceive the senior employees as models.

To maintain consistency and conformity to your standards, train all employees—even those with experience—who come into your department. Since bad habits are very quickly developed and hard to break, teach new employees immediately. Take time to teach the right way first. Each person must be taught, and taught the same way. Otherwise, confusion results and all employee standards sink to the level of those with the lowest standards.

Long-term employees should also be sent through the training program on a regular basis for retraining. If a housekeeping trainer isn't training new housekeepers during a given week, for example, the experienced housekeepers can be sent through a retraining session so that any bad habits can be corrected and new processes can be properly learned.

Types of Training

Training program formats usually fall into one of three general categories: learner controlled, group, and individual instruction.

Learner Controlled Instruction. Learner controlled instruction programs are also called **self instruction.** They enable trainees to work alone and set their own pace for learning. Learners work largely without an instructor, and one teaching unit is required per trainee. These programs take such forms as videotape presentations, **programmed instruction** manuals, and **computer interactive training programs.**[4] They can usually be used at the times which are best for the trainee, making them an efficient use of time for both the trainer and learner. They can help cut travel costs when the number of employees to be taught is so small that it wouldn't be practical to send a trainer to a unit site.

Learner controlled instruction programs are usually used when there are repetitive tasks, many employees doing the same job, high turnover, or a large number of on-call or temporary workers who need training. They can also be useful for general orientation, general product knowledge, or goal communication. They are generally recognized as the most effective way of training people to standardized routines and patterns because of the high degree of consistency and adherence to standards they can provide. They may also be helpful to the manager who doesn't have good training skills.

However, such programs are usually associated with very high initial costs. It takes a great deal of time to develop the programs, and competent instructional designers are required. Furthermore, updating is an ongoing process requiring much time and attention. In fact, if the procedures in question are changing very rapidly, the shelf-life may be too short for practicality.

Trainees must have the time to use the program, and there must be a strong payoff for them upon completion. If not, less-motivated people may

---

[4]For further information, see Forrest. Also, the Educational Institute produces interactive video presentations for the hospitality industry. Currently available presentations teach guest relations and front office skills. The Institute expects interactive videos teaching professional housekeeping, dining room service, sales, and interviewing to be available in the near future. For more information, contact the Educational Institute, P.O. Box 1240, East Lansing, Michigan, 48826.

not make it through the program. In addition, some may feel threatened because of a lack of prior education or because they have been out of school for a long time. They may find their reading and study skills inadequate and structured book work intimidating.

As stated earlier, learner controlled instruction is largely training without a trainer. However, our primary focus in this chapter is on training that more directly involves managers and/or trainers. Therefore, the rest of the chapter examines individual and group training in some detail.

Individual Training

The method of training most often used is individual instruction, also known as **on-the-job training (OJT)**. Used for all new people once a facility has been opened, it's generally the fastest, most flexible, and cheapest method of training.

Preparing for Training

You must prepare some guidelines for the job you're going to teach and the manner in which you'll teach it. Your **job outline** should be in writing and, in one form or another, ought to contain information in these four categories:

1. Purpose and accountability—how the job helps the company achieve its goals, and any areas of specific responsibility

2. Procedures—the basic elements of the job and how they're performed

3. Rationale—why each procedure or portion of a procedure is performed

4. Standards—the observable, measurable benchmarks by which you decide when the job is well done

Rely on your own experience and knowledge of the job to help you break it down into its basic elements, or procedures which can be taught in independent units, then list these elements in order of their importance. You may feel that some procedures will be easier to teach if broken down again into still smaller steps. Consider the learner's background, education, and experience in making this decision. In general, it's a good idea to develop a basic training program with the average employee in mind. If you plan it for the fast learners, the majority will be frustrated. On the other hand, if you aim it at the slow learners, you risk losing the others' attention.

If you have an additional breakdown, these smaller steps should be taught in a logical sequence—in chronological order if it's relevant. If not, train from easiest to hardest or build on what they already know.

For instance, in planning to train a new cashier, you might begin by defining the job's responsibilities and purpose. For example:

Ensures that each guest leaves the restaurant satisfied by being friendly, fast, accurate, and helping other employees if needed, while maintaining a pleasant appearance and a clean work area. Accountable for all cash, guest checks, charges, and related reports for the restaurant during the shift.

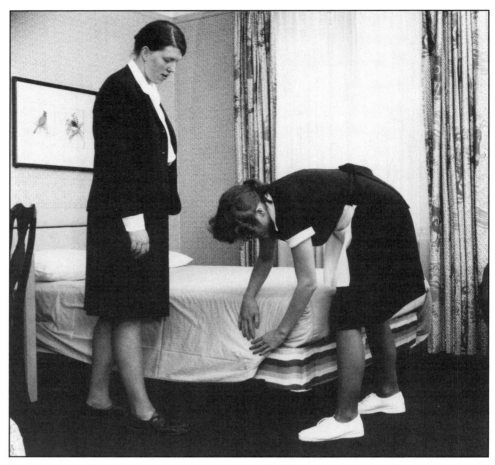

On-the-job training is generally the fastest, most flexible, and cheapest method of training.

Try to arrive at about six to eight basic elements that are part of the job, such as:

1. Friendliness
2. Appearance
3. Teamwork
4. Opening duties
5. Operating duties
6. Closing duties
7. Reports
8. Equipment

Note the placement of friendliness, appearance, and teamwork as the first three elements on the list. While these three may not take as much time to teach as operating duties or equipment, their successful implementation can have an equal or greater impact on the guest in the service environment,

Exhibit 7.4   Procedure Breakdown for Friendliness

PROCEDURE: Friendliness

Step	Why	Standards
Establish eye contact	Make a good final impression	Speak with or establish eye contact with every guest within 15 seconds of their approach
Ask if guest enjoyed meal (if not, report it)		Treat each person as an individual
Thank guest for coming		
Time permitting, engage in small talk (talk to children)		
Be consistent, friendly, warm, and happy		

and they must be given equal emphasis in training. Don't assume these elements will be obvious. You must cover each item that's important to the job.

You can break elements of the outline down into additional steps. Exhibit 7.4 does this with friendliness. Only one statement is necessary to indicate why all of these steps are important. Steps for appearance would probably itemize the complete uniform and dress code. Standards could include having a name tag on, and might also spell out that hair should be worn no longer than the collar and shoes must be shined. These three items are well-chosen as the standards because they're among the easiest to neglect. If they're given proper attention, the chances are good that the employee will follow through on the rest of the list.

Keep your outline simple, and try to avoid getting so caught up in the mechanics of a writing project that you lose sight of your objective of helping people learn. It isn't necessary to detail in writing how each step is done or why. Areas of confusion can be clarified as the item is presented to the trainee. Also, plan and prepare your job aids as you outline the job so that you can use them in teaching the procedures of the job.

Whether your guidelines are broken down into "elements," "tasks," "procedures," "functions," "units," or "steps" isn't nearly as important as your own ability to identify and convey the essence of the job itself in a logical order.

Trainer Preparation. Be aware of the processing and first-day information that have been handled by the human resources function or department, and be prepared to coordinate the first days of training with the necessary introductory procedures.

Before you start training, gather all the materials and training aids required. Select a quiet location as close to the work area as possible, and set up the work station properly. Since you're the role model, make sure that your dress and grooming standards set the example you wish others to follow.

Exhibit 7.5 Guidelines for Training Adults

- Adults must want to learn.

- Adults must feel a need to learn.

- Adults learn best by doing.

- Adults demand a realistic training focus.

- Adults learn best in an informal setting.

- Adults want guidance and coaching, not reprimands and criticism.

Source: Educational Institute of the American Hotel & Motel Association.

Either arrive early to make the necessary preparations or have the employee begin late. Since the start of a workshift is often a busy and confusing time, consider starting the new employee's first day later in the shift, on a slow day, or during a time other than peak business hours. Otherwise, training will suffer.

Keep in mind that the best relationship between a trainer and a trainee is one of openness, so that each is able to talk directly and honestly with the other. You can't make everyone the same, so bring out the best that each person has to offer.

You'll always like some trainees better than others, and some will always perform better than others. Do the best you can to maximize each one's individual strengths, and try not to be judgmental.

Presentation. As you begin, keep in mind the guidelines for training adults listed in Exhibit 7.5. Ignoring these guidelines makes successful training much unlikelier.

Begin to create the right environment by putting the trainee at ease. All employees going into something they don't know are nervous and uncomfortable, so you should be relaxed. Smile, establish eye contact, shake hands, establish a first-name basis, and go over the schedule for the day. Review your background so the trainee knows who you are. Encourage the person to ask questions. Help eliminate fears by reassuring the trainee that he or she will be able to learn the job.

Explain what will be taught and why it's important. People want to know they're doing important work and how it affects others. Avoid comments like, "If you learn how to be a good desk agent, someday you'll be promoted to supervisor," which is, in effect, a way of telling people that they're nothing until they're something else. It's better to say, "This job you're about to learn is very important, and I want you to do it right." You don't need to hold the incentive of promotion in front of your employees. Those with high potential will distinguish themselves anyway.

Find out what the trainee knows. Most trainees have a preconceived notion of the job and many already have specific knowledge. Ask them their ideas of the job and what they need, and they're likelier to think of you as helpful, not preaching.

Everyone is different. People come to their jobs with varying degrees of knowledge and levels of intelligence, different motivations and interests, and all sorts of cultural and educational backgrounds. Some are fast learners;

some are slow learners. The presentation must be adapted to the individual. Let the trainee set the pace, and don't talk over anyone's head.

Explain the whole job and how it fits into the department and the entire organization. We build on things we already know, so try to relate the job to experiences the trainee has had. Try to explain familiar things first, but be careful not to presume knowledge the trainee may not have.

Teach those skills that are likeliest to be needed on the job first. Don't teach skills that won't be needed for a long time. Explain all the equipment, materials, tools, and trade terms. Use the job outline to go over the quality and quantity requirements of the job.

Demonstrate by going through the job at the normal pace and then repeating it at a slower pace. The hand is always quicker than the eye, so make sure you slow down your demonstrations. Explain each step and test for comprehension, usually by questioning as you go along. Don't just ask, "Do you understand," though, since the trainee may assent too quickly in order to avoid appearing to be a slow learner.

While you're demonstrating, explain not only what you're doing, but also why it's done that way. When people understand why they're doing something, their retention, consistency, and commitment all increase markedly. Use humor occasionally. As you're explaining the job, tell the trainee about some of your own experiences or "war stories." Allow the trainee to interrupt and ask questions or even to disagree. Teach for three or four minutes at a time. Repeat the sequence and ask the trainee questions to check comprehension. Then have some practice sessions. As soon as the trainee has demonstrated mastery of the function, go on to the next task.

Practice. Emphasize even during practice that the first objective is for each person to maintain 100% compliance to the standards, regardless of speed. Once the steps and standards of a procedure are understood, repetition is used to develop the skill to perform more quickly. Stress that if speed is part of the standard, it will be gained through practice.

After you've communicated the what, how, and why of the procedure, let the learner practice immediately, going through the steps several times slowly, asking questions whenever necessary. Work in a quiet area with a minimum of interruptions, but keep the practice area as close to the actual work area as possible. It's best not to put anyone into an actual work situation immediately.

Encourage creativity by remaining receptive to differing viewpoints and challenges to the procedures being trained. Show respect for the opinions of others. When an employee disagrees, listen carefully to find out why. Some disagreement is normal. If a trainee gets frustrated, listen and keep in mind that people sometimes react to uncomfortable situations with anger or rudeness. Don't get into an argument. The best way to win one is to avoid it.

When a trainee is very nervous, go back and spend a little more time on the things he or she knows best before proceeding in order to continue to build on successes. Talk about things that will help the trainee relax. Don't push. If necessary, take a break.

Permit the trainee to make mistakes in order to experience doing something the wrong way, then ask, "What would happen if you did it differently?" Just as you wouldn't try to discipline your spouse or a friend because you know it would destroy the relationship, never humiliate or belittle a trainee. Keep corrections friendly. Questions like, "Why do you think that happened?" or "Can you think of any other ways to solve this problem?" help people begin to think for themselves, solve their own problems, and take responsibility for their own actions. If you want employees who think on their feet and take risks to make guests happy, you must allow them some freedom to fail without being punished.

Avoid the temptation to move in and take over when a trainee fumbles a few times. When someone is learning a new job, he or she feels uncomfortable with the new techniques and hasn't completely forgotten old habits. Mixing the new and old frequently results in temporary confusion. Be patient and provide plenty of reassurance and feedback.

Feedback. Praise is an essential part of teaching. It builds self-confidence and encourages the trainee to try harder. Use compliments freely. A person needn't do the job perfectly in order to deserve a compliment. Improvement, even though slight, is sufficient basis for praise. Comment when you see progress at each step. Don't overdo it, however. There must be a good reason for each compliment or it will be seen as insincere.

Be sparing with criticism, and avoid it if possible. Your sole motive for criticism should be to improve job performance, and the trainee must be able to see and believe that's the case. If you correct every single thing, the trainee's self-confidence plummets and the corrections become annoying and destructive. Just show how the job could have been done better, and try to compliment before you criticize an action: "You did a good job that time, but here's a suggestion that might help." Talk about your own mistakes, and make the fault seem easy to correct.

Always correct the procedure and not the person. That is, emphasize *what* the cause is, not *who* the cause is. Express the consequences of the error in terms of how it affects others.

The best of all techniques is to let trainees correct themselves. Simply ask if they can think of anything that would have made their performance even better. This method also helps set up the pattern of ongoing self-evaluation and acceptance of personal responsibility that you want to instill in each employee.

Even after a trainee is ready to work alone, don't abandon him or her. Part of feedback is providing good role models to reinforce training, so see to it that the new employee knows whom to go to with questions. Ongoing feedback also includes day-to-day, and even minute-to-minute, supervision at first. If you see that the standards aren't being maintained, make corrections on the spot. Don't wait until the end of the shift when the employee is about to go home to mention a mistake made earlier in the day. Managers who procrastinate never seem to have any more time later on and feedback is neglected.

Managers should take corrective action at the time they see the need for it, even if it means doing so in front of guests or fellow employees. Take the employee aside and handle the correction tactfully and with sensitivity.

Mistakes happen to everyone, but negative feedback can be discouraging, especially to someone who's just learning a job. This is particularly true of service people, who are usually good at service at least partly because they are very sensitive to people. Their feelings may be hurt more easily. A lot of positive words of encouragement can help counteract these minor setbacks. Don't inspect to find mistakes; inspect to find achievements.

Rewards. Provide positive recognition through praise. If you are the trainer, you can praise the employee as he or she progresses. If you have a designated trainer, see that he or she brings the trainee back to you when reporting a job well done. Other forms of reward might include a certificate, a letter to the home, badge or uniform changes, a formal status change at the end of the probationary period, or a raise.

Don't underestimate the sense of personal achievement as a form of reward. An employee who reaches a certain production level has a right to be proud of this accomplishment, and the trainer should acknowledge it.

Group Training

Group training is a useful approach in various situations. When you have several employees to be trained for the same task—like opening a new facility or learning how to use a new piece of equipment—and individual training isn't practical, group training should be considered. It's also the most effective method when teaching human relations skills like conflict resolution, team-building, or problem solving. Group training is often an important part of a company's human resources strategy and its attempt to create a positive organizational culture.

We've seen that employees tend to place themselves in loosely structured work groups, each having its own values, standards, rules of acceptable behavior, and informal leaders. Those who don't accept the group's norms are usually rejected by the other members. Thus, employees who come back from a training program and operate above or below the accepted standards of performance may well be excluded. Because of this impact on the individual's values and productivity, *unmanaged group influence can nullify employer attempts at training or standards modification.* That's why the manager's highest training priority must be directed toward the group rather than individual skills training. The best way to start the group off on the right foot is through the proper general company orientation.

General Orientation

Each training step should be designed to answer the questions that are in the mind of the average employee at that time. The initial job training centers on job skills and procedures. After learning their jobs and adjusting to co-workers, supervisors, work schedules, and procedures, new employees are more willing to make a long-term commitment. Generally, two weeks to a month after hiring, the average line employee is ready to make a genuine commitment to the company as a whole.

Orientation is run by the human resources department in large companies and by the general manager in smaller operations. Either way, top management must show visible support and involvement.

As with any training program, when a general orientation program is initially installed, first have your existing employees go through. In addition, you should send your key and training employees for reorientation every year, and all other employees every other year. Your property should consider inviting spouses to the orientation program. Obtaining family commitment now can prove valuable later when you have to ask the employee to work a double shift without notice.

Employees who don't work for your company, but work within the same building (in leased operations such as a gift shop, flower shop, or newsstand, for

During general company orientation, a tour of the facility should highlight special features.
(Courtesy of Amway Grand Plaza Hotel, Grand Rapids, Michigan)

example) might also be invited. Guests frequently assume those employees work for your company, so make them feel they're part of the operation, keep them well-informed, and obtain their commitment as well.

The program should be designed for the type of people hired most, probably the entry-level positions. This program must be meaningful to them or it's a waste of time. Employees should be paid for time spent in orientation. Top management should attend the programs, and even speak to the group.

Orientation should be approached like any other sales program—it's worth putting time and money into the presentation. It should creatively capitalize on your company's uniqueness. One hotel wouldn't copy another hotel's advertising campaign—neither should it use someone else's orientation plan. Its people need to understand and identify with its unique differences.

For the general orientation to be credible, it cannot say things the employees already know aren't true, so it must reinforce current experiences. In the way they were hired and during their first days on the job, you should already have been communicating your goals and values.

The orientation presenter must set the right environment. He or she must be believable and sincere, and must create a feeling of belonging, pride, teamwork, and a commitment to the goals and values of the company.

General orientation doesn't need to cover specific details, since its purpose is to evoke feelings and generate commitment. The presenter should sell security, caring, and peace of mind by talking in general terms about benefits, employee recognition programs, and wage and salary policies. Details of the health insurance coverage, for example, don't need to be covered during orientation and would probably be forgotten anyway. They can be covered in a booklet. People should be encouraged to read the booklet, and then told where to get more information when it's needed.

Employees want to be part of a successful team, so orientation should emphasize the points that make your company successful. The presenter might read complimentary guest letters and magazine articles, mention awards and accomplishments of the various departments or other people who work for the company, offer testimonials from other employees, and highlight special features or functions during a tour of the facility.

Even during high turnover or movement of management, companies can ensure continuity with a well-done general orientation program. Such a program can build a commitment which is strong enough that the group can maintain its high standards in spite of a poor department head or even no department head. Employee groups can maintain their standards indefinitely if the company's values:

- Consistently encourage employees to take responsibility for their own actions

- Are supported by employee involvement techniques and participative management practices

- Are reinforced by regular employee general meetings

Planning for Group Meetings

The group meeting is an important tool for maintaining commitment, sharing ideas and information, and influencing employee attitudes, as well as for training. Whether it's a simple daily pre-meal meeting, a weekly supervisors' meeting, or a formal training session when you're implementing new procedures, every manager must be adept at planning and conducting group meetings.

The size and purpose of your meeting will dictate how you adapt these steps to meet your needs. We'll address here the requirements of a large, all-day session.

Preparation is the key to any training program. A professional teacher often spends three to eight hours in preparation for every hour of training time. To assist in your preparation, you will need:

- A **training plan** to provide the key information, broken down into the main points to be covered, how they'll be covered, and the approximate time it will take

- A checklist of materials needed—handouts, equipment, and training aids

The Training Plan. In addition to helping you organize the logistics of your meeting, the training plan can help you plan the presentation of the material itself. You may wish to use your job outline to help you prepare the breakdown of key information, which may range in length from a few index cards for smaller meetings to several pages for a major presentation. Exhibit 7.6 is a sample group training plan.

Spell out the course objective and keep it in mind at all times. What do you want the trainees to think and feel when they leave the training session? Express in one or two lines the idea you want to communicate. Also take time to clarify why people should learn it. If you can't complete these steps, perhaps you shouldn't be having a class.

In the first column of the presentation section (using Exhibit 7.6 as a model), list key points that you want to cover. Use the next column to note what you want to stress, and to identify any quotations, handouts, equipment, audiovisual aids, or assistance that will be required. Indicate whether you'll use demonstrations or guest speakers, and whether your format will include lecturing or involvement techniques like role-playing.

The last column begins with the meeting's starting time and expresses the time needed for each subsequent step in terms of its starting time. The listing should be by clock time—9 a.m., 9:10, 9:25, for example—so that you can quickly spot whether and by how much you're falling behind.

Develop reading material, homework assignments, and job aids beforehand. When making up materials to hand out, always prepare about 10% more than you think you'll need; you'll find you always pass out more than anticipated. Arrange this material in order of use.

The Training Room Checklist. Go over your meeting room requirements with the person who will be taking care of the physical arrangements. For this purpose, a checklist is helpful (see Exhibit 7.7). Arrange for the room to be set up at least an hour early to allow time for you to inspect it and make any needed adjustments.

When you select a location, consider the size of the room. A room that's too large can be more harmful than one that's too small. The feeling of personal contact is lost, and it may even seem that almost no one showed up for the meeting. On the other hand, adequate space should be allowed for each person attending.

Check to make sure ventilation, heating, and air conditioning are acceptable. Try to eliminate distractions like outside noises, squeaking door hinges, noisy air conditioning vents, or windows with distracting views. The room should be close to a restroom and telephones.

You or the designated trainer should always check before scheduling to ensure that training sessions don't interfere with other key meetings, such as regular departmental meetings. The best training time seems to be in the morning, when people are fresh, so more detailed presentations should probably be covered then. The next most productive time is probably after lunch. When many departments are closed over weekends, Mondays and Fridays generally become busier than other days. For this reason, the days of the week which seem to produce better results are Tuesday, Wednesday, and Thursday.

Exhibit 7.6   Group Training Plan

GROUP TRAINING PLAN

Course_____   Housekeeping Announcements/Notes:

Day/Date_____   _____

Location_____   _____

Time of Meeting_____   _____

Scheduled Breaks_____   _____   _____

PREPARATION CHECKLIST
- ☐ Announcements   ☐ Attendance List
- ☐ Name Tags/Place Cards   ☐ Pre-Reading Mailed
- ☐ Meeting Room Checklist   ☐ Diplomas
- ☐ Handouts (List):_____
- ☐ Homework Assignments   ☐ Souvenirs   ☐ Other Handouts
- ☐ Demonstration Materials (List):_____
- ☐ Visual Aids (Videotape, Slides, Film, Audio Cassettes, Show Cards, Overhead Transparencies)
- ☐ Supplies (Markers, Masking Tape)   Other_____

COURSE OBJECTIVE_____

_____

IMPORTANCE TO PARTICIPANTS_____

_____

_____

PRESENTATION

Key Points	Trainer Notes	Start Time

Plan to spread training out over several sessions with practice time between each session. Several short sessions are often better than one long session.

Short meetings can have a coffee break beforehand or afterward so that attendees' personal business with each other won't cause disruption to the meeting. For longer meetings, one morning break of about fifteen minutes is generally adequate, while two brief breaks may be needed in the afternoon.

Exhibit 7.7   Training Room Checklist

TRAINING ROOM CHECKLIST

Course_____ Number of Attendees_____ Day/Date_____

Location_____

Time: Set Up By_____ Starting_____ Ending_____

Breaks:_____ _____ _____

MEETING SPECIFICATIONS (Attach Drawing)

☐ Style of Setup:
  ☐ Schoolroom
  ☐ Rounds   Number_____
                 Persons Per Table_____
  ☐ Conference
  ☐ U-Shaped
☐ Other Meeting Tables:_____
☐ Registration Table
☐ Coffee-Break Table
☐ Brochure Table
☐ Head Table
☐ Podium: ☐ Table-Style   ☐ Floor-Style
☐ Risers
☐ Telephone: ☐ On   ☐ Off
☐ Message Board
☐ Coat Storage
☐ Light Dimmers
☐ Wall Covering
☐ Parking

ROOM EQUIPMENT/SUPPLIES

☐ Carpet clean, in good repair
☐ A/V Cords taped down
☐ Table/Chairs lined up
☐ Tablecloths level, clean, pressed, in good repair
☐ Table Skirting
☐ Drinking Water/Glasses: _____ Attendees
                            _____ Trainer
☐ Note Pads clean, enough pages
☐ Pencils sharpened
☐ Ashtrays
☐ Mints/Candies
☐ Wastebasket(s)
☐ Motel Bulletin Signage
☐ Your Special Signage Requirements
☐ Flipchart Pad full of clean paper
☐ Chalkboard: ☐ Yellow Chalk/2 full pieces
                ☐ Clean Eraser
                ☐ 3-Foot Pointer
☐ Easel

AUDIOVISUAL REQUIREMENTS

☐ Microphone: ☐ Podium-Style   ☐ Lavaliere   ☐ Long Cord
☐ Screen
☐ 16mm Sound Projector: ☐ Projectionist   ☐ Take-up Reel
☐ 35mm Slide Projector: ☐ Remote With Long Cord   ☐ No. of Trays
☐ Tape Player: ☐ Cassette   ☐ Reel-to-Reel   ☐ Sync With Slides
☐ Video Player: ☐ VHS   ☐ Beta
☐ Video Monitor With Stand
☐ Overhead Projector: ☐ Opaque   ☐ Translucent
☐ Extension Cords
☐ Other_____

_____
_____

A juice and coffee break set up in the morning and a soft-drink/coffee break in early afternoon should be considered. The third break, late in the afternoon, can be a simple ten-minute stand-up break to get a quick cup of coffee. You may wish to place candy bars or other snacks on the table.

If your meeting is going through a meal period and nearby restaurants aren't adequate to get your participants in and out during the meal break, valuable time could be lost, so you may want to arrange a planned meal function. If you do, it's generally better to serve light foods. Many times a large meal, particularly with beef, can make members of the group sluggish in the afternoon.

Decide what you're going to do about smoking and any other special requirements. If you're planning to use slides, videos, filmstrips, or movies, make sure the meeting room lights can be controlled by dimmers and windows can be darkened.

Consider whether or not a telephone should be allowed to ring in the room. You may prefer to ask the operators not to ring the room unless it's an emergency. For large groups, messages can be taken and placed outside the meeting room on a message board that can be viewed during breaks.

To ensure that your meeting room is set up according to your specifications, draw an exact plan of where you want every item and give it to the person taking care of the physical arrangements. A copy of this diagram should also be attached to your training room checklist.

The room should be laid out so that you can maintain eye contact with all the participants. If you're using a lecture format, a standard schoolroom or V-shaped setting with three feet of table space for every participant is normal for large meetings. U-shaped, horseshoe, or conference tables are best for smaller meetings. Round tables are particularly desirable when you're going to have groups working together on projects, with six to eight at a table. The exit should be at the rear of the room.

Head tables are used if you have demonstration materials and handouts. A table podium can be used for your introductory comments and training plan, but the main speaker should stand in front of this table so that there are no barriers between the speaker and the audience. Risers are used in groups of over a hundred to help the instructor maintain eye contact and to improve visibility for demonstration materials.

Flipcharts can be used in a well-lit room. They should be kept simple, with no more than six lines per page, six words per line. Concise statements are more effective than lengthy ones. Use dark colors, like black, blue, or green, for emphasis. Make sure all printed material is large enough to be clearly visible to each participant. It's much more convenient to tape the pages on the walls around the room for future reference and re-examination than to flip back and forth through the pages. If you do plan to tape up pages, make sure the wall coverings won't be damaged by masking tape.

Chalkboards make many adults uncomfortable. Use them only when you need a large writing surface.

Microphones should normally be used for groups of 50 or more. If your voice is weak, the room has a high ceiling or poor acoustics, or you're having a long meeting, you may want a microphone with 30 or more people. To develop a rapport with your group, use a lavaliere microphone with a long cord to permit you to walk around the room.

If you're considering using video equipment, review your specifications. Standard-sized television monitors start to lose their impact with more than 25 people. Be sure everyone in the audience can see. When using a film projector, check the ceiling height for the screen. Place the projector in back of the audience to minimize the effects of operating noise, and use a stand that allows it to project above their heads.

The size of the movie screen should be determined by the room arrangement and the size of your audience. One easy method to decide how large a screen to use involves the "**2 × 6**" **rule**. The width should be half the distance from the first row of seats to the screen, and the height should be one-sixth of the distance from the last row of seats to the screen.[5]

The commonest type of movie projector is the 16-mm with 16-mm optical sound track. The film should be pre-threaded and focused and the sound level adjusted before the meeting. Be familiar with the equipment so that you don't fumble around with it during the presentation. Make sure the lens is clean and appropriate for the size of and distance to the screen. Have extra bulbs on hand and know how to change them.

Films and videos are usually shown at the end of the lecture as a demonstration of things discussed. Some trainers like to allow time to stop a film at key points to reinforce ideas by discussing them, or at least to conduct a critique after the film is over. Never rewind the film during class time.

The most commonly used slide projector is the 35-mm. Even though they have to be changed less frequently, avoid 140-slot slide trays, because the slot openings are too narrow and the slides may not drop properly. The 80-slot tray is more reliable. Don't combine vertical and horizontal slides; if necessary, have the scenes in question re-shot. The picture should fill at least three edges of the screen.

The overhead projector is one of the most effective visual training tools. You don't have to darken a room in order to use it, so you can look at people and move around the room to achieve more personal contact. It can be used for groups of any size. You can often maintain better control over the group through your ability to switch the overhead on and off, write on it, and uncover only those portions currently under discussion. If you use it, keep the presentation simple, and make sure all printed material is large enough to be clearly visible to each participant.

Preparing Trainees

Use the notice you send to participants to prepare them for the meeting and to set the proper expectations. State the purpose of the session, who is coming, locations, and times. Include an agenda and any pre-meeting reading material. You may also want to touch on such items as parking, dress codes, what to do about food, and how to handle telephone calls. If some of the attending employees wear pagers or beepers, ask them to leave them with someone else.

Well in advance of a training session, send memos to the immediate supervisors of all attending employees, giving the same information that the employees are receiving. Be sure they understand who's going, why they're going, and what you expect attendees to get from the program. Inform managers why the company is conducting the session and what support is expected from them.

A monthly training summary (see Exhibit 7.8) can be used to keep a record of department training.

Implementation of the Group Training Program

There's no substitute for planning and rehearsal to give you the polish and assurance to teach with confidence. Know your material very well. Practice your presentation, but don't memorize it, and never read it. If you think you may be nervous getting started, you may memorize the opening lines, but after that, plan to talk informally. Use an outline if necessary.

Feel good about your appearance. Dress comfortably and appropriately.

---

[5]*Convention Liaison Manual*, 3rd ed. (Washington, D.C.: Convention Liaison Council, 1980), p. 69.

Exhibit 7.8 Monthly Training Summary

MMI HOTEL GROUP

MONTHLY TRAINING SUMMARY

Hotel _____   Month _____ Year _____

DEPARTMENT TRAINING

DEPARTMENT			DEPARTMENT		
Date	No. Attending	Topics	Date	No. Attending	Topics

DEPARTMENT			DEPARTMENT		
Date	No. Attending	Topics	Date	No. Attending	Topics

NOTES/COMMENTS:_____

ORIENTATION SESSIONS

Date _____ No. Attending _____ Date _____ No. Attending _____ Date _____ No. Attending _____

MM-P18
(Rev. 3-85)

Courtesy of MMI Hotel Group, Jackson, Mississippi.

Don't wear new clothes if you're not sure how comfortable they'll be.

Arrive in the room early and walk around so that you're familiar and comfortable with the layout. See that all of your supplies are in order. Check all the equipment and make sure you know how to operate it.

Presentation. Greet people as they come in. It helps you get started and puts trainees at ease. As people come into the room, try to break up the cliques.

Start on time. Waiting for latecomers only encourages them to come late again and penalizes the people who are prompt. Use the first few minutes of the training session to cover non-essential items—a short welcome, an ice-breaker exercise, or a funny story—so that late arrivers do not miss a key point in the presentation.

Introduce yourself, and ask the participants to introduce themselves if the class is small enough. If you're going to have group exercises later, spend a few minutes now letting the members at each table get acquainted; then have each person introduce someone else to the group. Ask people what they expect to learn.

Think about what you want people to feel when they leave the session. Often, the way you say something is more important than what you say. If you believe in what you're saying and you care about it, you should be able to convey the feelings that you want to evoke in others. People want to know how much you care before they care how much you know. Being open and genuine is more important than being skillful at making presentations.

Try to establish an informal, unthreatening environment. Eliminate physical barriers between yourself and the learners, and maintain eye contact with them. If you want to create a more informal atmosphere, take your coat off, roll up your sleeves, sit on the edge of a table, or walk around.

Tell attendees why the class is important to them—perhaps the job will be easier, the workplace will be safer, job security will be increased, or raises or promotions may result. A supervisor may be excited by the potential for increased productivity or sales if a new procedure is introduced, but line employees may view it as just more work. Tell them what they'll be expected to learn and what they'll be able to accomplish when they're finished. Keep expectations realistic, but be sure your learners understand how the training is going to help them.

Use your training plan to help you keep your presentation straightforward, simple, and orderly. For each aspect of the job being taught, tell the trainees what has to be done and what the standards are for the completion of the procedure. Explain why if it's not obvious.

Center the presentation on real work problems and relate them to the employees' specific areas. Regularly review why the procedure you're talking about is important. Statements like, "This will help you when you're faced with this situation," help improve attention. Frequent summaries are also helpful.

Next, they must see the procedure performed successfully, either through a live or audiovisual demonstration.

Teach tasks in a logical order. Certain skills may have to be taught before others. When it's possible, starting with easier or more familiar procedures and progressing to the more difficult can provide positive experiences on which to build.

Keep things interesting. People who are excited about what they're learning often work long and hard. If they're bored, they'll be tired in ten minutes. Watch the body language in your class. Is there more fidgeting? Are people glancing at their watches, folding up their books, or starting to have side conversations?

Group participation is one of the most effective ways to overcome boredom. Involve as many people as possible. Have someone write on the flipchart or run the projector. Ask people to write down key points. Have them discuss real problems that relate to their work. For example, have a front desk agent talk about an experience with a difficult guest before you introduce the topic of guest complaints.

Improve retention with frequent summaries, examples, catchy phrases, slogans, and even humor. Ask questions to keep students involved and to see if the material is being absorbed. There are four general types of questions that instructors use.

Group participation is one of the most effective ways to overcome boredom. (Courtesy of Amway Grand Plaza Hotel, Grand Rapids, Michigan)

- The **overhead question** is a lead-off question used to get the discussion rolling and is generally addressed to the whole class. Phrase it so that you elicit extended answers, instead of a yes or no. State your questions clearly and slowly. Ask easy questions at first. Some sample overhead questions might include: "Will someone please explain for us. . . ." "What does the group think about. . .?" "Can anyone see another side to this issue?"

- The **direct question** is used to elicit a specific answer. When addressing a specific individual, be sure you have the person's attention. Call the individual by name and then ask the question; for instance, "John, what's the first thing you do when a guest walks up to the counter?"

- The **rhetorical question** is asked largely to get the audience to think about the answer. It may be discussed or answered by the questioner; for instance, "What do we mean when we say the hotel is the ambassador to the community?. . . Well, perhaps we're talking about. . . ."

- The **relay question** helps the trainer avoid doing all the talking or giving an opinion. You may relay the question back to the person who asked it or on to another person so that you remain in the background and promote group discussion. Sample relay questions are: "John's question is, what should the average turnover be for a hotel? Can anyone answer that?" or "How do you feel about John's question?"

Start with the easy questions and proceed to the more difficult. As you begin, pick one of the less aggressive people in the room first. If someone is unable to answer a question, don't allow a person to flounder indefinitely, and don't intimidate or embarrass anyone. Just smile and move on to someone else: "Can someone help Jane with that?" As participation increases, satisfaction increases as well. People tend to remember, give more support to, and make a greater commitment to things that bring satisfaction.

Ask questions on a random basis to keep people alert. Rotate your questions so that people sitting around the room have a chance to speak. Ensure that the person who answers a question replies to the group. If one person keeps answering all the questions, ask, "How do the rest of you feel about that subject?"

If two or three people are speaking among themselves, sometimes all you need to do is just remain silent until they stop. If not, ask them a question, or suggest pleasantly, "If you're commenting on what we're talking about, maybe it's something the whole class would like to hear." Never use sarcasm.

If one person starts to monopolize the group discussion, try saying, "Many others have questions; I'll get back to you if there's time." If someone wanders from the subject being discussed, you might ask, "How does that relate to the subject we're talking about?" Maybe it is relevant for that person.

Be prepared to respond to questions, and be open to suggestions and opinions of the group. If you don't have an answer to a question, offer to find out and respond later.

Try to maintain a trusting atmosphere in which all members feel free to participate. All questions and comments should be regarded as of equal importance and treated with respect. Never display a negative attitude toward anyone for participating. Avoid answering questions with remarks like, "Well, that's obvious." Don't rate questions. If you respond, "That's a good question," to one inquiry, you may have to use that response to all. Watch your own body language—don't fold your arms, point at people, or put your hands on your hips.

A group trainer should keep discussions moving along. Be a good listener and try to remain neutral. When someone asks a question, give your complete attention. Look directly at the person, nod your head, and say, "Uh-huh" or "I see what you mean." Help put feelings into words and, if necessary, summarize the question, but wait for the questioner to finish before you answer. Repeat any question the group is unable to hear.

If you're having a question-and-answer period, don't let it end on a negative question or comment. Always end on a positive note by allowing time for a summary. Do not, however, announce that you're summarizing or that you have just one more point to cover, or you may lose the group's attention. Just say something like, "Let's see what we've learned here so far" or "Let's put the comments up on the flipchart." Get the members to participate and summarize. You can hand out your own summary later, along with any checklists or job aids. You might also want to let each person work on his or her own action plan individually for the last few minutes and then share it with the group.

Try to finish ten minutes ahead of schedule. People are happier and leave with good feelings. Since their minds are already moving ahead to other things, the last few minutes are usually non-productive time, anyway.

While two major goals of the group training session are to communicate ideas and get the group's commitment, you don't need to get a total commitment from everyone to be successful. If the majority of the group accepts the idea, the others will probably go along. Try to reach a group consensus that supports the idea. Then, try to get participants to take significant action to carry out the new mission, and to accept the idea of 100% compliance to standards.

Practice. Experience is the best teacher, and good habits are learned through repetition. It's certainly better to have trainees practice on each other than on a guest, and the sooner they can put what they've been learning to use, the better they'll retain it.

For simple techniques, a written quiz may give adequate practice, or trainees might turn to a person nearby. For more difficult skills, you may want to break up into small groups. This way, no one has to demonstrate in front of a large class and everyone will feel more at ease. Five to six members usually provide the best interaction. These groups can be assigned to different corners if there's enough privacy; or you can use separate meeting rooms, called **break-out rooms**, for practice sessions.

If you're going to break up into smaller groups, before the participants leave, give them the specific details of their assignments and what they must accomplish. If a report of what went on in the group is necessary, ask them to select a recorder or group leader. Tell them how much time they have and ask them also to designate a timekeeper, so time won't be wasted while everyone waits for one group to return.

Once they start their teamwork, your only purpose for checking in on the groups is to see if any clarification is needed or to provide periodic time checks—"Five minutes left," for example. Don't get trapped into doing the group's work.

Group Training Techniques. Participatory techniques commonly used for group training meetings include the following:

- **Brainstorming** involves participants in generating new ideas and solutions to help solve problems, particularly with new and unusual approaches. Emphasis is on quantity instead of quality, and no attempt is made to moderate or evaluate suggestions.

- **Case studies** are actual cases taken from real business situations. The participants read the fact sheet and then discuss the solutions. The emphasis is on the development of the problem-solving process and the interaction of the participants, rather than the actual solution.

- **Role-playing** requires people to assume roles and act out parts in the training setting, thus allowing them to learn and practice newly-learned skills in a realistic situation.

- **Simulation** is a form of role-playing in which the person practices in a more realistic environment, perhaps even in the actual work area. As the last step or dress rehearsal, simulation allows you to check the employees thoroughly before using a new procedure for the guests. For instance, you might invite off-duty employees or their friends to check into a hotel and stay overnight shortly before the grand opening to simulate actual working conditions for on-duty workers.

When working with techniques like case studies or role-playing, use real situations involving real people. Keep the case studies brief, simple, and general. Avoid adding so much reality that the participants get caught up in details, like, "But the bellperson doesn't take bags out of the car—the door attendant does that."

Feedback. Make sure you structure your training process with plenty of immediate and relevant feedback, so that participants build on successes. Feedback can be spoken, written (as with quizzes and tests), or as elaborate as videotaping to permit employees to see themselves practicing.

Give information back to group members about how they did. You can do this yourself, have other members of the group provide feedback to an individual or group, or you can rate one group against another. Such competition not only provides feedback, but also builds team spirit within the individual groups and improves attention, participation, and, most importantly, commitment. Be careful to keep the competition light, however, to avoid resentment. Never permit anyone to be victimized.

Rewards. The final step in a successful training program is rewarding the group members. Souvenirs, mementos, or pins are types of immediate rewards, as are memos sent to the participants' department heads (in cases where the manager is not the trainer) complimenting their performance. Memos from top management to the employees, complimenting them on their progress, are often kept for years by the recipients. Certificates are particularly good motivators in areas where general schooling is lacking. A story in an in-house publication or on bulletin boards should also be considered.

On a long-term basis, make sure that attendance at the training session is mentioned in the permanent **personnel file** for future reference during salary and status reviews.

Evaluation

In any training program, individual or group, the instructor should ask trainees to write down how their new skills will help them improve their performance and how they plan to use what they've learned on the job. This plan should be shared with others in the class and with their supervisors. An individual might even be asked to make a presentation to the department about what he or she learned in order to inform co-workers of a new procedure or technique.

Evaluation forms should be handed out to the participants of every training program. The forms should ask them to rate the instructor and to indicate whether the program met their expectations and how it could be improved. Exhibit 7.9 is a sample training evaluation form.

Check with trainees within two weeks after a training program to find out whether the techniques learned are being used. If, for example, you were doing a seminar on suggestive selling, look for increases in the size of the average check. If so, give the group additional recognition. This might range from a simple note from the general manager all the way to a more formal incentive bonus plan. To evaluate success in training for customer service, measure repeat business and compare guest comment cards from before and after training.

All training will result in some short-lived improvements. Just being selected for training is a form of recognition and motivation. Don't think that early improvements ensure the success of the training. As time passes, you should verify that short-term improvements have become permanent improvements.

Exhibit 7.9   Sample Training Evaluation Form

Day Learning Center

Name:_____

Dates attended:_____

Please rank the DLC overall: ☐ Unsatisfactory   ☐ Good   ☐ Excellent

If I had designed the daily schedule, I would have_____

_____

_____

Topics that addressed my needs included_____

_____

_____

I suggest that from now on, to improve their presentation, the instructors_____

_____

_____

I especially enjoyed the class time when instructors would_____

_____

_____

I would have liked to learn more about_____

_____

_____

The first thing I am going to put into practice when I return to my property is_____

_____

_____

General comments, suggestions, issues:_____

_____

_____

Courtesy of Days Inns of America, Inc., Atlanta, Georgia.

When industrial plants began to put gauges on their machinery so people could see how they were doing, quality, consistency, and production went up. In the service industry, hanging a bar chart or poster that resembles a thermometer on the wall to plot the increase in sales could have the same effect.

Ongoing assessment is the only way to determine whether your training investment is paying off. All training programs should be reviewed at least annually to ensure that content is current and the program is still needed and effective.

Key Terms

brainstorming
break-out rooms
case study
computer interactive training
    program
department trainer
direct question
job aid
job outline
learner controlled instruction (LCI)
needs analysis
on-the-job training (OJT)

overhead question
performance standard
personnel file
programmed instruction
relay question
rhetorical question
role-playing
self instruction
simulation
training director
training plan
2 × 6 rule

Discussion Questions

1. What are some of the characteristics of a good trainer?

2. What are some of the elements a manager should consider in doing a departmental needs analysis?

3. Why would a manager need to train a new employee who already has experience?

4. Under what circumstances might it be most appropriate to use a learner controlled instruction program?

5. What is wrong with evaluating trainee performance with a system that uses rating terms such as *unacceptable, poor, acceptable, good,* and *excellent*?

6. Why should the manager's highest training priority be directed toward the group rather than individual skills training? How is this principle put into practice?

7. What steps should you take to prepare for a group training meeting?

8 Management Development

Although no hospitality business can succeed without effectively recruiting, interviewing, evaluating, hiring, and training competent line employees, line employees alone do not make a business a success. Every business also needs competent management, from the supervisor to the chairman of the board. Because the importance of and need for good managers is so great, companies cannot afford to let management positions be filled haphazardly. Rather, a systematic approach to finding and developing managerial talent is called for.

A company's approach to management development is centered on three basic areas:

1. Training current managers and keeping their skills up-to-date

2. Promoting people from within

3. Setting up programs for those hired as management trainees

The programs associated with all three of the above areas represent a major expense to the company and usually eat up most of the company's training budget. Management training involves more sophisticated training techniques, and is likelier to be handled by professional trainers or specialized consultants. Changing behavior also becomes more difficult at the managerial level; it requires a great deal of time and isn't always successful without extensive follow-up and reinforcement.

With the emphasis in the service business on the management of people, the subjects now being taught in management development include such areas as team-building, conflict resolution, managing change, assertiveness training, dealing with stress, and developing creativity.

Teaching these subjects and allowing managers to practice the skills usually involves group training sessions with other managers, which also increases the cost.

Succession Planning

Before embarking on a course of management development, upper management must first decide what is needed. Progressive medium-to-large companies use succession planning to ensure that they have enough properly trained key managers and professional employees coming up through the system to support their growth and turnover. Succession planning will give a company a current picture of the strength of its management and professional staff, but its primary use is in helping to plan for long-term management staffing needs.

The succession planning process has several steps:

1. The key positions within the company that need to be tracked and their **feeder jobs** (positions from which people can be promoted into key positions) must be identified.

2. The short- and long-term staffing needs of the company must be defined. They should be tied directly to the business plan by outlining expected growth. Retirement and turnover factors should be considered as well.

3. Once it is determined how many managers are needed, those who are capable of being promoted into those positions must be identified (see Exhibit 8.1 for a career review form which can be used in succession planning). Two or three candidates should normally be pinpointed for each position, for two reasons: One person may be qualified for promotion into several jobs, and allowance must also be made for turnover and for the employees who don't want to move. Some hard decisions may be required with respect to people who are the best performers, those who aren't promotable, and those who should be replaced. At this stage, the company may find that key arteries for developing managers and professionals are clogged with low-potential individuals around whom good people can't pass. This identification process begins by having existing managers rank their people from the best to the worst in terms of their potential. This information is passed up to middle and then top management for further ranking and classification. The collection of data involves making some highly subjective judgments. It doesn't include any feedback from the employee at this time, as the objective is to obtain a broad, long-term staffing planning tool, not an individual career development plan. Decisions are usually more related to skills than behavior. For example, a front office manager may need to have housekeeping experience before being promoted to rooms division manager.

4. Management must determine what skills the promotable employees need, how they're going to get them, how soon they must be ready, and who's accountable to ensure that they obtain the skills.

5. Upper management then reviews the succession plan semi-annually or annually to ensure that people are progressing and that the company will be able to fulfill its staffing demands.

6. After determining what shortages exist, the company decides how many new people it would like to bring in each year and in which areas.

The succession planning program must be individually designed for each company. The size and diversity of the company, the lead time to

Exhibit 8.1 Sample Career Review Form

HILTON CAREER REVIEW   Today's Date_____

NAME_____ LOCATION / HOTEL_____

POSITION TITLE_____ REPORTS TO_____
                                                                    (Title)

PERFORMANCE RATING (Circle One—Transfer Performance Rating from Performance Review Document)

  1   2   3   4   5

ESTIMATE OF PROMOTION POTENTIAL (Circle One)

Employee is PROMOTABLE

☐ **YES,** Next Logical Position(s) For Promotion Consideration:

_____

_____

  PROMOTION READINESS is (Circle One)

  A. NOW   C. Next Twelve Months   E. Next Thirty-Six Months

  B. Next Six Months D. Next Twenty-Four Months

☐ **NO,** (Circle and / or Check One)

  1. Better Suited For Another Position

    _____ A. At Same Position Level

    _____ B. Below Present Position Level

  2. Should Remain In Present Position For At Least One More Year.

TRAINING & DEVELOPMENT ACTIVITY *Indicate the training and development objectives for the next 12 months designed to improve performance on the job.*

_____

_____

_____

INDIVIDUAL PREFERENCE *Indicate the employee's personal career goals and aspirations.*

_____

_____

Courtesy of Hilton Hotels Corporation, Beverly Hills, California.

develop specific individuals, their ability to relocate, and even foreign language requirements are some areas that may be significant to a company's plan. It's important, however, that the program be kept as simple as possible. In large multi-unit corporations, control and tracking should be pushed down to the regional or divisional level.

If your company has such a program, you will be provided with the information relevant to the employees below you. The plan, which includes

The in-house seminar is an excellent way to keep managers current. (Courtesy of Days Inns of America, Inc., Atlanta, Georgia)

the identification and ranking of high-potential employees, should be treated confidentially. The listings of who is promotable and who should be replaced shouldn't be general knowledge within the company either. None of this information should be shared with the individuals or placed in personnel files.

Once staffing needs have been defined and key people have been identified, a company can more accurately predict its management training needs and where it should spend its time and training dollars.

Training Current Managers

Shifting customer demands, market segmentation, rapid growth, new laws, and expanded liabilities are some of the factors combining to make managers' skills obsolete almost as quickly as they're acquired. All managers and supervisors, not just those on the succession plan, need training and updating of their skills. Their managers must see that they get it.

As specific skills and management needs are identified, upper management must decide whether to provide in-house or outside training sources. When a large group needs a particular skill on a recurring basis, it may be more economical to strengthen the training department and provide that instruction in-house. If a highly technical skill is required on a limited basis, outside seminars can be used.

In-House Training

In-house seminars could include not only current managers, but also management trainees and other employees who wish to be promoted from within. It may be possible to have company managers lead seminars. For example, the controller could teach an in-house seminar on accounting, the director of marketing on sales, or the director of human resources on discipline or hiring.

Cross-training during slow periods is also helpful. For example, having the front office manager spend time in housekeeping will not only help the person acquire additional skills, but may even improve communications between departments and force the assistant front office manager to grow as well.

There are many other things that can be done in-house that will help improve the existing managers' skills or keep them current. An in-house company library with books, development tapes, and magazines can be made available. Outside industry speakers can be invited in. Managers can be encouraged to join and even assume positions in professional and civic organizations. (Their joining such organizations also helps represent the company in the community and professional circles.) They can be encouraged to subscribe to and write for professional journals and business magazines, to speak at professional meetings, to publish a textbook, or teach at local schools. These activities help managers become more capable and confident as they acquire more knowledge and skills, develop contacts, keep abreast of recent developments in their fields, discuss work-related problems with other professionals, and gain professional recognition among their peers and colleagues.

More and more companies are providing support through additional time off, financial aid for travel and membership fees, technical support for research in writing manuscripts or speeches, and secretarial support for typing publications, photocopying, and distributing speech materials.

When employees train in an area that's directly job-related, it's considered by wage and hour law to be time for which they must be paid. When the training isn't directly job-related, the law isn't so clear. In this case, the legal determination will probably be based on the extent to which the company may benefit in the foreseeable future.

Outside Seminars

If the skills identified can't be provided within the organization, outside seminars can be used; however, they're often expensive. Exhibit 8.2 presents several guidelines to consider when selecting an outside seminar.

Before sending someone to an outside seminar, the attendee's supervisor should consider having the person write up a proposal indicating how the company will benefit and how the employee will be able to use the skills on the job. This proposal could be part of an agreement the employee signs which also states that if the employee leaves within a specified time, all costs which the company paid must be repaid to the company. All of the financial arrangements should be clearly outlined in writing, and the entire agreement should be reviewed and approved by upper management. The total cost of the seminar—including travel expense, lodging, meals, wages paid while attending, and the cost of the course—should be itemized on the approval form.

Anyone returning from a seminar should complete an evaluation form before the company sends additional attendees. A manager should also spend some time with the attendee discussing how the knowledge gained from the seminar can be used to improve the existing operation and when the improvements can be made. A copy of this discussion can be placed in a follow-up file—often called a **suspense file**—for several months so that the manager can later check to see whether any of the improvements have actually been made. Consideration should also be given to having the attendee speak at the next management meeting to share new information with others.

Exhibit 8.2   How to Choose an Outside Seminar

- Identify the people you want to train and what specific skills they need.
- Look for a program that will involve all three types of learning: visual, reading and writing, and practice.
- Is the program simply lecture or does it involve the trainees?
- Will the format hold their attention? An all-day (or longer) seminar shouldn't be all lecture. The format must be varied to keep interest.
- What is the background of the instructor? The person should have credibility with your trainees.
- What is the class size? How much time will be available for trainees to ask questions? The instructor needs to be able to give some individual attention and answer questions.
- Is this seminar attended by many people from your industry or by the level of management you have in mind? Get the names of companies similar to yours that have used this seminar, and call them for references.
- Is there any material your trainees would find helpful to read before the seminar?
- What is the ratio of presentation time to practice time?
- Never select a seminar simply by reading a brochure about it—ask that more information be sent to you.

Once a company has in place the necessary training to help its existing managers stay current as well as improve and grow, it can begin to make plans for an effective program of promotion from within.

Promotion from Within

Employers should not overlook their main source of new management talent. In the hospitality business, most managers come from within a company's own ranks. The hospitality industry survives on promotion from within. Unfortunately, the success rate for many of these potential managers has not been high. Since both individual companies and the industry in general can ill-afford to lose these people, the special problems associated with the transition of a line employee to management must be addressed.

One of these problems involves the employee's own expectations. Often, the person wishing to be considered for promotion has an inaccurate perception of the management function and is merely fantasizing about more money, long lunch hours, better benefits, more authority, and status symbols like a private office. Be certain your candidates for promotion have a clear and realistic understanding of the job of manager. It's a career change and involves entirely different skills and responsibilities, many of which they may not want to assume.

A second problem in promoting from within is the apparent difficulty many existing managers have in selecting the proper candidates. They often promote the best worker on the incorrect assumption that someone who does the job well must also be able to manage people. However, the best food server isn't necessarily going to be the best restaurant manager. Unfortunately, promoting good employees into positions about which they know nothing seems to be the rule rather than the exception in hotels and restaurants. Some feel the hospitality industry epitomizes the "Peter Principle," according to which people are continually promoted until they reach a point where they can no longer perform well, and there they stay.[1]

A wrong choice can be costly both from the standpoint of training and from the damage done to the department. The company loses all the way around—it loses one of its best workers when it promotes the employee; it loses productivity in the department because of lower morale and higher turnover when the person performs poorly as a manager; and it loses everything it has invested in training the person. Furthermore, it will probably ultimately have to fire the unsuccessful manager, who may then choose to sue for wrongful dismissal.

The fact is, the skills required to be good at a line job are simply not the same skills that it takes to be a successful manager. Since line employees don't use supervisory skills—like leadership, discipline, and delegating—in doing their jobs, it's extremely difficult to identify potential managers from among their ranks.

Assessment   In spite of almost a century of scientific study, we still don't have a proven list of the traits of a successful manager. Looking at performance reviews isn't very helpful, since (as we've seen) just being good at a current job doesn't always make a person promotable.

More often, a variety of other factors must be considered. If a department has a particular problem, an attempt may be made to promote someone who has skill in that area. Choices may be limited to the candidates who'll be ready for promotion at the right time. One may have just bought a house and be unwilling to transfer. Another may have a sick spouse. Some may too recently have been moved into a position, while others have no back-ups to replace them if they're moved out. In some cases, selection is based on the candidate's need to pick up experience in a specific area as part of management's overall succession plan. This far-from-complete list begins to illustrate the complexity of the promotion process and the importance of having a company succession plan supported by an assessment center and career pathing. (Assessment centers and career pathing are discussed later in this chapter.)

An important step in the promotion process is the clear **paper trail**. Without adequate documentation of the reasons surrounding each promotion—made at the time of the promotion—it's virtually impossible to go back later and justify the decisions that were made.

Spotting Potential Managers. Although there are no foolproof methods of determining who will make a good manager, there are some observable characteristics which may help you recognize potential leaders. Good candidates should:

1. Be able to cope with unfamiliar situations, deal with problems impartially, and ask for help when it's needed.

2. Be able to act without having everything spelled out for them.

[1]Laurence J. Peter and Raymond Hull, *The Peter Principle* (New York: William Morrow & Company, Inc., 1969).

3. Be open-minded, tolerant, and unbiased.

4. Admit their mistakes and accept the consequences rather than trying to blame others.

5. Be good team players, tactful, and sensitive to others.

6. Be calm and competent, rather than moody and volatile.

7. Have the physical stamina for the job.

Look around your department. Don't overlook those who speak out or even complain frequently. Often, they have a strong interest in the department's success, the drive to make change happen, and extensive job knowledge—all qualities which might be indicative of leadership ability.

Ask around. Get the opinions of managers in different departments which interact with your staff. Ask your own supervisors. They have more knowledge of the people who report to them, and their ratings may be closer to the mark than yours.

Talk to other line employees, since their judgments may also be very accurate. Cooks know a lot about food servers, for example. Try asking your own employees, "If I were going away for two weeks, who do you think should run the department?" "Who would you go to for help in a tough situation?" or "Which person in the department is the best at handling people?" You may be surprised by how accurate and objective they can be.

Psychological testing can be useful, providing the assessor is well aware of the organizational environment and the norms of your specific industry and department. Unfortunately, the comparative profiles are sometimes averages for unrelated industries. A large hotel chain once began to assess all its general managers using manufacturing-oriented profiles and norms. The assessors rejected many of its top general managers as unsuitable until the profile was adjusted to conform to hotel industry norms.

Assessment Centers. The **assessment center program** is one of the most effective tools available to assist the employer in identifying employees with a high potential for success when promoted. In them, employees must complete a series of exercises which use skills needed in a managerial role. As they work their way through the exercises, they are watched by trained observers who record their competency in the different areas. A better indication is given of how the person will perform as a manager than on-the-job observation might provide.

Such centers can be set up and run by outside companies or developed and operated in-house. Either way, for maximum success, the skills measured must relate specifically to the company's needs. Exhibit 8.3 is an assessment center summary form used to assess candidates for supervisory positions.

Since an assessment center's results are more objective than those derived from on-the-job observation, employees feel that promotional decisions are fairer. You may also find it easier to justify your choices if later required to do so by the Equal Employment Opportunity Commission or other agencies. In addition, after going through such a program and realizing what is involved in the management role, some employees may decide they really don't want to become managers and may then choose to pursue professional skills enhancement instead.

At the end of an assessment center program, employees are given

Exhibit 8.3   Assessment Center Summary Form

Amway Grand Plaza Hotel
SUPERVISOR ASSESSMENT CENTER

Candidate_____

Supervisory
Position Sought_____

	Needs Development Less than required to perform at this time			Acceptable As required to perform at this time			Excellent More than required to perform at this time		
	1	2	3	4	5	6	7	8	9
Work Standards									
Stress Tolerance									
Interpersonal Skills									
Decisiveness									
Leadership									
Planning, Scheduling and Organization									
Cooperative Work									
Verbal Communications									
Problem Solving									

Ratings Guide

1: None of this skill was demonstrated; unable to perform as a Grand Plaza supervisor.
2–3: A little to some of this skill was demonstrated; less than required to perform as a Grand Plaza supervisor.
4–6: A barely satisfactory to highly acceptable amount of this skill was demonstrated; about the same as most Grand Plaza supervisors I've known.
7–8: A lot of this skill was demonstrated; more than most Grand Plaza Supervisors I've known.
9: A great deal of this skill was demonstrated; the best I could expect in any Grand Plaza supervisor.

NEEDS DEVELOPMENT ☐   ACCEPTABLE ☐

RECOMMENDATIONS:

feedback about what the assessors see as their strengths and weaknesses. Quite often, this is followed by a career pathing session in which the company makes recommendations about how they could improve their management skills.

Career Pathing   Personal growth and development and job satisfaction have become serious priorities for today's work force. Managers are dealing with more and more employees who want to transfer, be promoted, or change careers. Some have the abilities and some don't. In either case, managers need to handle their inquiries properly to keep workers motivated in their jobs, to provide them with meaningful assistance, and to help the company by developing people to their full potential.

A clear and important distinction has to be made between **career**

pathing (or career planning) and life planning. Life planning includes setting down long-term financial, family, religious, and other goals beyond the company's scope. Furthermore, when employees really don't know what they want to do in terms of career growth, it isn't the manager's place to decide for them. In that case, the best approach may be to refer the person to a professional career counselor.

In career pathing, the manager deals with employees who wish to move up or to another job within the organization. The employee usually takes the first step by going to his or her immediate supervisor, because most initial moves will take place within the same functional area. The employer's role is merely to provide information and guidance about company needs. Inquiries of this kind should never have any negative consequences and must be handled in a serious manner, since the employee is obviously concerned.

Not all employee requests are actually motivated by a desire to move, however. People often ask to transfer not because they want to do another job, but because of dissatisfaction with the current job. Frustrations over lack of recognition, shifts worked, co-workers, or rate of pay may lead them to the conclusion that a job change is needed.

Experienced managers know that true career success involves a sense of belonging to the organization, doing meaningful work, feeling good about oneself, having some control over one's environment, and growing to the extent of individual abilities—much of which can be accomplished within the existing job. Be sure your employees are recognized and know their work is important and appreciated.

When employees ask you for business advice, give it freely within the sphere of your own knowledge as a manager. You can suggest skills you believe would be helpful, outside reading, or cross-training. It's advisable to preface such advice and suggestions with the observation that these are, indeed, just opinions:

- "As I see it. . . ."
- "My feelings are. . . ."
- "I can only speak for my department (or our company). . . ."
- "This is out of my area of expertise; I can only discuss what I know about the different jobs."

When someone seeks to change to a position beyond their current abilities, you might suggest the person do some relevant reading and self-analysis. Many companies have literature on career choices in their libraries, as well as **self-analysis forms**. Such forms generally ask for the following information:

1. Types of work duties, hobbies, and activities employees enjoy doing the most.
2. Skills they have which aren't currently being used.
3. Their strongest skills.
4. Their weakest areas.
5. Types of jobs within the company that they'd like to do. Here, employees must define goals stating what they really want to do; later, these can be matched to the company's needs.

6. Skills needed for jobs they'd like to do. Employees can list skills they feel they need, and these can be supplemented by you, by the human resources department, or by other members of management.

7. How skills can be acquired. Again, the company's primary role is to provide information based on its own needs and job requirements. In this section of the analysis, you and the employee can agree on specific action steps and set target dates.

Exhibit 8.4 (a career inventory sheet) and Exhibit 8.5 (a career counseling session summary) show useful forms which serve a similar function. The process should be under the employee's control at all times. Any needed action steps are the responsibility of the employee, not the company.

It's also a good idea to contact the human resources department and the appropriate department head. If you have an employee who's interested in a position in another department, help the person learn more about the position by setting up an interview with the manager of that department. These interviews should be friendly and cooperative, since these are your current workers, usually highly-motivated and loyal. You don't want to de-motivate them during this process. Remember to give their inquiries treatment which is the same as or better than that which an outside applicant would receive.

The outcome of such an interview should include straightforward and honest feedback. Don't allow someone who is clearly unqualified to leave still clinging to false hopes. If the employee doesn't have the basic qualifications, the interviewing supervisor should make it plain, emphasizing the job requirements for that position rather than focusing on what may be wrong with the applicant. At the end of the meeting, the employee should have a realistic understanding of the training that will be required and how it can be accomplished. This will allow the employee to decide whether the results are worth the time and effort involved.

Any recommendations for seminars, cross-training, and so forth should be reviewed and approved by the immediate supervisor, the supervisor's manager, and the human resources department. Employee progress should then be tracked so the company has some idea of whether employees are following through, and whether they'll be ready should positions open. Following up also demonstrates the manager's interest and support.

Tuition Reimbursement

Continuing education is a necessity for any professional career. Some companies feel that all self development in order to get ahead is the individual's responsibility. Other companies see value in helping their employees gain further education. Whatever the decision, it's generally based on company philosophy, rather than on any sense of employer obligation.

Although company policies vary from a position of paying nothing for employee education to paying for everything, it is common today to have a **tuition reimbursement program** which provides employees an additional opportunity to supplement work experience with technical and professional education not available from within the company.

The tuition reimbursement budget should be carefully managed. Such programs are expensive and, if they are not controlled, they can quickly get out of hand and be difficult to bring back under control. Funds should be allocated to areas where training needs are greatest. Exhibit 8.6 is a sample tuition assistance application form.

Exhibit 8.4 Career Inventory Sheet

CAREER INVENTORY SHEET

Name _____ Date _____

Position _____ Hotel _____

Employment History (start with current position)

Date From	Date To	Position	Location	Salary
	present			
				Reason for Leaving

RADISSON / OTHER

Education	Name/Location	Major	Degree
College or University			
High School			
Vocational School			
Other/Courses			

What is your long term career goal? _____

What are your 3 to 5 year career objectives? _____

What interim positions do you think would aid you in reaching these goals? _____

Summarize your achievements, strengths, and special job related activities and interests. _____

In what areas do you feel you need additional development and what actions have you taken to achieve your goals? _____

Preferences or limitations on relocation: _____

cc: 2-RHC Personnel   1-Personnel Director   1-Employee

Courtesy of Radisson Hotel Corporation, Minneapolis, Minnesota.

If an employee is asked to take a course, the general policy is to reimburse all expenses in advance. However, if the person asks to take a course that's directly job-related, one common approach is for the employer to reimburse the cost of tuition, books, registration, and lab fees upon successful completion.

Exhibit 8.5   Career Counseling Session Summary

THIS WAY UP

Career Counseling Session Summary

Name _____   Position _____

Hotel _____   Date in position _____

Date of hire _____   Date of counseling session _____

What position is your 3 to 5 year goal? _____

I. Following are the six major skills for the position of _____

Your current rating on each of these skills uses this scale:

    4=Surpasses normal skill expectations   2=Meets most skill requirements
    3=Meets all necessary skill requirements   1=Needs development in skill area.

        Skill   Rating   Comments on Development

1. _____
2. _____
3. _____
4. _____
5. _____
6. _____

II. Following are the six key areas of technical knowledge for the position of _____
Your current rating uses the scale in section 1.

        Technical Knowledge   Rating   Comments on Development

1. _____
2. _____
3. _____
4. _____
5. _____
6. _____

III. Following are positions which contain experiences which may be helpful to achieving your career goal:

1. _____
2. _____
3. _____

IV. After reviewing resources to aid your career development, we agree on the following strategies and timeframe:

1. _____
2. _____
3. _____

Supervisor's signature _____   Employee's signature _____
cc: 1-Personnel Director   1-Employee

Courtesy of Radisson Hotel Corporation, Minneapolis, Minnesota.

When an employee wants to take a course that isn't directly job-related but is industry-related, companies frequently reimburse as much as half of the cost upon successful completion. However, many employers prefer to make this decision on an individual basis. For example, if a stockroom clerk

Exhibit 8.6   Tuition Assistance Application Form

DAYS INN   Tuition Assistance Application

Personal	INSTRUCTIONS: Your application for tuition assistance must be approved before you begin the classes. Fill out this form with a ball-point pen, pressing firmly. Have your department head sign the application, and send all copies to the Director of Personnel for final approval.

Name
FIRST   MIDDLE INITIAL   LAST

Address
STREET   CITY & STATE   ZIP

Job
TITLE   DEPARTMENT

EMPLOYMENT DATE   SOCIAL SECURITY NUMBER

School
NAME OF SCHOOL

Courses
1
COURSE TITLE FROM CATALOGUE   COURSE NUMBER

2
COURSE TITLE FROM CATALOGUE   COURSE NUMBER

Semester/Quarter
COURSE 1 BEGINS: _____   ENDS: _____
MONTH   DAY   YEAR   MONTH   DAY   YEAR

COURSE 2 BEGINS: _____   ENDS: _____
MONTH   DAY   YEAR   MONTH   DAY   YEAR

Tuition Cost $

Degree   Are these courses part of a degree requirement?   ☐ YES   ☐ NO

Which degree: _____

_____   ☐ GRADUATE   ☐ UNDERGRADUATE

Benefit to Job

Applicant's Signature
NAME   DATE
The courses listed   ☐ will   ☐ will not   help the applicant do a better job or achieve a reasonable promotion objective.

Department Head
SIGNATURE   DATE

Personnel Director
SIGNATURE   DATE
☐ APPROVED   ☐ DISAPPROVED

Accounting Only
AUDIT   EXT. OK.   FINAL APPROVAL   DATE
☐ Return check to applicant   ☐ OTHER _____

ACCOUNT NUMBER								AMOUNT					

Days Inns of America, Inc., 2751 Buford Highway, N.E., Atlanta, Georgia 30324

White-ER   Yellow-Employee   Pink-A/P

Courtesy of Days Inn of America, Inc., Atlanta, Georgia.

wants to take a bartending course, someone must determine whether the person has the other necessary qualifications to become a bartender and how badly more bartenders are needed.

Most employers don't reimburse someone who wants to pursue education for a career in an area outside the industry. Companies don't want to allocate funds to pay for people to train to leave them. Employees are simply advised that, because training funds are limited, they must be used in those areas in which needs are greatest.

There's normally an annual limit to the dollar amount of reimbursement, and the benefit is usually available only to full-time employees who have been with the company a required amount of time. The courses must be approved in writing in advance and be offered by a reputable school or company. If funds are available through other sources, such as the Veterans Administration or scholarships, the employer should direct the employee to these sources. If these other sources do not cover the entire expense, the employer will then often pay the difference.

As with seminars, it's customary for the employee to sign a statement agreeing to repay the company in full if he or she resigns before a certain time. Employees should be advised that reimbursed funds may be taxable.

Documentation of all education completed by an employee, whether under the tuition reimbursement program or at the individual's expense, should be placed in the personnel file.

Making Promotions Work

Once a decision has been made to promote from within, there are some steps that will significantly improve the newly promoted manager's chances for success.

If possible, the promoted manager should be transferred to a different department or even a different property—if not permanently, then at least during training. If the person stays in the same department, the first two weeks should be spent outside the department, going through an orientation similar to the one all other new managers receive. Time should also be spent in other relevant departments to develop a better understanding of the overall operation. For example, a housekeeper being promoted to floor supervisor should spend time in areas like the front desk and the laundry. In addition, this person should work other shifts, trail a current floor supervisor, spend time in the housekeeping department office, and learn the other functions that will be under his or her supervision.

Upon returning to the department in the new position, the promoted employee should have a different uniform, name tag, or other visible symbols of the change. Having different days off and working a different shift are also helpful if they can be arranged.

The new supervisor should be enrolled immediately in a formal supervisory development program that will improve the needed skills, such as delegating, discipline, assertiveness, and communications. If such programs aren't readily available, the company library should maintain some books and audio or video cassette tapes on these subjects. This kind of self-study program will need to be monitored closely, however, to ensure that it's completed properly.

As the new supervisor's manager, you play the key role and must be prepared to spend time with the person and to provide extra support during the adjustment. You must be sensitive to the fact that, in order for new supervisors to succeed, they'll have to be extremely responsive and make quick decisions on scheduling, changes to procedure, and guest problems. If they don't know exactly how much authority they have or don't get a show of complete support, they'll be afraid to make those decisions and their authority will be regarded as questionable. They and those who report to them may also quickly begin to feel that upper management isn't behind them.

During the training and installation of new supervisors, communicating some of the following attitudes about management may be helpful to new supervisors.

McDonald's 80-acre Hamburger University provides state-of-the-art training and career development to its managers, staff, and franchisees. Many courses even lead to college credit. (Courtesy of McDonald's Corporation, Oak Brook, Illinois)

- Don't be afraid to ask for help, even from line employees.

- Don't say, "I'll check with my boss." Instead, make a decision or say, "I don't know—I'll check on the information and get back to you." Then do it promptly.

- After making a decision, be assertive and firm. Don't vacillate. Even an incorrect decision is better than indecision.

- It's all right to make a mistake—everyone does. Be willing to admit the mistake and correct it. Honesty, dependability, and integrity are more important than perfection.

- Be consistent and avoid highs and lows of mood or temperament.

- When uncertain about how much authority to assume, it's generally better to overestimate than to underestimate.

- Be friendly without being friends. It's more important to be respected than to be liked.

- It's preferable not to go back to eating with other workers in the department. If it's unavoidable, talk about impersonal things like business, sports, or the weather rather than personal matters. (Upper management or trainers should even assign other members of management to have meals with the new supervisor, if necessary.)

- It's better to be too formal than too casual. You can "loosen up" later.

Newly promoted supervisors should be told what to expect. Most will face two enormous obstacles: the attitudes of their former co-workers and the attitudes they develop themselves. After about three months, fellow employees may begin to present difficulties. Many are envious because they didn't get the promotion. Others resent the authority of the new manager who was once their peer. They may view the person as having become insensitive, unfriendly, and uninterested in the needs of the workers, and as having deserted old friends. They may even deliberately resist the new supervisor's attempts to manage their work.

During transition periods, new managers are unsure where they belong. They no longer belong to their former group of friends and don't yet feel like a part of the management group. They may even have no one with whom they can eat comfortably. The majority of new supervisors who fail do so because they fall into one of two traps. They'll either let the power go to their heads and play executive roles, becoming excessively distant and authoritarian; or they'll go to the other extreme and try to prove they haven't let promotions go to their heads by just becoming "one of the gang" again. It may take as much as a year or two for someone to establish a new identity and complete the transition.

Nothing a company can do will force employees to respect and accept any new supervisor. Respect must be earned, and managers who practice "Do as I say, not as I do" management techniques won't be respected. They must be prepared to work harder than anyone else in the department and plan to work different shifts at times. They'll have to act as positive role models and motivating forces for their employees.

They must also earn the respect of fellow managers by knowing their own jobs and departments, learning how to forecast and set priorities, becoming familiar with the profit and loss statement, and learning how to work with upper management—including knowing the latter's goals and keeping them informed.

Management Trainees from Outside the Company

Even when its recruiting, management development, and promotion-from-within programs are working, a company may still need more sources for new managers. Many companies have developed special programs to help these **management trainees** bridge the gap between their schooling or other job experiences and the new work environment.

Internship Programs

Student internship programs are an excellent source of future managers and give a company a head start on its program for management trainees. Most graduates return to work for the companies where they've served their internships. Thus, companies not using internship programs may already have lost the majority of the best candidates by the time they get to the campuses to interview graduating seniors.

Participating in such programs offers a number of advantages. You have the opportunity to observe potential managers before you actually hire them. The student interns bring knowledge of the latest technology and research

Newly promoted supervisors can't earn the respect of their employees by playing executive roles.

data from the schools into your unit. Their enthusiasm for and commitment to the industry often have a strong positive impact on peer employees with whom they work. Their energy levels, questions, and activities all have a tendency to keep their supervisors challenged. Most of them must accomplish special projects during their internship programs and these projects can usually be assigned by the company. Special studies can be completed relatively inexpensively by using interns.

Perhaps the greatest advantage of participation in such programs is that it helps the schools do a better job of training people for our industry. Only when hospitality businesses provide support for and develop closer working relationships with the schools can we expect to produce enough graduates who will really meet our needs.

If you choose to use such a program, be prepared to make a good impression. Otherwise, the dissatisfied students may return to their campus and tell others to avoid your company.

While some companies use interns only to fill existing positions, others add a position to their payroll. Some will simply hold one position open year-round for interns and have it filled on a rotating basis.

Programs for Management Trainees

When recruiting candidates, don't oversell your training program. As we have already discussed, unrealistic expectations can have disastrous effects. This is especially true for high-potential employees. They have firm ideas about where they're going and what they expect to achieve when they get there, and they're willing to work and sacrifice for it. Many idealistic management trainees already believe they'll be general managers within three years; it doesn't take much additional encouragement to have them assuming they can do it in two. Comments like, "The sky's the limit around here," or

The lack of furnished short-term housing is the major problem facing internship programs. Some companies have responded by renting and sub-leasing apartments. Others, like Walt Disney World, have their own entire housing projects.
(Courtesy of Disney World, Lake Buena Vista, Florida ©1989 The Walt Disney Company)

"Once you get your foot in the door, you can go as far as you want," may quickly lead to exaggerated expectations.

Most management trainee programs are designed to help the average potential manager, but some rapidly growing companies have developed a second level of programs to advance the high-potential managerial candidates more quickly. This latter, referred to as a **fast-track program**, hasn't been a mainstay of management development, however, because only large organizations can afford the two-level system. Also, generally speaking, the fast-track individuals will get to the top quickly even without a second level of training programs. As with any program a company develops, the need must justify the cost.

Management training programs vary. Some have elaborate training manuals. In some places, everyone goes through the same program, regardless of background or interest. The program should be formal. The main consideration is to have someone who is totally accountable for its success. This person should have regular meetings with the trainee and make sure that what was promised at the time of hire is actually delivered.

Recent graduates are accustomed to more feedback and structure than the business world offers. The person who oversees management training should take the time to provide these things. One of the biggest complaints management trainees have is that they feel lost in the company. Regular progress reviews with upper management can help alleviate this problem.

The department heads that trainees work under play a key role in the success of the program, so upper management should make sure they are the best department heads. Some managers just aren't good trainers, and forcing trainees on them is self-defeating.

Exhibit 8.7 is a sample training schedule for a management trainee specializing in the rooms division.

On-the-Job Training

When training is taking place in a specific department, the immediate supervisor is the best person to coordinate the on-the-job training. The supervisor will know more about it than anyone else, and can provide immediate feedback and effective rewards for learning.

The same coaching techniques used for a line employee will work when providing a management trainee with hands-on training. However, you should involve management trainees more in the management process. Include them in decision-making. Ask them to make recommendations concerning a problem, or consult them before taking action. Have trainees represent you at various meetings such as budgetary or staff meetings, sit in on hiring or disciplinary interviews, do the scheduling, or handle other management problems as they arise.

Key Terms

assessment center program
career pathing
fast-track program
feeder jobs
management trainee

paper trail
self-analysis form
suspense file
tuition reimbursement program

Exhibit 8.7   Sample Management Training Flowchart

HYATT HOTELS CORPORATION   HYATTRAIN

MANAGEMENT TRAINING FLOWCHART

NAME ___Jane Doe___   PROPERTY ___Cambridge___ DATE ___April 10, 19XX___

Refer to Personnel Policy Manual, section 504.IV.C. for instructions and requirements for the flowchart.

DEPARTMENT	TIME PERIOD	DATES
ORIENTATION PHASE	3 months	
FOOD & BEVERAGE		
Banquets/Catering	1 week	
Restaurant	2 weeks	
Stewarding	1 week	
ROOMS		
Front Office	2 weeks	
Housekeeping	1 week	
Reservations	1 week	
SUPPORT		
Sales & Marketing	1 week	
Human Resources	1 week	
Accounting	1 week	
CONCENTRATION PHASE		
ROOMS		
Front Office	2 weeks	
Housekeeping	4 weeks	
Reservations	2 weeks	
Guest Services	2 weeks	
Hotel Assistant Manager	2 weeks	

AREA OF CONCENTRATION

TRAINEE _____   PERSONNEL DIRECTOR _____

Courtesy of Hyatt Hotels Corporation, Chicago, Illinois.

Discussion Questions

1. How does succession planning differ from career pathing?

2. If an employee wishes to attend an outside seminar at company expense,

what information should the employee's supervisor obtain about the seminar?

3. Why isn't the best employee in one position always the best candidate for promotion?

4. What are some of the characteristics that could indicate management potential in an employee?

5. What are some of the problems encountered when an employee is promoted from within the company? What steps can be taken to minimize the problems?

6. What are the benefits for an employer in having an internship program? For the student?

9 Motivation and Communications

The success of managers and their companies is determined by the work their employees do. Since motivated employees are more productive, managers have a clear interest in finding out what motivates them. The only way to learn what motivates employees, and then to motivate them, is to communicate with them. Managers need to appreciate the differences among people, to see that what motivates one employee may not motivate another.

In the past, authoritarian management styles concentrated on downward communication and relied on the worker's insecurity and the manager's power for motivation. Today, the work force frequently no longer accepts this arrangement. Workers want satisfying jobs. They want to be involved, to have their opinions heard and respected. Although downward communication clearly remains important, companies which also have effective upward communication benefit in at least two ways: they make better use of all of the resources available to them, and their employees see that management values their thoughts.

Employees who feel appreciated are generally happier and likelier to be motivated. They are more willing to go out of their way to help others. While happy workers aren't *necessarily* more productive, production improvements certainly won't be made in an atmosphere of low morale.

Although they are related, an important distinction must be made between morale and motivation. Employee activities aimed at raising morale—such as picnics, ball teams, or Christmas parties—aren't motivators in and of themselves and hold no promise of improved production. Motivation is the result of a person's own drive to satisfy personal needs, wishes, and desires. It is an aspect of one's total outlook and is based on many things— experiences, environment, wants, needs, feelings, and perceptions.

Workers need to be able to see how they can best satisfy their own needs while achieving the objectives of the entire organization. This integration of purpose is crucial to motivation. The manager's role is to show employees how meeting the company's goals is the best way to realize their own goals, and then to provide the environment in which that is possible. To do so, the manager must also understand what each employee's needs and goals are. The managers who increase productivity will be those who communicate with and know each worker personally—his or her family, life goals, and needs. Successful managers recognize and appreciate individual differences while being able to make each worker an integral part of the team.

Attending to the Basics

Some aspects of the workplace are not effective motivators in themselves, but they're so basic to worker performance that they have a strong negative impact on morale and motivation if they're neglected by managers. The most significant of these factors are security, salary, working conditions, and status. These factors must be handled properly before worker motivation can be addressed.

Security

Most companies offer the general security of insurance benefits, retirement programs, and savings plans. Still, some workplaces cause employees to feel insecure, anxious, and stressed. Workers who are worried about whether they'll have jobs next week aren't likely to be very responsive to employee participation programs.

Fear of job loss is still a primary source of distress for many workers. In some ways, federal and state governments have alleviated this fear. The current trend in legislation is a shift away from **employment at will** (the philosophy that the employer can terminate an employee at any time for any reason; see Chapter 11). In addition, responsive employers are providing published company policies of appropriate and consistent discipline and **alternative dispute resolution committees** (groups of line and management employees who review disputes over employment issues). Some employers even use employment contracts.

Arbitrary, inconsistent, unpredictable, or incompetent supervision is another cause of insecurity and anxiety in the workplace. A chaotic environment results when workers don't know where they stand or what the company's goals are. Employees need boundaries within which to operate and must have confidence that they'll be treated fairly. Problems with company policies or administrative practices should be handled through a fair and accessible grievance procedure. In addition, workers want to know how they're doing, and managers should tell them.

Salary

Wages must first be perceived as internally fair; that is, consistent and equitable within the organization. They should also be considered comparable within the community and the industry in general.

Payday should be one of the happiest days of the week. Payroll's first priority is to get paychecks processed correctly and delivered to workers on time in a friendly manner. Few managers realize how many paychecks either must be reissued because of mistakes or are delayed because of improper procedures. If an employee's paycheck can't be found or if employees have to wait in line for their checks, the payroll system is not operating as it should.

In many companies, the managers hand out paychecks to their employees. This gives managers an opportunity to talk to employees and thank them for a job well done.

Working Conditions

Low productivity is often misdiagnosed as a motivational problem. In fact, working conditions can often be a cause of low productivity. Workers need adequate equipment, space, heating, lighting, and ventilation. Noise should be kept to a minimum (although the right type of music may have a positive effect, particularly in break areas or places associated with highly repetitive jobs, such as the dish room).

Color also has a significant impact on the work environment. Management may spend thousands of dollars to determine the right colors for a

Original art and prints can be borrowed or rented for a nominal charge from many local libraries and museums to enhance the environment of the employee cafeteria and other break areas.

dining room, in which guests dine for perhaps an hour. Unfortunately, management may completely fail to consider color when designing the employees' cafeteria, locker room, or support areas, where employees spend forty hours a week.

Art may also improve the working conditions. In some cases, art not only enhances the environment, but also has a positive effect through the power of suggestion. A poster of a sleeping baby or a quiet forest in the dishwashing area may remind employees to help reduce noise.

Restrooms and lockers should be clean, secure, and well-maintained. If you're providing employees with clothing to wear, employees should look and feel comfortable in their uniforms.

In high-stress industries, it's important that employees have a pleasant, relaxing break area. If your company has an employee cafeteria, it should have its own name. The cafeteria service attendants should be pleasant. The dining area should be clean and relaxing. The cafeteria should offer a variety of foods which are nutritional, presented well, and served at the proper temperatures. The food provided should be the same for line employees as for managers. Managers, including top executives, should be expected to eat at the cafeteria except when entertaining. If it's not good enough for managers, it shouldn't be considered good enough for line employees.

Status   Today's workers believe that everyone deserves equal treatment. Most employees can readily accept the idea of higher pay for positions of more responsibility or expertise. However, they want to see the same rules applied to everyone. If line employees are required to wear name tags, they feel that managers should wear them also. They don't think top managers should get bonuses when line workers are getting laid off.

Many companies today are eliminating the typical status symbols of the past, such as stuffy titles, special parking areas, separate dining rooms or meal privileges, different entrances, or special benefits. Many managers encourage employees to address them by their first names. Some employers are even getting rid of timeclocks to avoid sending the message that hourly employees can't be trusted or must be treated as second-class. Their idea is to remove the unnecessary trappings that set up artificial barriers and distinctions between line and management employees. In the future, these types of distinctions may have to be minimized if genuine employee involvement and motivation are to take place.

Creating a Positive Motivational Environment

As previously stated, the most productive work environment is one which permits employees to find their own motivation—to fulfill their own goals and needs while serving the organization's best interests. The employer should provide an environment of acceptance, confidence, mutual trust, and openness toward employees. At the same time, the company should have an unshakable set of values within which employees can operate.

Workers should be given some influence over the elements affecting them and their work. This self-direction shouldn't be confused with permissiveness or indulgence. Being too "soft" and giving workers everything they want can create as many problems as being autocratic; employees start to expect more and more while giving less and less, and still job dissatisfaction grows.

People need to feel that they've earned what they've gained in order to achieve self-esteem. Each person's self-esteem is a prerequisite for a relationship of mutual respect and esteem between worker and manager. Without genuine self-worth, mutual respect, and responsibility, there can be no arena for motivated improvement.

Elements of a positive motivational environment include:

- Achievement
- Recognition
- The work itself
- Responsibility
- Growth and advancement

Achievement
People like to achieve goals, to keep busy, to face challenges, to solve problems, and to do so with high standards. Nothing reduces motivation more quickly than a manager who is indifferent to quality or who has low standards.

Employees can find achievement in simple things, such as trying to sell ten gallons of fresh orange juice before ten o'clock in the morning. To be motivated, people need to be excited, and building a business is something people can get excited about. Contests like "most improved sales figures" help keep your employees motivated. While it may be harder for employees to get excited about controlling costs, if that is what your facility needs to do, make it more interesting with a campaign or contest. If the environment is right, the achievement will be its own reward.

WESTIN
HOTELS & RESORTS

PREMIER
PERFORMERS

WEEK OF_____

I nominate

_____

for Front of House Employee ☐

for Back of House Employee ☐

Observed Performance

_____

_____

_____

Employee Department

_____

Manager Signature

6201-5   Printed in U S A

1988 EMPLOYEE OF THE WEEK NOMINATION FORM

GUEST COMMENT CARD

7890-7

WESTIN
HOTELS & RESORTS

PREMIER
PERFORMERS
EMPLOYEE RECOGNITION PROGRAM

I would like to recognize:

_____
(Name of Employee)

_____
(Employee Department)

for extending outstanding service to me during my stay
at this Westin Hotel.

Nominate the All-Star Employee
and Win $100!

Thank you for participating in our Premier Performers
Employee Recognition Program. In the event that the employee you nominated becomes a Premier Performers
All-Star for the most outstanding achievements, you will
receive a check from Westin for $100!

Just fill out this card and return it to the front desk, and you
may be $100 richer in September!

_____
(Guest Signature)

Guest Name (Please Print)   Date of Stay

_____

Guest Address

_____

Thank you

PRINTED IN U.S.A.

Westin's Premier Performers employee incentive program rewards employees for outstanding service to guests and fellow employees. The program includes Employee of the Week selections, based on nominations from supervisors, and the distribution of Premier Dollars (redeemable for awards), based in part on guest comment cards. (Courtesy of Westin Hotels and Resorts, Seattle, Washington)

Recognition
While respect from others isn't valued unless it's deserved, appropriate recognition and appreciation can certainly contribute to confidence and a sense of competence. Recognition can be the easiest, cheapest, and fastest way to improve production, yet time after time, managers hold it back. They seem to be reluctant to say, "Thank you." Simply praising someone privately when you notice the person doing something right may be one of the best motivators.

For recognition to be effective as a motivator, it must be:

• Deserved
• Prompt

- Perceived as fair to all employees

- Appropriate for the effort expended

- Attainable

A reward will motivate only if employees know about it, perceive it as a reward, and want it. To motivate employees, the reward must be appropriate and worth the effort involved; the payoff must be seen as fair. If the "Employee of the Month" selection is viewed as a political appointment, it won't serve as a motivating program.

No one reward program will be effective for every company. A company should first determine its values and the behaviors it wishes to encourage in employees, and then set up appropriate recognition programs. They should have a cost-to-value relationship and make financial sense for each specific operation. For example:

- If a company is opening units across the country, it could make heroes out of those who have been transferred six times in six years by giving them special awards.

- If a company is an independent and its roots are in one area, it may want to encourage employees to take an active role in the community by offering special community service awards.

- If a company needs to emphasize teamwork, it could reward group efforts and achievements by giving prizes, bonuses, or time off.

- If a company has an absenteeism problem, a program to recognize good attendance makes sense.

- If a company has a turnover problem, a length-of-service award pin for five years' service may come too late. The company may want to provide a salary increase after three months, additional benefits after six months, and so on.

A seasonal operation or one in which most employees work part-time may need a different kind of program.

Other areas that companies choose to acknowledge include retirement, suggestions, safety, sales, production, training, customer service, and quality. The types of recognition used include awards, bonuses, gifts, plaques, pins, certificates, buttons, accessory jewelry, letters to the home on anniversary dates, notes on the bulletin board, articles in the in-house newspaper, memos, news releases to hometown papers or trade magazines, paid advertisements in local newspapers, a free room or dinner, or free groceries or parking for a given length of time.

A cash award is always a welcome form of recognition, but its impact is short-lived. On the other hand, allowing the employee to select an item from a gift catalog offers excitement when the catalog is received, perks the interest of co-workers, and involves the family in the selection process. Later, when the gift arrives, the employee and family are motivated again, and the gift serves as a lasting reminder.

Most companies have some form of program which designates at least one employee per month who has done an exceptional job in a given category. If a company wants to emphasize risk-taking and going outside the job

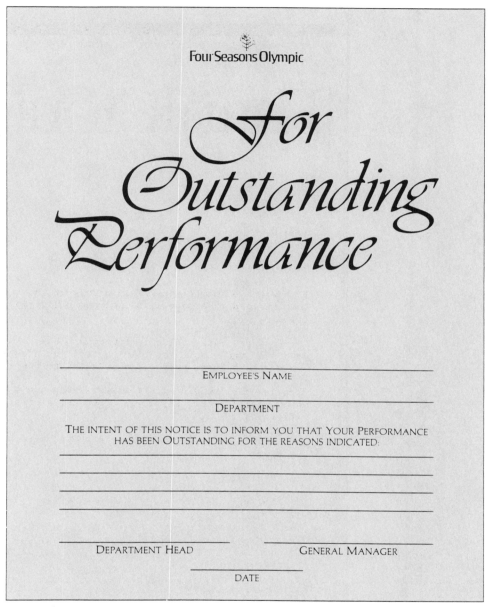

A well designed certificate is a popular and effective way to recognize employee achievements. (Courtesy of Four Seasons Olympic Hotel, Seattle, Washington)

description to help a guest or co-worker, then these criteria should be used to select the employee-of-the-month.

One employee per month may be adequate for a small operation, but may not be enough if your operation has several hundred employees. In this case, management may consider recognizing a team of employees from different departments. This allows employees from different departments to meet, reinforces the values of teamwork, and spreads recognition around.

Many managers miss the point behind recognition awards. They think that such awards should be given only to someone who is perfect, and that to

Amway Grand Plaza Hotel · Pearl at Monroe, Grand Rapids, MI 49503

Thank You!

March 3, 19XX

John Doe
Bentham's Restaurant

Dear John:

I thought you might appreciate a copy of the attached guest
comment card. We have also included a copy in your personnel
file.

When a guest makes the effort during a busy schedule to remember
your name and then takes time to fill out a comment card, it is
one of the highest personal awards in the hospitality industry.

Through your individual effort you have made a lasting impression
on another person. As you can see, extra effort makes the
difference.

Keep up the great work! We are proud to have people like you on
our team.

Congratulations!

Dave Wheelhouse

Dave Wheelhouse
Director of Human Resources

Attachment

cc: Department Head
     Personnel File

A note on special "Thank You" stationery is a nice way for a manager to show appreciation to good employees.

do otherwise would be lowering the standards. These managers lose sight of
the fact that the purpose of recognition is to encourage people to do better,
not to acknowledge perfection.

If recognition is to serve as a motivator, it must be given for achievements that most of your workers believe are within reach. Such a program
might call for you to rank all of your employees in each job category and
then give special attention to the top two or three in each category. Employees don't have to be doing everything perfectly to be recognized. You can still

recognize the things they're doing well, the ways in which they help others, or the improvements they've made. You might want to emphasize an area of work that's difficult or unpleasant for many.

A recognition program should bring attention to all of the people who keep the place going. It should, therefore, include employees from every shift and department. Another mistake that managers make in using recognition programs is to select only the people they see. Thus, the awards list ends up heavily out of balance with office staff, people from the accounting and sales departments, or day-shift employees. To help avoid this tendency, allow line employees to make some of the nominations. This approach also minimizes the questionable practice of managers selecting each other's assistants or secretaries as favors.

Workers need to know that they're doing useful work and doing it well, and that they have the respect of their co-workers. The goal of your recognition program should be to meet this need. Much of the energy of the program comes from emotions. When people are excited about work and committed to a goal, their motivation can be extremely high.

The Work Itself

Job satisfaction is the best predictor of job longevity and one of the best guarantees of performance. Among the greatest sources of job satisfaction is the knowledge that the job is meaningful, that it serves a purpose in meeting the goals of the organization.

In some areas or departments, it may be necessary to do some restructuring or redefinition of jobs to give each position an identity and a sense of purpose. Try breaking down a department of a hundred cooks and food preparers, for instance, so that each small group works for one of the restaurants. This gives each worker a special identity as one of a few. Workers can identify with the goals of the restaurant team, rather than merely feeling like one of many people who do the same thing all day.

Instead of giving each worker in the dishwashing area one specialized task to perform repeatedly, teach everyone all the steps and let them move around. Pay could be based on how many jobs a person can do, rather than on how many units of work are produced.

Sometimes, completely eliminating the monotony or unpleasantness from a job isn't possible. In those cases, compensation, working conditions, and work group relationships may take on greater significance. More recognition may be needed, with emphasis on the sense of personal achievement and contribution to the team effort.

Responsibility

People won't commit themselves if they're unable to contribute. They want to be involved and have a voice in what affects them. They need to know what they can do to improve productivity.

Regardless of the nature of the work, every employee should expect to be held personally accountable for the work he or she does. Employees who deal with the public should wear name tags and give their names when they answer the telephone. When a maintenance person makes a guestroom repair or a housekeeper cleans the room, he or she could leave a signed card.

When delegating work or decision-making responsibilities to workers, be supportive and positive. Communicate clearly what responsibility you're delegating, and indicate exactly what results you expect. You can often express your expectations in terms of the company's goals and values. Give the employee the necessary authority, and be sure that everyone else

The *Yes I Can!* Training Program Structure

The Training Program consists of eight units of instruction and a graduation. Units are:

Unit 1 **Understanding *Yes I Can!*—**Explains what *Yes I Can!* stands for and the Radisson Hotel Corporation's commitment to it. At the end of the unit, employees are asked to make their own commitment to service.

Unit 2 **Understanding Quality Service—**Describes what service is, what factors make up quality service, and how to measure quality service. The unit places heavy emphasis on *value-added* service.

Unit 3 **Understanding Guests—**Explores the importance of peoples' emotions in their buying decisions. Employees examine the kinds of treatment guests do and do not like. They also look at reasons we don't always treat guests like we know we should.

Unit 4 **Understanding Guests' Expectations & Your Role in Meeting Them—**Points out that all guests bring expectations with them. The unit also discusses how guests' expectations are formed. Employees learn that we must surpass guests' expectations to achieve a competitive advantage in the marketplace.

Unit 5 **Understanding Yourself—**Looks at how employees, as individuals, benefit when they provide quality service. Also discusses ways each of us can provide better service and increase job satisfaction by injecting our personalities into our work.

Unit 6 **Understanding the Team: Your Supporting Cast—**Helps employees identify co-workers who can assist them in serving guests. Explores when team members should ask for help and when they should offer it.

Unit 7 **The "Right Stuff" of Service—**Introduces communication skills: observing non-verbal behavior, speaking, and listening as important customer relations skills. Also discusses the knowledge and attitudes of service professionals.

Unit 8 **Dealing with Difficult Situations—**Offers specific steps for effective handling of complaints and other difficult service situations. Actions to avoid during difficult situations and methods of dealing with job stress are also addressed.

Radisson's "Yes I Can" training program, outlined above, is a unique combination of training and motivation to make guest service every employee's first priority. (Courtesy of Radisson Hotel Corporation, Minneapolis, Minnesota)

involved—including other supervisors—knows about the person's additional responsibility and authority. Offer support and feedback. Be available to give advice if asked, but don't permit the employee to delegate the work or decision back to you.

Participative management involves seeking and, when appropriate, using the employees' input in decisions that affect their work. For instance, a manager might break the department down into self-management teams of eight to twelve people, teach them how to measure their own performance, and let them get help from other workers when they need it. A self-management team should be given well-defined objectives and the resources and authority to accomplish those objectives. Participative management will not succeed without the support of all levels of management. There must be a commitment to allocate the people and resources to implement and maintain the program.

If participative management is used merely in an attempt to manipulate people into thinking they're doing something important, it will be more destructive than useful. If management isn't ready to let workers control aspects of their jobs, such a program should not be introduced.

Employees often assume more responsibility by participating in other programs, such as quality circles, problem-solving task forces, and safety committees. These programs are discussed later in this chapter.

Of course, not every employee wants more responsibility. Nevertheless, pride in a good job should always be a standard. You can insist that each person accept responsibility for doing his or her own job well.

Growth and Advancement

Identify the high achievers in your department and keep them challenged with new opportunities for growth and advancement. If you don't, you may lose them.

However, being promoted is only one of the ways in which a person can grow and advance on the job. Not everyone wants to be the general manager. If the only motivator you're using is possible promotion, you're simply not going to motivate everyone.

Don't assume that what motivates you will motivate your employees. Some people don't want **job enrichment**; they're happy with routine. Some don't want to do the work of a manager, but would like to learn more about their current jobs. Others would like to learn another job, even though no promotion or pay increase is involved. Get to know employees, focusing on their needs and interests. Know how to place them in the right jobs and determine how they can be integrated into the company's goals.

Special Considerations for Middle Managers

As top managers address worker dissatisfaction and attempt to create an environment that encourages improved productivity, they should keep in mind that their middle managers have needs as well. The unhappy manager is very likely to have an unhappy staff. The manager who doesn't get praise won't give it either. Awards and recognition programs should be scheduled for managers as well as line employees.

Some companies are responding to middle managers' needs through better management job design, shifting their middle managers' emphasis away from long-range planning and toward implementation. Companies are trying to get their middle managers to spend more time on the floor and less in the office filling out forms for accountants and analysts. Promotions and evaluations are being based less on paperwork and reports, and more on action, implementation, and quality of supervision.

Business Communication

To find out whether an organization is communicating well, ask the top executives what the priorities are, then ask the middle managers, then the line employees. See how well their answers coincide. As an alternative, try sitting in the employee cafeteria during the third shift and listening to employees' distorted views of the meeting held earlier in the day. You may be quite surprised at how poorly a company communicates facts, priorities, and values. Numerous barriers to effective communication must frequently be overcome (see Exhibit 9.1).

Exhibit 9.2 presents the results of a survey which indicates another aspect of poor communication—there is quite a difference between where employees actually get their information and where they would prefer to get it.

Business communication may be formal—that is, planned and administered by the employer—or informal. It generally falls into three categories:

Exhibit 9.1   Barriers to Effective Communication

- The speaker assumes knowledge the listener doesn't have.

- The message is incomplete or ambiguous.

- Some of the words used can have more than one meaning.

- The attitude of the speaker or listener (or both) is one of superiority, distrust, or defensiveness.

- The listener's expectations, assumptions, or past experiences distort the message.

- The listener listens selectively, hearing only what he or she wants to hear and believe.

- The listener may be uninterested, inattentive, or possess poor listening habits.

1. **Downward communication** refers to information traveling from higher levels of the organization to lower levels.

2. **Upward communication** refers to information traveling from lower levels of the organization to higher levels.

3. **Lateral communication** refers to information traveling among all sectors of a company.

Communication between various levels of management and employees can be visualized as a pyramid of interlocking rings or links. The line employee is linked to the department head via the supervisor; the supervisor is linked to the division head through the department head; and so on. At the same time, peers in different divisions should be linked to each other. All levels must be considered when planning business communication.

Inadequate communication inhibits cooperation and coordination, and fuels the rumor mill. On the other hand, excessive communication can waste time and money. Many companies are guilty of over- or under-communicating simply because the communication program hasn't been carefully considered. An ad hoc committee or project team, including supervisors, secretaries, and managers, might be a good place to begin to plan and control the dissemination of information. Each form of communication should have a specific purpose and detailed parameters, and its cost should be justified.

All forms of communication used within an organization should be coordinated to avoid confusion and duplication. Instead of several people sending separate memos for each activity, for example, the executive secretary might be able to send out one memo for the coming week. This memo could list the time and place of division meetings, staff meetings, orientation meetings, and other key events. It could also indicate which managers are on vacation. This type of memo would reduce paperwork and secretarial time, and would inform managers about the availability of others with whom they need to talk.

Exhibit 9.2 Actual and Preferred Sources of Information for Employees

Current Actual Sources (Percentages indicate the number of employees who agreed that this was a major source of information)		Preferred Sources (Percentages indicate the number of employees who agreed that this was a major preferred source of information)	
Rank Source		**Rank Source**	
1. Immediate supervisor	59.7%	1. Immediate supervisor	92.3%
2. Grapevine	40.4%	2. Small group meetings	63.0%
3. Small group meetings	33.1%	3. Top executives	55.5%
4. Bulletin boards	30.1%	4. Annual business report to employees	45.8%
5. Employee handbook and other booklets	26.6%	5. Employee handbook and other booklets	41.2%
6. Regular general employee publication	21.2%	6. Orientation program	41.1%
7. Regular local employee publication	19.2%	7. Regular local employee publication	40.4%
8. Annual business report to employees	16.8%	8. Regular general employee publication	38.5%
9. Mass meetings	16.6%	9. Bulletin boards	37.1%
10. Top executives	13.3%	10. Upward communication programs	33.8%
11. Orientation program	12.9%	11. Mass meetings	30.3%
12. Union	12.3%	12. Audio-visual programs	23.2%
13. Mass media	10.5%	13. Union	20.4%
14. Audio-visual programs	9.3%	14. Grapevine	10.5%
15. Upward communication programs	9.1%	15. Mass media	8.8%

Source: International Association of Business Communicators/Towers, Perrin, Forster & Crosby Management Consultants, *Employee Views of Communication*.

Meetings   Regular informational meetings may include 5-minute pre-meal conferences, weekly department head meetings, and monthly departmental meetings. Such meetings should be scheduled for the same time and place to allow attenders to plan for and schedule around these regular meetings.

For the weekly department head meeting, the general manager should include as many levels of management within the organization as possible, particularly line supervisors. Line supervisors are a crucial link in management's communication to line employees. They will have to implement the decisions and be able to explain them.

Before planning other kinds of meetings (for instance, problem-solving and decision-making sessions), be sure you really need them. Meetings are time-consuming and expensive, and they aren't always the best way to make a decision. If a meeting is needed, keep attendance under a dozen people when possible.

For any meeting you're running, keep the following suggestions in mind:

1. Carefully select who must attend—those who need to be informed, to give input, or to be involved in some other way.

2. Provide an agenda and notify attenders well in advance of the purpose, expected results, beginning and ending times, and place.

3. Don't schedule the meeting at a time that conflicts with business or other important matters. Attenders won't be able to give their full attention.

4. Be organized to avoid wasting time in the meeting.

Incomplete communication is a major cause of poor guest service.

5.   Start on time. Waiting 5 minutes only encourages lateness and penalizes those who arrived on time. It also wastes the time of the people who are there. When a group of 30 has to wait 10 minutes, your company has lost the equivalent of 5 employee hours.

6.   Stick to the agenda. It's fine to encourage discussion, but don't let the meeting get sidetracked. For instance, you shouldn't permit two people to carry on a discussion that doesn't affect the whole group.

7.   Summarize and set timetables for follow-up action.

8.   End on a positive note and on time.

9.   If recorded minutes were needed, they should be prepared within 24 hours.

The All-Employee Meeting

The employer may get as many employees as possible together three to six times a year for an all-employee meeting. The all-employee meeting helps the employer to hold teams together and to renew employee commitment to company goals. These meetings usually cover general topics, such as the status of business and the competition, new developments, and changes. Sometimes, they cover short-term campaigns, such as controlling costs, suggestive selling contests, or a United Way drive. Besides communicating important information, all-employee meetings can be light-hearted and entertaining, with a format much like a pep rally.

Downward Communication

Downward communication is from higher levels of the organization to lower levels. Channels of communication chiefly used by managers for downward communication include memoranda, policy manuals, employee handbooks, newsletters, magazines, annual employee reports, paycheck stuffers, table tents for the employee cafeteria, posters, and bulletin boards. The list is virtually endless.

Each item issued should have a specific purpose. Write clearly and concisely, using language appropriate for the audience. Keep words to a minimum, sentences simple, and paragraphs short. A policy statement will have more impact if it is worded in the active voice ("Report all accidents to your supervisor immediately") instead of the passive voice ("All accidents should be reported immediately").

The Employee Handbook

The employee handbook is the most important employee document. In many states, it's regarded as a contract in the absence of a formal one. It should be updated yearly and reviewed by an employment law attorney before each printing.

In spite of its weighty legal implications, the handbook should be kept under 16 pages and written in a language suitable for its readers. Its main purpose should be to communicate with employees. Far too often, it's written in language which suggests that its main purpose is as a legal document designed to protect the company. If it's too long and complicated, it will serve no purpose, since no one will read it anyway. If a company needs more than 16 pages, it should use separate flyers for topics like insurance coverage and tuition reimbursement programs.

Special Notices

Paycheck stuffers can be effective if used with restraint. Regularly attaching memos to paychecks will guarantee that none of them will ever be read. They should involve no more than a short, simple message that can be read at a glance.

Important notices can also be mailed to the employee's home. Items mailed to the home two or three times a year get a significant amount of attention and involve the rest of the family.

Employee Publications

Companies large enough to have a human resources department often produce a variety of employee publications—for example, newsletters. The human resources department usually handles these publications.

All employee publications should maintain a central theme that is part of the organizational culture and is associated with the mission, image, or location of your property. A facility on a ranch in the Southwest, for example, might employ a western theme and use headings like "The Round-Up" or "Bunkhouse Chatter."

Adopting a mascot which supports this theme can also get attention and improve the effectiveness of downward communication. A locker room sign showing a cowboy sweeping off a cabin porch and saying, "Pardner, let's all help keep our bunkhouse clean," would earn more attention and cooperation than a sign saying, "NOTICE: Keep Locker Room Clean. (Signed) The Management." The mascot can become management's goodwill ambassador, acting as an informal spokesperson in many sensitive areas.

A human resources department shouldn't continue publishing anything that's not being read. If it is unsure whether a publication is actually hitting the mark, it should conduct a survey asking employees how many times they've read the publication, if they read it from cover to cover, and if they remember the features in the last two issues. Did they take the latest copy

The Amway Grand Plaza Hotel's employee handbook, "On with the Show," helps to carry out the show business theme used in the employee cafeteria and other employee publications. (Courtesy of Amway Grand Plaza Hotel, Grand Rapids, Michigan)

home, pass it along to someone else, or throw it away? The department should also find out what features the employees would like to see; after all, an employee communication tool should have employee input.

Newsletters and Magazines. Employee newsletters and magazines are in-house publications that often fail to properly communicate the information needed at the line level. If such publications are to be successful, they must involve input from more than one person. Representatives from all levels and every department should pass along information for possible inclusion.

In-house publications often fall prey to certain standard cliches used issue after issue, such as the same regular columns or the same tedious format. Stock items like the general manager's letter, birthdays, guests who stayed in the hotel, and recent promotions all have value. If that's all there is to write about, however, people may stop reading. Exhibit 9.3 is an example of the successful formula Disney uses for its weekly employee newsletter, *Eyes and Ears*.

The people in charge of these publications should add variety by using different paper colors, changing captions and artwork with each issue, having different managers write the "manager's message" on a revolving basis, and/or including feature articles about employees' special achievements off the job. If there's something to say, they should say it; if there isn't, they shouldn't try to invent something. Also, the layout should be designed with a purpose in mind. If employee recognition is one of the reasons for the

Exhibit 9.3 Disney Newsletter Masthead and Formula

A Weekly Newsletter Formula

FORMULA INGREDIENTS:

Communicating and reinforcing the Disney corporate culture through. . .
- —Historical perspectives
    - Stories on past achievements
- —Current success stories
    - Recent outstanding gains
- —Future plans
    - Visions, artists' renderings, projections

Providing knowledge to cast members that will help them perform their jobs, answer guest questions, and be Disney PR representatives through. . .
- —Current company news
    - Special events
    - Progress toward company goals, projects
    - Organizational updates, changes
    - Operational notes
    - Information on new guest services, products

Showing appreciation and recognition through. . .
- —Individual achievements within the company
- —Individual achievements outside the company
- —Guest letters
- —"It Takes People" Employee Profiles
- —Retirement honorees
- —Employee roles in current news

Informing cast members of benefits and services through. . .
- —Cast Activities announcements
- —Discounts, special offers
- —Cast member want ads

Courtesy of Walt Disney World, Lake Buena Vista, Florida.

magazine, for example, every employee's name should be underlined or printed in bold letters.

If the publication is to be timely and informative, it will probably have to be issued on a frequent basis; no one wants to read yesterday's newspaper. The items in a quarterly newsletter, for instance, could hardly be regarded as news. Information about such events as birthdays or promotions would be out of place in a quarterly publication; feature stories would be more appropriate. If your property doesn't have a need for feature stories, it may want to consider a weekly newsletter.

The Employee Annual Report. The **employee annual report** has a mission similar to that of the stockholders' annual report. It can be issued at the corporate and local levels. It usually contains a message from the chairman or general manager, highlights the key events of the year as they relate to employees, summarizes the company's current status, and talks about the year ahead. It often includes a financial review, written at the employee level, and talks about the social responsibilities undertaken by the company within the community. The largest portion of the report is devoted to feature stories on employees and their individual accomplishments. Employee annual reports are quickly gaining in popularity as employees become more involved in managing the company.

Posted Communications

Posters or company bulletin boards can be located in a number of back-of-the-house areas, including the employee entrance, the uniform room, the locker room, the employee cafeteria, and service elevators or elevator landings. Tent cards can also be used on tables in the employee cafeteria. These are all excellent methods for communicating information quickly and effectively. However, they shouldn't be placed in spots where people will be too hurried to read them (for example, by the timeclock) or where stopping to read them would create a traffic jam.

When posted communication is used, someone should be responsible for removing or replacing the postings when their usefulness has ended. Otherwise, people will learn to ignore them.

Required bulletins and posters should be posted in locked, glass-fronted cabinets in prominent locations in the personnel office and employee cafeteria. Required postings cover such topics as equal employment opportunity, unemployment and workers' compensation, age and sex discrimination, the Occupational Safety and Health Act, the location of available medical facilities in the event of industrial accidents, and minimum wage.

The employee bulletin board, particularly the departmental bulletin board, is one of the most effective, versatile, and cheapest communication channels available. An interested employee should be assigned to maintain it. All posted notices should be cleared through this person and signed for authority. They should be posted and removed on a schedule. Permanently posting items, such as the employee cafeteria rules and regulations, doesn't improve readership and serves only to add more clutter to the overall layout.

The board should be attractive and well-designed. Cork can be covered with fabric. Instead of always using plain paper or photocopied notices, try using felt-tipped pens or colored paper. Eye-catching headlines add interest and can be tied in with the theme of the rest of your employee communication programs.

Notices should be timely. In general, bulletins shouldn't remain up for more than three days. Important bulletins should remain for no more than one week. Even a blank bulletin board is effective in telling people that when you do have something to put up, it's significant.

Regular bulletins about which people need to know, such as work schedules and daily activities, should be maintained with consistency. People have to know this, will seek it out, and should be able to locate it quickly. Keep them in the same location on the board and always use the same caption and

Exhibit 9.4   Techniques for Effective Listening

- Stop talking.
- Look at the speaker.
- Don't prejudge what is said because you don't like something about the speaker.
- Don't interrupt or change the subject.
- Make a conscious effort to prevent your attention from drifting.
- Don't be distracted by bits of information. Focus on the important points.
- Listen for what is meant—not just what is said.
- Show your responsiveness vocally by paraphrasing or restating some of the important points and by asking questions.
- Show your responsiveness through body language as well, by sitting still, smiling, nodding, or offering a sympathetic gesture when appropriate.

even the same color as a border around the notice. On the other hand, new or irregular items to which you want to attract attention, such as guest letters or special announcements, should be moved around, matted with different colors, and varied in headings.

Set aside a section for employee notices. If someone wants to place something on the board, require that it be approved and signed or stamped to indicate the approval. All such notices should be screened in accordance with your policy of prohibiting all solicitation (this policy is discussed in Chapter 16).

Upward Communication

The greatest changes in employee communication in recent years have probably come in the area of upward communication. Good new programs are being developed to respond to the employee's need to communicate and contribute, and old programs are being brought up-to-date and improved. However, managers must be aware that listening to their employees implies taking their input seriously and, when appropriate, acting on it. Management must be willing not only to listen (see Exhibit 9.4), but also to provide the time and resources to institute the necessary changes.

If managers are to create an effective channel of upward communication, many of them should be prepared to change some assumptions. Managers often assume that they know what employees want and that employees will feel comfortable coming in and talking to them. This won't happen for many managers unless they change their basic style. Managers should encourage more frankness from their employees and make themselves more accessible. They need to show a willingness to hear, support, and reward ideas which are new, even offbeat. They must also be prepared to accept criticism without retaliating.

Many managers must also accept that they don't always know the problems on the job as well as they think they do. In the hospitality business, most managers have come up through the ranks and have actually held the positions they now supervise. While their experiences are valuable, they often forget that procedures change with time. They respond to employees' problems by saying, "That's the way I did it 15 years ago and it worked for me," or "I've done that job and I know how long it takes."

Managers must be committed to making the company's upward communication system work well. Upward communication includes open-door policies, exit interviews, suggestion or communication boxes, speak-up meetings, attitude surveys, and employee committees. Some of the traditional elements of upward communication are not likely to work well unless they are modified to take modern circumstances into account—for example, the suggestion box. Other elements may never work well because of inherent problems—for example, open-door policies. Before discussing effective upward communication channels, let's look at a popular approach which unfortunately has very limited value.

Open-Door Policies

Traditionally, managers have relied on what they thought of as an **open-door policy**: any employee who had something to say could always bring it to the manager, whose office door was "always open." Managers seemed to operate under the delusion that employees felt comfortable with such a program.

In fact, the contrary is much likelier to be true. Workers usually don't tell their supervisors how they feel, especially if the supervisor is contributing to a problem on the job.

Many employees don't respond to the open-door policy because they feel that expressing their true feelings about the company to a manager is dangerous. Further, they fear that disagreeing with the manager will block any chances for promotion. There's also a widespread belief that management isn't interested in employees' problems. Indeed, quite often when an employee does bring up a problem, the manager appears unresponsive. A busy schedule and other priorities may mean that, at best, the manager only has time for a quick, temporary solution. At worst, the manager may be totally inaccessible, either deliberately because of a desire to avoid dealing with people or inadvertently through a failure to set the proper priorities.

Another major reason for employees' reluctance to accept an open-door policy is that employees aren't rewarded for good ideas. In spite of all this, an astonishing number of managers continue to believe that they understand employees' problems well, and that employees communicate with them openly.

There is certainly nothing wrong with managers having open-door policies. They simply need to realize the limitations and recognize that other forms of upward communication will be needed.

Exit Interviews

In a formal **exit interview**, a company representative other than the immediate supervisor meets with a terminating employee to discuss the termination, the job, and the company. Many employers have begun to question whether conducting an exit interview with everyone who leaves provides enough reliable information to justify the investment of time and money. You probably already know why most people are leaving, such as involuntary termination, moving out of town, graduation from school, having a baby, or retirement.

Furthermore, it's difficult to get complete and accurate information. Some departing employees aren't willing to "burn bridges" by complaining about things that they no longer have to deal with every day. Others may take the opposite approach and try to damage someone unjustly. Another

Four Seasons Olympic Hotel
SEATTLE

EMPLOYEE COMMENT CARD

EMPLOYEE NAME _____
(Optional)

DATE _____

DEPARTMENT _____

	Exceeds Expectations	Meets Expectations	Below Expectations
ARRIVAL/DEPARTURE			
5th Avenue Entrance (Well lit, clean, dry)	☐	☐	☐
YOUR UNIFORM			
Cleanliness	☐	☐	☐
Condition (Proper size, no missing buttons, etc.)	☐	☐	☐
Attitude of Staff	☐	☐	☐
EMPLOYEE LOCKER ROOM			
Cleanliness (Please note time of use _____ a.m./p.m.)	☐	☐	☐
Maintenance	☐	☐	☐
Amenities	☐	☐	☐
Condition of Locker	☐	☐	☐

	Exceeds Expectations	Meets Expectations	Below Expectations
EMPLOYEE CAFETERIA			
Quality of Food	☐	☐	☐
Attitude of Staff	☐	☐	☐
Cleanliness (Please note time of use _____ a.m./p.m.)	☐	☐	☐
EMPLOYEE LOUNGE			
Cleanliness (Please note time of use _____ a.m./p.m.)	☐	☐	☐
Maintenance	☐	☐	☐
YOUR WORKING CONDITIONS			
Cleanliness	☐	☐	☐
Safety Conditions	☐	☐	☐
YOUR SUPPLIES			
Enough Supplies to Perform Job	☐	☐	☐
Proper working order of equipment	☐	☐	☐

YOUR COMMENTS
(Please be specific as possible)

_____
_____
_____
_____
_____
_____
_____
_____
_____
_____
_____
_____
_____

THANK YOU FOR
YOUR INTEREST

Similar in format to the guest comment card, the employee comment card is an excellent example of upward communication. (Courtesy of Four Seasons Olympic Hotel, Seattle, Washington) problem is that it's difficult when sensitive issues arise to be sure that confidentiality can be maintained, especially in smaller companies.

There are times, however, when conducting exit interviews on a selective basis may prove helpful. Typical cases include:

- When there is a major problem in one department or with a particular position

- Anytime an employee asks for an exit interview

- When you're trying to collect and keep a record of the facts and events surrounding a difficult termination

Collecting facts about a difficult termination can assist your company's defense against potential post-employment lawsuits. It can also help defuse the situation by giving the employee the opportunity to air his or her feelings.

In cases where an exit interview is appropriate, some steps can help you improve the reliability of the information obtained. If possible, conduct the exit interview during the final week, but don't wait until the last day; too many other things are happening then and the discussion may be rushed. You may wish to follow up in one to three months by mailing out a questionnaire with a postage-paid return envelope or by asking employees to call or come in if they're reluctant to put their feelings in writing.

Always assure the person that no one in the company will retaliate, regardless of what is said, by promising as much confidentiality as possible. Anonymity for interviewees is one of the best assurances of obtaining reliable information. Exiting employees will know whether the employer has a history of confidentiality and no retaliation for such interviews. Top management should enforce such a policy by disciplining managers who do retaliate.

The quality of any information received will be strongly influenced by the relationship that exists between the interviewer and interviewee. Having a stranger handle the interview is sure to minimize its effectiveness. On the other hand, the employee's immediate supervisor should *not* conduct the exit interview. Either a level of management should be skipped (so that the immediate supervisor's manager conducts the interview) or the interview should be handled by the human resources department.

Most employees will offer safe and acceptable reasons for leaving, such as more money or a better job. When you interview such employees, your goal is to find out if there were other, less obvious reasons. Determine what factors made them decide to start looking when they did. To get the person talking more openly, try asking general questions like "What do you think the next person coming into the job should know about it?" or "What did you expect when you started here? How did things differ from your expectations?" Another tactic is to ask about specific aspects of the job, such as working conditions, work group relationships, or the adequacy of the training, equipment, and supervision.

Ask the interviewee for opinions on what could be done to improve the company or the department. Find out what the person liked and disliked about the company. Responses to these kinds of questions can help you determine whether the termination was the result of an initial mistake in hiring. Perhaps the employee didn't have the right values and goals to fit within your organizational culture.

Finally, use the exit interview information. It certainly isn't worth going through all the trouble to obtain this information if it's then merely filed away. It should be used along with turnover statistics to identify problem areas. Pertinent information should be passed on to those who can benefit from it, keeping in mind the need to protect anonymity. A consistent pattern of complaints about wages, for instance, might indicate the need for a wage survey. (Exit interviews are discussed further in Chapter 15.)

The Communication Box

A classic example of disregarding employee input is found in the way many companies have handled the long-suffering **suggestion box**. Companies often wonder why they don't get any helpful suggestions. Yet when people do put in suggestions, management makes no attempt to let them know, in terms they can understand, why their ideas can't be used. The suggestions may never even get any recognition. Boxes such as this generate more bad morale than good.

Many companies have replaced the standard suggestion box with a more general version of a **communication box**, sometimes called a **hot line**. Some companies have the general manager's office open the box daily, so that employees have the opportunity to send communication directly to the top in just one day. Employees are encouraged to deposit not only their suggestions, but also their complaints, questions, and any other information they want to bring to the attention of top management. Management may then respond through one of the company's other channels of communication, such as an employee newsletter or bulletin board. If confidentiality is a consideration, a response may be mailed to the employee's home.

The communication box has many purposes. It provides employees with a channel for airing complaints and anxieties in addition to the formal grievance system. Since it's difficult to anticipate everything employees need to know, a method for responding readily to their questions and concerns helps to head off false rumors. Because the box is available 24 hours a day, it's also a good way for employees to return survey data (such as how many guests they're bringing to the company picnic) or order forms when they've been offered a catalog gift selection as an award.

Despite the potential benefits of the suggestion box, managers often lack the time and interest necessary to respond to submissions. Before establishing any form of information, suggestion, or communication box, a company must be prepared to respond promptly to every submission and to take each one seriously. This kind of commitment takes a lot of time and interest on the part of top managers. If they're unwilling to commit, the company is better off not having such a program.

The Speak-Up Meeting

In a **speak-up meeting**, sometimes called a **round-table discussion**, the general manager meets with a group of line employees from a specific department without the department manager present. This provides an effective means for top and line levels to communicate without having the information filtered. Any topic can be discussed, any complaint or problem aired.

For these meetings to be effective, the person in charge must be open-minded and not defensive. Responding to complaints with arguments or justifications will quickly discourage employees from speaking up. In choosing to preside at a speak-up meeting, the general manager conveys that all concerns expressed will be treated confidentially and with dignity, and will result in action where warranted.

The communication box should be attractive and readily accessible to all employees.

Of course, the feelings of the middle managers have to be considered. Everyone should understand that the object of the meeting is to inform and involve top management. The implicit goal is to improve the operation of the department, not to circumvent or malign the department head.

Attitude Surveys

The employee attitude survey provides information about the opinions, attitudes, and needs of line employees. In this way, the attitude survey helps diagnose organizational health. It also provides an indication of employee job satisfaction.

To ensure confidentiality, attitude surveys are generally conducted by an outside company. This company will typically destroy the original survey forms after tabulating the results. Without the assurance of this protection, true candor wouldn't be possible.

The survey questions may be prepared in-house, purchased commercially, or custom-developed by a consultant. The number of questions may run from 20 to 100, but 60 is usually sufficient to determine trends.

Questions should be designed to measure those elements that relate to job satisfaction, such as commitment, promotional opportunities, job content,

Exhibit 9.5 Sample Employee Attitude Survey Questions

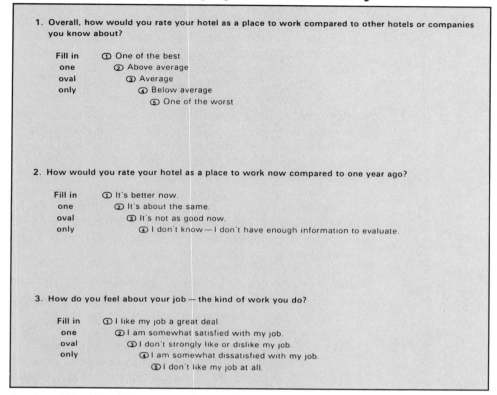

1. Overall, how would you rate your hotel as a place to work compared to other hotels or companies you know about?

Fill in
one
oval
only

    ① One of the best
      ② Above average
        ③ Average
          ④ Below average
            ⑤ One of the worst

2. How would you rate your hotel as a place to work now compared to one year ago?

Fill in
one
oval
only

    ① It's better now.
      ② It's about the same.
        ③ It's not as good now.
          ④ I don't know — I don't have enough information to evaluate.

3. How do you feel about your job — the kind of work you do?

Fill in
one
oval
only

    ① I like my job a great deal.
      ② I am somewhat satisfied with my job.
        ③ I don't strongly like or dislike my job.
          ④ I am somewhat dissatisfied with my job.
            ⑤ I don't like my job at all.

Courtesy of Hyatt Hotels Corporation, Chicago, Illinois.

supervision, wages, benefits, working conditions, co-workers, and communication. If an employer is interested in how well goals are being communicated, employees could be asked how often their managers talk about the goals of the company. Just as it does with the communication box, asking for information implies action. If the company isn't prepared to change in certain areas, they shouldn't be covered in the survey. Exhibit 9.5 presents sample questions from an employee attitude survey form.

Generally speaking, employees are asked to respond to each question based on whether they strongly agree, agree, don't feel strongly either way, disagree, or strongly disagree. After the questions, space is usually provided for employees to write in any additional comments they choose to make. These are typed up exactly as written and included with the tabulated responses to the survey questions.

The survey should be open to all employees. Many employers feel that, to be effective, they need the participation of 80% or more. Before employees are asked to respond, they should understand that management is seeking their honest and thoughtful replies and that great care is being taken to ensure the confidentiality of all responses. Management may find it useful to categorize respondents by general work area, by level, or even by sex or length of service. However, any further breakdown (such as by individual departments) doesn't provide enough anonymity to respondents; the supervisor could well be able to determine who said what. Once employees sense this possibility, the survey becomes practically useless.

The timing of the survey is significant. It shouldn't be conducted when employees may feel unsettled, such as during major organizational changes. Employees should not be surveyed when they may be experiencing extremes of attitude—positive or negative—such as during the Christmas season or when business is particularly slow. Regardless of when the survey is conducted, it shouldn't be a one-time procedure. Conducting surveys regularly, every 12 to 18 months, is important to their success and effectiveness.

Survey results represent employees' subjective responses. Whether their attitudes, feelings, opinions, and reactions are justified or not, they must be addressed. Regardless of how damaging it may seem to a manager, the survey still offers the best feedback for improving his or her performance. Therefore, no manager should fear the survey or feel threatened by it. Certainly, no one should ever be fired as the result of bad survey results.

Since upper management's concern is with your employees, comparing your survey results to national averages or those of other properties really has no significance. Managers should address their own specific areas of concern and use the survey results in planning the budget and setting priorities for dealing with those concerns.

After each survey, you can see whether you've improved since the last one. For example, if employee response indicated that promotions were perceived as being handled unfairly, the company could implement an assessment center program. If the program is effective, the next survey should show that people are happier with the promotional process. Any question that has more than a 20% negative response should be addressed.

The results of the survey should also be communicated to the employees as quickly as possible. Management should share the results with employees and state how it plans to respond. Committees that include employees can be formed to define the problem areas more specifically and to suggest possible solutions.

Employee Committees

Employee committees provide input from line employees for use in the problem-solving process. Most project teams or ad hoc committees are assigned to a specific problem and then dissolved once the mission has been accomplished. Others, such as quality assurance and safety committees, are ongoing.

Involving the line employees in committees has a number of advantages. People actually doing the work bring their job knowledge as input. The solution is usually better and can be implemented more quickly when more people are involved; they understand not only the problem and its solution, but why that solution is best. Furthermore, committee members become peer group experts and can become very powerful communicators for the company. Their suggestions have credibility with their co-workers. Since they have a personal involvement, the quality of their recommendations is high and they're committed to seeing that the solutions are correctly implemented. Being part of a group often gives them the courage to choose a bolder course of action. In addition, the committees can contribute to lateral communication (discussed in the next section) by bringing people from different departments together.

In Chapter 16, we'll see that any group of workers that's formed to deal with work-related issues might under certain circumstances be considered a union according to the terms of the National Labor Relations Act. Management can take some steps to avoid this with any ad hoc committee. It should select participants from among those workers who indicate an interest. It should *not* allow them to be elected by other employees. It must be clear to all that the function of the committee is to advise, not negotiate. The membership of an ongoing committee should be rotated or changed on a regular basis. Two people might be replaced each month, or about every six months a whole new committee could be designated.

It should be clear that management wants information and advice and will take all recommendations seriously. A committee generally comprises three to twelve people, depending on its purpose, with larger groups sometimes splitting into smaller teams to accomplish specific projects.

One manager should be assigned to guide, assist, and coordinate—but not control—the committee. Committee members should also have access to any technical people they may need temporarily. The continuing support of top management can be demonstrated by its participation in the first meeting, by its appearance at the committee's conclusion to express thanks, and by its responsiveness to the committee's suggestions.

As with any communication or problem-solving vehicle, the need for an ad hoc or ongoing employee committee must justify its cost. The problem addressed by the committee should be significant enough to merit the expense, with enough alternatives to make the committee a reasonable option. For instance, assume you're selecting uniforms for a soon-to-open restaurant with a definite theme. If only two choices can be delivered in time, a uniform-selection committee wouldn't be appropriate. On the other hand, if workers in your department are going to need new uniforms in a year or so, an ad hoc uniform review committee might be very productive. Other possible assignments for ad hoc committees include planning picnics, developing a child care center or flexible hours plan, reducing excessive paperwork, and cutting costs.

Each committee should have a specific designated goal to prevent its meetings from getting side-tracked. It's the job of the manager-advisor to provide enough guidance to members to keep them on course. If quality assurance is the team's mission, the type of quality must be specified. A committee working on improving the quality of the guest experience shouldn't be hearing complaints about messy locker rooms or poor food in the employee cafeteria. Of course, if such areas of dissatisfaction keep coming up, management should address them, perhaps through the use of a different ad hoc committee.

To improve effectiveness, committee members need some training. Problem solving, goal setting, return on investment, group dynamics, and teamwork techniques are all good topics for a short course on committee participation.

The costs of employee committees can readily be justified by the contributions to morale and motivation of those involved. Employees feel increased job satisfaction, more control over their environment, and more pride and interest in their work. Ideally, employee committees improve cooperation among employees and produce better relations between management and workers. Such committees also assist the development of leadership skills in employees who may someday become managers.

Lateral Communication

Lateral communication is the interchange of information and ideas among all sectors of a company. Effective lateral communication is an

Line employees on a quality assurance committee inspect a guestroom for compliance to standards.

essential element of the teamwork for which every manager is responsible. Without this interchange, the structure of your organization would be no different from an office building with many separate companies all working independently. Rather, a hospitality company is a group of people working together and helping each other to serve and satisfy guests.

Perhaps the greatest loss of time and efficiency in a company results when people are required to go through official channels unnecessarily. Using official communication channels generally involves many busy people when only two may be needed. If an employee needs to talk to another employee in a different department or division, the system should recognize and allow for it.

Consider the case of the bellperson who wants to get an arriving guest's luggage into the hotel promptly, but has no way of knowing when the door attendant has removed the bags from the car. Ideally, after notifying their respective supervisors of the problem, these two employees could get together to work out a simple solution themselves. While not expected to make policy changes, the two employees should feel able to take the initiative to structure their work so each can give the best possible service to the guest. Of course, they should tell their supervisors of their solution.

Many of the programs previously discussed can serve to improve lateral communication if consideration is given to such matters as who should attend meetings and receive copies of memos.

Informal Communication

Informal communication includes all the unofficial and unplanned communication that occurs continuously at all levels within a company. In the form of rumors heard through the grapevine, it is frequently controlled by informal leaders who are gossip-prone and who have a reputation for knowing what's going on.

The grapevine may be reliable information traveling ahead of the official communique. As a manager, you should be aware of it and be prepared to listen to it, since it can indicate employee reactions to the information that is about to come down officially. By identifying the informal leaders, you can even use the grapevine to your advantage, obtaining through them a kind of "straw vote" opinion poll or giving through them an early warning to soften the blow of unpleasant news.

If based on damaging or inaccurate information, the grapevine can be detrimental to the company. Just how harmful it can become depends largely on the climate within the company. If the employees don't trust management, damaging rumors will find acceptance.

If you hear a false rumor, correct it. If it affects another area, contact that department's manager. If it could have serious ramifications, contact higher levels of management to find out what can be made public to combat it. Call in your key people and explain the situation as soon as possible. In some cases, the people responsible for the spread of a harmful rumor can be dealt with through disciplinary action.

The most effective method of controlling damaging rumors, however, always involves providing correct and adequate information from the start. By supplying the facts on a regular and timely basis, you remove the uncertainty on which the rumors depend. Management should avoid delaying memos and should make announcements soon after plans and decisions have been made. Otherwise, rumors based on speculation and incomplete information will precede the facts. Employees then develop negative or uncooperative attitudes. The actual decision, when finally reported, has less chance of acceptance because employees are unable to separate the facts from the fiction. Any similarities between the facts and the false rumors are likely to be emphasized by those using the grapevine in an attempt to illustrate their own credibility and knowledge.

Key Terms

ad hoc committee
alternative dispute resolution
   committees
communication box
employee annual report
employment at will
exit interview

job enrichment
hot line
open-door policy
round-table discussion
speak-up meeting
suggestion box

Discussion Questions

1. Why is the personal relationship a manager has with each of his or her employees so important in employee motivation?

2. What are the roles of job security, salary, working conditions, and status in motivation?

3. What are some of the ways a manager might use to encourage employees to accept responsibility for their own actions?

4. What are some steps you might take to make the next meeting you run more effective?

5. Why doesn't the open-door policy work as well as many managers think?

6. What are the advantages of using an employee committee to find a solution for a work-related problem?

7. How would you deal with the problems created by the spread of false information in your department?

10 Wage and Benefit Administration

In the past few years, the prices we've charged for our rooms and restaurant services have jumped substantially to offset rising expenses. Many feel that the marketplace will not tolerate further rate increases at such a rapid pace. Unfortunately, the already rising cost of an employer's single largest expense—labor costs—is expected to rise even more sharply in the future.

In the hospitality sector, labor costs—including pay and benefits—average about a third of total sales.[1] The shrinking labor market and the rapidly growing service economy have been forcing wages and other expenses up simply because of the laws of supply and demand. Because of rising deficits, we can also expect that local, state, and federal governments will continue to transfer much more of their burden of social care onto private industry. For example, the government currently pays 40% of all medical bills in the United States.[2] However, the legislative trend is toward compelling businesses to provide more of this coverage—through mandatory insurances, increased social security contributions, benefit provisions extending beyond periods of employment, and faster vesting of retirement plans.

To make matters worse, workers are becoming increasingly dissatisfied with the wages and benefits they're receiving. Some sources of dissatisfaction include supervisors making less than the tipped employees working under them; managers making less than the highly-skilled professionals they manage; a rising minimum wage that diminishes the difference between unskilled and skilled compensation; and the resentment caused when top managers get additional, special benefits which the hourly workers don't receive.

Clearly, a primary objective for every hospitality business is getting the most for every dollar spent on labor costs. One way to do this, as we've already discussed, is through the motivation of employees to higher productivity and quality of service. In addition, managers must be skillful and aggressive in supporting and using the company's wage and benefit programs.

In a unionized company, pay rates and practices are normally determined through contract negotiations between the employer's representative

---

[1]*Trends in the Hotel Industry—1987 USA Edition* (Houston, Texas: Pannell Kerr Forster, 1987), p. 44.
[2]U.S. Bureau of the Census, *Statistical Abstract of the United States: 1988*, 108th ed. (Washington: U.S. Department of Commerce, 1987), p. 88.

and the union. Incentive pay plans, bonuses, even contests and promotions will probably have to be negotiated. All managers must comply with the contract's terms. They may have very little control over the design and administration of wage and benefit programs.

A non-union company will have a wage and salary program which serves the same purpose as the union contract and which should be followed just as strictly. However, managers usually participate more in the design of its wage and benefit programs. They also have more control over how programs are administered and more freedom to modify pay rates, job responsibilities, staffing, hours, and so on to meet the needs of their respective departments. Because of their greater input and involvement, managers in a non-union company need a better understanding of the principles behind pay policies and practices, pay as a motivator, pay for performance, incentives, and so on.

While pay isn't the ultimate satisfier, it's still the ultimate dissatisfier. The wage and salary program must be well thought out, administered with consistency, and tightly controlled. Companies can no longer afford to have hourly employees in the same job starting at different rates or to have the general manager signing off on substantial increases because of a manager who overrates and overpays all of his or her employees. All of the implications must first be considered.

Many managers feel they know what's best for their employees and their department, and they usually do; but they're often unaware of the impact such decisions have on the overall company program. An improper or poorly controlled wage and salary program will create more employee dissatisfaction than anything else you can do.

The effectiveness of the program often comes down to the quality of the research and preparation that went into its development and the expert judgment of the wage and salary administrator.[3] While operational managers' input should be sought to evaluate jobs within their own areas, in the final balance, the total package has to support the company's business plan and not the line manager's personal perceptions.

Wage and Benefit Decisions for Top Management

It is the company's philosophy and values that should set the tone and direction for controlling and managing labor costs. Its philosophy should give managers the guidelines they need to make important decisions and maintain consistency within and between departments. These guidelines include:

- Setting the philosophy and direction for a long-term plan for managing a company's labor costs

- Establishing controls and guidelines for the size of the work force, including giving careful consideration to the contribution made by every job

---

[3]While it isn't the function of wage and salary administrators to decide who deserves an increase, it is their job to ensure that the system the company has devised operates with consistency and fairness. They're also responsible for helping managers get what they need to run their departments effectively while staying within the guidelines of the wage and salary program, as well as federal and state laws.

- Developing the principles and policies of the wage and salary programs
- Directing the design, administration, and maintenance of employee benefit programs

Corporate leaders must determine whether the company will be controlled with a large central office staff or decentralized. Even the location of the corporate office—that is, whether it's in a high or low cost of living area—will have a tremendous impact on the fixed overhead and operating expenses of a company. How many levels of management should there be? What will be the role and size of staff functions at the corporate and unit levels? Where should the staff priorities be placed? If you're building your reputation on good service, investment in concierge departments might receive high priority. If your reputation is based on good food, staffing and funding for wages, training, and other expenses in the food areas would get additional consideration.

How to handle human resources during both good and bad times should also be considered. Companies today can no longer manage and control their payroll costs by staffing up in good times and laying off in bad times. Most service companies today no longer have a philosophy that allows for staff buildups in busy times.

Rather, flexibility should be built into the wage and salary programs to allow for fluctuations in business. For instance, some employers are incorporating other forms of compensation, such as incentive pay plans, profit sharing, and stock options, in order to reward workers well when they increase their productivity during busy periods. This allows the company to keep its fixed and base pay at a level it can live with during slow periods without cutbacks and layoffs. This approach is more effective than simply giving everyone large increases during the good times which must then be sustained when business slows down.

More consideration is also being given now to such practices as having geographic differences built into the pay programs. Companies using these **area cost allowances** increase wages as their managers transfer into high cost of living areas. When managers transfer into lower cost of living areas, the adjustment is backed out.

Different budget amounts are also being allocated to different key jobs or divisions. In the past, companies may simply have set a budgetary figure of 5% for pay increases for all departments. Now, they're likelier to put the money where their priorities are—for example, budgeting 3% for staff functions, 5% for service positions, and 7% for key or critical skills areas.

There is also more of a trend toward long-term results, with pay and incentive programs reflecting this emphasis. Far too often, short-term objectives and values encourage managers to devise solutions with immediate results. One common example is the corporate practice of evaluating the general manager of a facility based solely on the unit's profit in any given year. Thus, instead of spending large sums of money to correct major problems, managers may use cheaper "patching" techniques which merely mask the problem while allowing it to grow worse. The manager's goal is to postpone the major expenditure and to be transferred to another hotel before an even greater expenditure is required.

As with any aspect of the human resources strategy, wage and benefit

Pay for performance is a better motivator.

programs should support the organizational culture and the values and beliefs of the company.

Finally, wage and benefit programs must be developed and administered with a business orientation. If a company is in business to make a profit, it must be competitive and offer consumers good value for their money. Programs that result in operating at a loss can hardly be considered effective.

In the discussion which follows, we will focus first on wage and salary concerns and then on benefits.

How Pay Is Used

Several approaches to and ideas about wages and salary have developed or arisen over the years. In today's marketplace, wage and salary administrators find some of these approaches and ideas problematic. Unfortunately, efforts to change them often meet with resistance.

For example, tradition has helped to establish the concept of the **entitlement** of workers to certain wage increases. The idea that wages should go up with both inflation and length of service, irrespective of productivity, involves deep-rooted beliefs. Most people aren't going to abandon them readily.

Another approach to wage administration has been the **fixed-rate** form of payment, typified by union contracts, under which everyone gets the same rate and the same increase, regardless of skill, effort, or length of service.

Over the years, wages have also come to represent a method for people to keep score of how well they're doing on the job. So far, industry has done very little to change this attitude or provide alternatives, such as adequate feedback, recognition, and job redesign.

Wage and salary administration is experiencing something of a shift in emphasis, however. For many companies, the concept of **pay for performance** is beginning to replace the old ideas of entitlement, fixed-rate payment, and keeping score.

Pay as a Motivator

Opinions differ widely about the effectiveness of pay as a motivator. We've seen that it can serve as a source of dissatisfaction if improperly administered. There are at least some indications that it can also provide incentive to employees under certain circumstances:

- Money must be a goal for the worker. The more strongly someone wants more money, the more production will improve. As with other needs, when a comfortable level is reached, the power of pay to motivate declines, so after getting large increases, employees will sometimes slow down. They may then start pushing for more time off and the satisfaction of other needs.

- Workers must believe strongly that good performance will lead to more money. Often, in fact, workers actually don't believe that a relationship exists between performance and pay.[4]

- Employees and managers must maintain a high level of trust. Otherwise, increases may be perceived as preferential treatment.

- Increases must be based on objective, measurable, and attainable standards.

- The negative impact of being a good performer must be eliminated or at least minimized. In spite of any wage incentive, peer pressure puts ceilings on output. Work group members who violate the group's standards for the extra income may be labeled "rate busters" and suffer retribution from their peers.

- The time span between the effort and the reward must be short. One raise a year for entry-level positions may be too infrequent to encourage improved performance.

- The differential between the reward for greater performance and the standard increase must be enough to make the effort worthwhile.

---

[4]Walter I. Jacobs, "Human Resources Cost Containment: Trends and Strategies," *A Strategic Report: Linking Employee Attitudes & Corporate Culture to Corporate Growth & Profitability* (Philadelphia: Hay Management Consultants, 1984), p. 125.

Getting only small increases over the average worker would minimize the effect of pay as a satisfier.

Problems Encountered. The pay-for-performance system is catching on, but rather slowly. This isn't hard to understand, given that hospitality managers have many obstacles to overcome, including the following:

- Making reliable distinctions between different levels of performance for service jobs is often difficult, since there are few easily measurable standards like piecework on which to base decisions.

- The company's budget must be large enough and flexible enough to allow for larger-than-normal increases for outstanding performers.

- Most pay-for-performance programs reward individual performance, which can be counter-productive in establishing team efforts. To build teamwork, employees must be able to see how they benefit from the good performance of others before they will be encouraged to help one another.

- Many employees prefer the security and guarantee of automatic increases.

For these reasons, most managers would prefer to take the easy way out and give all their people about the same amount of increase. To help counter this tendency, the switch to a pay-for-performance system should be supported by a strong management training program in how to use the system. Regardless of the obstacles, if a hospitality company doesn't recognize and reward performance, it isn't going to increase productivity.

How Pay for Performance Works

How does a pay-for-performance system work? When you allot a budget amount for pay increases, use most of it to reward the better performers. For instance, if the budgeted raise amount averages ten cents an hour per employee, when it's time for increases, you might give poor performers somewhere between nothing and five cents an hour. The average people would get the average amount. The outstanding employees might get 15 to 20 cents an hour. Your own well-kept records of performance discussions, lateness, absenteeism, and warning notices should provide the justification for your decisions. See Exhibit 10.1 for an example of how such a system works.

Companies are also paying for growth. If an employee takes a course in sanitation or CPR, it's worth an increase of a given amount per hour. So is learning another job and becoming more valuable to the company. The increases don't have to be large, but they should be enough to send a clear message that one way to get a raise is to learn additional skills.

Elements of the Wage and Salary Program

The basic objectives of the wage and salary program are to help the company attract and keep qualified people, provide equal pay for equal work, reward good performance, control labor costs, and maintain a cost parity with direct competitors.

Exhibit 10.1   A Pay-for-Performance System

MONTHLY PAY REVIEW ANALYSIS

Department* __XYZ__   Pay Reviews for __July, 19X2__   Date Issued __06-12-X2__   Due Date __06-23-X2__

APPROVALS: Department Head _____   Date _____   Division Head _____   Date _____

Human Resources _____   Date _____   General Manager _____   Date _____

Name*	Position*	Next Review Date	Last Increase Date	Last Increase Amount	Current Rate	Budgeted Amount	Recommended Amount	Reason#
		07-23-X2	01-22-X2	.15	5.05	.15	.15	
		07-02-X2	HIRE	.00	4.75	.10	.10	
		07-02-X2	07-10-X1	.10	8.05(C)	.20	.00	red-circled
		07-16-X2	01-15-X2	.15	4.90	.15	.05	lateness
		07-23-X2	01-22-X2	.15	5.75(B)	.15	.15	
		07-16-X2	01-15-X2	.20	5.60	.15	.25	outstanding worker
		07-16-X2	01-15-X2	.05	4.90	.15	.00	on final warning
		07-23-X2	01-22-X2	.10	5.05	.15	.15	
		07-09-X2	01-08-X2	.25	5.90	.15	.20	good worker
		07-09-X2	01-08-X2	.15	5.40	.15	.05	poor quality work
		07-16-X2	04-16-X2	.50	8.00(A)	.25	.25	
		07-23-X2	HIRE	.00	4.75	.10	.20	good worker

KEY: A – Green-circled
B – Over Mid-Point of Pay Grade
C – Red-circled
\# – Reason required for any amount other than budgeted

*Department, Employee Name, and Position would normally be shown on this form.

The purpose of the elements of a wage and salary program is to provide the program with structure, objectivity, and fairness. Managers should never get so concerned with format and forms that they lose sight of the company's overall philosophy and goals. The elements of the wage and salary program should simply provide managers with a framework within which they may handle pay decisions and from which they may make intelligent exceptions.

A company must first decide what position to take—does it want to be known as the highest paying, the lowest paying, or somewhere in between? Many companies strive only to have their wages fall in the upper 25%. They feel that working conditions, benefits, location, and other factors will still allow them to attract the best candidates, even though they're not paying top dollar. Some companies choose to open a new operation at the top of the scale, then don't adjust starting salaries for a number of years until other companies catch up.

Management must also decide what percentage of the total compensation package will come from wages and what percentage from other benefits, including insurances, uniforms, meals, pensions, and time off. If a company wants to attract young employees, it may wish to have higher starting salaries and fewer benefits. If it has a mix of ages or mostly older workers, it may want to increase the benefits ratio. In the average hotel today, benefits represent about one-third of payroll.[5]

Generally, the wage and salary program has five key elements:

1. Job analysis
2. Job evaluation
3. Wage surveys
4. Structure and design
5. Maintenance and control

Tying all these pieces together should be policies and procedures written in language that everyone can understand. Some of the items that should be covered by wage and salary policies and procedures include:

- How, when, and by whom performance reviews are handled
- Who handles wage surveys
- How pay decisions are made at the time of hiring, transferring, promoting, or demoting
- How jobs get re-evaluated when there's a change in duties
- How new jobs are graded and put into the system when created
- Who's responsible for administrating the program
- To whom employees go when they have a question or complaint about their pay

---

[5]*Trends in the Hotel Industry*, p. 44.

Job Analysis

The **job analysis** is a brief definition of each job. It enables the company to assess the relationships and differences between all its jobs (see Exhibit 10.2). Job analysis is the heart of the wage and salary program. If jobs aren't rated properly, it will be a source of endless dissatisfaction. There may be complaints ("Why do I make less than a desk clerk? My job is just as hard"), bickering, adjustments, loss of confidence in the system, and eventually a complete collapse of the program leading to spiralling labor costs.

In addition to the job title, department, and division, the job analysis usually also includes the following:

1. The fundamental purpose of the job, usually a one-paragraph job description

2. Work assigned or performed, including specific tasks, areas of responsibility, and the amount of time spent in each area of responsibility

3. The position's scope, including areas of accountability or authority, such as "responsibility for a hundred-thousand-dollar inventory"

4. The supervision received and exercised—in other words, to whom this position reports and who reports to this position

5. Working conditions, including the environment and any unusual circumstances, such as extra physical effort, high stress, hazards, or equipment to be operated

6. The minimum requirements of the job, particularly skill level, ability, education, and experience

The person who functions as wage and salary administrator collects the necessary information from all departments and coordinates the overall program. This person ensures that the job analysis is accurate, current, and consistent. Many companies have found that it's worth having one or more full-time people to handle job analysis.

Job Evaluation

Job evaluation is a system of ranking all of the jobs in an organization according to their relative value or contribution to the company. Since relative value can readily become a subjective and elusive concept, most companies have chosen to adopt the method offering the most objectivity, the **point factor analysis** approach. Because of its greater objectivity, this approach also seems to be the most acceptable to employees and labor unions.

The Equal Pay Act of 1963, which defines equal pay requirements for both sexes, designates four elements common to all jobs—skill, effort, responsibility, and working conditions—that may be used as a basis for determining equal work. These elements also serve as a useful basis for the job evaluation procedure, particularly when they're broken down into more detailed factors to meet the needs of individual employers.

Based on its own goals and priorities, a company assigns a maximum weight, or point value, to each factor (see Exhibit 10.3). In some industries, education gets more weight than experience as a factor of Skill. In some places, physical demands will be outweighed by mental effort under Working Conditions. There's no one correct point value total. Depending on the size of a company and the number of different job titles, the total might work out to be 100 points, or it might be 500.

Exhibit 10.2   Sample Job Analysis

SAMPLE JOB ANALYSIS

Job Title: Reservations Manager   **Date:** May 2, 19XX
Division: Rooms Division   **Dept:** Reservations
Reports To: Rooms Division Manager   **Promotion To:** Front Office Manager

JOB SUMMARY: Supervises entire Reservations Department. Initiates both staff development and training. Maintains group and convention information. Assures smooth flow of information between Reservation Agents and Front Desk Agents. Sells the entire hotel and determines controls for maximizing revenues. Fills in for Guest Service Manager and Front Office Manager upon request.

SCOPE: Direct responsibility for every room reservation made into the hotel. Maintains a staff of eight Reservation Agents.

SUPERVISION EXERCISED:
Directly: Reservation Agents
Indirectly: Front Desk Agents, Bellpersons, Concierge

SUPERVISION RECEIVED:
Supervisor: Rooms Division Manager
Supervision Received: Works under general direction

RESPONSIBILITIES AND AUTHORITIES:
1. Maximizing potential room revenues through upselling.
2. Achieving guest satisfaction through product knowledge and honest communications.
3. Control and support of staff personnel.
4. Maintaining limitations of staffing guides.
5. Staff development and employee relations through constant interaction with current staff.
6. Selling of rooms, food/beverage, Health Club, etc., within the hotel. Selling guests on the city, local highlights, shopping, and activities the area has to offer.

QUALIFICATIONS:
1. High school and at least two years of college level courses, preferably in the area of hospitality.
2. Three years of experience in the hospitality industry.
3. Previous experience dealing with employees on a supervisory level.
4. Good public relations skills with strong emphasis on written and oral communications.

SPECIFIC DUTIES:
1. Training and retraining of Reservation Agents for the purpose of better product knowledge and performance.
2. Planning and presenting departmental meetings once/twice a month.
3. Constant updating of employee records, i.e., performance reviews, Personnel Action forms, etc., to ensure equal treatment to entire staff.
4. Providing support services for employees. Listening to concerns and guest input. Offering suggestions for future use. Acting as a pressure reliever in tense situations.
5. Maintaining all group- and convention-related information. Monitoring all group blocks cutoff dates. Communicating with hotel and non-hotel staff convention coordinators regarding certain aspects of the groups.
6. Maintaining rate restricting calendars for the Reservation Agents' use when selling rooms.
7. Gathering information and compiling the 30–60–90 day forecasts, including occupancies and revenues.
8. Analyzing occupancies and creating weekly forecast reports used primarily for department scheduling.
9. Supplying monthly payroll forecasting and adhering to the forecasts.
10. Initiating information pertaining to the monthly recap report, including gathering of information from the previous month.
11. Reviewing employees and distributing praise and discipline when necessary.
12. Recognizing and responding to the need for improved ideas and methods within the department.
13. Maintaining a steady flow of work-related responsibilities and monitoring problem areas.
14. Monitoring Telex for central reservations system. Updating system on sold out nights.
15. Attending meetings as requested: Sales, Credit, Rooms.
16. Maintaining and adhering to annual budget figures.
17. Performing other duties as requested.

Exhibit 10.3   Sample Point Value Assignments

SAMPLE POINT VALUE ASSIGNMENTS
(For Job Evaluation in a Medium-Sized Hotel)

Element	Factor	Factor Breakdown	Maximum Points	Total Points
SKILL:				40
	Job Knowledge	Education	10	
		Experience	20	
	Judgment and Ingenuity		10	
EFFORT:				15
	Physical		10	
	Mental		5	
RESPONSIBILITIES:				30
	Supervision		10	
	Contacts With Others (Verbal and Written)		5	
	Financial Impact/Consequence of Error		10	
	Equipment		5	
WORKING CONDITIONS:				15
	Surroundings (Stress, Third Shift)		10	
	Hazards		5	
TOTAL				100

The next step is to determine the point value of each job in the organization by assessing the extent to which it requires each factor on the list of point value assignments. The total of points for a job becomes its point value. Once all jobs have been evaluated, they're lined up in order of their point values. Pay grades can then be assigned to groups of jobs with the same or nearly the same point value.

Clearly, the point factor approach can become fairly complicated. It may not be necessary for all companies, particularly smaller ones. Some companies prefer the simple **ranking process**, whereby a manager ranks all the positions in a department or unit, or the **classification system**, which involves fitting jobs into pre-assigned pay grades. Both of these methods are more subjective than the point factor approach, and could therefore result in more inconsistencies and greater employee dissatisfaction. They're useful, however, when the number of job titles and pay grades is small.

For example, in engineering, if you had job titles for Carpenter, Electrician, and HVAC (heating, ventilation, and air conditioning) Specialist, and all had different starting rates, the ranking or classifying system might not be sophisticated enough. On the other hand, if all of your skilled maintenance people are classified as Engineering Craftsmen and have the same starting salary, the simplicity of the ranking and classification system can serve you well.

Many companies use a combination of all three methods to develop their wage and salary program. For example, they may use the classification system and on a departmental basis rank the positions to see if wages are in or out of balance. Companies that don't have time to do a point factor comparison of all positions may do them only for the **benchmark jobs**—those jobs readily recognized in the industry and that have easily-defined and stable job duties. A benchmark position is one for which you usually have a large number of employees, is generally representative, and is at the mid-range within the pay grade. Once these jobs are evaluated, others can often be compared to and ranked around them with fewer steps.

After finishing the job evaluation, the program's designer will check the results to determine whether the individual jobs still fit together in a relevant manner. He or she will compare the jobs that are grouped together with one another to check the weightings. Any necessary adjustments to the point values and rankings are then made. If, for example, the point values indicate that the front office supervisor—who works weekends and on whatever shift needed—could transfer into accounting as a clerk answering the telephone Monday through Friday, nine to five, for the same pay, the point values assigned to those job titles may need to be re-evaluated. Perhaps not enough weight was given to working condition factors like third shift and stress.

Wage Surveys

To be sure that they remain competitive in the labor market, companies conduct periodic **wage surveys**. Some retain professional compensation consultants to conduct surveys for them, while others conduct their own. Efforts range from making a few telephone calls to performing a rather extensive survey involving many jobs and companies. Exhibit 10.4 is a sample area wage and benefits survey sheet.

To keep its wages current, a company should conduct complete wage surveys regularly—usually every one or two years, depending on inflation and competition. If it becomes difficult to recruit or keep people in a specific job, a quick survey can be done for that position. Often, your company's recruiting representatives can tell you when you get out of balance. They see what people are making on every application, and they know when they're beginning to lose the best applicants.

Be wary of national surveys, because they're usually too general in nature. It's hard to get useful information from a survey of general managers' salaries when the sampling includes everything from "Mom and Pop" operations to luxury hotels. Such surveys are usually also too old, since it takes so long to compile the data. In addition, the differences in pay between areas like New York City and a small north central town can render such general surveys useless.

To avoid placing yourself at an economic disadvantage with your competition, you should survey similar companies. If you poll only the top paying establishments in your area, you may end up paying substantially more for labor than your competitors. You may then be forced to charge your customers more.

Survey other companies within the labor market from which you recruit. Companies recruiting nationally for general managers of luxury hotels, for example, need national statistics for like jobs. If you find yourself competing for employees with employers from other industries, you may want to include those companies in your survey.

You also have to know your recruiting area. If your maintenance personnel don't have the credentials to get a job at a highly-automated factory near you, then you don't have to compare yourself to that firm. If you find many

Exhibit 10.4 Area Wage and Benefits Survey Sheet

AREA WAGE AND BENEFITS SURVEY SHEET

Company _____ Date _____

Contact _____ Phone _____

No. of Employees _____ Union _____ Non-Union _____

Wage Survey

How often are employees eligible for a wage review/increase? _____

Position/Title	No. of Employees	Starting Salary
Convention Set-up		
Bartender – Front		
Bartender – Service		
Bellperson		
Busperson + % of Tips		
Food Server		
Cashier – Restaurants		
Front Desk – Clerks		
Front Desk – Cashiers		
Front Desk – Reservationist		
Front Desk – Night Audit		
Cook I: 1–2 Yrs Experience		
Cook II: 2+ Yrs Experience		
Cook III: Supervise, etc.		
Pantry I: Vegetable Prep, etc.		
Pantry II: Veg Prep + Experience		
Custodian – Houseperson		
Custodian – Specialties		
Dishwasher		
Maintenance – General		
Engineering II – Trades		
Host/Hostess		
Housekeeping Floor Supervisor		
Housekeeping Uniform Attendant		
Laundry – General		
Laundry – Presser/Valet		
Laundry – Wash Person		
Painter I: Rolling		
Painter II: Color Matching		
Accounting I – Entry/No Experience		
Acctg II – 2 yrs Exp/Some College		
Acctg III – Degree/3 yrs Experience		
Purchasing Clerk – Entry/No Experience		
Secretary I: Receptionist		
Secretary II: Typing		
Secretary III: Executive		
Telephone Operators		

Benefits Survey

Item	Yes	No
Life Insurance (Amount –)		
Medical		
Dental		
Vision		
Cost to Employee for Coverage (Amount –)		
Cost for Dependent Coverage (Amount –)		
Free Meals		
Paid Holidays (How Many –)		
Pension Plan		
Uniforms Provided		
Uniforms Cleaned by Company		
Third Shift Premium (Amount –)		
Sick Pay (Specifications –)		

Vacations: _____ weeks off after _____

_____ weeks off after _____

_____ weeks off after _____

_____ weeks off after _____

Do you have any other *major* benefits such as transportation assistance, day care, etc.?

of your people are going to work for a particular company, perhaps you should survey that company.

Include all of your benchmark positions in the survey. Make sure you're comparing like jobs, perhaps by providing a short job description—job titles don't always represent the same work in different companies. Survey data can be as simple as asking what the starting salary is for a given position, or as detailed as asking for the number of employees in each position and what their current rates are. You should also inquire about practices such as offering third shift premiums or increases after a probationary period.

This statistical data helps you determine three things about the pay rates for each job:

1. The mean—the total of the pay rates of all employees in a job, divided by the number of employees.

2. The median—a mid-point at which half the people are above and the other half are below. Unlike the mean, the median isn't affected by extremes in pay and is a more reliable indicator of the central pay distribution.

3. The mid-range—the lowest and highest rates of pay for the middle 50% of employees reported for a particular job. This means that 25% of the employees receive higher than the mid-range and 25% receive lower.

Knowing all three of these can help your company set and assess its own pay ranges.

Regardless of how carefully you analyze the data, remember that the survey is only a window into the market. It will only reveal what other companies have done—not what your company should do. It won't indicate whether the other companies have internal problems with pay grades, or whether they're attracting the same caliber of people that you want.

Although you should treat the information confidentially, it's normal to provide the companies that have participated in your survey with your results. However, you must take steps to avoid even the appearance of illegal wage-fixing or direct exchange of information with competitors. Make it plain that the information is intended only for spotting trends, not for use in any collective rate-fixing agreements. Then, list the companies involved separately from the rate structures reported, so that no specific organization's pay rates can be identified.

Structure and Design

Establishing the structure and design of a wage and salary program involves many elements. Management must set starting rates, look at job design, create the staffing guide, analyze labor costs, implement pay grades, and determine what to pay salaried employees and whether to pay commissions and bonuses.

Setting Starting Rates. All hourly employees hired into a job should start at the same rate or severe morale and equal pay problems may occur.

As the labor market shrinks, particularly for entry-level jobs, a word of caution is in order. While starting salaries will continue to rise, don't look at increasing them as the answer to all your recruitment problems. Paying higher wages won't create more people where none exist, nor will small

Exhibit 10.5 Sample Restaurant Staffing Guide

STAFFING GUIDE							
Department & Title	**EEO.1 Report Code**	**Exempt**	**Grade**	**Staff Needed**	**Shift**	**Status**	**Starting Rate**
COFFEE SHOP							
Manager	MGR	Y	—	01	Var.	FT	– – –
Line Cook	CRAFT	N	08	02	Var.	FT	xx.xx
Host/Hostess	SER	N	06	03	Var.	FT	xx.xx
Cashier	SER	N	05	03	Var.	FT	xx.xx
Prep Cook	SER	N	04	02	Var.	FT	xx.xx
Dishwasher	SER	N	03	04	Var.	FT	xx.xx
Busperson	SER	N	02	03	Var.	FT	xx.xx
Food Server	SER	N	01	10	Var.	FT	xx.xx

increases expand the size of your labor market by attracting people who are more qualified. You would have to pay a great deal more than a few cents per hour to change your labor market. You might merely end up paying more to the same people you would have hired anyway. Your competitors would probably adjust their rates to meet your wages, so that any short-term advantage would quickly be lost.

Job Design. As we've discussed, today's workers want their jobs to be interesting. They want to be involved and have an identity. The clear trend is toward breaking large departments down into smaller work units where people can feel that they have a meaningful part to play. It's far more satisfying, for example, to feel like part of a small group of dishwashers playing an important role in the restaurant than it is to feel like one of 50 people in the stewarding department being assigned anywhere they're needed. Using smaller work units not only improves job satisfaction, but also helps control payroll.

In a standard restaurant, for example, you may have to staff the bus help first thing in the morning to get the tables set and coffee and water poured. The dishwasher isn't really totally productive until the end of the shift when all the soiled dishes are returning. At this time, the dish room must be staffed up, and the bus help is going into a slow period. Bus people are then sent home to cut payroll—which creates turnover because they're not getting a full day's pay—while extra dishwashers are brought in to work, perhaps on overtime. Instead of using this approach, have the buspeople help out with dishwashing for their restaurant. Conversely, when demands on bus help are again at a peak, have dishwashers help set up tables or fill in as pantry workers to help with food preparation. In such a restaurant, every employee feels like a member of a team working together with guest service as the goal.

This philosophy of broadening job descriptions works particularly well when built into the staffing guide.

The Staffing Guide. The **staffing guide** (see Exhibit 10.5) is a determination of the number of workers needed to achieve optimum productivity and quality.

Arriving at that determination requires extensive job knowledge, experience, and judgment. It probably will involve the combined efforts of the department head and the wage and salary administrator.

The person responsible for overall control and coordination of the staffing guide's development should understand the organization's operation in great detail, the human resources strategy, and the levels of service and quality the company is trying to achieve. He or she should be someone able to train, influence, and command the respect of all the other managers. However, every manager should be involved and committed to both the careful development of and subsequent adherence to the staffing guide if the company is to achieve the control it must have over labor costs.

While industry averages and area practices provide a basic starting point, each company is unique. Your own job analysis and job evaluation should give you the input you need for adapting industry and area averages to your staffing guide.

For example, if your area's practices and industry standards suggest to you that one room attendant can clean between 13 and 16 rooms per day, make sure this standard applies to hotels comparable to your own. You should look at the size of the rooms in your facility, percentage of double occupancy, average length of stay, how far room attendants must travel between rooms, whether a houseperson is available to run linens and supplies, and a host of other considerations. If comparable hotels are getting 16 rooms per day from each room attendant and you set your standard at 12, the price you have to charge guests in order to cover your labor cost may not be competitive. Whether industry standards appear to be right or wrong, staying in line with them (known as maintaining a **cost parity**) is an important consideration for every employer.

Working from the job analysis, decide how much can be accomplished by one person. Consider such factors as the size, nature, and quality standards of your operation; the time required for each duty; the amount of time allowed for completion of duties; and available assistance, equipment, and other job aids.

Use your business forecasts to determine how much work will be required of the job in a year's time. Divide predicted units of business for the year by corresponding units of work that one person can do. The result is the approximate number of workers you'll need in that job title for the year ahead. In larger departments, you may also have to make allowances for vacations, leaves of absence, and other sources of extended vacancies. Exhibit 10.6 presents a sample staffing guide calculation.

On the surface, it would appear that this method would work well only when predicted business is spread evenly through the year—which almost never happens. Staff levels vary as business fluctuates, and these variations are the real challenge in the staffing process. If you overstaff, no one has enough work or wages. If you understaff, everyone is overworked and service suffers. Either way costs go up.

To deal with these fluctuations, you must determine your business cycle. If the increase in business is seasonal, you may want to add seasonal help. If the increase is just for a few days, you can arrange work schedules so that everyone works during the peak periods and days off are scheduled on the slow days that week. If the increase is for a longer period—two weeks or more—your first option is to increase the hours of your part-time employees, if you have any. Then consider using employees in other departments who

Exhibit 10.6 Sample Staffing Guide Calculation

Problem: Determine the number of room attendants needed in a hotel with 200 guestrooms and an average expected occupancy rate of 70% for the coming year. The area standard for comparable hotels is 16 rooms cleaned per day per room attendant.

200	guest rooms
× .70	occupancy rate
140	average daily occupancy
× 365	days in a year
51,100	expected yearly occupancy
16	rooms daily per room attendant
× 5	working days per week
80	rooms per week per room attendant
× 50	weeks worked per year
4,000	rooms per year per room attendant

51,100 ÷ 4,000 = 13 room attendants needed

aren't engaged in priority work. Finally, you can go into overtime.

Many managers feel that incurring overtime is to be avoided at all costs. However, running as much as 10% overtime may be the cheapest alternative to adding staff or hiring temporary workers. You pay only for those hours actually needed, rather than hiring additional help at full eight-hour increments. Also, your full-time staff is far more productive and will maintain your quality standards and service. At the busiest times, you need your best people working harder, not slowing down to supervise new employees. There's also less overhead, since there are no hiring, training, benefit, uniform, or other related employment costs. For many minimum wage employees, having some overtime helps make ends meet, which will help to stabilize your work force.

Temporary employees are less productive, generally provide lower levels of service, and are involved in more accidents, breakage, and pilferage. When you lay them off, you incur sizable unemployment compensation costs. Weigh all of these expenses carefully before adding temporaries to your staff.

Managers must be equally skillful at reducing payroll when business is slow. Your first priority should be to protect the core group of employees called for in the staffing guide.

Traditionally, many hospitality managers have responded to the unpredictability of business by hiring more help during peak periods and laying people off and cutting back hours when things slowed down. However, laying people off and cutting back hours generates another set of problems. If you cut back the hours of some or all workers when business slows down, you can't expect them to maintain any loyalty or commitment. People who are laid off several hours one week aren't going to work harder for you the following week just because business improves. In some states, workers whose hours are cut can also collect partial unemployment; they may actually be able to collect more working part-time than they could working full-time.

It is possible, however, to reduce your labor costs in slow times without undermining morale. First, don't rush to replace those who leave. Tell employees well in advance when business will be slow and have them schedule vacations according to business fluctuations. Find out which employees might like to have extra time off—many people today would gladly trade some wages to have time off to take care of personal business. This is also the time to get rid of the non-performers you may have been carrying in order to get through a busy season.

Employees who get used to less work when business volume is down may have a hard time getting back up to standard productivity levels when volume picks up again, so it's vital that everyone has enough work to do all the time. Keep odd jobs and special projects lined up for slow times. Having the convention service housepersons make repairs and wash down banquet chairs or banquet room walls is far more productive than laying them off and then hiring more people in housekeeping to do that work. Most people would rather be productive at something than to be idle and try to look busy. Having employees do their own clean-up, maintenance, and repairs also encourages them to take care of their equipment and work areas.

If employees can move to other departments to help out or cross-train, so much the better. This is particularly effective in convention hotels, where customers frequently arrive in groups. You may get people from different departments to help on a busy check-in. Once all the guests are checked in, the employees can go back to their normal duties. Perhaps a few desk clerks could then even help out in other areas. If people know that this is part of the job when they are hired, they won't object when it's time to do it, and morale and commitment are maintained.

The staffing guide establishes the total number of people your operation requires for all positions. From this figure, the company can plan the appropriate number and types of uniforms, locker space, insurance programs, vacation expense, and other budgetary considerations. Adjustments to the guide can be made as the operation changes.

In departments with fixed staffing, such as sales, accounting, engineering, security, and personnel, once the number is set it should be difficult to add an extra person. Before adding people to these areas, consider other ways to make the department more productive. Look carefully at workflow, time management, job design, adding or improving equipment, and resetting work priorities by either postponing non-critical work to a slower period or eliminating it altogether. It takes more time to be this careful, but when you add a person, you're adding a major expense to your fixed overhead in a non-service or non-revenue department. The greater the overhead, the harder it will be to remain competitive and make a profit.

Before adding people in any department, also look at the business volume to see if it's increasing. If overtime rates are up, try to determine whether performance is dropping temporarily because of such factors as a general decrease in morale or increased turnover. Perhaps better management or training could solve the problem.

Labor Cost Analysis. Once staffing guides are established, managers should occasionally look at labor costs and productivity to see that they're staying in line with original standards. For example, are housekeepers still cleaning the standard number of rooms per shift? This kind of checking should be done at least once a week, with trends and details being examined each month.

Some companies use a daily payroll control system in an attempt to monitor labor costs. Others feel such a system requires too much time from managers. They believe that managers essentially become bookkeepers trying to analyze yesterday's results when they should be on the floor responding to today's guests and controlling today's costs. Another concern is that maintaining such records can quickly cost more in labor than the results justify, especially if they are too vague or inaccurate to be of real use.

For a daily labor cost figure to be meaningful, it must be adjusted for all the factors that may affect it. For instance, if an employee is transferred to another department for a few hours, those hours must be properly allocated. If the kitchen is doing prep-work one day for a banquet scheduled for the following day, work hours must be adjusted so that the current day's labor costs don't appear to be out of line with production standards. In addition, if payroll costs aren't adjusted for time spent in training—for new employees, for instance—proper training won't be done. Again, a decision has to be made about whether the expense involved to produce such accuracy is justifiable.

Whether payroll is monitored on a daily or weekly basis, labor cost analysis must be kept in proper perspective. It's a tool to help managers evaluate their operations, not to judge their effectiveness each day.

Many companies aren't giving labor cost control the attention it requires. They may invest in the latest technology, equipment, and talent to calculate and manage food and beverage costs, but then neglect to address the payroll expenses that can sometimes double the food costs figures. Others who do make some effort to control labor costs in a few departments (for example, food and beverage) still fail to control or even review the expenses in other departments (such as engineering, accounting, and sales).

Whether labor cost analysis is the responsibility of the human resources department, the accounting department, or the property's manager, the company's philosophy and values must control the analysis process.

Pay Grades. All jobs with the same starting wage are assigned to the same **pay grade** (see Exhibits 10.7 and 10.8). Each grade has a fixed minimum, which is its starting rate, and a maximum which represents the top pay for that grade. Industry practices and company policy usually influence the number of different pay grades, but most employers try to have as few as possible.

If job titles are placed into grades according to their point values, they'll generally be clustered around the benchmark jobs. Having a different pay grade and starting salary for each job title that has a different point value would be impractical. To avoid this, the difference in point values between grades is often as much as 18 to 20% of the benchmark's value. If the benchmark job has a value of 27 points, for instance, it would be likely that all other job titles within a range of about 25 to 30 points would fall into the same pay grade.

As you jump to another pay grade, the starting rate goes up significantly. For example, in the lower-paying grades, the increase between grades might be around 25 cents. As grades go up, the differences between starting salaries often escalate as well, and may go up to 50 or even 75 cents between grades at the top end of the range.

Not only does the practice of grouping job titles help to simplify wage administration by minimizing the number of pay grades, it also facilitates

Exhibit 10.7   Sample Pay Grade and Rate Schedule

	HOURLY PAY GRADE AND RATE SCHEDULE		
PAY GRADE	MINIMUM	MIDPOINT	MAXIMUM
1	3.75	4.35	4.90
2	4.25	4.90	5.50
3	4.75	5.70	6.65
4	5.00	6.00	7.00
5	5.25	6.30	7.35
6	5.50	6.60	7.70
7	5.75	6.90	8.05
8	6.00	7.20	8.40
9	6.25	7.80	9.35
10	6.50	8.15	9.75
11	6.75	8.45	10.15
12	7.00	8.75	10.50
13	7.50	9.40	11.25
14	8.00	10.00	12.00
15	8.50	11.05	13.60
16	9.00	11.70	14.40
17	9.50	12.35	15.20
18	10.00	13.00	16.00
19	11.00	14.30	17.60
20	12.00	15.60	19.20

compliance with equal pay for equal work requirements. A small operation may need as few as 10 grades, while a major organization might require as many as 60.

The range from starting to maximum within the grade permits a company to reward performance. Within the lower grades, the top rate might be 30% above the starting point. As the grade goes up, the maximum also increases proportionately (see Exhibit 10.9 for a graphic depiction of this increase using information from Exhibit 10.7). Within the highest grades, the top pay rate might be 60% above the starting point, for a number of reasons. People who have reached the higher grades will have fewer opportunities for future upward movement. The broader responsibilities of their jobs provide more room for variations in individual effort and contribution, and should be compensated accordingly. Furthermore, jobs at the higher levels are generally held by experienced, talented people whom management wants to retain. The wider range of pay rates prevents these skilled employees from reaching their maximums too quickly.

Most ranges have a mid-point which serves as a flag to the manager. When an employee reaches this point, you may choose to reduce the amount of each increase and advise the person that the top of the range is near. You may also want to begin training the employee to move into a higher-rated job.

Ranges for different grades will often overlap. This overlap can result in

Exhibit 10.8   Sample Partial Listing: Hourly Pay Grades

Grade 5: $x.xx (insert current rate of pay)

          Night Bell Service
          Garage Cashier
          Food Server/Cashier (Gourmet Shop)
          Room Service Food Server
          Lobby Attendant (Dining Room)
          Checkroom/Phone (Dining Room)
          Roll/Cocktail Server (Cafe)
          Banquet Cashier ($x.xx)*
          Concessions Worker ($x.xx)*

Grade 6: $x.xx

          Employee Cafeteria Supervisor
          Floor Supervisor, Housekeeping
          Valet Parking Captain
          Assistant Bell Captain
          Purchasing Clerk
          Lead Houseperson, Housekeeping
          Night Cleaning Lead, Stewarding
          Housekeeping Penthouse Attendant
          Steward Lead

                 . . . . . .

Grade 17: $x.xx

          Restaurant Cook Supervisor
          Assistant Beverage Manager
          Lead Baker
          Lead Bake Shop Decorator

Grade 18: $x.xx

          HVAC Mechanic
          AV/TV Technician
          Executive Secretary to General Manager
          Guest Service Manager

* Show individually if different from grade rate.

experienced employees' earning as much as or more than inexperienced employees in slightly higher grades, or even more than their immediate supervisors. When these situations arise, the manager whose department is affected may have to make some decisions based on subjective criteria: Is the supervisor likely to be upset by it? If so, should the employee get the raise anyway? How can both best be prepared for the changes in order to minimize problems? Each situation of this sort will have to be addressed individually.

Even if you have a policy of pay for performance, there *has* to be a practical limit on what a job is worth to an employer if the company is to be profitable. People who reach the top of a pay range are sometimes called **red-circled employees** and require some additional decisions from the company. They can no longer be handled in the same manner as everyone else, yet treating situations on a case-by-case basis can result in inconsistency or preferential treatment. Since going above the range of a job's pay grade would be paying more than the job is worth, you must decide whether to exceed the

Exhibit 10.9   Proportionate Growth of Maximum Pay Rate

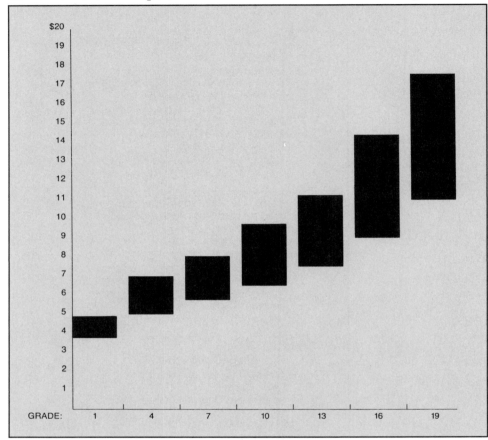

top of the range for such employees, freeze their wages, reduce the amount of increases, or extend the period between increases. Some employers choose to freeze wages but extend additional perks like more time off or longer vacations.

Providing professional development and career pathing for your top performers so that they can move to higher grades is a vital part of the program. Top employees usually have the capability to take on new or additional responsibilities which could justify a higher grade. You must look ahead to these possibilities before people reach the top of their grades, so that you and they will be prepared. An aggressive career development program can help you implement and enforce a firm no-increase-beyond-the-grade policy, which is the key to a fair and effective wage and salary program.

Salaried Employees. The administration of a wage program for salaried employees has the same basic format as the hourly wage program, though there are a few differences. The rate-setting process requires that a substantial number of benchmark positions be compared with outside sources. This survey data is the key to the effectiveness of the salaried program.

Companies may also wish to have a different evaluation system for salaried positions. Since the salaries are so dependent on market conditions, detailed point analyses are less effective. It may be adequate to use only three elements: skill or know-how; judgment, including various levels of problem solving; and accountability, which is the scope of the manager's authority and responsibility.

While the minimum salary is the least amount a company expects to pay for a minimally acceptable candidate, and the mid-point represents the "going rate," the experienced candidate is often already making more than the going rate and receiving extra perks as well. It's not uncommon to offer a 10 to 20% increase over the current rate to induce someone to make a change. Such a practice can mean bringing people in at or near the maximum of the range. This may create serious morale problems with other employees doing similar work, set you up for potential equal pay violations, and increase your labor costs more than you need to. You may also find the new employee is quickly frustrated at finding little room for pay or career advancement. All are good reasons to practice promotion from within and keep your turnover under control. One alternative is to give the candidate a one-time sign-on payment as an incentive to make the change. This can help you keep your wage and salary structure in line over the years.

Commissions and Bonuses. Consideration is often given, particularly in sales areas, to paying commissions, and they can be used effectively in certain situations. The plan must be easily understood, simple to administer, and directed at a specific, measurable target, such as weekend business, off-season business, short-lead business, or new accounts. Commissions can be awarded for individual or group achievement. Unless accomplishments can be easily perceived and clearly measured, however, commissions should be avoided.

Furthermore, since the commission is designed to focus attention on a specific objective and provide incentive to accomplish that goal, care must be taken to ensure that this objective is not achieved at the sacrifice of other areas such as customer service or overall profitability.

Companies have experienced such difficulties administering commission programs that many return to straight salary plans. This is particularly the case when:

- Salespeople get most of their leads from incoming inquiries
- Factors affecting the sales are too numerous and complex
- The value of the business can't be measured accurately

For example, when a salesperson books a convention three years out, but the possibility exists that the customer could cancel six months prior to the date, does the commission get paid or not, and if so, when?

When executive bonus plans are used, the factors for which the bonus will be paid will determine how the executive will manage. Thus, it's critically important to ensure that the executive is rewarded for performance *beyond* the normal requirements and that the emphasis is on long-range as well as short-range performance.

Program Maintenance and Control

Once the basic grades have been established and positions assigned within the grades, additional decisions can be made. For example, a night-shift premium or extra pay for additional responsibilities, such as training new employees or assuming opening and closing duties, can be built in. These increases would be over and above the earnings determined by position in the pay range.

Policies with regard to promotions can also then be handled with consistency. If someone is moved into a higher-rated position, the employee might get either the starting rate for that job or an increase equal to the difference in starting salaries of the old and new pay grades.

Generally speaking, giving promoted employees an increase of up to 15% at one time should be sufficient. If this doesn't bring them up to the starting salary for the new job, they should be **green-circled**, which means that their salary reviews and salary increases should be accelerated until they reach the minimum of the job.

An employee whose salary is already above the minimum but below the mid-point should still be given an increase when promoted. Someone who's already above the mid-point should probably be transferred in at the same rate or given a token increase.

Careful consideration must be given to transfers or the program can quickly lose its balance, particularly when people are transferred to a lower grade. Every effort should be made to maintain their current rate without creating inequities in the departments to which they're being transferred.

As stated earlier, an area cost allowance can be used to compensate people moving into higher cost of living areas, including those who work in foreign countries. Since these adjustments are only made for the period of time that the employee is in the higher cost area, the pay system remains intact.

If the basic wage and salary program is sound, it will be easier for managers to deal with unusual situations. In fact, one of the responsibilities of the wage and salary administrator is to review all the implications of exceptions to the wage and salary program. Variations must always be considered carefully before exceptions are granted. With the mood of workers today, the legal emphasis on equal pay and comparable worth, and other concerns, exceptions to policy can lead to severe morale problems and major lawsuits.

If, for example, a company hires one new manager and refuses to pay relocation costs, then agrees to do so in negotiations with the next new manager, it may be asking for trouble. At best, the relationship it has with the first manager will probably be poor. It sends the message that the company can't be trusted, that employees must fight for everything they get, and that what they're entitled to is arbitrarily decided by the whim of the manager who hired them.

If decisions are made which are exceptions to the wage and salary program, they should be documented and a paper trail left explaining why the exception was made so the company can defend its actions.

Benefit Administration

Benefits must be viewed as an integral part of the company's total compensation philosophy.[6] In the final accounting on profit and loss, labor costs are combined to include direct pay (including bonuses, incentive pay, commissions, and the like), mandatory expenses associated with labor (FICA, FUTA, SUTA, workers' compensation), and voluntary benefit plans. Instead of leaving the design of benefit plans to whatever the insurance companies are marketing, top managers should become as much involved in benefit program design as in other pay programs. Executives should consider—at

[6]See Chapter 15 for a further discussion of certain benefits.

Exhibit 10.10   Rising Cost of Health Care

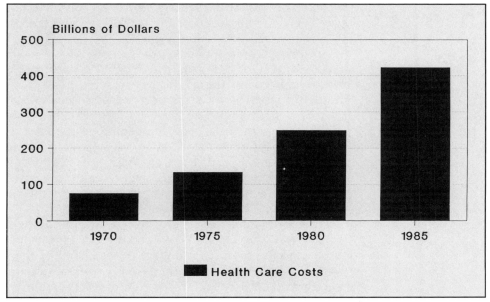

least annually—how much they would like to pay their staffs, how much they must pay to attract and retain the best people, and how much the company can afford.

Employers first began to offer benefits because they could furnish them more cheaply on a group basis than their employees could obtain the same things individually. The system offered financial advantages for both the company and the employee, and goodwill was a by-product as the company gained an image of caring about the well-being of its employees. These were once referred to as "fringe" benefits. The employer generally regarded them as a slowly escalating fixed expense and gave them little attention.

Today, managers have been forced to take a much greater interest in benefits. There's nothing "fringe" about them anymore. The cost of benefits represents between 30 and 40% of payroll, often making benefits the second-largest expense category in the company. And it's growing at an alarming rate, primarily because the cost of health care in this country is out of control.

Health care costs have soared in the past two decades, far surpassing inflation (see Exhibit 10.10). Improved medical care has extended the lifespan of the average person, meaning more people need health care and for a longer time. Adding another dimension is the shocking cost of what was once miracle surgery—such as the organ transplant—but is now an everyday occurrence. As if the actual costs of medical treatment weren't bad enough, the high incidence of fraudulent patient insurance claims, hospital billing errors, and mammoth lawsuit settlements compounds the problem. Insurance companies have had to respond to both the growing demand for health benefits and the rising expenses of medical care by increasing their charges.

Every manager must stay up-to-date on the laws regarding benefits, since a company and its management representatives can be held accountable for misrepresentation of certain benefits. In other words, employees have the right to sue their managers personally. In fact, certain violations are treated as criminal infractions which can result in jail terms for managers.

The changing needs of the work force and the increasing dissatisfaction employees feel about their benefits are forcing employers to rethink their basic approach to the concept of benefits: are they compensation or benevolence, optional or requisite? Much of society tends to view benefits as entitlement and not something left to the discretion of the employer. The fact that more and more benefits are being taxed indicates that the government now regards at least some of them as a form of compensation.

It's not surprising, then, that employees want to have more to say about the benefits they receive. They're not willing to pay taxes on programs they don't want or need. For example, if an employer provides more than $50,000 worth of life insurance to employees, they must pay taxes on the premiums paid for the life insurance coverage over the $50,000, whether they want the coverage or not.

Benefit plans, originally designed around the idea that the average worker was a young male with a wife at home and 2.3 children, must also respond to the significant impact of the changing demographics of the labor market. Single-parent homes, two-income families, and women in the workplace are all on the rise. The population is also aging rapidly, and their needs are changing. Companies that have traditionally provided continuing benefits to their retirees are just realizing the cost, and many may face serious financial challenges. These benefits are currently costing U.S. companies hundreds of billions of dollars and are escalating rapidly.[7] How these costs will be paid is becoming a major issue. The average Fortune 500 company had 12 active employees for every one retiree in 1974. By 1987, that ratio had fallen to only three active workers per retiree.[8] As people retire earlier and live longer, the ratio could get even worse.

Government Legislation

The Employee Retirement Income Security Act of 1974 (ERISA) provided legislative coverage of employee benefit and welfare plans that was far more comprehensive than anything previously enacted. Aimed at protecting workers' rights to certain retirement benefits, it covers such areas as participation and vesting of employees in pension and profit sharing programs, funding, administration, and disbursement of funds.

The 1986 Consolidated Omnibus Budget Reconciliation Act (COBRA) requires that employers with 20 or more workers provide employees, their spouses, and dependent children the opportunity to continue health care coverage under the employer's plan at group rates (plus a 2% fee paid to the employer for handling the account) if coverage terminates under certain circumstances.

The Tax Reform Act of 1986 is the most sweeping legislation ever enacted in the area of benefits and compensation. It's effecting radical changes in the way corporations and individuals are taxed and in the approaches taken to the provision of pensions and other benefits.

In addition, there are aspects of other legislation, such as the Age Discrimination in Employment Act (ADEA), the Deficit Equity and Fiscal Responsibility Act (DEFRA), the Tax Equity and Fiscal Responsibility Act (TEFRA), and Section 89 of the I.R.S. Code (which deals with non-

[7]Laura Jereski, "The Silent Killers," *Forbes*, February 23, 1987, p. 112.
[8]John Nielsen, "Sick Retirees Could Kill Your Company," *Fortune*, March 2, 1987, p. 98.

discrimination testing of benefits) that also affect benefits. All of these laws are extremely complex and are driving up the cost and complexity of benefit administration.

How Companies Are Responding

Because of the amount of money involved—not to mention the employee morale at stake—corporate management is demanding more from the human resources area. Management expects the benefit plan design and administration to comply with legal and tax obligations while meeting the needs of employees. It wants aggressive cost control. It also wants the human resources area to communicate the many complex and related issues and changes to everyone in the organization.

The position of benefit manager is among the fastest growing professions. This function is being added to corporate staffs and individual units. Even very small independent operations are placing professional benefit consultants on retainer and paying for additional assistance from their insurance companies. Exhibit 10.11 presents guidelines for selecting a benefit consultant or insurance company.

Designing the Benefit Program

It would be impossible in one chapter even to list all of the different kinds of benefits being offered to today's workers, much less to try to include everything a manager would need to know to design a benefit program. In designing such programs, employers aim to address the human concerns for security, safety, and freedom from worry about major financial disasters that could ruin lives. Employees generally expect the employer to furnish benefit coverage in five areas:

1. Health

2. Death

3. Paid time off

4. Disability

5. Retirement

Each benefit has a specific purpose. Each company must analyze its own objectives within the human resources strategy and the needs and makeup of its work force. It then must make individual decisions about specific programs. You can't expect to adopt another company's plan and achieve the same results it did.

In order to respond to the egalitarian work ethic and to facilitate compliance with federal laws, employers are merging the benefit programs of their hourly and salaried personnel. Separate dining arrangements, VIP parking, employee stock ownership programs and other perks are frequently eliminated in favor of one total benefit program for all workers.

Along with the traditional programs offered, the changing needs of workers have led to a number of new benefits, such as day-care centers, flextime, pre-retirement counseling, and a variety of insurance options.

Employers are also taking new approaches to providing benefits, such as offering their workers more choices. Within any single benefit, employees might be given a basic plan and the opportunity to obtain more by paying for it themselves. An employer might furnish medical coverage with a $500 annual deductible, for instance, but offer workers the chance to lower their

Exhibit 10.11   Guidelines for Choosing a Benefit Consultant or Insurance Company

- Have a clear idea of what your company's needs are before you talk to a consultant or agent—they can't define your values and goals for you. In addition, your preparation will help you avoid buying more than you need.

- Ask your network contacts for recommendations. Find out what firms they've used, what services they received, and if they're still using them. If not, find out why.

- Talk to more than one firm. Insist on meeting the people who will be working directly with people in your company. Are they professional and competent? Do you like them? Will they be able to relate to others in your organization with whom they'll have contact?

- Invite the consultant's representatives to visit your operation so they can meet the people with whom they'll be interacting and the employees for whom the program is intended.

- Do they listen to you as you outline your company's needs? Are they paying attention, taking notes, asking pertinent questions? Or are they just salespeople, trying to sell you one of their packaged programs?

- Does the firm have the time and interest to give your company the personal service you need?

- Are the firm's philosophy and culture compatible with yours?

- If they're going to be handling only one portion of your benefit program, will their program be compatible with others you're already using?

- Are the firm's areas of strength—such as controlling costs or employee communication—the same ones you need to emphasize?

- Can they tailor their program to meet your specific needs?

- What kind of support and follow-up will they provide?

- Ask for a list of current clients. Is their typical client similar to your company?

- Check their references. Call the companies that are similar to yours in size and service requirements, and ask what they like the most and the least about the consultant.

- Visit the consultant's office to find out how professionally the operation is run and to evaluate the size and caliber of its support staff. Ask what kind of turnover they have.

- To find out how they explain their programs to the employees themselves, ask to attend an employee presentation for one of their current clients. Is it interesting? Does it communicate with the employees on the appropriate level?

- Ask for a written proposal, and look for the following:
  - Is it professionally done?
  - Can you understand it?
  - Does it show that they perceived clearly what you were saying and understood your needs?
  - Does it touch on all major points you had discussed?
  - Does it show attention to details?
  - Does it spell out what their responsibilities will be and what's expected of you?
  - Does it provide a timetable with specific deadlines?
  - Are the costs and terms of payment clear and acceptable?

- Finally, total all the costs, including hidden expenses like employee time, ongoing administrative costs, and printing. Weigh these against the program's value to your company.

deductibles by paying the additional premium costs themselves. Another company might give workers the option of taking a salary reduction in exchange for an equal amount of employer-paid child care, which would be tax free for the employee. The same approach can be taken to increasing many other benefits, including life insurance and pension accumulations.

The idea of having employees pay for even a small part of each of their benefits is gaining popularity because it helps to combat the notion of entitlement. Employers also feel that workers will better appreciate the value and cost of their benefits if they share the cost. Furthermore, if the employees don't want the coverage enough to pay for it, they can choose not to have it. With this arrangement, the company doesn't end up paying for unappreciated coverage.

Flexible Benefit Plans. Another popular approach to giving workers more choices in their benefits involves the concept of **cafeteria** or **flexible benefit plans.** The flexible benefit approach allows employees to choose the benefit programs they want, eliminating unwanted items or unnecessary duplicate coverage that may be provided by a working spouse's employer.

Implementing a flexible plan has some serious ramifications, however, particularly in the area of insurance coverage. Since workers will choose the kinds of coverage they intend to use the most, there's little of the group cost savings that would normally result from including people who aren't likely to make claims. For example, term life insurance coverage for employees has been relatively inexpensive in the past because the premium paid for younger workers included in the plan served to offset the cost of benefits to older workers. With flexible benefits, young people might prefer more vacation time and less life insurance, making the cost of insuring only the older workers a great deal more expensive. Thus, under a flexible benefit plan, the employer may not be able to obtain the same amount of life insurance as previously provided for the same rate.

These cost changes should be carefully considered and allowances made for them before a flexible plan is implemented. Employees should be aware that selecting from a variety of benefits doesn't mean a dollar-for-dollar trade. If you convert to a flexible benefit program and budget the same amount that you had allotted for fixed benefits, people will get less value for what you pay. However, they may still be more satisfied if they're getting more of what they want.

How well informed they are when they're making their choices will have a marked influence on the degree of employee satisfaction. Along with administration and recordkeeping, employers have a major and costly challenge in the areas of communications and education if a flexible program is to be successful. Furthermore, they'll have to decide how to handle the fact that employees won't always make intelligent choices. Should an employer permit an employee with a dependent spouse and children, for example, to forgo life insurance coverage completely in favor of more days off? What happens when one of your workers falls ill without any medical coverage? These are considerations companies must address before they choose to offer a flexible benefit program.

Employers may be better able to control some costs through a flexible plan, because they can determine the amount of the benefit allowance they give to employees and the timing of any increases to it. Employees then select the benefits and levels of coverage based on the dollar limits available to them.

FourSeasons Olympic Hotel

VACATION REQUEST FORM

VACATION REQUESTS MUST BE SUBMITTED TO PERSONNEL THREE WEEKS PRIOR TO VACATION

| EMPLOYEE | PLEASE COMPLETE AND SUBMIT TO YOUR DEPARTMENT HEAD FOR APPROVAL |

DATE _____

EMPL ID # _____   NAME _____

DEPT. _____   HIRE DATE _____

DAYS REQUESTED _____

DATES REQUESTED _____

☐ VACATION PAY IN ADVANCE   **(MUST BE APPROVED BY PERSONNEL)**   DATE REQUIRED _____

| DEPARTMENT HEAD | IF VACATION TIME APPROVED, PLEASE SIGN, DATE AND RETURN TO PERSONNEL |

SIGNATURE _____   DATE _____

| DIRECTOR OF PERSONNEL | PLEASE COMPLETE AND SUBMIT TO DIVISION HEAD FOR APPROVAL |

VACATION PAY IN ADVANCE APPROVED   _____

DAYS AVAILABLE _____   VERIFIED _____

DAYS PAID   _____

DAYS REMAINING _____

COMMENTS _____

_____

_____

SIGNATURE _____   DATE _____

| DIVISION HEAD | PLEASE SIGN, DATE AND RETURN TO PERSONNEL |

SIGNATURE _____   DATE _____

WHITE - PERSONNEL   YELLOW - PAYROLL   PINK - DEPARTMENT

Proper administration of the benefit program contributes to employee satisfaction and facilitates company control. (Courtesy of Four Seasons Olympic Hotel, Seattle, Washington)

Employee Satisfaction. In the design and administration of any benefit program, ensuring employee satisfaction must be a priority. If it's to be perceived as a benefit, it must be something the employees want, and it must be administered efficiently. If an insurance company is reimbursing employees slowly or making numerous errors in responding, for instance, many of the morale-building advantages of the health care program are lost. Similarly, the phrase "paid vacation" can be a mockery to the employee who's packed and ready to take the family to Disney World and shows up to collect a vacation paycheck that isn't there because someone forgot to authorize it.

Controlling Costs

Medical Insurance. In the area of soaring health care costs in particular, employers are trying a number of new approaches:

- Alternate payment methods, such as new funding vehicles, third-party claims administration, and self-insurance

- Reduction of coverage by eliminating payment of first-dollar expenses and raising deductibles (transferring responsibility to employees for a portion of the cost of medical treatment makes them question the necessity and frequency of such treatment while they shop around for the least costly service that's appropriate for them)

- Cost containment measures, including health maintenance organizations (HMOs), preferred provider organizations (PPOs), hospice care, birthing centers, ambulatory surgery centers, use of generic drugs, and second-opinion surgery

- Education and prevention through wellness programs

Finally, employers are scrutinizing their health plan expenses far more closely than ever before. Since the costs of billing errors and misrepresenting insurance claims are actually passed back to the company, monitoring and controlling all of the medical costs and claims can result in substantial savings. Employers are also teaching employees how to shop for and use medical services more carefully and providing more guidance and assistance in preparing and submitting claims.

Time Off. With the rising cost of labor, companies are also adopting policies to address more directly the problems encountered with employee time off. For instance, establishing a three-day wait before sick-pay goes into effect and then using the savings to provide a system of days off for good attendance is a more positive approach than paying employees to be sick.

Companies are also giving fewer holidays and extending vacation time that can be taken during slow periods. By substituting floating holidays, such as birthdays or personal days, the employer has to pay less premium pay, since not everyone takes the same day off. Service is also better because the operation doesn't have to run with a skeleton crew on holidays.

To help combat the negative impact these kinds of changes can bring, employers should keep in mind many benefits that cost next to nothing which are high on goodwill and the sense of security they generate. Such programs might include setting up special funds for flood, fire, or other disasters experienced by employees; or a policy of continuing to pay wages or health care costs for three months to survivors of an employee who dies.

Communication

Because of the increasing costs, employee dissatisfaction, and the variety and complexity of options available today, the communication of benefit information to the worker is a vital part of benefit administration. Employees must understand what they have, what their choices are, and how to use their benefits wisely. The company should also communicate that these are the *current* benefits. This helps to minimize the feeling of entitlement and to put people on notice that their benefit package will change from time to time.

Employees should also realize the value represented. Few employees

Your Hospital Services Checklist

When you are hospitalized, the following checklist can help you keep track of the services you receive. You may bring it to the hospital or fill it out as soon as you get home, whichever is more convenient. It's easy to use. Just indicate the dates of your hospitalization in the spaces provided. Record the services you receive in the column under the appropriate date. Add extra columns on a separate sheet of paper if your stay exceeds 6 days.

Services Received:

Dates Of Hospitalization

Services						
1. Transportation by ambulance to or from the hospital						
2. Private room (PR), semi-private (SP), ward (W) or intensive care (ICU)						
3. Blood tests						
4. X-rays						
5. Tests on your heart: A. Electrocardiogram (EKG or ECG) B. Echocardiogram C. Stress test D. Halter monitor						
6. Therapy A. Intravenous D. Radiation B. Physical E. Occupational C. Respiratory F. Speech						
7. Ultrasounds						
8. Scans						
9. Oxygen						
10. Blood transfusions						
11. Drugs						
12. Operating room						
13. Anesthesia						
14. Recovery room						
15. Equipment to take home such as a cane, walker or crutches						
Maternity Patients Only						
16. Labor room						
17. Nursery (should be no charge for a newborn kept in your room)						

Your Checklist And Hospital Bill— Do They Match?

Be sure to ask the hospital to send you an *itemized bill*. Then match your bill against your checklist. Make sure the admission and discharge dates are correct.

If you find errors or have questions about any charges, call the hospital billing office and ask them to review your records. If you find an overcharge, don't forget to get a corrected bill!

It's Worth A Second Look

Hospitals and other providers can and do make mistakes on their bills. Don't assume yours is correct. Use the hospital services checklist to carefully check your bill. Your participation can help control health insurance costs and a second look may save you money!

Many employers are getting help from their insurance providers to involve employees in managing health care costs by distributing paycheck stuffers and other information pieces like the one above. (Courtesy of Aetna Life Insurance Company, Hartford, Connecticut) realize that each thousand dollars they receive from their insurance company in payment of medical costs is equal to a 50-cent-an-hour increase for an entire year.

Also, since benefit costs probably equal around 33% of your annual payroll, try asking your employees to consider whether they'd rather have their current benefits or a 33% increase in wages. If they say they'd rather have the wage increase, you haven't done an adequate job of communicating and selling your benefits. If you had, employees would realize that, in all probability, they couldn't go out on their own with *double* that amount—even tax free—and buy the benefits that you're providing under your group plans.

If they could find such a program on an individual basis, the cost might well exceed 100% of their wages, particularly for minimum-wage workers. What's more, if they purchased their own benefits and you gave them the 33% increase, they'd have to pay taxes on the additional income (perhaps even in a higher tax bracket), thus reducing the size of the actual raise.

Some communications pieces, such as the Summary Plan Description (SPD) explaining medical, pension, and other major insurance programs, are required by law. Most companies choose to produce a more extensive summary of all of their benefits and often hold benefit explanation meetings as well. Since these explanations are becoming more complicated and time-consuming, the benefit explanation meeting is frequently not conducted at the time of hiring. Instead, it is usually scheduled right before the major benefits go into effect.

To reinforce this information, the benefit manager could also attend various departmental meetings, elaborating on one benefit each time and answering employees' questions. Since keeping managers informed is so extremely critical, the same approach should be used at department head meetings, too.

Insurance companies can usually assist in the communications process. They often offer posters, paycheck stuffers, and other materials for their clients' use, or they know of companies that publish such materials. Sometimes, they also rent or lend audio or video tapes.

In-house publications should be used to keep reinforcing the value of the benefit program. For example, right before a holiday, an article could come out about the cost of holiday pay. It could be reinforced by the memo sent out to announce the holiday. Timed to coincide with the vacation season, information about vacations and their cost might accompany an article about where people will be going, keeping the value of this benefit in the minds of employees.

Bulletin boards, table tents in the cafeteria, letters to home, and employee meetings are all vehicles that could be used effectively to communicate benefits and their value. An individualized summary of benefits could also be distributed to each employee annually.

Put vacation checks in brightly-colored envelopes, or in greeting cards thanking employees for the efforts of the past year and wishing each individual a safe vacation. Having managers deliver these envelopes personally is far better than just sending out vacation checks with regular payroll and letting employees go off without anyone noticing. The same is true for other kinds of payments, such as insurance and tuition reimbursement checks. Employers that merely send benefits through inter-office mail miss a wonderful opportunity.

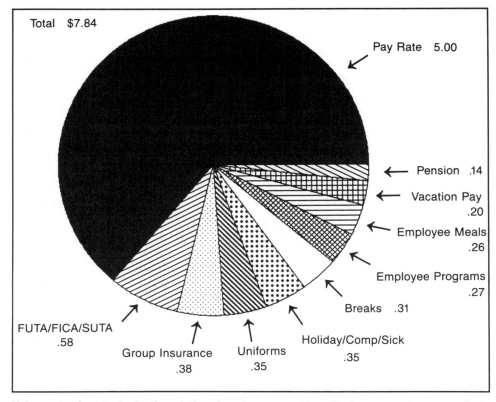

Total $7.84

Pay Rate 5.00

Pension .14

Vacation Pay .20

Employee Meals .26

Employee Programs .27

Breaks .31

Holiday/Comp/Sick .35

Uniforms .35

Group Insurance .38

FUTA/FICA/SUTA .58

Using a pie chart to depict the relative size of wages and benefits is one way to communicate the value of benefits to employees.

The problems facing employers in the areas of wages and benefits may seem overwhelming. However, well-thought-out programs with efficient design and flexibility, along with aggressive and continuous education of employees and supervisors, can result in a positive message about your company as a great place to work.

Key Terms

area cost allowance
benchmark job
cafeteria benefit plan
classification system
cost parity
entitlement
fixed rate
flexible benefit plan
green-circled employees

job analysis
job evaluation
pay grade
pay for performance
point factor analysis
ranking process
red-circled employees
staffing guide
wage survey

Discussion Questions

1. Under what circumstances is pay likely to be effective as an incentive to workers to improve performance?

2. What is wrong with increasing starting salaries to recruit more people?

Communicating the value of benefits helps promote employee satisfaction. (Courtesy of B.B.D. Enterprises, Burger King, Grand Rapids, Michigan)

3. What are some of the factors a department head should consider before making an exception to the company's wage and salary program?

4. What are the advantages of running overtime instead of hiring temporary workers?

5. What problems occur when a company hires a highly-skilled professional at a pay rate above the organization's existing range for that job? How can these problems be avoided?

6. What are employers doing to respond to the increasing costs of providing health care insurance to their employees?

7. What are some of the reasons a manager needs to be thoroughly conversant with the benefit program his or her employer provides?

11 Employment Laws

Keeping up with employment laws and the changes to them is fast becoming one of an employer's major responsibilities. The employer's managers must then implement those laws and changes within their organizations by setting up the procedures and forms, educating the employees, and monitoring compliance. They must also deal with the rash of lawsuits that usually follows each new law.

Most companies find it necessary to retain a law firm specializing in employment law relations. Many large operations even have their own staff of employment law attorneys. Among the services such a firm or staff can provide are:

- Furnishing regular notification to their clients of new laws and changes

- Recommending appropriate means and steps of implementation

- Advising ways to prevent possible lawsuits

- Reviewing employee handbooks, personnel policies, and other personnel forms before they're printed or reprinted

- Counseling on any termination that may suggest potential litigation problems

- Assisting in the preparation and defense of employment-related lawsuits

There are many other ways this legal counsel can assist an employer. Still, even this short list makes it clear why the law firm should specialize in the employer's particular industry and have many clients in the employer's state.

Even with the law firm on hand, however, most managers look to the director of human resources to keep them informed on a wealth of current information. Some of the ways the human resources director keeps up include joining personnel and trade associations, reading newsletters and other publications, and attending seminars and conventions.

Some understanding of how a law, once passed, is interpreted and defined can help every manager. Legislation passed either federally or by a state usually spells out intent and sets parameters for the administration of the law. The agency or other body assigned to administer and enforce the law prepares procedures, designs and issues relevant forms, and outlines the details and many of the regulations, including penalties.

Under the statutory system in practice in the United States, as lawsuits alleging violations of the statutes are brought, decisions are made by trial judges and appeals are handled by appellate judges. Until it's handled by the U.S. Supreme Court, there can be many different interpretations as to the meaning or application of a law. Actual specifics and clear guidelines won't be realized until many cases have been heard and precedents set. As a result, the older a law gets, the better defined and more specific it becomes.

Achieving compliance with these laws as they change and develop is indeed complex. The task is further complicated by the fact that the federal government may pass one piece of legislation and the state governments may enact more rigid versions, or even develop their own laws. Much of the legislation developed to protect the worker carries with it personal liability and penalties against the manager who violates the law. In some cases, these penalties include fines—which can't always be reimbursed by the company—or even jail terms. Judgments against companies found to be in violation can soar into the hundreds of thousands of dollars. This is why it's important to understand the intent of the law and follow it in spirit. An employer acting in good faith will generally minimize the potential liabilities.

This chapter is designed to give a broad overview of some of the federal employment laws as they apply to the hospitality industry, to outline briefly the intent of and areas covered by the law, and, where possible, to consider some of the commonest problems employers face with the law. *This is by no means a complete review of each law.* In addition, many states have laws to cover these subjects. The state laws may affect more employers or be stricter or more comprehensive. To achieve a working understanding of the complexities and ramifications of all the employment laws in this country and in each state, you would have to pursue reading materials far beyond the scope of these pages.

Wage and Hour Legislation

The **Fair Labor Standards Act (FLSA)** of 1938, commonly referred to as the **Wage and Hour Law**, establishes regulations relevant to pay and hours worked. Administered by the **Wage and Hour Division** of the U.S. Department of Labor, the Act regulates the payment of wages including overtime and deductions, limits the employment of minors, and enforces equal pay for men and women performing equal work. The Act covers every employer, regardless of the number of employees, who has employees engaged in interstate commerce. While the Act has been in existence since 1938, service workers were exempt from coverage until 1967. In fact, with respect to many major issues and provisions, the hospitality industry was only brought into full compliance in 1979.

We'll look briefly at a few of the major areas covered. There are many others, and every employer is expected to know and follow all the regulations. Furthermore, many states also have their own wage and hour laws, and they must also be followed. As with any legislation, you must conform to the more stringent of the two versions.

Payment of Wages

The Act sets the **minimum wage** that can be paid and defines the exemptions and exceptions to minimum wage. Every covered employer must pay employees at least that amount, although a sub-minimum wage category does exist for some full-time students, employees in special education programs, and other special categories, such as agriculture.

In addition, certain credits may be used in the calculation of the minimum wage. For instance, where meals, lodging, or other facilities are provided for the benefit of the employee, the reasonable cost of these facilities can be considered as wages and used in calculating the minimum wage. (The employer's cost of providing uniforms isn't generally allowable as such a credit, because uniforms are usually regarded as being of more benefit to the employer than the employee.)

Another credit, and one of the most commonly used, is the **tip credit**. A tip or gratuity is a discretionary amount of money beyond the amount billed, left voluntarily by a customer for a specific employee. In calculating the minimum wage of tipped employees, the employer can take a tip credit no greater than the actual amount of tips earned by the employee. The tip credit also can't exceed 40% of the minimum wage.

The workweek is defined as seven consecutive 24-hour days. Each week must stand alone in compliance with many of the regulations, such as the reporting of tips and payment of overtime, even if an employer pays every other week.

Take the case of the employee who earns a large amount of tips one week but minimal tips the next, so that the amount of tips reported the second week doesn't bring the total earned, with wages, up to minimum wage for that week. An employer paying every two weeks couldn't average the totals for the two weeks in order to use the tip credit for both weeks. Instead, the employer would have to pay additional wages for the second week to make up the difference and bring the total earned for that week up to minimum wage.

Gratuities automatically added to guest checks, such as in banquets and room service, are not considered tips. Tip credits can't be taken for them. (According to federal law, however, these employees can be considered **high-commission employees**; this means that if they make more than one-and-a-half times the current minimum wage and more than half of their total income comes from these automatic gratuities, they can be exempt from overtime and their hourly rate can be less than minimum wage.)

An employer taking a tip credit must advise its employees of this fact in writing and tell them how much it is (see Exhibit 11.1). Employers must also advise employees that they're free to keep their tips. Employers who force an employee to pay a percentage of the tip to other employees violate the tip credit exception unless a voluntary tip pooling arrangement has been agreed upon. Some states have stricter provisions; others don't allow wage credits at all.

Deductions

It's also a violation for an employer to take a deduction from an employee's pay if doing so would reduce the wage below minimum, unless deducting for certain specified exceptions, such as income tax, credit union, or union dues. No deductions are allowed for such items as breakage, lost checks, uniform maintenance, and deposits on uniforms or locks if such deductions will reduce the employee's wages below the minimum.

For example, requiring someone to make a deposit on uniforms you

Exhibit 11.1   Notice to Tip Employees

NOTICE TO TIP EMPLOYEES

If you receive over $30.00 per month in tips, you are required by Federal Income Tax Law to report the full amount of such tips. The report is to be submitted to your employer at the end of each pay period.

Failure to report such tips is considered a crime. You may be liable not only for back taxes, but also an additional penalty equal to 50% of the tax, plus 6% interest. Tax evasion is also punishable by imprisonment.

Internal Revenue Code Section 6053 and 6652 (c)

HIRING AGREEMENT ADDENDUM FOR TIPPED EMPLOYEES

1

I understand that I am being paid _____ per hour and that my employer is taking a tip credit of _____. I further understand that as my wages change my employer will continue to take tip credits as allowed by the Federal/State Wage and Hour Laws.

2

I have also been informed that it is not a condition of employment to share my tips with anyone, and, if I choose to share my tips, it will be because I voluntarily wish to do so. I understand that any tips I receive are mine to do so with as I choose.

3

I have also been advised that Federal Law requires that I report all my tips to my employer. I agree to report all my tips in the space provided on my time record at the end of each pay period.

| DATE | EMPLOYEE'S SIGNATURE | WITNESS'S SIGNATURE |

issue or to buy a uniform such as a tuxedo would be illegal if the deduction were to reduce the wages to less than minimum wage for that week. The employer can't spread the cost of the purchase over several weeks to avoid bringing that one week's wages to less than minimum. Additionally, if cleaning costs would reduce earnings too much, the employer must clean uniforms or pay for employees to do so. When paying employees for such cleaning, in the absence of any specific costs, such as using a rental service or specific dry cleaning bills, the rule of thumb is one hour's pay per week.

A uniform is defined as any clothing required for the job that isn't basic street wear. Black leather shoes would be considered street clothing and wouldn't be considered a uniform, even when the employee is required to wear them at work.

Deductions for such items as breakage, missing cash, or lost keys can also be taken only if they don't reduce earnings below the minimum, and if the employee so authorizes without any fear, threat, or intimidation. This means you can't tell an employee to pay back missing funds or be fired. In the case of theft, the employer may make deductions that reduce the employee's pay below the minimum, but only if the employee has been convicted. Your best approach with employees who handle cash or other items of value is to establish a policy stating clear and detailed procedures, outline the penalties—such as termination—for *not following the procedures*, and then enforce the policy strictly.

Employee's Daily Record of Tips

Employer's name

Month | Year

Date	a. Tips received directly from customers and other employees	b. Tips received on charge receipts	c. Tips paid out to other employees
1			
2			
3			
4			
5			
6			
7			
8			
9			
10			
11			
12			
13			
14			
15			
16			
Sub-totals			

(Continued on back) — Form **4070-A** (Rev. 5-84)

Date	a. Tips received directly from customers and other employees	b. Tips received on charge receipts	c. Tips paid out to other employees
17			
18			
19			
20			
21			
22			
23			
24			
25			
26			
27			
28			
29			
30			
31			
Sub-totals			
Sub-totals from front			
Totals			

Tips (col. a plus col. b minus col. c). Report this amount on Form 4070.. ▶

Form **4070** (Rev. May 1984)
Department of the Treasury
Internal Revenue Service

Employee's Report of Tips to Employer
▶ For Paperwork Reduction Act Notice, see back of this form.

OMB No. 1545-0065

Employee's name and address

Social security number

Employer's name and address

Month or shorter period in which tips were received
from , 19 , to , 19

Tips $

Signature

Date

A tip employee fills out and retains Form 4070-A, the Employee's Daily Record of Tips. This employee also fills out Form 4070, the Employee's Report of Tips to Employer, and turns it over to the employer.

Overtime

Overtime, as defined by federal law, is one-and-a-half times the regular pay rate and must be paid after 40 hours unless the employee is exempt. Union contract or company policy may provide for overtime pay after less than 40 hours or at a rate higher than one-and-a-half times the regular rate.

Exhibit 11.2   Sample Overtime Calculation

Mary worked 40 hours in one week at her regular job at $5.00 an hour. In addition, she worked 10 hours for the same employer in the same workweek as a banquet server at $3.75 an hour; but she also received tips for this work equivalent to $7.00 an hour. Her employer-provided meals are valued at $.25 an hour for both jobs.

To determine the **rate** at which overtime will be paid,

Add:

Regular pay ($5.00 × 40 hours)	$ 200.00
Value of meals ($.25 × 50 hours)	12.50
Value of banquet service work ($3.75 × 10 hours)	37.50
Value of tips	70.00
Total value of the 50 hours of work	$ 320.00

Divide:

$320.00 ÷ 50 hours worked = $6.40/per hour average for the week

Multiply:
$ 6.40
× 1.5
$ 9.60   **rate** at which Mary's overtime will be paid

Multiply:
$ 9.60
× 10   hours of overtime Mary worked

96.00 overtime pay
+ 200.00 regular pay
$ 296.00 total pay for Mary for the workweek

Even when an employee who puts in 40 hours in one department goes home and comes back later to work extra hours in another department, the extra hours worked must be paid at time-and-a-half, generally based on the weighted average of all earnings. This means you would add the earnings from the regular job, the part-time job, and all tips, and divide the sum by the total number of hours worked on both jobs to come up with an average hourly wage for that week. Overtime must be paid based on this average hourly wage, unless you have specified in an agreement signed in advance by the employee that extra hours paid at time-and-a-half will be paid at the rate of the job in which the person was working when he or she went into overtime. Exhibit 11.2 presents a sample overtime calculation.

Basically, four types of employees are exempt from overtime regulations: outside sales, professional, executive, and administrative. The outside sales exemption requires that the employee make sales away from the place of employment in excess of 90% of the workweek. Inside sales personnel aren't included in this exemption.

The professional exemption was designed for doctors, lawyers, and others whose work is predominantly intellectual and non-routine. In the hospitality industry, few positions, if any, have been able to meet the specifications of this exemption. In spite of the training and special skills required of a sous chef or garde-manger, for example, the Wage and Hour Division has generally declined to recognize these kinds of positions as a "profession."

The exemption most often used in the hospitality industry is the executive exemption. Employees who meet the following four tests can be exempt from the overtime provisions of the Wage and Hour Law as executives:

1. They must supervise two or more other employees.

2. Their salary must be $155 or more per week. (The minimum amount is determined by the Wage and Hour Division.)

3. They must have the power to hire and fire, or their recommendations must carry significant weight.

4. Their primary duty must be managing, meaning they can't do non-exempt work more than 40% of the time in any given workweek. As a rule of thumb, they can't do the work of the people they supervise, such as seating customers, setting tables, or handling the cash register. They must be able to exercise discretionary powers and set policies on the job. The prevailing attitude about this test has been that only the manager of the department can set policies within that department, and all others follow those policies. Hence, only one person in a department is usually considered exempt using the executive exemption status. However, the Wage and Hour Division has recently been interpreting this rule to allow an assistant manager who is working on an entirely different shift from the manager to be exempt if the other requirements are met.

In addition, an exempt employee who earns more than $250 a week may perform work not directly related to the exempt executive status as long as it doesn't exceed 50% of the working time.

The next most commonly used exemption in the hospitality industry is the administrative exemption. An administrative employee is one who performs office or non-manual work. This work must directly assist an executive; it must be done only under general supervision; and the bulk of the work must be specialized or technical, requiring special training, experience, or knowledge. The worker must be able to make discretionary judgments and must not perform non-exempt work more than 40% of the workweek. Examples of positions that meet these criteria would be purchasing agents, safety directors, and many inside salespeople. Positions such as head bartenders, paymasters, credit managers, and convention service coordinators must be closely examined against the administrative criteria.

Child Labor   The Wage and Hour Law defines a child or minor as anyone under 18 years of age. Children between the ages of 14 and 16 may work in occupations other than manufacturing and mining. There are certain positions in which minors can never be employed, such as work around hazardous equipment, driving motor vehicles, or jobs in establishments selling or serving alcohol. State and local laws may provide other restrictions as well.

People 14 through 16 years of age can be employed only under certain additional circumstances. They may not work:

1. During school hours

2. Before 7 a.m. or after 7 p.m.

3. More than three hours a day on school days

4. More than 18 hours a week during the school week

5. More than eight hours a day on non-school days

6. More than 40 hours a week in a non-school week

7. More than four hours straight without a break

Any employer hiring minors must set up the controls to ensure that they don't violate these guidelines, since the penalties for violation are severe. The human resources department must also be sure the minor provides an age certificate and a work permit, copies of which should be kept in the personnel file.

Equal Pay

The **Equal Pay Act** of 1963 is basically an amendment to the Fair Labor Standards Act, and covers employers subject to the FLSA. However, since 1979, it has been administered and enforced by the EEOC. It guarantees that pay differentials for substantially similar jobs in the same establishment shall not be based on the sex of the employee.

Before you may assign one job a higher wage than another, you must be able to prove that there's a substantial difference between the two jobs, based on skill, effort, responsibility, and performance under difficult working conditions. Examples of the latter might include hazardous duty pay or night shift differentials. While there's not always a simple way to distinguish between the amount of skill, effort, and responsibility needed for two different jobs, one rule of thumb is that the higher-paying position must be 15 to 20% more difficult. The positions of housekeeper and houseman, for instance, have been litigated. The courts have found no substantial difference between the two jobs; therefore, the pay must be the same.

Note that experience and education are not on the list for justifying a difference in pay. The practice of using either of these for pay distinction, particularly in higher-level management jobs, must be backed up with substantial justification.

Differences in wages on the same job in the same establishment may be allowed. Defenses used to justify differences in pay practices include merit increases, incentive increases, seniority increases, or plans involving production or piece rate. An employer may assign an employee temporarily to another assignment and continue to pay that employee at his or her regular rate. Such temporary assignments shouldn't exceed 30 days.

The Equal Pay Act also covers other forms of compensation such as overtime, benefits, and working conditions.

Garnishments

The Wage and Hour Division also administers and enforces the **Federal Wage Garnishment Law**. Part of the Consumer Credit Protection Act passed in 1968 and effective in 1970, this law limits the amount of an employee's disposable earnings which may be garnished in any one week and prohibits discharging an employee because of a garnishment for any *one* indebtedness. The term "one indebtedness" refers to a single debt, regardless of the number of levies made in order to collect it.

APPLICATION FOR DEVIATION ON HOURS FOR MINORS

MICHIGAN DEPARTMENT OF LABOR

BUREAU OF EMPLOYMENT STANDARDS

WAGE HOUR ADMINISTRATION

By authority conferred on the department of labor by Section 20 of Act No. 90 of the Public Acts of 1978, as amended, being 409.120 of the Michigan Compiled Laws, the Director of Labor may grant a deviation from hours when it is determined to be in the best interest of the minor and the community.

Business Name
and Address
where minor
will be
employed

NAME _____ PHONE _____

STREET _____

CITY & STATE _____COUNTY_____
Zip Code

We wish to employ _____, Birthdate_____
Minor Employee's Name

as a _____
Type of Job

to work until _____ on _____ Sunday through Thursday, and until _____on Friday
Time   Number of Nights   Time

and/or Saturday nights for a maximum of _____ hours per week, school and work combined.

Signature of Employer or Representative _____
Signature   Title

PARENT OR GUARDIAN

We give our permission for _____ to work the above stated hours.
Minor Employee's Name

Signature of Parent or Legal Guardian _____

SCHOOL REPRESENTATIVE

_____attends school _____between _____ am. & _____ pm.
Employee's Name   Hours Per Week

I believe that working the above stated hours will not be detrimental to school work and/or attendance.

SCHOOL _____ SIGNATURE _____
Title

EMPLOYER MUST PROVIDE CLOSE ADULT SUPERVISION

See information on reverse side

Before hiring a minor, employers are required to obtain the proper authorizations from parents and school and keep them on file.

Again, the federal law works in tandem with various state laws, and the employer must follow the regulations which result in the smaller garnishment amount being taken.

Compliance Audits

Since the Fair Labor Standards Act is the law most frequently violated by employers, a company can expect to be audited for compliance at some time. Most audits originate as the result of a complaint, but the investigating officer may audit not only the area of complaint, but also all other areas covered under the Fair Labor Standards Act.

The investigation will probably include reviewing personnel and payroll records and even interviewing employees. Any instance of non-compliance, even unintentional, may be investigated, and the employer forced to make amends. Thus, a single miscalculation that occurs on a daily basis, such as interrupting an employee during a meal period or not paying for time to change in or out of uniform, can add up over a year or two to a major sum of money.

Since the impact of these investigations can be substantial, it's important that the employer contact an employment lawyer upon being notified of an investigation. It's preferable even to have counsel present at the time the investigator arrives.

Employment Discrimination

Many types of employment discrimination are prohibited by many different acts. One of the most important of these acts is the **Civil Rights Act**, passed in 1964 and amended numerous times since then. The section of this Act known as **Title VII** covers employment and guarantees everyone the privilege of being hired and working in an environment free from discrimination on the basis of race, sex, religion, or national origin. The Act established the **Equal Employment Opportunity Commission (EEOC)** to oversee its enforcement and administration. It covers all employers engaged in interstate commerce with 15 or more employees.

Title VII clearly spells out that the employer can select or pay a person based only on the following criteria as they relate to the specific job in question:

1. The person's ability
2. Established job standards
3. The physical requirements of the job
4. Experience
5. Education

If you use any of the above for selection, you must be able to prove that there's a direct relationship between those criteria and the performance on the job for which you're hiring, and you must use the same standards consistently.

In an industry which encourages promotion from within and in which competition for employees is fierce, it's tempting to relax standards occasionally and hire someone with less than the established qualifications, particularly when business is slow and you have time to train. Once you do so, however, it will be very difficult later to justify returning to the higher standards. For example, if you would like to require that a person in the accounts receivable department have prior front office experience, but in the past you've hired a person without it, you may be accused of discrimination if you turn down an otherwise qualified minority applicant who doesn't have the front office experience.

The only exception to using the above-listed criteria for selection would be a **bona fide occupational qualification (BFOQ)**. A BFOQ allows an employer to hire people based on the need for a specific age, sex, religion, or national origin for the performance of the job. Positions to which the BFOQ would apply include models, restroom attendants, and actors. You could require that the entire front of the house of a French restaurant be able to speak French. However, if you hired a busperson who couldn't, you would lose the BFOQ for the whole restaurant.

Many practices that were justified in the past as "business necessity" are now being ruled illegal, including the following:

- Decisions based on preserving the company's image—for example, keeping all male waiters in a formal dining room or hiring young, attractive receptionists

- Refusing to hire women because they can't lift heavy objects, when in fact lifting such objects occurs only on an occasional basis (you may even be required to buy a piece of equipment to assist the female worker if such equipment is available and reasonable)

It's possible to be in violation unintentionally. For instance, if your business is located in a predominately white neighborhood, and you rely mainly on walk-in and word-of-mouth recruiting, any imbalance that already exists in your work force will be perpetuated. Even though you didn't intentionally discriminate, your recruiting method would have an adverse impact on the employment of minority group members.

The Act also specifies that it's the employer's obligation to provide a work environment free of discrimination and bias. If an employee is discriminated against by another employee, the company may be liable *even if unaware of the discriminatory practice*. The employer may also be liable for violations if policies or practices have an effect of discrimination even though none was intended, such as permitting ethnic or racial jokes or slurs. Management should publish and conspicuously post statements that reflect a policy of fair treatment and permitting no discrimination (see Exhibit 11.3).

Dress code and appearance standards must also be considered in light of Title VII. You can have different grooming standards for each sex, as long as they're reasonable, appropriate, and equally restrictive. Consistency is also important. If one restaurant within a hotel requires male employees to be clean-shaven and gives the reason as customer contact, the entire front of the house—which may include the front desk, bell service, and other restaurants—must have the same policy. If the requirement is said to be made because those in the restaurant handle food, then all food handlers must be clean-shaven. Such subjective standards should be set company-wide and not decided by individual managers, since each new manager may have a different interpretation and point of view.

Exhibit 11.3   Sample Fair Treatment Statement

> Every employee, regardless of position, will be treated with respect and in a fair and just manner at all times. All persons will be considered for employment, promotion and training on the basis of qualifications without regard to race, color, national origin, religion, age, sex, disability or veteran status.
>
> We recognize that, being human, mistakes may be made in spite of our best efforts. We want to correct these as soon as they happen. The only way we can do this is to know your problems and complaints. No member of management is too busy to hear the concerns of any employee.

Courtesy of Marriott Corporation, Washington, D.C.

Even company-wide standards must be based on business need. In particular, unless there's a valid reason, an employer can't refuse to allow items that are symbolic of national or religious heritage. You can't require a black employee to shave off a goatee, since it's regarded as a symbol of the race and to make such a requirement could be a violation of Title VII. Also, many black employees have a skin condition which makes shaving impractical. In such a medical situation, they must also be allowed to keep their beards.

Most companies have a policy in their dress code which states that whatever style is worn must be conservative and in keeping with the conservative image of the company.

Religion

It's illegal to refuse to hire someone who must have time off for religious observance at a time when the person would be needed at work. Some religions allow the person to satisfy the religious obligation on more than one day. If not, time off for religious observance must be given unless the company can prove that undue hardship on the business exists and that the job can't be performed by anyone else. It's generally wise to check with an employment law attorney before refusing to hire someone or refusing to give time off under these circumstances.

Sexual Discrimination

Settlements of sex discrimination lawsuits are among the costliest in employment litigation.

Once enacted as a form of protection, state laws limiting women's hours and working conditions have now been declared illegal. Other actions that could now be interpreted as discriminatory include:

- Establishing minimum or maximum weight or height requirements that would discriminate against women, unless those requirements are mandatory for successful completion and are essential elements of the job

- Refusing to hire women because of a lack of adequate uniforms, locker space, or other such facilities

- Denying employment because of pregnancy

Pregnancy must be treated as any other illness (see Exhibit 11.4). A pregnant employee can't be removed from the job unless she's unable to perform it, or for other health or safety reasons. The Federal Pregnancy Discrimination Act of 1978 provides that:

Exhibit 11.4   Sample Request for Leave of Absence

Request for Leave of Absence

NAME_____DEPT._____DATE_____

I hereby apply for a leave of absence for _____ consecutive days, from
_____ through _____.

I am requesting this leave for the following reason(s):

MEDICAL	**PERSONAL**
☐ Personal Illness	☐ Family Illness
☐ Accident	☐ Personal Leave
☐ Pregnancy	☐ Other

Please explain_____.

In the event a Leave of Absence is granted, I understand and agree that:

1. I must turn the following in to the Personnel Office before I leave:
    A. Photo-I.D.   B. Meal ticket   C. Keys and/or Bank
    D. Uniform card   E. Name tag   *F. Parking Card
    *In order to have my space held for me, I realize that I must continue payments during my leave.

2. A leave for MEDICAL REASONS MUST BE ACCOMPANIED BY A DOCTOR'S STATEMENT setting forth the nature of the illness and the estimated length of disability. A written clearance from the doctor must be presented to the Personnel Office prior to my return to work.

3. It is my responsibility to contact the Personnel Office regarding:
    A. Disability pay   B. Pre-paid parking
    C. Continuation of insurance   D. Extension of dependent coverage
    Failure to contact Personnel on the above matters may result in loss of coverage.

4. Accepting other employment while on leave of absence will result in the termination of my employment with the Amway Grand Plaza Hotel.

5. My service date will be adjusted, which will cause my vacation and wage evaluations to be delayed by the length of my leave.

6. My return to work will be subject to employment conditions existing at the time of my return.

7. If I am unable to return by the above date, I must notify the Personnel Office in writing at least five days before the expiration date to request an extension. This request must set forth the reason for needing the extension, the length of time required, and be supported by a DOCTOR'S STATEMENT if the leave is for MEDICAL REASONS.

THIS LEAVE IS NOT APPROVED UNTIL *ALL* SIGNATURES ARE OBTAINED.

Signed_____(Employee)

I recommend this request
be granted_____(Dept. Head)

I recommend this request
be granted_____(Personnel)

Date_____Approved_____(General Mgr.)

(1) Yellow, Personnel; (2) Green, Payroll; (3) Blue, Department; (4) White, Employee

Courtesy of Amway Grand Plaza Hotel, Grand Rapids, Michigan.

Women affected by pregnancy, childbirth, or related medical conditions shall be treated the same for all employment-related purposes . . . as other persons not so affected, but similar in their ability or inability to work.

The beginning and ending dates of maternity leave are now based on the woman's choice rather than on arbitrary dates set by the employer. Most employers now provide unisex uniforms and allow employees to buy or make their own maternity clothes so that they can continue working.

Title VII doesn't protect homosexuals, transsexuals, or transvestites. However, the Federal Rehabilitation Act and many states laws do prohibit discrimination on the basis of sexual orientation. Therefore, it would be a practical mistake to discriminate against an individual because of sexual preference.

Sexual Harassment

There are two forms of sexual harassment—*quid pro quo* and hostile environment. In *quid pro quo* harassment, submission to unwelcome sexual advances is made a condition of employment, either in terms of threatening some detriment or promising some benefit in return for sexual favors. In hostile environment harassment, the employer creates or condones a hostile or offensive working environment, whether or not the employee suffers any tangible economic loss or harm. A hostile environment would include obscene jokes, pictures on bulletin boards, suggestive or insulting sounds, repeated touching, pinching, or leering, and any other conditions that make a person feel uncomfortable.

If the employer knew or should have known of sexual harassment by any employee—especially by supervisors—it may be held liable because it didn't take remedial action or because, in the case of supervisors, it gave them the authority over others and is responsible for how that authority is used (or abused).

The company must take steps to prevent both forms of harassment. An employer should provide the following:

- A written policy statement which prohibits sexual harassment in the workplace (see Exhibit 11.5)

- A well-publicized in-house grievance procedure for handling sexual harassment complaints

- Training for managers so that they're aware of their responsibilities to maintain an environment free of any sexual harassment

All complaints must be investigated promptly, thoroughly, and fairly by the people designated by the grievance procedure. Don't treat them lightly, with such statements as, "I can't believe it. Are you sure?" Listen carefully to find out what the complainant feels and believes would be required to resolve the situation. Take prompt action to end the harassment and prevent recurrence. Such action can range from verbal warnings to discharge, depending on the circumstances.

The employer is responsible if it "fails to take immediate and appropriate corrective action." After such action has been implemented, it's a good idea to send out a memo restating the policy to emphasize further that the company wants to prevent future sexual harassment.

Exhibit 11.5 Sexual Harassment Policy

HILTON HOTELS CORPORATION SEXUAL HARASSMENT POLICY

In view of the rather substantial number of sexual harassment decisions and the increased publicity the subject is getting, we feel it is appropriate at this time to reiterate Hilton's long standing policy concerning sexual harassment.

Hilton Hotels Corporation is committed to providing a work environment that is free of discrimination. In keeping with this commitment, Hilton has long maintained a strict policy prohibiting sexual harassment in any form on the part of supervisors or co-workers.

The Federal Equal Employment Opportunity Commission (EEOC) defines sexual harassment as unwelcome sexual advances, requests for sexual favors, and other verbal or physical conduct of a sexual nature. According to the EEOC, such conduct becomes actionable not only when it adversely affects an employee or applicant, but when it has as its purpose or effect, the creation of an intimidating, hostile or offensive working environment.

In order to provide a documentation of our guidelines and the understanding and support of all major department heads, we are asking each of you to periodically review Hilton's policy prohibiting sexual harassment with all your employees.

The EEOC and many courts hold an employer strictly liable for sexual harassment by a supervisor, regardless of whether the specific act complained of is not authorized or even forbidden by the employer and regardless of whether the employer knew or should have known of its occurrence.

Any action or activity that you may be aware of or may suspect should be immediately brought to the attention of the Director of Human Resources for investigation.

All employees should be informed that if he/she is being harassed by a co-worker or supervisor, he/she should promptly report the facts of the incident and the names of the individuals involved to his/her supervisor, or in the alternative, to the Director of Human Resources. Supervisors should immediately report any incidents of sexual harassment to the Director of Human Resources and take appropriate corrective action. All employees should be informed that failure to adhere to Hilton's sexual harassment policy will result in disciplinary action up to and including termination.

Courtesy of Hilton Hotels Corporation, Beverly Hills, California.

National Origin

Any practice that would directly or indirectly discriminate against a person because of national origin is also a violation of Title VII. Forbidding an employee to use his or her native language, unless dealing with the public in a situation which would require English, is illegal.

Age Discrimination

The **Age Discrimination in Employment Act** of 1967 is administered and enforced by the EEOC. The basic intent of the law is to forbid any employment practice which discriminates against a person over the age of 40 (as amended in 1987). For example, if an EEOC investigator were to find the resume of a person over the age of 40 who was passed over for promotion but who had better experience than a younger person who was promoted, a *prima facie* case of discrimination would exist. The company would then have the burden of proving that no discrimination took place.

Providing different benefit programs, refusing to put older workers in training programs, not promoting older workers, and forcing older workers to retire are all considered to be forms of age discrimination. As the population continues to age, this Act will become more significant to managers, since it's likely to lead to more and more age discrimination cases.

Handicaps

Some of the most significant legislation in recent years has been in the area of protecting the rights of the handicapped. The definition of what constitutes a handicap is being interpreted very broadly, with more areas being included all the time. Alcoholism, AIDS, allergies, and other areas are now being defined as handicaps.

In general, you can't refuse to hire someone who's handicapped simply because you lack the proper facilities. You must show a good-faith effort to provide reasonable accommodation for all potential employees, or be able to establish undue hardship if they're not provided.

Veterans

While Title VII doesn't require that private employers take affirmative action in employing veterans, other laws and Executive Orders now require government contractors to do so, even in areas of their business that are unrelated to the government contracts.

Veterans are protected by the rights granted to them under the **Veterans Reemployment Act** of 1942. Two main provisions of this act affect employers:

- A company is required to rehire an employee who left for military service, whether voluntarily or after being drafted, within 90 days after military discharge, should the employee re-apply. There can be no loss of seniority, although the person doesn't continue to build seniority while in the armed forces.

- A company is required to give an employee time off without pay, in addition to vacation time, to meet reserve status obligations.

Additional Employer Obligations

Job-related decisions should be based on objective criteria to the extent possible. While subjective qualities and judgments are still permitted, the courts look on them with suspicion. A system of promotion based on subjective evaluations and one supervisor's recommendation is risky. Two people should be involved in virtually every decision affecting people.

If you fire someone who's a member of a protected category, you must be prepared to defend the action with tangible and reasonable evidence or you may be accused of discrimination. You can no longer safely terminate an employee because of a claim of bad attitude, since attitude is so subjective and hard to prove. You can't allow an atmosphere of discriminatory harassment and then fire the victim of the harassment for not getting along with fellow employees. If a minority employee can show evidence of having been placed in a situation that made discharge inevitable, the firing may be ruled illegal. In fact, firing an employee on the grounds of incompetence when it was understood training would be given but none was provided would probably also lead to charges of discrimination if a person in a protected category is adversely affected.

Many states have set up their own civil rights commissions, primarily to expedite complaints. In those states, employees must file with the state commission first. The EEOC won't review the case until the state body has made its decision.

The penalties for violations of Title VII can add up to millions of dollars, particularly in **class action suits**, in which the company's procedures have been perceived as having an adverse impact on an entire class of people.

EEO.1

Once a year, every employer with 100 or more employees or federal contractors with 50 or more employees and with contracts of $50,000 must fill out an **EEO.1 Report** (see Exhibit 11.6) and submit it to a regional EEOC office. This report summarizes the number of people employed by the company in each of nine job categories: official and manager, professional, technician, sales, office and clerical, craft, semi-skilled, service, and unskilled. Within each category, the numbers of workers are categorized by sex and minority status.

The EEOC, using Standard Metropolitan Statistical Area (SMSA) data available for every area of the United States, may compare an employer's percentages with the norm in the event of a discrimination claim.

Affirmative
Action

Every federal contractor is required to have an **affirmative action program**. Many other companies implement them voluntarily or as part of a settlement with the EEOC of a discrimination case. Such a program is extremely complex and usually requires at least one full-time administrator.

An affirmative action program first divides the various jobs in the company into dozens of different categories as outlined by EEOC guidelines. It then arranges them into a breakdown of the company's work force by sex, race, and national origin. This breakdown of the work force is then compared by each job category to the corresponding category in the SMSA for the company's recruiting area. For management positions, an employer may recruit nationally and would then use the national SMSA. For line employees, the company may recruit locally and would need to compare to local SMSA statistics. In order to do all this, every employer has to keep records on where its applicants come from.

If the comparison with the appropriate SMSA indicates that a particular group (for example, women) is "under-utilized" (if, for instance, the company has fewer females in management than the data would suggest is appropriate), it will be required to set up targets for achieving parity, as well as target dates based on turnover, transfers, staff increases, and other data. Once these targets are determined, the company then develops a plan of action to reach them.

Employment of Aliens

Anyone who isn't a citizen of the United States must have an **Alien Registration Receipt Card** (commonly referred to as the **green card**, even though it's no longer green) in order to reside in the United States and thus be eligible to work.

Students from other countries attending schools in this country are generally not allowed to work. They take an oath before they enter this country that they can sustain themselves through their own funds and won't work in the United States. If they work, they violate their status and can be deported. The employer can also be fined. After one year, if their situation changes so that they need to work, students can file for a temporary work permit. This permission is usually stamped on the back of their Form I-94, or Arrival-

Exhibit 11.6   EEO.1 Report

Standard Form 100
(Rev. 5–84)
O.M.B. No. 3046–0007
EXPIRES 3/31/85
100–211

Joint Reporting
Committee

- Equal Employment
Opportunity Com-
mission
- Office of Federal
Contract Compli-
ance Programs (Labor)

EQUAL EMPLOYMENT OPPORTUNITY

EMPLOYER INFORMATION REPORT EEO–1

Section A—TYPE OF REPORT
Refer to instructions for number and types of reports to be filed.

1. Indicate by marking in the appropriate box the type of reporting unit for which this copy of the form is submitted (MARK ONLY ONE BOX).

    (1) ☐ Single-establishment Employer Report

    Multi-establishment Employer:

    (2) ☐ Consolidated Report (Required)

    (3) ☐ Headquarters Unit Report (Required)

    (4) ☐ Individual Establishment Report (submit one for each establishment with 50 or more employees)

    (5) ☐ Special Report

2. Total number of reports being filed by this Company (Answer on Consolidated Report only) _____

Section B—COMPANY IDENTIFICATION (To be answered by all employers)

OFFICE USE ONLY

1. Parent Company

    a. Name of parent company (owns or controls establishment in item 2) omit if same as label

    a.

Name of receiving office | Address (Number and street)

    b.

| City or town | County | State | ZIP code | b. Employer Identification No. |

2. Establishment for which this report is filed. (Omit if same as label)

OFFICE USE ONLY

    a. Name of establishment

    c.

| Address (Number and street) | City or Town | County | State | ZIP code |

    d.

    b. Employer Identification No.   (Omit if same as label)

    e.

Section C—EMPLOYERS WHO ARE REQUIRED TO FILE *(To be answered by all employers)*

☐ Yes ☐ No   1. Does the entire company have at least 100 employees in the payroll period for which you are reporting?

☐ Yes ☐ No   2. Is your company affiliated through common ownership and/or centralized management with other entities in an enterprise with a total employment of 100 or more?

☐ Yes ☐ No   3. Does the company or any of its establishments (a) have 50 or more employees AND (b) is not exempt as provided by 41 CFR 60–1.5, AND either (1) is a prime government contractor or first-tier subcontractor, and has a contract, subcontract, or purchase order amounting to $50,000 or more, or (2) serves as a depository of Government funds in any amount or is a financial institution which is an issuing and paying agent for U.S. Savings Bonds and Savings Notes?

    If the response to question C–3 is yes, please enter your Dun and Bradstreet identification number (if you have one):

☐ Yes ☐ No   4. Does the company receive financial assistance from the Small Business Administration (SBA)?

NOTE: If the answer is yes to questions 1, 2, or 3, complete the entire form, otherwise skip to Section G.

NSN 7540–00–180–6384

Exhibit 11.6 *(continued)*

SF 100 Page 2

Section D—EMPLOYMENT DATA

Employment at this establishment—Report all permanent full-time or part-time employees including apprentices and on-the-job trainees unless specifically excluded as set forth in the instructions. Enter the appropriate figures on all lines and in all columns. Blank spaces will be considered as zeros.

JOB CATEGORIES		OVERALL TOTALS (SUM OF COL. B THRU K)	MALE					FEMALE				
			WHITE (NOT OF HISPANIC ORIGIN)	BLACK (NOT OF HISPANIC ORIGIN)	HISPANIC	ASIAN OR PACIFIC ISLANDER	AMERICAN INDIAN OR ALASKAN NATIVE	WHITE (NOT OF HISPANIC ORIGIN)	BLACK (NOT OF HISPANIC ORIGIN)	HISPANIC	ASIAN OR PACIFIC ISLANDER	AMERICAN INDIAN OR ALASKAN NATIVE
		A	B	C	D	E	F	G	H	I	J	K
Officials and Managers	1											
Professionals	2											
Technicians	3											
Sales Workers	4											
Office and Clerical	5											
Craft Workers (Skilled)	6											
Operatives (Semi-Skilled)	7											
Laborers (Unskilled)	8											
Service Workers	9											
TOTAL	10											
Total employment reported in previous EEO–1 report	11											
(The trainees below should also be included in the figures for the appropriate occupational categories above)												
Formal On-the-Job trainees — White collar	12											
Production	13											

NOTE: Omit questions 1 and 2 on the Consolidated Report.

1. Date(s) of payroll period used:

2. Does this establishment employ apprentices?
   1 ☐ Yes   2 ☐ No

Section E—ESTABLISHMENT INFORMATION (Omit on the Consolidated Report)

1. Is the location of the establishment the same as that reported last year?
   1 ☐ Yes   2 ☐ No   3 ☐ No report last year

2. Is the major business activity at this establishment the same as that reported last year?
   1 ☐ Yes   2 ☐ No   3 ☐ No report last year

OFFICE USE ONLY

3. What is the major activity of this establishment? (Be specific, i.e., manufacturing steel castings, retail grocer, wholesale plumbing supplies, title insurance, etc. Include the specific type of product or type of service provided, as well as the principal business or industrial activity.)

f.

Section F—REMARKS

Use this item to give any identification data appearing on last report which differs from that given above, explain major changes in composition or reporting units and other pertinent information.

Section G—CERTIFICATION (See Instructions G)

Check one
1 ☐ All reports are accurate and were prepared in accordance with the instructions (check on consolidated only)
2 ☐ This report is accurate and was prepared in accordance with the instructions.

Name of Certifying Official	Title	Signature		Date
Name of person to contact regarding this report (Type or print)	Address (Number and street)			
Title	City and State	ZIP code	Telephone Area Code	Number	Extension

All reports and information obtained from individual reports will be kept confidential as required by Section 709(e) of Title VII
WILLFULLY FALSE STATEMENTS ON THIS REPORT ARE PUNISHABLE BY LAW, U.S. CODE. TITLE 18, SECTION 1001

Departure Record, which is attached to the person's passport. The work permit will allow the student to work up to 20 hours a week during the school year and full-time from June first through Labor Day.

The **Immigration Reform and Control Act**, which applies to *everyone* hired after November 6, 1986, requires the employer to affirm each employee's citizenship status and legal right to work in the United States. You may not ask for this information before the applicant is hired. After being hired, however, the employee must furnish documentation of the right to be in the country and authorization to work, such as a green card, work permit, or proof of U.S. citizenship. Within three days of the date of hire, the employer and employee must complete the Employment Eligibility Verification Form, or Form I-9 (see Exhibit 11.7), which confirms that the employer has verified the employment authorization.

Once the Form I-9 has been completed, it must be retained in a file separate from the personnel file. These files must be maintained for a period of three years from date of hire or one year from the date of separation from employment, whichever is later. (Keeping copies of the documents shown as proof of authorization isn't required. However, if the employer decides to make and keep copies of some documents, it should make and keep copies of the documents every newly-hired employee presents.)

Fines for an employer's first-offense violation can range from $250 to $2,000 for each unauthorized alien. For a second offense, they can go up to $5,000 for each unauthorized alien. For subsequent offenses, the penalties can go as high as $10,000 for each unauthorized alien. In addition, fines for inadequate documentation or failure to complete the Form I-9 can result in penalties of from $1 to $1,000 for each violation.

Administration and compliance is handled by the U.S. Immigration and Naturalization Service (INS).

Invasion of Privacy

In recent years, laws relating to the privacy of citizens and workers have proliferated rapidly, both at the federal and state levels. Legislative standards are being set concerning such issues as the collection and retention of information, locker and personal inspections, polygraph tests, drug tests, AIDS testing, background investigations, and disclosure.

Generally speaking, if employees have an expectation of privacy and if that expectation is reasonable, they're entitled to it. For example, most people would have an expectation that they would have privacy while changing their clothes. Therefore, surveillance cameras in the locker room may be an invasion of privacy. There are some general areas of which every manager should be aware in order to avoid lawsuits based on defamation, libel, slander, and a host of other actions.

Personnel Records

Applicants, current employees, and former employees have a reasonable right to expect that information about them will be treated confidentially. Only authorized persons with a need to know should be allowed access to such information.

Records constituting the personnel file, generally known as **type 1** records, include information that could identify an employee and that has been or could be used in connection with the employee's qualifications for

Exhibit 11.7 Form I-9

EMPLOYMENT ELIGIBILITY VERIFICATION (Form I-9)

1 EMPLOYEE INFORMATION AND VERIFICATION: (To be completed and signed by employee.)

Name: (Print or Type) Last	First	Middle	Birth Name

Address: Street Name and Number	City	State	ZIP Code

Date of Birth (Month/Day/Year)	Social Security Number

I attest, under penalty of perjury, that I am (check a box):

☐ 1. A citizen or national of the United States.

☐ 2. An alien lawfully admitted for permanent residence (Alien Number A _____).

☐ 3. An alien authorized by the Immigration and Naturalization Service to work in the United States (Alien Number A _____ , or Admission Number _____ , expiration of employment authorization, if any _____).

I attest, under penalty of perjury, the documents that I have presented as evidence of identity and employment eligibility are genuine and relate to me. I am aware that federal law provides for imprisonment and/or fine for any false statements or use of false documents in connection with this certificate.

Signature	Date (Month/Day/Year)

PREPARER/TRANSLATOR CERTIFICATION (To be completed if prepared by person other than the employee). I attest, under penalty of perjury, that the above was prepared by me at the request of the named individual and is based on all information of which I have any knowledge.

Signature	Name (Print or Type)

Address (Street Name and Number)	City	State	Zip Code

2 EMPLOYER REVIEW AND VERIFICATION: (To be completed and signed by employer.)

Instructions:

Examine one document from List A and check the appropriate box, **OR** examine one document from List B **and** one from List C and check the appropriate boxes. Provide the **Document Identification Number** and **Expiration Date** for the document checked.

List A — Documents that Establish Identity and Employment Eligibility	List B — Documents that Establish Identity	and	List C — Documents that Establish Employment Eligibility
☐ 1. United States Passport	☐ 1. A State-issued driver's license or a State-issued I.D. card with a photograph, or information, including name, sex, date of birth, height, weight, and color of eyes. (Specify State)_____		☐ 1. Original Social Security Number Card (other than a card stating it is not valid for employment)
☐ 2. Certificate of United States Citizenship			☐ 2. A birth certificate issued by State, county, or municipal authority bearing a seal or other certification
☐ 3. Certificate of Naturalization	☐ 2. U.S. Military Card		
☐ 4. Unexpired foreign passport with attached Employment Authorization	☐ 3. Other (Specify document and issuing authority) _____		☐ 3. Unexpired INS Employment Authorization Specify form #_____
☐ 5. Alien Registration Card with photograph			
Document Identification #_____	**Document Identification** #_____		**Document Identification** #_____
Expiration Date (if any) _____	**Expiration Date (if any)** _____		**Expiration Date (if any)** _____

CERTIFICATION: I attest, under penalty of perjury, that I have examined the documents presented by the above individual, that they appear to be genuine and to relate to the individual named, and that the individual, to the best of my knowledge, is eligible to work in the United States.

Signature	Name (Print or Type)	Title

Employer Name	Address	Date

Form I-9 (05/07/87)
OMB No. 1115-0136

U.S. Department of Justice
Immigration and Naturalization Service

employment, promotion, transfer, raises, or disciplinary action. Exhibit 11.8 presents a sample employee personnel file jacket.

Type 2 records may include such information as medical records, workers' compensation records, I-9 forms, and other such data that shouldn't be used in evaluating employees. They should be kept separate from the personnel file.

Type 3 records pertain solely to investigations of employees' criminal misconduct perceived to be harmful to the employer. Also in this category would be records that contain the names of other employees which, if disclosed, would infringe upon their privacy. In some states, upon completion of an investigation or after two years—whichever comes first—the employee must be notified of the investigation and of being suspected of criminal activity. Upon completion of the investigation, if disciplinary action isn't taken, the investigative file and all copies of the material must be destroyed.

In many states, employees have a legal right to see their personnel files. An organized, systematic policy should be set up to accommodate this disclosure. At a minimum, it should incorporate whatever requirements may be imposed by state law. For example, if the law permits requiring notice before a file may be reviewed, a company's policy might require that an employee make an appointment before viewing the file. It might also allow for making photocopies of anything in the file if the employee pays the actual cost of the copies, and if permitted by state law.

The employer should require any request by an employee to review the file to be made in writing. If an employee disagrees with information and asks that it be removed, the company is not required to do so unless otherwise provided by law. However, the person can respond with a written statement explaining his or her position which must be added to the file.

A company isn't required to open every file for employees to review. Information that should be kept in a separate file, not available for viewing, includes employee references, materials which disclose staff planning, personal information concerning another employee, records relevant to criminal or grievance investigations, and notes made by executives which don't leave their possession. Such notes made by managers should be kept in a separate departmental file. As long as that file is maintained by the department head for his or her sole and exclusive use, with the freedom to discard items at will, it need not be considered part of the personnel file. The employee has no right to see it, unless the manager discloses information from the file to a third party—at which point the employee may have the right to see it. Of course, providing information to a third party on anything but a strict need-to-know basis could constitute an invasion of privacy.

Certain states say that nothing more than six months old can be transferred from the manager's file to the personnel file. This means that managers can't keep warning notices until they're ready to fire someone and then bring them to the human resources office, because notices over six months old couldn't be used to support the termination. That's one reason a copy of any record that could have a bearing on such matters as hiring, transfers, raises, promotions, and terminations should be sent to the human resources department immediately.

Searches   If a company believes it's necessary to inspect lockers, to search purses and packages going in and out, to search employee vehicles parked on company property, to perform tests for drugs, or to institute any other form of

Exhibit 11.8   Sample Employee Personnel Jacket

Last,   First,   Middle   Department/Position   Date Hired

Preferred Name

Social Security No.   Relatives Employed?   Yes   No

Date of Birth   Service Date   Effective Date of Insurance   Emergency Contact

Telephone Number ( )   Dependent Coverage Date   Relation   Phone No. ( )

Home Address   Locker No.   Termination Date   Last Day Worked

Date	Reason	Department	Position	Stat	Rate

Date	Reason	Department	Position	Stat	Rate

Information in this file is the property of the Amway Grand Plaza Hotel and is confidential.

search or test, it should establish the acceptance of same as a condition of employment. It should also have the employee sign an agreement authorizing the company to make the searches and tests, agreeing to cooperate, and acknowledging that failure to cooperate may result in disciplinary action up to and including termination.

Regular entrance or exit searches or periodic personal searches or tests can be appropriate when conducted for legitimate business reasons and pursuant to a publicized employer policy. If an employer intends to do unannounced locker inspections, for instance, it should also provide the locker and the lock and advise employees in the handbook and with a posted sign in the locker room that there are regular, unannounced inspections.

When there's a reasonable cause to believe that an employee is in possession of alcohol, drugs, or company property, an employer may conduct a search. There must be a justification for the intrusion on the employee's privacy, and there must be a balance between the need and the degree of intrusiveness. Pat-down and strip searches, for example, would be considered too much of an invasion of privacy. However, asking an employee to empty pockets or remove a hat or shoes would be acceptable. Searching an employee in the presence of co-workers would probably also infringe upon privacy rights.

Polygraph Testing

The **Employee Polygraph Protection Act** of 1988 prohibits most pre-employment polygraph and lie detector tests. Post-employment testing is also severely restricted. An employer may request an employee to take a polygraph test from a licensed polygrapher in connection with an investigation involving economic loss or injury to the employer's business. To do this, the employee must have had access to the property in question and the employer must have a reasonable suspicion that the employee was involved. The employer must fulfill a number of recordkeeping and notification obligations, including advising the employee in writing in advance of the test, and providing the questions that will be asked and the reasons for giving the test. The employee has many rights under the Act, such as the right to refuse to take the test and the right to have legal counsel present during testing. Employment decisions may not be based solely on the test results or on the employee's refusal to take it.

Many states now prohibit polygraph and lie detector tests altogether, and even suggesting that an applicant or employee take a test to establish innocence could be construed as a violation of rights. If an employee were to provide the results of such a test voluntarily, the information still could not be used in making any employment decisions. (For more information on searches and testing, see Chapter 13.)

Third Party Disclosure

The federal **Credit Reporting Act** restricts the collection and dissemination of information about employees. In some states, an employee must be advised within three days if reference information is requested from a credit agency.

The employer's hiring procedures should include telling employees of the company's policy on references. They should be told that the only reference information that will be provided in response to subsequent inquiries is dates of employment, job title, and verification of salary if specified in the inquiry, unless the employee submits a written authorization to release additional information. While there's no law requiring an employer to obtain a release before turning over information on a current or former employee to a third party, it's a good idea to do so. A company may even include such a release on the bottom of the application form. These kinds of inquiries should all be directed to one person in the company, such as a human resources department representative. Before giving information, the representative should inquire about the purpose of the request, and know who he or she is dealing with by asking for verification. Disclosing salary information to a spouse's attorney in a divorce action, for example, could violate an employee's rights.

Any third party who asks a department head for information should be referred to the human resources department, which should give only information about the employee's job performance. No mention should be made or questions answered about age, physical or mental abilities, political activities, attitudes, lawsuits, or other claims or charges the employee has filed against your company or others. In fact, any response to questions regarding this information should be handled with care. Often, silence can convey an impression as effectively as a verbal response, and either may result in later claims of privacy infringement. To avoid misinterpretation, the company's policy should be to state that only job-related matters will be discussed.

Many companies require that the caller send a letter asking the questions in writing. This allows the company time to review and edit its comments and to keep copies of both the inquiry and its response. This practice is particularly important when an employer gets a reference check on someone who has a record of poor performance.

Finally, don't talk about employees' problems outside the business setting. Informal remarks made away from work in social settings may be regarded as slanderous.

Conducting Reference Checks

Conduct a reference check on every potential employee as a matter of policy. Verify that all applicants are who they say they are. If you only check references when you suspect a problem or need information, you may develop a pattern that indicates you're doing more reference checks on minorities, which would be a form of discrimination.

By all means, get reference information *before* someone is hired. Firing people can create much more bitterness and resentment than not hiring them in the first place. But avoid asking about garnishments, political activities, lawsuits filed, conviction records, credit problems, marital status, or other subjects not related to the job. (For additional information on reference checking and giving references, see Chapters 5 and 15.)

Employment Litigation

The term **employment litigation** applies to any legal action taken by a past, present, or prospective employee in a civil court against an employer because of an event arising out of the employment relationship. One type of employment litigation, suits for wrongful discharge, didn't come about until the early 1980s, but it has already become one of the major sources of litigation against employers. The verdicts juries render against employers can be devastating.

In addition to determining whether the claim was justified, juries are now also deciding on such issues as:

- Compensation for emotional distress the employee has suffered

- Punitive damages, an amount in excess of or addition to actual damages, where the employee can show that the employer's conduct was extreme and outrageous beyond the bounds of all decency

- Injunctive relief—that is, court orders compelling someone to perform or refrain from performing a particular act

- Back pay or loss of future pay

- Attorney's fees, which can sometimes be more than the settlement the plaintiff receives

Since these trials can take several years, the employee is also granted interest on the judgment.

Many employers have traditionally felt that the employment-at-will doctrine—which suggests that companies may hire and fire as they choose—means that they don't have to justify their managers' actions. However, the expansion of public policies restricting the employer's rights is resulting in many more exceptions to the at-will doctrine.

The United States is the last industrial nation that still allows the firing of an employee for reasons other than **just cause**. However, the intent and mood of the country are clearly changing toward providing an employee with an inherent right to a job and ensuring that the person may only be fired for just cause. To understand and be able to work in this new environment, it's important to understand how the trends and policies have evolved.

The basis of the at-will doctrine was the idea that the non-union employee hired without a contract could be terminated at any time for any reason. This doctrine began to erode with the passage of legislation which outlawed terminating employees because of race, sex, religion, national origin, or physical handicaps.

The next area of erosion for the doctrine involved restrictions on terminations contrary to the terms of an agreement. The definition of an employment agreement has been expanded greatly in favor of the employee. A contractual arrangement may exist not only in written form, but also if it's simply *implied* through what's said, what's left unsaid, or by conduct. Any terminology regarding length of employment should be handled with care. Whether spoken or written, expressed or implied, employees can accept what you say as a contract.

In recent years, courts have ruled that the employee handbook can be a form of contract even when it contains a statement or disclaimer informing the employees of their status as at-will employees. Courts have ignored such disclaimers where they have found that the employer's conduct negated the disclaimer. Also, the language of the handbook may give the impression that it's a contract or that job security can be inferred. A probationary period statement that says, "You are on probation for the first 90 days and you can be fired at any time," may imply that, after the probationary period, the employee can't be fired at any time except for good cause.

The courts in some states have also taken the position that an employer and an employee have a mutual contract and are both bound to act in good faith toward each other. This means that if an employer were to fire an employee in order to avoid paying a commission or pension, or just to make room for a preferred person such as a relative to be hired, it could be

Any comments regarding length of employment should be made with care. Many such statements can be interpreted as an expressed or implied contract.

construed as failure to operate in good faith. Such actions may be unlawful or cause for a judgment against you in a legal action.

The third area that has caused erosion to the at-will doctrine involves employment practices that are sometimes referred to as "exceptions to public policy" and are generally considered to be illegal. Indicating the trend in this type of legislation, some of the actions now commonly considered to be illegal are:

1. Retaliation against an employee who reports an employer's criminal activity or exposes violations by others. (This employee action is often called "whistle blowing.")

2. Discharge for exercising statutory rights such as filing a workers' compensation claim.

3. Discharge for performing public duty, such as jury duty, or for refusing to give false testimony, fix prices, or conduct other activities that are against the law; in fact, even if you have other good reasons for firing this employee on the heels of such an incident, the appearance of retaliation would probably cause a judge to disallow the dismissal.

Exhibit 11.9   Sample At-Will Employment Agreement

I am fully aware of all the provisions set forth in the manuals, policy guidelines, general policy manual, and handbooks of ____(Name of Company)____ and I agree that my employment and compensation can be terminated for any reason at any time, with or without cause and with or without prior notice, by either me or ____(Name of Company)____. I understand that no supervisor, manager, or other representative of ____(Name of Company)____ other than the President has any authority to enter into any agreement for employment for any reason or for any specified period of time, or to make any agreement contrary to the foregoing provisions. I further agree that any promises made by the President are not binding upon ____(Name of Company)____ unless made in writing.

_____
Date

_____
Employee (Agent)

_____
Company Officer

_____
Title

(This statement can be added to the employment application and/or the employee handbook.)

4. **Constructive discharge**—that is, setting up a situation that forces an employee to resign or be discharged.

5. **Negligent evaluation**—courts are beginning to take the viewpoint that an employer can't fire an employee for poor performance if dissatisfaction wasn't indicated on the performance reviews. Even giving an undeserved or normal wage increase can show negligence. If you're negligent in addressing shortcomings during a review, you may find yourself in court with no defense for a later dismissal.

6. **Intentional infliction of emotional distress**—that is, intentionally or recklessly causing emotional injury to an employee, such as intentionally making the person's working conditions intolerable or using stressful interrogations when the employee is suspected of theft.

While the basis of much of this legislation has arisen out of the employment-at-will doctrine and the precedent-setting cases dealing with wrongful discharge, the applications of the concepts are now spreading to cases involving no discharge, such as grievances, refusals to hire, promotions, transfers, fringe benefits, and other employment conditions.

What Can Employers Do?

An employer should have a lawyer specializing in employment law review the employee handbook and other documents to eliminate any language suggestive of permanent employment. The human resources representative should have the employee sign an at-will statement (see Exhibit 11.9). Managers should refrain from making such statements as, "If you do a good job around here, you have nothing to worry about."

Some companies are moving to put every employee on a contract which specifies exactly what the damages can be if the employee is fired for just cause and what the employee is entitled to if fired for no reason. Employers are also reviewing all of their policies and procedures, placing tighter restrictions on their managers' ability to fire and make other employment decisions, and setting up employee review boards or other internal dispute resolution mechanisms to avoid litigation.

The successful managers of the future will be those who operate from a base of honesty and integrity, and who approach all employment decisions in good faith.

Key Terms

affirmative action
Age Discrimination in
    Employment Act
Alien Registration Receipt Card
bona fide occupational
    qualification (BFOQ)
child labor laws
Civil Rights Act
class action suit
constructive discharge
Credit Reporting Act
EEO.1 Report
Employee Polygraph Protection Act
employment litigation
Equal Employment Opportunity
    Commission (EEOC)
Equal Pay Act
Fair Labor Standards Act

Federal Wage Garnishment Law
good faith
green card
high-commission employee
Immigration Reform and
    Control Act
just cause termination
minimum wage
negligent evaluation
overtime
punitive damages
tip credit
Title VII
type 1, 2, and 3 records
Veterans Reemployment Act
Wage and Hour Division
Wage and Hour Law

Discussion Questions

1. According to the federal Wage and Hour Law, what is an exempt employee?

2. Under what circumstances can a deduction be taken from an employee's pay for breakage or missing company property?

3. What are some of the circumstances that might allow for a pay differential for two employees—one male and one female—both doing the same job in the same company?

4. Why is it important to have company-wide standards for appearance and dress?

5. What factors should be considered before you decide whether to hire a person who refuses to work on Sundays for religious reasons?

6. What kinds of behavior characterize the hostile environment of sexual harassment? How should an employer respond?

7. How does an employer lay the groundwork in order to be able to conduct unannounced locker inspections when they're deemed necessary?

12 Employee Appraisals

In one form or another, employee appraisals are an integral element of every manager's job. Managers must evaluate their employees on a broad spectrum of issues and concerns, and the appraisal process has been developed to meet this need. Over the years, the appraisal process has undergone many changes. As the interests and demands of the work force have evolved, the scope of the appraisal process has been widened in an attempt to better meet these needs. Employers have also modified the process in an attempt to avoid some of the barriers to its success.

The Traditional Performance Appraisal

The appraisal process had achieved widespread acceptance by the 1920s in non-union plants as a means of justifying pay increases. A manager would simply fill out an evaluation form once a year and send it to personnel or payroll with the recommended salary increase. Seldom did the employee see this evaluation.

Later, perhaps influenced by the principles of scientific management, managers began to link this review process to their efforts to increase the productivity of assembly line workers. Very specific standards were set, actual production records were kept, and, at periodic intervals, the records were compared to the standards. The appraisal was the attempt to realign employee performance with the established standards. At this point, performance appraisal was actually an auditing and controlling function.

Still later, employers began to adapt the appraisal system to their efforts to increase productivity in white collar and management jobs. Since these jobs had more variety, the format of employee appraisals became increasingly sophisticated, complex, and varied.

Some employers are continuing to refine and develop more sophisticated appraisal forms. Others are conducting reviews more often than once a year. Many employers involve the employees more by having them do self-appraisals which they then compare with their managers' appraisals.

The practice of conducting an annual, formal performance appraisal is declining. In fact, most managers probably haven't had one in years. Still, they remain productive because they know how to keep score and take responsibility for their own actions. They're able to determine how they're doing from the amount of responsibility and authority they're given, the

Exhibit 12.1   Barriers to Successful Performance Appraisal

- Service skills and productivity are hard to standardize, rank, and measure.
- It's hard to cover all the possible objectives in one meeting and do them all well.
- Once a year is not often enough.
- Appraisals take too much time.
- Managers dislike sitting in judgment on their employees, and employees dislike being judged.
- Appraisals don't always improve performance.
- The manager doesn't always know the job well enough.
- Turnover is high among managers.
- Many factors are beyond the employee's control.
- Some of the manager's shortcomings may make the appraisal unreliable.

overall performance of their departments, how much weight their comments and recommendations carry, whether their supervisors show any personal interest in them, and the frequency and size of raises. As our culture changes, more and more employees are adopting this work ethic.

Barriers to Successful Performance Appraisal

Some companies have stopped conducting formal employee appraisals altogether. One reason for this is that there are several substantial obstacles to their success. These are highlighted in Exhibit 12.1 and detailed in the following paragraphs.

Service Productivity Is Hard to Standardize. The original appraisal process was based on established, well-defined standards that were clear-cut and measurable. These were usually accompanied by a job description, job specifications, established production rates, inspection guidelines, and a uniform format for recording production. Such a system is only possible in a stable, structured, highly regimented setting, where many jobs are alike.

In the service environment, where few jobs are identical, it's often very difficult and time-consuming to break each job down into key elements, rank the elements, and develop standards against which performance can be measured. It would be impossible to quantify, measure, and rank creativity, risk-taking, responsiveness, attitude, teamwork, showmanship, judgment, personality, and all the other elements that have to be considered in determining the performance of a person whose primary function doesn't fall within the assembly-line category. To ignore these traits, however, would be to eliminate the personal element of the job, which is the main product of the service industry.

You Can't Do Everything at Once. Traditionally, managers have tried to achieve too many objectives with one annual employee appraisal meeting. Along with pay adjustments and performance evaluations, they may also have tried to provide information for such varied functions as succession planning, career planning, final warnings, termination, promotion, transfer, making training decisions, goal setting, and team building. At the same time they're doing this, managers are trying to improve their relationships with their workers and to learn more about their life goals, their interests, and their families. Too much may be going on for anything to be done well.

If employees are thinking about how much more money they're going to get, a manager will have little success talking with them about their good and bad traits. By the same token, the manager who has just had to express dissatisfaction with someone's performance is going to have a difficult time trying to move on to the subject of setting goals that will stretch the person's talents.

Once a Year Isn't Often Enough. Waiting a year to provide feedback, give praise, make suggestions for improvement, and assess training and equipment needs, while trying to remember objectively what someone did or didn't do ten months ago, is useless. Setting goals once a year is waiting too long, as well. Business and priorities are changing too fast. Goals set months earlier are meaningless.

They Take Too Much Time. The average manager has too little time on the floor as it is. To give each appraisal meeting the research, preparation, and meeting time that would be required in order to cover each topic thoroughly with every employee would be an overwhelming task.

Managers and Employees Dislike Them. Many managers feel that the formal performance appraisal puts them in the position of sitting in judgment on their employees. They dislike the idea of issuing a "report card," and feel more comfortable in a coaching role.

Today's workers don't even want to be managed, much less judged. They want information and regular feedback so that they can manage themselves.

They Don't Improve Performance. Most workers rate their own work as above average and better than it actually is. When the manager rates an employee as average, it frequently has such a negative impact that it takes a devastating toll on the person's self-esteem and on the manager's relationship with the employee. Performance often goes down for a period of up to three months after an employee review.

Managers Often Don't Know the Job. As originally conceived, the performance appraisal was conducted by a manager who had started at the bottom and worked up through the company, learning all the jobs on the way up. However, managers today are often thrust into positions of management with very little hands-on experience. The enormous changes in the business have also changed the nature of many jobs, so that even experienced managers may not know the jobs they once performed. Often, the worker in the job knows far more about it than anyone else.

Turnover Is High Among Managers. A new manager who knows little about the company or the department may be faced with making pay and performance decisions without being acquainted with the employee or the quality of performance. He or she may not be able to evaluate the person or the situation properly. Further, a new manager usually brings new priorities, standards, and rules and may begin by making many changes to the operation. Thus, the guidelines formerly in effect become irrelevant and workers have to learn how to adjust to the new manager.

Many Factors Are Beyond the Employee's Control. The most significant factor in performance is the management leadership style. When performance deteriorates in a department, the manager should first conduct a self-appraisal. The overall organizational climate will also have a strong influence on employee values and subsequent productivity, as will peer pressure. The people on whom they depend and with whom they interact often influence workers more than anything a manager can say. Other factors include changes in the workplace, such as staffing, supervisory, and schedule changes.

The Appraisal Is Unreliable. Regardless of how well-defined the process may be, rating another's work still involves a great deal of subjectivity. It is open to all the human shortcomings and idiosyncrasies of the person conducting the evaluation. Some common errors affecting the reliability of the performance appraisal are:

- The **central tendency**—the manager gives everyone an average rating.

- Leniency—weak managers may try to make everyone happy by giving them all high ratings.

- Unrealistic expectations—managers who are too strict or demanding may rate workers too low.

- The halo effect—one quality that the manager likes influences the manager to give a rating that is higher overall than the worker actually deserves.

- Evaluator inconsistencies—the evaluator's attitude, mood, and health can affect the outcome. An appraisal done in the morning may be different from one done by the same individual in the afternoon, after the manager is fatigued from the efforts of the day.

- Timing—if workers are rushed during a busy period that happens to occur just before an appraisal session, and don't take time to do an adequate job, their appraisal for the entire year may be influenced by their performance level for that one short period.

- Contrast—after an outstanding employee has just been evaluated by the manager, average workers may look worse than they really are. Conversely, following a poor performer, average workers may get a better rating than they actually deserve.

- Personal bias and favoritism—neither is appropriate during an appraisal.

- Poor documentation—managers can't possibly remember everything about each of their employees for a year. They need to keep adequate records of discipline and performance, such as written notations of lateness or absenteeism, if they're going to have a reliable basis for making an objective appraisal.

The Future of the Appraisal Process

Despite all of these problems, employees do need to know where they stand. Therefore, in lieu of the traditional, all-encompassing annual meeting, a trend seems to be emerging in which employers separate the objectives of an appraisal session. They then address only those elements required for a

HYATT MANAGEMENT TRAINING PROGRAM

QUARTERLY EVALUATION — CORPORATE MANAGEMENT TRAINEE

TRAINEE NAME _____ PROPERTY _____ DATE _____

QUARTERLY EVALUATION NUMBER: 1 2 3 4 (CIRCLE ONE)

O=OUTSTANDING G=GOOD S=SATISFACTORY M=MARGINAL U=UNSATISFACTORY

		O	G	S	M	U
GUEST RELATIONS	Success at promoting guest satisfaction and goodwill	☐	☐	☐	☐	☐
HUMAN RELATIONS	Success at dealing smoothly and effectively with fellow employees at all levels	☐	☐	☐	☐	☐
DEPENDABILITY	Success at producing desired results on assignments	☐	☐	☐	☐	☐
QUALITY OF WORK	Thoroughness, accuracy, attention to detail, neatness	☐	☐	☐	☐	☐
VOLUME OF WORK	Uses time productively, expected quantity of work achieved	☐	☐	☐	☐	☐
LEADERSHIP	Ability to take charge, motivate and guide others to achieve results	☐	☐	☐	☐	☐
PERSEVERANCE/ DRIVE	Desire to excel; willingness to work through difficulties	☐	☐	☐	☐	☐
INITIATIVE	Originates action; self-starter; looks for things to get involved with	☐	☐	☐	☐	☐
SELF-CONFIDENCE/ SELF-RELIANCE	Looks to self first in handling situations; resourcefulness; willingness to make decisions	☐	☐	☐	☐	☐
ASSERTIVENESS	Formulates own ideas and opinions and states them in a professional manner; not intimidated by others	☐	☐	☐	☐	☐
ADAPTABILITY	Ability to adjust readily to new and unforeseen circumstances	☐	☐	☐	☐	☐
LEARNING ABILITY	Ease in assimilating and understanding new ideas and concepts	☐	☐	☐	☐	☐
ANALYTIC ABILITY/ JUDGEMENT	Ability to think things through, evaluate situations, and to find causes for, and solutions to, problems	☐	☐	☐	☐	☐
CREATIVITY	Ability to generate new ideas, to find new and better ways to accomplish goals	☐	☐	☐	☐	☐
EMOTIONAL MATURITY	Objectivity; self control; common sense; appropriateness of behavior	☐	☐	☐	☐	☐
ATTITUDE	Enthusiasm, interest, commitment	☐	☐	☐	☐	☐

SPECIAL PROJECTS UNDERTAKEN AND SUMMARY OF RESULTS

_____

HOTEL MEETINGS, SEMINARS, CLASSES ATTENDED/COMPLETED

_____

OVERALL EVALUATION OF PERFORMANCE THUS FAR IN MANAGEMENT TRAINING PROGRAM

SPECIFIC AREAS OF STRENGTH	SPECIFIC AREAS OF WEAKNESS

CURRENT PROGRAM STATUS

☐ Outstanding Performance (PROGRAM COULD BE ACCELERATED)
☐ Satisfactory to Good Performance (NORMAL STATUS)
☐ Presently Marginal Performance But Has Demonstrated Some Potential (PROBATIONARY STATUS—CORPORATE OFFICE MUST BE NOTIFIED)
☐ Unsatisfactory Performance—Has Not Demonstrated Sufficient Potential (RECOMMEND RESIGNATION OR TERMINATION—CORPORATE OFFICE MUST AUTHORIZE)

TRAINEE COMMENTS/PLANS TO CORRECT WEAKNESSES (IF APPLICABLE)

_____

PERSONNEL DIRECTOR'S COMMENTS/PLANS TO ASSIST TRAINEE IN CORRECTING WEAKNESSES (IF APPLICABLE)

_____

SIGNATURES

PERSONNEL DIRECTOR _____ DATE _____

GENERAL MANAGER _____ DATE _____

TRAINEE _____ DATE _____

New employees require feedback more often. The form above is used to provide new management trainees with quarterly evaluations. (Courtesy of Hyatt Hotels Corporation, Chicago, Illinois)

particular employee at a given time. When it's time for a pay increase, for instance, that's all the manager and worker talk about during that meeting. If someone wants to talk about career planning, the manager sets aside time to discuss that topic exclusively with the employee. Since the interview has just a single well-defined purpose, satisfactory results can probably be achieved more quickly.

Every company must tailor its own appraisal program to help managers reach their goals and manage their employees. In order for managers to support it, the program must meet their needs. Therefore, they should be involved in its planning and design.

Almost every aspect of management involves some form of employee evaluation. The rest of this chapter focuses on three significant areas in which a manager needs professional appraisal skills. They are the performance discussion, the annual planning session, and the pay review.

The Performance Discussion

Whether they like it or not, managers are paid to use their judgment and to evaluate. Just as they evaluate business decisions, they must also evaluate people—who's hired, who's fired, who's promoted, who gets increases, who's producing, and who isn't. The person who won't accept this responsibility can't be a manager. As with all decisions, some decisions about people will be right and some wrong. Managers must be able to live with this fact.

When you have an employee whose performance is slipping, act immediately. You can't wait until the annual review to make adjustments and provide feedback. For this reason, many companies are installing a formal employee **performance discussion** procedure to assist managers in dealing with poor performance.

If there's a performance problem in your department, your first step as manager should always be to ask yourself what *you* did to contribute to the situation. Have the department's goals been adequately communicated? Are employees getting the feedback they need to judge and manage themselves? In the hospitality industry, the performance of a department depends heavily on team spirit, within both the department and the company. Having a few individuals get high ratings means nothing if the team is losing all of its games. The manager must form an effective unit, and everyone should use the same scorecard. If food cost is important to the chef, all the cooks should know it and it should be equally important to all of them.

Often, a department functioning well as a whole has one or two people experiencing performance problems. In this situation, the manager should immediately have a performance discussion with the employee whose performance is down. The performance discussion helps the manager assess whether the employee needs counseling or additional training, or whether a motivation or discipline problem exists.

Once the manager determines that an employee is a chronically poor performer who shows no prospect of improving, no further performance discussions should be conducted. In this case, go directly to the methods of the discipline procedure (see Chapter 14). Performance discussions should only be held when the employee has a future with the company.

In determining whether a performance discussion is in order, you must know the job well enough to be able to determine what level of performance you expect. Know which elements of the job are important and which take the most time. Don't overemphasize insignificant aspects simply because they're easier to measure. When you're reviewing the mistakes people have made, remember to contrast them with the number of decisions they have to make. No one is going to be right all of the time. Worry more about patterns than about one-time mistakes.

Be sure you're evaluating results and not just activity. A housekeeper may be meeting your standard of cleaning 13 rooms per day, but how well they're done is just as important. Consider what the results would be if you had the best possible worker in the job and use that as your standard. Keep in mind, however, when measuring people against your best worker, that your objective is to get the best from each employee. Just because one person stands out as a great worker doesn't mean everyone else isn't making a contribution.

The performance discussion has four steps: preparation, presentation, problem solving, and feedback.

Preparation

While it's commonly believed that performance appraisal is a far too important task for the department manager to delegate, employee performance discussions can often be handled successfully by a responsible and well-prepared assistant manager. If a line supervisor just one level up from the employee can handle the review without inequities or resentment surfacing, it may be more comfortable for the employee.

Many times, the only preparation that's necessary is to walk up to the employee and say something like, "I've noticed that your performance is slipping a little, and I'm worried about it. I'd like to sit down with you and see if I can help. Why don't you think about it overnight. Can we get together at ten tomorrow morning to discuss it?" Or you might say, "It seems like this new system is a little harder than we expected. I'd like to get your perspective on what we can do about improving it. Why don't you think about it tonight, and we can get together at ten tomorrow." Try to be reassuring so the employee won't feel threatened. With this approach, you identify what you'd like to talk about, involve the employee by asking for his or her analysis, and establish a definite meeting time that will be convenient for both of you.

Preparation time for the meeting should be kept to a minimum. You just need to put together the facts that will help you present the problem effectively. If the preparation process is too time-consuming or complex, it won't happen.

The better you know the job and its standards, the better you'll be prepared for the discussion. You should also know each employee as an individual. An older person may resent your views. A new or insecure person may need a lot more encouragement. Marginal performers need more positive feedback, so you should know and emphasize their strengths to show your confidence in them.

If you want cooperation, don't undertake a performance discussion soon after a disciplinary interview. Pick a time when you won't be interrupted and try to eliminate unnecessary distractions. As with any personal interview with an employee, you should have a place that's quiet and enough time to talk without interruptions. If you don't normally sit behind a desk, doing so may be a barrier to your conversation. On the other hand, if you spend a lot of time sitting at a desk, doing otherwise during this kind of discussion would be out of character. Either inconsistency can make the employee more uncomfortable.

The skills needed to perform in the hospitality industry are harder to measure and rank than those needed in manufacturing. (Courtesy of Walt Disney World, Lake Buena Vista, Florida © 1989 The Walt Disney Company)

Presentation: Identifying the Problem

Take a negotiatory approach to the discussion. The idea of negotiation isn't so unsettling when you realize that most people inherently want to improve and that their realistic involvement is the best way to elicit their commitment to change. Employees want to do a good job, and performance can slip for many reasons, some of which you can correct and some you can't. That must also be understood. Causes may range from temporary personal problems to worn-out equipment, a lack of supplies, a bottleneck in a new system, or inefficiencies in the job design. Whatever the cause, you must discover it in order to identify what you can do to help.

Keep an open mind. Your attitude should be supportive instead of judgmental. You're not there to blame, or even discuss, the person, but rather to solve a problem. Use a "we" approach, and focus on performance only.

How you say something is as important as what you say. Be spontaneous and sincere. Show enthusiasm for the process—if you're not interested, it's certain the employee won't be either. Speak straightforwardly and approach the person as an equal. Be empathetic, but not patronizing. Maintain frequent eye contact and good body language. Don't speak too loudly or too softly. Aim for a friendly, warm, well-modulated tone.

If either of you has any anxiety over this meeting, deal with that first by acknowledging that it's typical to feel uncomfortable about this kind of discussion. If the person is doing good work in other areas, say so and express your appreciation for those efforts. Developing someone's strengths is far likelier to be successful than trying to correct weaknesses. Whether conveying praise or criticism, however, remember always to focus on the work performance and not the person.

Outline specifically and as briefly as possible what you want to discuss. If performance is lacking in more than one area, start with the simpler problem and work up to the more complex. Don't try to accomplish too much in one meeting.

In the performance discussion, the employee should do most of the talking, so once you have outlined the problem, ask the other person for his or her opinions and suggestions. Encourage the expression of all feelings, including negative ones. Giving someone the opportunity to air feelings early in the conversation helps get past any defensiveness. Help your employee get started by saying something like, "Why don't we start with your giving me your perspective on the problem?"

Your major role at this point is to listen, which both connotes and evokes acceptance. It tells others you're interested in their problems. Listening to people talking freely about themselves is the surest way to get to know them—their attitudes, values, and even their abilities. It doesn't necessarily suggest that you believe or agree with everything you hear, but it does show that you're willing to hear it. Listen actively by nodding your head and commenting, "Yes, I understand," or "Can you clarify that?"

When two people have differences of opinion, each wants to convince the other of his or her rightness. This usually involves listening to the other person's viewpoint only long enough to refute it. The biggest challenge lies in listening carefully enough to understand the other person's position. The natural tendency is to shut out any message which threatens your own viewpoint. Demonstrating to the employee that you've listened, heard, and understood strengthens the possibility that he or she will make a similar effort to listen to your position. Each position usually has some validity.

Remain impartial as you listen, and avoid jumping to conclusions. Accept, don't judge, each statement. Don't question the validity of perceptions or try to determine who's right. As the person tells you his or her opinion or viewpoint, don't agree, disagree, criticize, interrupt, analyze, or diagnose. Don't let the discussion degenerate into a debate—it's the kind no one can win.

Deliver your criticism in a matter-of-fact manner, with little or no emotion. Be direct and describe the problem specifically, simply, and candidly. Holding back does no one a favor.

Don't use accusatory terms such as "your fault," "mistakes," or "weaknesses." Avoid making evaluative statements like "Just use more common sense" or "Everyone should know how to do that." Don't dwell on past errors, or assess someone's personality or character. Concentrate on what the person did or didn't do and the work problem it caused, keeping your emphasis on the important elements of the job. When you're not dealing with specific facts, use phrases such as, "In my judgment," or "I feel that . . . ."

If you need more information, use open-ended questions that deal with what, when, how, and why, much as you would in your standard interviewing techniques. Asking questions helps the employee achieve some insight and provides an opportunity to modify or clarify without confrontation or loss of face.

When people overrate their own performance, find out what makes them think they're that good. Try asking them to compare their work to others in the department.

If the employee appears to be blaming someone or something else, use reflective questions, such as, "Then you feel it was a budget problem?" or "If I understand what you're saying, you feel that Jane was really responsible, but was there anything you could have done to work around it?" In response to people who point out all the good they've done, you can say, "Yes, I know that, and I appreciate it, too; but is there any other way we can improve this situation?" If someone dwells too long on a problem, summarize it and say, "Now let's go on to the next area," or "We can talk more about that later, but let's go on now."

When the employee is finished, summarize what you've heard. Acknowledge the areas in which you agree, outline those points on which you disagree, then give your reasons for disagreeing. Use phrases like, "I feel this way," or "Well, my approach would be . . . ." If you're partly at fault, admit it. This will make it easier for others to admit their mistakes.

Explain your reactions to what has been said. If you have experience on the job, use your own experiences to show how problems can be overcome, or suggest alternate ways of getting the job done. Don't be afraid to state your opinion. People want to know how they're doing and what their supervisors are thinking. You're a person who greatly influences their lives, and they want your viewpoint, subjectivity and all. Don't tell employees how they rate against their co-workers. Specifically mentioning another employee's poor performance will get out, and commenting about your outstanding employees will only create friction.

Ask the employee to restate what you've said. For instance, "OK, as you understand it then, what is my viewpoint on this?" The employee would probably then respond with something like, "You seem to feel that I should have seen this coming, and that I should have acted sooner."

Once each of you is satisfied with the other's summary and understanding, conclude by summarizing the areas of agreement and disagreement. Total agreement on all performance standards isn't necessary in order for both of you to reach an understanding of what the problem is and what you expect. Nor is total agreement necessary for you to be able to negotiate a solution, which is the main function of the performance discussion.

Goal Setting: Solving the Problem

After the problem has been identified, set up an action plan consisting of specific, realistic steps that will help improve performance. In this phase of the interview, the commitment to change can best be achieved through the active participation of the employee, who also has the best knowledge of the limitations and opportunities of the job.

Express faith that with the employee's ability and your support, together you can solve the problem. However, the responsibility for action still rests with the employee. Identify clearly the things you can do to help and those steps which the employee must accomplish. Since almost everyone works better with a deadline, set up a timetable for the completion of each step.

Don't promise rewards, such as raises or promotions, since the emphasis in the performance discussion should be on growth in the current job. Avoid telling people that correcting one fault would make them outstanding or eliminate all their problems. Never urge people on to achievements that really don't matter. Your employees can't maintain top performance at all times in all areas, so focus their efforts. Enforcing requirements that everyone knows aren't genuinely important can cause resentment.

If someone has a serious personal problem (such as substance abuse),

Exhibit 12.2 Sample Performance Discussion Memo

To: Departmental file of employee John Doe
From: R. Smith
RE: Performance Discussion
Date: 6/6/XX

This memo will document a conversation I had with John Doe in my office at 1:30 p.m. today. We discussed his inability to get meeting rooms set up on time, including three specific instances: the Blue Room on May 30th, the Cardinal Room on June 2nd, and the Clark Room on June 5th.

John agreed to give particular attention to the following:

—to watch his time more closely

—to keep his set-up schedule with him at all times

—to check his schedule after completing each task

—to report to me at once if he sees he is going to be unable to complete a set-up for any reason

concentrate only on how the problem has affected the job. Beyond that, the person must be referred to a professional within or outside the company who can deal with the problem.

Don't argue blindly for your own position. Remember, you're trying to help people to develop themselves, not remake them in your own image. Avoid the win/lose approach. If the other person doesn't accept the outcome, the performance discussion has accomplished nothing. When there's disagreement, a compromise must be negotiated. Select the next best alternative *that meets the needs*. It should be clear that, while the company will negotiate how to achieve its standards, it does not lower its standards just to accommodate poor performance. Don't change your mind simply to avoid conflict. Never apologize for being the manager or abdicate your ultimate responsibility.

The employee must be willing to take significant and enthusiastic action to carry out the plan. If objections are unrealistic, or no compromise can be reached because the person feels unable to comply or that he or she has been treated unfairly, listen fully and carefully to the complaints. Then, encourage your employee to follow the company's grievance procedure.

The negotiated performance objectives should result in personal growth and a greater degree of employee self-management—vital qualities in a fast-changing industry where the need for redirection is continuous.

Feedback   Marginal or insecure performers need feedback more frequently. Set a time when you can have another session to review progress and check whether objectives are being met. However, don't hesitate to point out at any time when an employee's performance is getting back on the right track.

You should document the discussion by writing up a memo for your departmental file (see Exhibit 12.2). This kind of information is confidential and should be kept no more than two years. Most people learn through trial and error and by analyzing their mistakes. Once the performance problem has been corrected and the employee has learned the correct way, the discussion form can be discarded.

The Annual Planning Session

Many employers have modified their annual performance appraisals by separating them from the pay and performance issues and emphasizing the planning process.

Like the performance discussion, the **annual planning session** should be a process in which the manager not only provides information and ideas to the employee, but also receives information and ideas from the employee. Unlike the performance discussion, the emphasis is on the future—developing the manager-employee relationship, setting goals, and making plans to improve performance—rather than on past problems, giving employees an overall "score," or ranking them against others in the department. (Such a meeting, however, would probably include a brief review of previous goal-setting sessions in order to set realistic goals for the future.) Such sessions also help companies ensure that managers make contact with *all* of their employees on a regular basis—winners and high achievers need time just as problem employees do. Exhibit 12.3 presents a sample annual planning session form.

The annual planning session helps managers and employees achieve a number of objectives.

It lets employees know where they stand. The annual planning session lets employees know how both they and the business are doing. It's a time to provide positive feedback and pass on information about any upcoming organizational changes, what's happening in the industry, and what customers are saying. Employees should also be given the opportunity to ask any questions they may have.

It allows managers to gain a better understanding of employees. Managers get to know their employees better and strengthen relationships by finding out about their families, interests, hobbies, and the like. They also gain insights into each employee's long-term career and personal objectives, unused skills, and relationships with co-workers. If an employee would like to pursue serious career counseling, it could be set up at this time.

It allows managers to gather information about the job and the department. Since the line worker has the greatest knowledge of the job, this is an excellent opportunity to obtain employee input, suggestions, and ideas for any improvements or changes, new equipment that might be needed, or problems that could be eliminated.

It allows managers and employees to set work goals together. Employees should be involved in making plans and setting their work goals for the coming year. You may review the past to help set direction and future goals, and you should review the goals of the department and the company for the coming year. Goals should be realistic, but high enough to challenge each person. As a manager, you should never make promises or allude to raises or promotions that may not come, nor should you overstate someone's capabilities. Simply give employees the information they require and let them choose which options to pursue. If it seems that a career pathing session is in order, another meeting should be arranged. Exhibit 12.4 presents several useful tips on writing performance goals.

It gains employees' recommitment. Reacquainting employees with departmental and company goals and showing them how each worker can

Exhibit 12.3   Sample Annual Planning Session Form

ANNUAL PLANNING SESSION

NAME_____ DATE:_____

DEPARTMENT_____ POSITION:_____

PART ONE: PROGRESS REVIEW

KEY AREAS	Exceeds All Standards	Exceeds Most Standards	Achieves Most Standards	Meets Minimum Standards	Meets Few Standards
Committed to the Goal of the Hotel. Goes out of the way to provide the finest in service and to be responsive to guests' needs. Enthusiastic about the job. Regularly performs duties outside the normal job to assist guests or improve quality. Shows pride and willingness to help the department and hotel become the very best. Believes in the values of the company. Enjoys helping others. Is a positive influence in the department.	☐	☐	☐	☐	☐
Comments:					
Quantity of Work. Continually meets or exceeds departmental standards for production. Organizes and plans work, manages time, sets priorities, follows directions and completes all assigned work on time. Energy level meets the demands of the job.	☐	☐	☐	☐	☐
Comments:					
Quality of Work. Consistently meets or exceeds departmental standards for quality. Has full knowledge of all aspects of the job. Work is accurate and complete and of the highest possible quality. Checks own work, maintains quality under pressure. Pays attention to details.	☐	☐	☐	☐	☐
Comments:					
Departmental Objectives. Helps department meet its budgeted revenue and expenses. Makes suggestions and works to improve revenue and control expenses. Up-sells to guests. Reduces waste whenever possible.	☐	☐	☐	☐	☐
Comments:					
Dependability. Is ready for work at the start of the shift. Does not overstay meal periods. Good attendance and lateness record. Notifies supervisor before leaving work area. Works until the end of the shift and spends worktime working. Good follow-up. Perseveres on tough jobs. Has good health.	☐	☐	☐	☐	☐
Comments:					
Work Habits. Keeps work area clean. Cares for equipment. Safety conscious. Dresses appropriately for work, uniform or clothing clean and pressed, shoes shined. Wears complete uniform, including name tag.	☐	☐	☐	☐	☐
Comments:					
Teamwork. Works other shifts, overtime, days off or in other areas as assigned by supervisor. Goes out of way to cooperate with fellow employees, guests, supervisors and people from other departments. Shows patience and flexibility. Accepts direction well. Willing to work overtime and weekends. Deals well with change and conflict.	☐	☐	☐	☐	☐
Comments:					
Extra Effort. Willing to accept added responsibility. Has attempted to learn other areas, takes the company approach. Shows strong interest in training and learning. Takes initiative, uses good judgement and can solve problems quickly. Good listening, verbal and written skills. Has shown the ability to influence other people. Works with minimum supervision. Participates in hotel meetings and committees.	☐	☐	☐	☐	☐
Comments:					

(continued)

Exhibit 12.3 *(continued)*

PART TWO: PLAN OF ACTION FOR NEXT 12 MONTHS

EMPLOYEE FEEDBACK: What suggestions, comments and ideas does the employee have to improve guest satisfaction and company (or personal) efficiency or productivity?

MANAGEMENT SUPPORT: What training, equipment or assistance can the manager provide to help?

COMPANY/DEPARTMENTAL OBJECTIVES: What are the overall company and departmental objectives for the next year?

EMPLOYEE OBJECTIVES: What would the employee like to accomplish during the next year, personally as well as at work? Have short or long term goals changed since the last discussion?

LAST YEAR'S PLAN OF ACTION: How well have the objectives from the last planning session been achieved?

NEXT YEAR'S PLAN OF ACTION:

Priority	Specific objectives have been agreed upon	Target Date

COMMENTS:

SIGNATURES: _____ / _____ / _____
EMPLOYEE — EVALUATOR — REVIEWED BY

Exhibit 12.4 Tips on Writing Performance Goals

There are at least three important criteria to consider when setting effective performance objectives and they are that they should be:

- Results-oriented
- Measurable
- Understandable

Performance goals/objectives should be written in terms of the output or results expected, rather than the activities to be engaged in to achieve those results. As an example, a salesperson should be accountable for revenue expected (dollars or percentage improvement) rather than number of sales calls to be made.

Effective performance goals/objectives should be clearly measurable. They should contain specifics and details so that both supervisor and employee can objectively agree when the desired results have been achieved.

To aid in drafting effective performance goals/objectives, use an action verb, followed by some form of measurement such as quality level, quantity, time factor, and/or cost. Some examples are:

1. Reduce the number of accidents as a percentage of labor hours by 20% from the previous year's percentage.

2. Develop and qualify five hourly employees for promotion to first level management positions by December 31.

3. Implement an energy conservation program designed to save the hotel $35,000 a year by the end of the year and at a cost not to exceed $15,000.

Courtesy of Westin Hotels & Resorts, Seattle, Washington.

best realize his or her personal goals by achieving the goals of the organization will help renew their commitment.

Questions. Listed below are examples of the kinds of questions you might raise during an annual interview:

- What do you like most about your job?

- What do you like least about your job?

- What areas do you consider your strengths?

- In what areas would you like to have additional training?

- Do you have talents that you don't feel you're using now?

- What parts of your job do you think you could do better? (Most people criticize themselves more readily than they can accept criticism from their supervisor.)

- What are your short- and long-term goals?

- Have you been doing anything that will help you increase your competence on the job in any way?

- How do you feel about the working relationship that you and I have? What do you think we can do to improve it?

- Do I do anything that makes your job harder?
- Is there any way that I can be of help to you?

Many companies choose to conduct the annual planning session on the employee's anniversary date, so that they don't all have to be done at once. Regardless of when it's held, a once-a-year interview will be meaningless if it isn't part of a continuing dialogue between manager and employee. If you're dealing with problems as they arise throughout the year, a brief annual session should hold no surprises or problems.

As with the performance discussion, the written records kept of the annual interview should be treated confidentially.

The Pay Review

The frequency and timing of **pay reviews** are dictated by union contract or the company's wage and salary program. The commonest pattern is to have two pay reviews a year, with all pay reviews occurring at the same time. Another common practice is to bring people in at one rate and adjust their pay at the end of a probationary period. Further pay reviews would then come at six- or twelve-month intervals. For salaried employees, annual pay reviews are still the commonest, since it takes longer to evaluate their effectiveness.

The guidelines for increases are also normally set by company policies, taking into account such factors as equal pay and minimum wage laws, profitability, inflation, local union contracts, and the going rate for the job in the labor market.

A person's pay is a very personal topic. Discussing it can generate a great deal of anxiety, and many sensitive issues may come up. Going through the employee's mind may be thoughts of how to make ends meet, or what to buy, or whether the increase is fair. The manager must be prepared for and able to deal with many such emotions and concerns. It's because of this employee "tunnel vision" during pay discussions that many companies have stopped combining them with performance reviews.

Determining the Raise Amount

There's a strong tendency for managers to inflate all their performance ratings if they're done as the basis for salary decisions. Managers may do this in an effort to get as much money as they can for their people and to avoid having to talk to anyone about poor performance. However, major legal liabilities can result for the company when this occurs. If an employee is later terminated, the company may be forced to defend the firing of someone who has had a number of flattering reviews. In terms of legal justification, it's probably better to have no review than to have one that's misleading.

Of course, some evaluation of the employee is necessary to justify the amount recommended. In these cases, the manager should rate the employee into one of three categories: non-performer, average, or top performer—thus permitting the top and poor performers to be handled differently from the average employee. This evaluation is based on the manager's assessment of the employee's performance over the period since the last review.

Before deciding on an amount, review the amounts and dates of prior increases, the standing within the grade, performance discussions, warning notices, and attendance records. If goals and objectives have been set,

The annual planning session is part of a continuing dialogue between manager and employee.

determine whether they have been met and, if so, how well. Talk to other people and get their opinions about an employee before making your pay evaluation. Two heads are better than one, and a line supervisor or the head of another department with whom the employee has had frequent contact may see things differently.

It's best to have all pay increases reviewed and recommended by two or more people—usually the manager and division head—and approved by one or more others, normally the director of human resources and general manager. While it's the manager's job to reward performance, the human resources department has some related responsibilities. It:

- Ensures compliance with Equal Pay, EEO, Wage and Hour, and other legal requirements

- Watches for and heads off patterns such as the central tendency or overly lenient or demanding supervisors

- Ensures that dates and amounts are correct and within budget and approved guidelines

Green-circled employees are often being paid less than the starting salary for their pay grade because promotions or other actions have moved them into jobs with higher pay grades. It's tempting to give substantial increases to bring them quickly into line, but this can be detrimental. In fact, quite often, the promising employees who have been promoted or transferred to a higher-paying and more demanding job don't yet have all of the skills to take on all of the responsibilities of the new job. Therefore, they shouldn't get the same pay as someone with more experience doing the same job.

Furthermore, employees may perceive a large increase as a signal that they've been underpaid and that the company has finally recognized it. When they get normal increases at subsequent salary reviews, they think something's wrong with their performance, and they're disappointed. Even cautioning people that the larger than usual raise is only a one-time event doesn't seem to help much to avoid this perception. Instead, plan to have pay reviews more often and adhere to the standard increase amount each time until the proper pay grade is reached.

The Pay Review Meeting

Only *after* increases have been given full approval should you discuss a raise or hold a pay review with an employee. Never tell people in advance how much you're going to recommend. If it's not approved, they'll take it as a sign that someone at the top doesn't like them, and morale problems can result. Furthermore, it will appear that you're not in control. At a pay review, the employee may see a manager who says, "I put in for a bigger raise for you, but it was turned down," as weak and ineffective. In fact, a common reaction among workers who hear this is to conclude that they don't really work for this manager after all. They may then speculate that they should be talking to the person who actually makes the decisions on their increases.

You should allow enough time for any necessary preparation—including obtaining required approvals—so that the pay review meeting can be held on time. Most employees know when their pay reviews are due, and any delays can cause unnecessary anxiety and even resentment about why they are not hearing from you. Making a regular increase retroactive because of late paperwork is no substitute for being on time. An overdue pay review meeting suggests a lack of control on the part of the manager. It can also communicate to employees that they and their livelihood are not considered important.

Arrange to discuss each salary review privately in your office. Employees receiving an increase should be told that you've reviewed their work and are pleased with their performance. Tell them the amount of the increase and the date on which it will appear in their pay.

If you are giving a larger than average increase to someone who has done an outstanding job, clearly explain the reasons for the increase. Always caution that it's unusual and shouldn't be considered as setting a precedent.

Inform people getting close to the top of their range that when they reach the top, their salaries will be frozen, delayed, or the amount of increases reduced, according to your company's policies. Cover these facts far enough in advance that they can begin to prepare for additional responsibilities, transfers, or promotions to higher grades if they're so inclined. If no raise is forthcoming because someone has reached the top of the pay grade, you should still have the meeting. Thank the person for the good job and offer to discuss what would be needed for transfer or promotion to a higher grade.

If an employee disagrees with the amount received, listen to the reasoning. After you've heard the arguments, reaffirm your opinions of this person's contribution to the overall performance of the department. It's important for employees to have the opportunity to express their feelings. If someone wants to know what's needed in order to get a larger increase, set up a time for a performance discussion.

If an employee is getting no increase because of poor performance, it shouldn't come as a surprise, since you should have had one or more performance discussions and perhaps even disciplinary discussions before the

FOUR SEASONS OLYMPIC

PAYROLL AND STATUS AUTHORIZATION

— CHANGE OR TERMINATION —

ACTION INITIATEL THIS FORM	
☐ POSITION CHANGE	☐ SICK PAY
☐ SALARY CHANGE	☐ S.T. D.
☐ PERSONAL DATA CHANGE	☐ LEAVE OF ABSENCE
☐ TAX OR BENEFIT CHANGE	☐ TERMINATION

ACTION EFFECTIVE ON >

SALARY CHANGES EFFECTIVE ONLY ON FIRST DAY OF PAY PERIOD

EMPLOYEE #	SOCIAL SECURITY #	LAST NAME	FIRST	MIDDLE I.

POSITION CHANGE

FROM		TO	
DEPARTMENT	DEPT. CODE	DEPARTMENT	DEPT. CODE
POSITION	POSITION CODE	POSITION	POSITION CODE
STATUS ☐ (1) FULL TIME ☐ (2) PART TIME ☐ (1) PERMANENT ☐ (2) TEMPORARY		STATUS ☐ (1) FULL TIME ☐ (2) PART TIME ☐ (1) PERMANENT ☐ (2) TEMPORARY	

SALARY CHANGE

	HOURLY	WEEKLY	ANNUAL	REASON FOR CHANGE	LAST INCREASE
PRESENT SALARY	$	$	$	☐ MERIT (Attach Review)	DATE:
				☐ POSITION CHANGE	
CHANGE ±	$	$	$	☐ PROMOTION	AMOUNT:
				☐ CONTRACT	REASON:
NEW SALARY	$	$	$	☐ OTHER	

PERSONAL DATA CHANGE

NEW ADDRESS - STREET	CITY	STATE	ZIP CODE

NEW PHONE # ( )	NEW MARITAL STATUS ☐ (1) MARRIED ☐ (2) SINGLE ☐ (3) SINGLE HEAD OF HOUSEHOLD ☐ (4) DIVORCED ☐ (5) WIDOWED

TAX OR BENEFIT CHANGE

NEW TAX STATUS ☐ (1) MARRIED ☐ (2) SINGLE ☐ (3) MARRIED, BUT W/H AT SINGLE	EXEMPTIONS

NEW BENEFIT DEDUCTIONS PER PAY PERIOD

1. MED 100% HOSP. _____	4. _____	7. _____
2. MED/DEN DEPENDENT _____	5. _____	8. _____
3. VOL. AD&D _____	6. _____	9. CR. UNION _____

SICK S.T.D.

☐ SICK ☐ S.T.D. ☐ L.O.A.	# OF WORK DAYS	DATES

LEAVE OF ABSENCE

DATES	REASON ☐ DISABILITY ☐ MILITARY ☐ PERSONAL ☐ OTHER

TERMINATION

REASON ☐ RESIGNATION ☐ LAYOFF ☐ DEATH ☐ DISMISSAL ☐ RETIREMENT ☐ OTHER	ELIGIBLE FOR REHIRE? ☐ YES ☐ NO	ACCRUED VACATION PAY DUE _____ DAYS

COMMENTS

APPROVAL	DEPARTMENT HEAD	DIVISION HEAD	GENERAL MANAGER	PERSONNEL DIRECTOR
DATE				

WHITE - PERSONNEL   YELLOW - PAYROLL   PINK - DEPT. HEAD

Only after increases have been given full approval should the pay review be held. (Courtesy of Four Seasons Olympic Hotel, Seattle, Washington)

salary review. At salary review time, however, you should still discuss with the person the reasons for his or her not receiving an increase and what must be done before a raise can be given.

Unlike the training session or performance discussion, this isn't a time for sandwiching criticism in with praise. The focus should be clearly on why the person isn't getting an increase. If you lead off with the good things about the worker's performance, the person may concentrate on your praise and fail to absorb or accept what you say about the problem areas.

Don't delay the review for a period of time, such as a month, and then give the increase. If for the past six months a person's performance has been so poor that no increase is merited, one month can't make up for it. The consideration of an increase has to wait for the next review period. Delaying the review by a short time or giving the full amount plus the amount lost at the next review are common errors managers make. These errors suggest to employees that they can perform below standards and still get the same pay as the hard workers.

When it becomes apparent that an employee who was passed over for an increase once is about to be denied an increase again at review time, consider terminating the person. No one should be passed over twice because of poor performance and kept on in your department. A manager shouldn't tolerate unsatisfactory work for that long a period of time.

In your discussion with the person who's not receiving an increase, establish the direct relationship between performance and pay increases. Caution the person that if there are no signs of improvement, he or she will be terminated. You might state:

> As you knew, your review was due; and I couldn't justify giving you an increase this time, based on your performance. We discussed this before in our performance discussions, and I haven't really seen any improvement. I hope at the time the next review comes around, there's an improvement in your performance. If not, I don't see how I can keep you in the department and let others carry the extra work load.

Even though no raise was given, be sure to keep a record of the discussion by making a note for your departmental file. The fact that no raise was given and the reasons for this should also be shown on the company's standard pay review form that is placed in the employee's personnel file.

Key Terms
annual planning session
central tendency
pay review
performance discussion

Discussion Questions

1. Why is it better to have different kinds of meetings between manager and employee to meet different needs, instead of having only one all-encompassing performance appraisal session a year?

2. Why do you think many employees dread performance appraisals? What can a manager do to dispel those apprehensions?

3. What are some potential shortcomings managers have to guard against in themselves when conducting employee appraisals?

4. What are some steps a manager can take in order to be adequately prepared to conduct the performance discussion?

5. What does the annual planning session accomplish?

6. What are some of the things that should be considered before the amount of a pay raise is decided?

7. If company policy is to conduct two pay reviews a year, what's wrong with delaying a borderline employee's review an extra month to give the person a chance to improve and still get an increase?

13 Health and Safety

Public awareness of and concern for health and safety have been on the increase in recent years. Both consumer and worker protection are receiving increased attention, with new legislation and the revision and expansion of existing laws.

A sickness or injury can mean serious personal discomfort, loss of income, and expensive medical bills to a worker. To an employer, either represents a major expense in terms of medical insurance costs and lost production. The United States spends over $500 billion a year on medical care,[1] but that's only the beginning. If not controlled, illness- and injury-related absenteeism and turnover produce additional enormous costs in the workplace.

Less evident is the toll taken by personal problems which affect the worker's physical and mental health—problems like stress, burnout, poor health and eating habits, mental illness, child and spouse abuse, financial difficulties, gambling addiction, and substance abuse. In addition to their impact on absenteeism and turnover, these kinds of health problems can run up major losses for companies through increased accidents and breakage and lower morale, productivity, and quality of service. As their first line of defense against these burgeoning expenses, employers should adopt policies and practices based on prevention.

Controlling Absenteeism

Employee absenteeism is one of the biggest sources of unnecessary expense and poor service in the hospitality industry. Many managers seem to accept it as a fact of life, which is a mistake. If managers generally accept absenteeism, the organizational culture and values will soon accept it as well. If an employee calls in sick and then goes deer hunting and co-workers don't get mad about it, the department has real problems.

On the other hand, if a company or manager values good attendance, has high expectations, maintains clear policies and records, disciplines offenders, and rewards those with good attendance, the organization will value good attendance. A positive approach to developing the right climate includes a four-step process.

---

[1]Kathleen McAuliffe and Howard Hiatt, "Sick about America's Health Care," *U.S. News & World Report*, June 15, 1987, p. 64.

Tell Workers What's Expected

Spell out your position clearly for each new employee. For example:

I put particular emphasis on good attendance and punctuality when it comes time for raises and promotions. I expect a person to be late (meaning five minutes or more) no more than five times in any two-month period, and absent no more than four days in a six-month period. Anything above this I consider to be excessive.

Remember, however, that employees see the manager's own tardiness and attendance as the accepted standard.

Have a Clear Procedure

Cover how to report absences. For example:

If you're going to be late, call me as soon as possible. I need at least two hours' advance notice in order to get someone else scheduled in. If I'm not here, call the next highest ranking person in the department and leave a message that you'll be late. If you're calling in sick and I'm not here, leave word with that person; but then you must call back later and discuss it with me personally. I'll need other information, like how long you'll be out and whether you'll need to provide any medical releases before you come back to work.

When an employee calls in sick, it's usually a good practice to pull the timecard so the person can't go back to work without first talking to you. The majority of one-day absences are unnecessary; requiring employees to sit down and look you in the eye is a strong deterrent to their calling in sick without good cause. By using a caring tone while asking such questions as, "Did you have to go to a doctor?" or "Did you have a fever?," you express your concern while finding out more about the absence. Employees who were legitimately sick won't object to your interest. Those who weren't actually sick may feel uncomfortable enough to think twice before calling in sick again.

If an employee is having an attendance problem, let the person know that you're concerned about it.

Maintain Good Records

Keeping good attendance records on your people is useful in a number of ways. It helps when it's time for salary and promotion reviews. It provides backup for performance, disciplinary, and termination discussions. It helps indicate cases where an employee assistance program (discussed later in this chapter) might be in order. Tracking the absence and lateness habits of employees (perhaps on a form such as the one shown in Exhibit 13.1) will enable you to spot quickly those who develop patterns—for example, those who are frequently absent the day after payday or after days off.

Reward Good Attendance

One approach to rewarding good performance involves revising health care coverage and sick-leave policies so that they do not cover one- or even two-day absences. The reasoning is that employees can overcome the absence of one or two days' pay, but must be protected for significant long-term illnesses.

The company instead implements a program to reward good attendance. The **comp-day program**, for instance, allows an employee to earn a complimentary day off for achieving a specified number of weeks of perfect attendance. Complimentary days can be used to cover the one- or two-day illness, added to vacation time, or taken as personal days off. Since they can be scheduled during slow periods, they're far less destructive to the operation

Exhibit 13.1 Attendance Record

Employee Calendar	ABSENCE CODE

ABSENCE CODE
U — Unexcused (No Pay)
E — Excused (Pay)
L — Late
V — Vacation
B — Bonus Day
H — Holiday

REASON CODE
1 — Illness (Employee) 6 — Leave of Absence
2 — Illness (Family) 7 — Unknown (AWOL)
3 — Injury (At Work) 8 —
4 — Injury (At Home) 9 —
5 — Personal 10 —

NAME
ADDRESS

SOCIAL SECURITY NO.
DEPARTMENT

JANUARY

Sun.	Mon.	Tues.	Wed.	Thurs.	Fri.	Sat.
1	2	3	4	5	6	7
8	9	10	11	12	13	14
15	16	17	18	19	20	21
22	23	24	25	26	27	28
29	30	31				

FEBRUARY

Sun.	Mon.	Tues.	Wed.	Thurs.	Fri.	Sat.
			1	2	3	4
5	6	7	8	9	10	11
12	13	14	15	16	17	18
19	20	21	22	23	24	25
26	27	28				

MARCH

Sun.	Mon.	Tues.	Wed.	Thurs.	Fri.	Sat.
			1	2	3	4
5	6	7	8	9	10	11
12	13	14	15	16	17	18
19	20	21	22	23	24	25
26	27	28	29	30	31	

APRIL

Sun.	Mon.	Tues.	Wed.	Thurs.	Fri.	Sat.
						1
2	3	4	5	6	7	8
9	10	11	12	13	14	15
16	17	18	19	20	21	22
23	24	25	26	27	28	29
30						

MAY

Sun.	Mon.	Tues.	Wed.	Thurs.	Fri.	Sat.
	1	2	3	4	5	6
7	8	9	10	11	12	13
14	15	16	17	18	19	20
21	22	23	24	25	26	27
28	29	30	31			

JUNE

Sun.	Mon.	Tues.	Wed.	Thurs.	Fri.	Sat.
				1	2	3
4	5	6	7	8	9	10
11	12	13	14	15	16	17
18	19	20	21	22	23	24
25	26	27	28	29	30	

JULY

Sun.	Mon.	Tues.	Wed.	Thurs.	Fri.	Sat.
						1
2	3	4	5	6	7	8
9	10	11	12	13	14	15
16	17	18	19	20	21	22
23	24	25	26	27	28	29
30	31					

AUGUST

Sun.	Mon.	Tues.	Wed.	Thurs.	Fri.	Sat.
		1	2	3	4	5
6	7	8	9	10	11	12
13	14	15	16	17	18	19
20	21	22	23	24	25	26
27	28	29	30	31		

SEPTEMBER

Sun.	Mon.	Tues.	Wed.	Thurs.	Fri.	Sat.
					1	2
3	4	5	6	7	8	9
10	11	12	13	14	15	16
17	18	19	20	21	22	23
24	25	26	27	28	29	30

OCTOBER

Sun.	Mon.	Tues.	Wed.	Thurs.	Fri.	Sat.
1	2	3	4	5	6	7
8	9	10	11	12	13	14
15	16	17	18	19	20	21
22	23	24	25	26	27	28
29	30	31				

NOVEMBER

Sun.	Mon.	Tues.	Wed.	Thurs.	Fri.	Sat.
			1	2	3	4
5	6	7	8	9	10	11
12	13	14	15	16	17	18
19	20	21	22	23	24	25
26	27	28	29	30		

DECEMBER

Sun.	Mon.	Tues.	Wed.	Thurs.	Fri.	Sat.
					1	2
3	4	5	6	7	8	9
10	11	12	13	14	15	16
17	18	19	20	21	22	23
24	25	26	27	28	29	30
31						

This form and the attendance control system are part of a total payroll services program provided by Automatic Data Processing, Inc.

than unplanned absences. Thus, the potential cost of one-day illnesses is reduced, while good attendance is encouraged and rewarded.

Flexible work schedules, job enrichment, and participative management are all programs that have helped to reduce absenteeism. Others that have been used successfully involve contests to draw attention to a company's or department's value on good attendance. Programs may not be needed in all areas. They often focus instead on problem departments. Everyone in the department who had perfect attendance for a week could earn trading stamps or be included in a drawing for a prize, such as free groceries for a week. To keep interest and participation high, these kinds of programs need to be changed frequently and adapted to the workers involved.

If your aim is to improve attendance among people who have a high rate of absenteeism, the goal must be attainable. Perfect attendance for six months or a year may seem easy enough to a manager. However, for many minimum wage workers with unreliable transportation and constant baby-sitting worries, even a goal of three months may be unrealistic. Providing

How can you earn $500 or more a year?

Here's how it works. The money you earn from your attendance points added to the money you earn from unused bonus days could total $500.00 or more.

$450.00   for attendance points (from Ex. 2)
202.50   for six unused bonus days (from Ex.2)
$652.50   TOTAL AMOUNT TO BE PAID TO YOU!

As you can see, this program rewards those employees who work as scheduled and assist the Hotel by working six or seven days in the same work week. How much money you make is up to you...you're in control!

Please keep in mind this important point: the money we once used for sick day pay and OHPAP, plus approximately $150,000.000 is being put in to these new programs. That's a lot of money! So, if you take bonus days, they will be *unpaid* days. If you don't take them, we'll pay you for them at your next service anniversary.

Above is an excerpt from an attendance incentive program that is helping Opryland control absenteeism. (Courtesy of Opryland Hotel, Nashville, Tennessee)

flexibility may also prove helpful. Those who miss one day during a contest may have no incentive for the remainder of the contest. For this reason, consider keeping the time period of the contest short or giving an award for the most improvement in attendance.

Annual certificates for perfect attendance help reinforce to your good employees that their efforts are noticed and appreciated. So does making it known that good attendance counts in the selection of the Employee of the Month and similar awards. Whatever the program to deal with absenteeism, its purpose is to communicate continually the value and importance of good attendance.

Wellness Programs

Companies have made major strides in recent years in the area of illness prevention through **wellness programs**. These programs aren't generally covered under medical plans, but rather are funded separately by the employer. Since the expenses involved are predictable and controllable, paying for insurance coverage for them would be defeating their purpose. For example, if you're going to provide an annual physical, you know exactly what the cost is, so there's no reason to insure yourself for it.

Education is the key to any prevention campaign. Employers can offer information or courses through their wellness programs that cover such topics as weight loss and diet, nutrition and eating habits, and physical fitness. They may offer clinics on how to stop smoking, cholesterol and blood pressure testing, and coping with problems like stress and hypertension. Preventive education is also proving to be useful in dealing with concerns like AIDS. Providing information and addressing the problems in advance is a much better way of managing than waiting until an employee has AIDS. If you fail to address the issue in advance, you may suddenly find other employees refusing to come to work and guests refusing to patronize your restaurant. Exhibit 13.2 summarizes several concerns relevant to AIDS in the workplace.

As part of their wellness programs, many employers are re-examining the kinds of food offered, and even the atmosphere, in their employee cafeterias and other break areas. Some companies also provide on-site exercise facilities or exercise club memberships.

Since results can only be seen over the long term, it's difficult to show a direct relationship to reductions in absenteeism or insurance costs. Nonetheless, there's no doubt that employees who are active and physically fit will feel better about themselves and be more productive, which means they'll also provide better service.

Smoking

The legal aspects of smoking in the workplace are still not clearly defined, and laws vary from state to state. Some people feel strongly that the employer has an obligation to provide a smoke-free working environment. Others feel just as strongly that people have a right to smoke when and where they wish. While this debate rages on, the legal trend is clearly toward having employers make reasonable efforts to accommodate those employees who want a smoke-free work environment. In certain states, employers who have failed to provide workers a safe, smoke-free environment have been found liable under workers' compensation for health problems caused by the effects of environmental tobacco smoke.[2]

Some companies have responded by establishing policies that restrict smoking to certain areas so that non-smokers won't be exposed. The designated areas commonly receive improved ventilation. If smoking can't be restricted in an area, it may be necessary to transfer any employee who wishes to work in a smoke-free area. Common areas are usually off-limits for smoking, but in a private office with an odorless ashtray, smoking might be permitted.

The company's first obligation is to satisfy any relevant state and federal laws. A reasonable compromise between the positions of different employees should be achieved. Adequate notice should be given before the implementation of a new policy. The typical smoker can't simply quit or put the habit on hold during the workday.

Many companies also pay for smoking-cessation programs for their employees, particularly before designating restricted smoking areas. Such courses may also help reduce costs because fewer breaks are taken. In

---

[2]Philip R. Voluck, "The Work Environment: Burning Legal Issues in the Workplace," *Personnel Journal*, June 1987, p. 143.

Exhibit 13.2   AIDS in the Workplace

The Preventive Program®

CONTAGIOUS DISEASES
Copyright 1988
STOKES, LAZARUS & CARMICHAEL

*Contagious Diseases
In The Workplace*

How does an employer treat employees who have contagious diseases? This brochure discusses the competing considerations an employer faces when addressing this problem. It is our opinion that an employer should have a uniform policy dealing with employees who have contagious diseases. The AIDS example demonstrates how individual rights often compete with the rights of employers.

AIDS, Acquired Immune Deficiency Syndrome, is a fatal, contagious disease affecting many thousands of Americans. It is believed that the HIV virus causes AIDS. Although the exact number of Americans infected by the HIV virus is unknown, the Centers for Disease Control estimates that millions of Americans may be infected by 1990. The percentage of people infected by the HIV virus who will actually come down with AIDS is unknown.

Medical evidence to date concludes that AIDS is spread by sexual contact and through sharing of intravenous drug needles, and not by casual, non-sexual contact. There are no reported cases of transmission of AIDS between co-workers through casual contact in the workplace. It should be noted that based on medical evidence to date, AIDS is unlike many other communicable diseases in that it cannot be spread by casual contact.

SOME CONTAGIOUS DISEASES MAY BE "HANDICAPS"

- Many federal, state and local courts, legislatures and agencies have ruled that AIDS, and other contagious diseases, are handicaps within the meaning of laws prohibiting discrimination on the basis of handicap. Many states have expressly declared AIDS to be a handicap, including the states of New York, California, Texas, Illinois, Pennsylvania and Florida.

- Several states, including California and Florida, specifically prohibit an employer from testing job applicants or employees for the existence of the HIV virus or making decisions based on the test results.

- Several cities, including Los Angeles, Boston, Philadelphia, San Francisco and Washington, D.C., have ordinances prohibiting discrimination based on AIDS.

- A few states, like Kentucky, have expressly declared contagious diseases like AIDS not to be a handicap.

- This area of law is rapidly changing and you must continue to update your knowledge to comply with applicable law.

UNIFORM COMPANY POLICY

We believe that every employer, in developing a uniform policy on contagious diseases, should do the following:

- Consider what is in the best overall interest of the employer.

- Keep in mind that, if you are an employer in the restaurant or hotel industry, you are held to a very high standard of care in protecting your guests from the risk of contagious infection. You may be sued by a guest if you are negligent in this regard.

- Keep in mind that the Occupational Safety and Health Administration (OSHA) requires that "each employer shall furnish to each of his employees employment in a place of employment which is free from recognized hazards that are causing or likely to cause death or serious physical harm to his employees."

- Consider the business cost involved in each AIDS situation. Health insurance may become more costly.

- Consult your attorney to determine if you are subject to laws relating to contagious diseases and AIDS.

- Appreciate that in many jurisdictions there is a likelihood that you may be sued for adverse decisions affecting employees with AIDS, or who are HIV positive.

- If you become aware that an employee has AIDS, do not disclose that information to other individuals.

- If an employee has AIDS, the law may require you to make reasonable accommodations for the employee to perform his or her job after determining the employee's medical condition. Reasonable accommodation does not mean the employer must sustain undue hardship.

- If an employee cannot perform the essential functions of his or her job, or cannot perform his or her job after reasonable accommodation, then you are not required to hire or retain the employee.

- Educate your employees with the facts about AIDS and other contagious diseases. This will eliminate many problems caused by ignorance.

For further advice about contagious diseases and AIDS in the workplace, consult the attorney of your choice.

Source: *The Preventive Program®*, "Contagious Diseases in the Workplace" © 1988 Stokes, Lazarus & Carmichael, Attorneys At Law, Atlanta, Georgia. Used by permission.

addition, fewer illnesses related to the harmful effects on the smokers themselves may result in less absenteeism and lower medical insurance costs for the company.

Employee Assistance Programs

Through the **employee assistance program (EAP)**, the employer provides to employees a company-sponsored counselor referral system for assistance with any personal problem—whether it be emotional, financial, familial, or alcohol- or drug-related. The referrals can be to internal or external counselors.

EAPs can be handled in several different ways, but all have some basic common components:

1. The program's purpose and policies should be clearly stated.

2. Supervisors should be well prepared and trained to identify the problems and either deal with them directly or refer the employee to someone qualified to help.

3. To be effective, the program must have a referral source trained in dealing with each specific problem, to whom the employee can be readily referred. These sources are usually outside the company, since dealing with such problems as alcoholism or marital strife is outside the expertise of the supervisor.

4. In many cases, the cost of initial services is free from state- and community-supported organizations. The company can also bear some of the expenses, either by setting up another benefit process or adjusting the health insurance plan to include such coverage. To help control costs, some employers offer this program only to employees who have been with the company a year or more. This policy better protects the employer's more valued employees.

5. The employee's use of the EAP should be kept confidential. While disciplinary action for such problems as absenteeism or job performance can be kept in the personnel file, the counseling information should be kept confidential with other medical records.

Employers often publish the names of people within the company to whom employees can go for confidential advice and referral to appropriate agencies. This furnishes an avenue for an executive to go to a fellow executive or a female to another female, with whom each may be more comfortable discussing personal problems. These individuals need specific training in employee counseling and identifying problems, an understanding of insurance coverage, and knowledge of the various referral agencies.

Managers need to learn to spot employees with personal problems. Some of the signs to be alert for are:[3]

• Marked personality change over time

---

[3]*"All he needs is a good swift kick in the pants"* and *Other Misunderstandings about Mental Illness,* American Mental Health Fund brochure, undated.

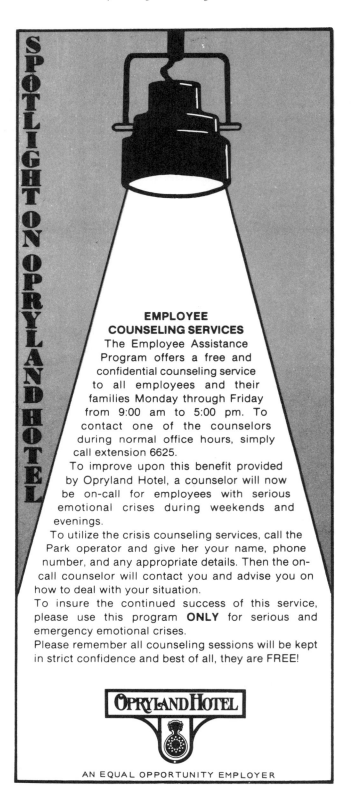

By helping employees and their families deal with personal problems, employee assistance programs reduce turnover and improve employee morale and guest service. (Courtesy of Opryland Hotel, Nashville, Tennessee)

- Confused thinking; strange or grandiose ideas

- Prolonged severe depression; apathy; or extreme highs and lows

- Excessive anxieties, fears, or suspiciousness; blaming others

- Withdrawal from society, friendlessness; abnormal self-centeredness

- Denial of obvious problems; strong resistance to help

- Thinking or talking about suicide

- Numerous unexplained physical ailments; marked changes in eating or sleeping patterns

- Anger or hostility out of proportion to the situation

- Delusions, hallucinations, hearing voices

- Abuse of alcohol or drugs

- Growing inability to cope with problems and daily activities such as school, job, or personal needs

In a diminishing labor market, keeping the experienced employees becomes more significant. This means treatment and rehabilitation are becoming more and more cost-efficient. Further, should a supervisor find during the disciplinary process that an employee's absences are the result of a personal problem, going to an EAP can be offered as a "last chance" before termination. Arbitrators are favorably impressed by companies that have made a reasonable effort to identify and treat personal conditions which affect performance.

Having an EAP also helps employees and the community see you as a caring employer and a good citizen. Employee morale and loyalty improve, along with your ability to recruit new employees.

Substance Abuse

Without question, the substantial rise in the rate of absenteeism in recent years and the growing number of personal problems adversely affecting worker health and job performance have been strongly influenced by the increased use of drugs and alcohol. Many states are now defining conditions like past alcoholism and drug addiction as handicaps, meaning that employees with these impairments are protected from discrimination in the workplace.[4] As with any other handicap, if the handicap prevents a person from doing the job, he or she can be fired or not hired. In the past, the general rule was to put up with the problem until it became intolerable and then fire the worker. Now, however, employers are being required to make a reasonable effort to diagnose and treat such employees before firing them.

Using information about health-related problems may be viewed in some cases as a violation of rights provided under the laws protecting handicapped workers. For instance, if you find that someone doesn't have a current

---

[4]Alfred Klein, "Employees Under the Influence—Outside the Law?" *Personnel Journal*, September 1986, p. 58.

Exhibit 13.3   Symptoms of Substance Abuse

- Decreases in performance—employees are less efficient or become distracted, forgetful, sloppy, careless
- Excessive tardiness or absenteeism, particularly after a day off
- Working an excessive number of hours to try to cover up inefficiencies
- Frequent trips to the restroom or water fountain
- An increase in accidents, usually caused by carelessness
- Wearing long-sleeved clothing in all weather
- Becoming careless about grooming and appearance
- Attitude changes, including a decrease in cooperation, rebelliousness, less openness, a decrease in enthusiasm
- Erratic mood swings, including depression or irritability
- Physical changes, including slurring of speech, very slow or very rapid eye blink rates, bloodshot or watery eyes, enlarged or very contracted pupils, excessive weight loss, bloating, trembling, or excessive perspiration

problem but had one in the past, you may not be able to refuse to hire the person because he or she may be protected by law from handicap discrimination.

Policy Regarding Substance Abuse on the Job

Employees must be advised that working under the influence of any substance is against company policy. "Substance" includes alcohol, illegal drugs, prescription drugs (whether obtained legally or illegally), and non-prescription drugs which may affect performance, such as cold tablets. "Under the influence" means any indicative behavior—such as slurring of speech or difficulty in maintaining balance—that's observable by a lay person or in the observer's opinion represents a safety hazard to the individual observed, to co-workers, or to the general public. Workers should also be told that violation of the policy will result in disciplinary action up to and including discharge for the first offense.

The employees should understand that it's their responsibility to seek assistance before problems like alcoholism or drug abuse influence their work performance.

Perhaps one of the most difficult areas concerns the use of marijuana, which is often handled legally as being no more serious than a minor traffic offense. Some arbitrators will sustain discharges for the simple use of marijuana and others won't. However, the case for discharge improves when policies have been clearly spelled out or when several instances of usage have occurred.

Companies are training managers to spot the warning signs and typical behavior patterns of substance abuse. Several of these signs and patterns are listed in Exhibit 13.3.

If employees are observed under the influence of any substance, the employer should remove them from the workplace and see that they get home safely. This includes taking reasonably prudent action to prevent them from causing risk or harm to others. If you send an intoxicated employee away who then injures someone while driving, the victim could bring action against you and your company. (The employer may also have this liability when employees are leaving office Christmas parties, picnics, or other such events.)

Anyone using legally obtained drugs as prescribed by a physician should be required to report this condition to the supervisor before going to work. Even when the drugs are legally obtained, employees shouldn't be allowed to work if their behavior is affected or they represent a safety hazard.

Policies are being expanded to address the possession or selling of alcohol or drugs. Employees who are living beyond their apparent means or receiving numerous telephone calls at work may be involved in the sale of drugs. Employees should be advised that any illegal activity conducted in the workplace is cause for immediate termination. An employer should also require that employees with knowledge of co-workers using illegal substances report it to their supervisor. Those who fail to do so may be subject to the same disciplinary procedures as the offender.

Screening and Testing

The general pre-employment physical examination is used to ensure that people are put into the proper job, and that they won't represent a hazard to themselves, co-workers, or guests. In conjunction with the physical, some companies have a stated policy (in states where it is legal—check with local counsel) that they may request blood, urine, and saliva tests or other drug/alcohol screening tests as part of the pre-employment procedure. This policy may also apply to current employees when reasonable suspicion exists that the person is using or under the influence of drugs or alcohol. The applicant is generally asked to acknowledge in writing that a refusal to take such tests may result in disciplinary action, up to and including termination.

Even with such pre-employment agreements, it's not always clear yet whether drug and alcohol screening are legal. Many people believe that such tests are an invasion of privacy. Others feel that when a legitimate workplace problem exists, testing does not represent an unreasonable intrusion.

State laws vary widely, so before your company institutes a screening program, it should consult an employment law attorney who is knowledgeable about your state laws. In addition, the employer should consider the size of the problem and weigh it against the expense, the delay in the hiring process, and the potential for liability where legal uncertainty still prevails.

A valid testing program has five basic and essential elements:

1. The person must be notified in advance of the test. For instance, an employer can't include a drug test in a routine pre-employment physical without the subject's prior knowledge. By the same token, if the company has a policy of requiring drug tests on all employees who have workers' compensation accidents, workers should be advised of it at the time they're hired.

2. The employer must obtain written consent from the employee, with the appropriate disclaimers to protect the company.

3. Test results must be reliable. The degree of reliability can vary greatly with the quality of testing and the kind of test. The employer should use licensed labs, spend the money to get a high level of quality, and stay on top of the program to ensure that it's properly handled.

4. The company should keep the results of the testing confidential. Along with other medical records, the information from test results should be kept separate from the personnel files. Even if an applicant refuses to take the tests and thus withdraws as a candidate for hiring, this action must also be kept confidential.

5. The employer has an obligation to ensure not only that the testing programs comply with the laws, but also that they're job-related. This means you can be selective in the group of people for whom you do pre-employment drug testing. You can, for example, choose to test the airport limousine driver and not to test the rest of the departments.

If test results indicate that an applicant is using drugs, your policy shouldn't allow for advising the applicant of the outcome nor for permitting a retest unless the laws in your state require that you do so. In general, you're not bound legally to tell someone why you didn't hire him or her.

Searches
The right to be free from unreasonable intrusions accords employees some protection against searches. Again, the best policy is to inform all employees clearly that they'll be subject to searches when a reasonable suspicion exists that the substance abuse policy has been violated. They should sign an agreement when they're hired that the company has a right to conduct a search at any time even without a basis for reasonable suspicion. In such an agreement, the employee usually authorizes the employer to make such searches for illegal drugs or alcohol, agrees to cooperate, and acknowledges that failure to do so may result in disciplinary action up to and including termination.

Even when an employee has signed such a statement, however, a personal search should be limited to the observation of whatever is in plain sight, such as loose and unsecured personal possessions, or asking employees to turn out their pockets and remove shoes or hats. Physical contact with the employee should be avoided.

Your policy might also include searching desks, tool boxes, company and employee vehicles, and packages or other containers brought onto or taken off of company property that might conceal alcohol or illegal drugs. Make it clear that employees shouldn't perceive lockers as their private property or expect them to be protected under privacy and protection laws. A statement in the employee handbook and a sign posted in the locker room saying that lockers will be inspected from time to time for various reasons, including insecticiding and cleaning, will help establish this point. Supervisors and security personnel should be instructed not to confiscate legal drugs from any employee under any circumstances.

Arbitrators dislike the requirement of searches and tests and frequently dispute the discharge of employees for refusing such searches or tests.[5] It's generally better to test routinely as part of the pre-employment screening or to use searches or tests to corroborate behavioral symptoms after they're observed on the job, rather than just doing them on a random basis. (For more information on screening, testing, and searches, see Chapter 11.)

---

[5]Klein, p. 62.

Employee Counseling

The format for confronting an employee who has a personal problem affecting work performance or workplace safety is similar to the interviewing, performance, or discipline session. However, the tone and technique will vary somewhat with the nature of the problem.

It's tempting to put off dealing with these situations out of pity, friendship, legal concerns, or just the hope that they will go away. They won't. Department morale will go down as the other employees who are aware of the problem wait for the manager to do something. Friends may try to help cover up mistakes. Once the manager has collected enough evidence, delaying the confrontation only makes it more difficult to deal with the problem. At the same time, managers must remain realistically aware that the process will take time. Instant results won't be evident after the first discussion.

Because each manager-employee relationship is different, there's no standard procedure that can be followed with absolute assurance. However, the confrontation should take place in private and begin in a positive tone by your mentioning some good things about the employee to show that you and others in the department care about the person. Beginning with an extreme approach, such as getting tough or angry or being especially nice or sympathetic, should be avoided. Instead, in very specific terms, address the purpose of the meeting and the problem.

Because the results of alcohol abuse are quite observable and readily identifiable, it's easier to be certain when the problem is alcohol-related. Unless someone is actually caught taking drugs, their use can be much more difficult to assess and handle.

Alcoholism is a disease and must be treated accordingly. Offenders often don't recognize or admit that they have a problem, and most will "hit bottom" before they do something about it. Gentle persuasion or coaxing will rarely produce any change in their behavior, so be prepared to deal authoritatively with the issue.

Don't refer to the person as a drunk or alcoholic or say that he or she has a drinking problem, but do approach the discussion head-on. Mention the times and dates of observed incidents and describe two or three instances in which the behavior has been observed. Then, very firmly indicate that unless help is sought or concrete steps taken, termination will result. The desire to hold onto a job is a very strong motivator for an alcoholic, but the employee must take the first step. You could have the telephone number of the local Alcoholics Anonymous on hand when you talk to the employee. However, even Alcoholics Anonymous requires that alcoholics call for themselves.

When the observed symptoms are less identifiable, avoid openly labeling the employee as having a drug problem, even if that's your assumption. Treat it as if you were addressing any other kind of personal problem. Use a nurturing approach and state that there seems to be a problem. Confront the employee with instances of poor work performance and offer your support in solving the problem, much as you would in a performance discussion.

In the face of denials, you might say, "Regardless of what you say, John, something is interfering with your performance, and it has to be corrected." Restating your own position over and over again (sometimes referred to as the "broken record" technique) may help force the person to deal with the issue. Statements such as, "Your behavior is alienating your co-workers, since it's making their work more difficult," help to illustrate the effect on the department. The manager's position should be expressed not as a threat, but merely as a fact of life. Avoid any diagnosis.

As a manager, you don't have the right to interfere with an employee's personal life without being asked. Your responsibility to the company and the department is to identify performance deficiencies and try to correct them. It isn't your job to be a professional counselor, and any attempt to provide counseling could complicate the problem.

You may help the employee start talking by saying that you understand that workers have problems from time to time. However, the employee has the problem and you must insist that he or she accept responsibility for its solution. Focus on the effects of the problem and the consequences to the employee if it's not corrected. Encourage the person to seek professional help.

Care should be taken not to demoralize the employee. Don't damage someone's sense of self-worth by consistently pointing out negative aspects of the performance. Don't isolate the person from others. As with other forms of employee interviews, you should seek to set up an action plan, and then follow up to see that the plan is implemented. You must also be prepared to take disciplinary action if the problem isn't corrected.

Employee Safety

Using prevention as the best approach to workplace safety isn't a new idea, although attention to the safety of the work environment is on the rise. One evidence of this increased attention is the growing concern of many employers with **ergonomics**, or human-factors engineering. This is an approach to the design of work environment and equipment that recognizes the mental and physical needs of workers to perform productively in comfort and security. Another area of growth is in the legislation that addresses the safety of the worker. Clearly, every employer has a responsibility to provide a safe working environment.

Corporations now hire people whose sole work assignment is to monitor and maintain employee safety. However, for the hospitality business, maintaining safety means maintaining service and facilities on site, not at corporate headquarters. Hence, the ultimate responsibility for safety rests on the shoulders of the unit's general manager and department heads. Unless managers at a local level display a genuine concern for and commitment to making workplace safety a top priority, employees won't learn about it, talk about it, or make safe habits a daily practice.

Managers have various resources to assist them. The security department usually handles such concerns as first aid, fire, bomb threats, and burglary. Engineering plays a major role in ensuring that the establishment meets and maintains the government's mechanical requirements. Purchasing can assist by ascertaining that products being purchased meet government-established standards and by obtaining the information required on certain products and chemicals.

However, the human resources department is responsible for providing the day-to-day support through:

- Employee training
- Prevention and awareness programs

The human resources department can provide support and training in the areas of health and safety by conducting prevention and awareness programs.

- The administration of workers' compensation
- Compliance with legal safety standards and recordkeeping requirements

It's in these areas that managers should expect the greatest support. A safety professional in the human resources department can assess potential risks and make recommendations that will not only minimize the liability, but can save a small company literally hundreds of thousands of dollars.

Because the liability for non-compliance is so huge, every manager should become fully informed on the provisions of all the laws relating to safety.

OSHA

The Williams-Steiger **Occupational Safety and Health Act** of 1970, now more commonly called the **Job Safety Act**, was enacted to assure all workers of safe and healthful working conditions. It established thousands of occupational standards with which employers must comply, requires regular safety committee meetings and plant inspections, and exacts substantial recordkeeping obligations.

		RYDER TRUCK RENTAL, INC.	DRIVER'S VEHICLE CONDITION REPORT		No. 6133368

TO_____ LESSEE

TRUCK/TRACTOR NO.	TRAILER NO.	DATE IN	TIME IN	MILEAGE IN	DRIVER SIGNATURE IN

PREVENTIVE MAINTENANCE INSPECTION DUE?   YES ☐   NO ☐   •   •   •   •   Neglecting a small defect today, may mean a major repair job tomorrow

Mechanic's / Driver's

Engine
- ☐ ☐ Check for Oil, Water and Fuel Leaks
- ☐ ☐ Knocks
- ☐ ☐ Misses
- ☐ Hard Starting
- ☐ Overheating
- ☐ ☐ Other_____

Clutch
- ☐ ☐ Check for Slipping or Grabbing
- ☐ ☐ Other_____

Transmission
- ☐ ☐ Noisy
- ☐ ☐ Hard Shifting
- ☐ ☐ Leaks
- ☐ ☐ Other_____

Steering
- ☐ ☐ Looseness
- ☐ ☐ Shimmy
- ☐ ☐ Steers Hard
- ☐ ☐ Other_____

Springs/Suspension
- ☐ ☐ Broken
- ☐ ☐ Other_____

Brakes
- ☐ ☐ Check Trl. Connections
- ☐ ☐ Parking Brakes
- ☐ ☐ Service Brakes
- ☐ ☐ Check for Air or Hydraulic Leaks
- ☐ ☐ Other_____

Rear Axle
- ☐ ☐ Noisy
- ☐ ☐ Grease Leaks
- ☐ ☐ Other_____

Instrument Panel
- ☐ ☐ Oil Pressure Gauge
- ☐ ☐ Ammeter
- ☐ ☐ Horn
- ☐ ☐ Windshield Wipers
- ☐ ☐ Speedometer
- ☐ ☐ Other_____

Electrical
- ☐ ☐ Check Trailer Light Cord
- ☐ ☐ Lights: Head, Tail, Stop, Turn, Clearance
- ☐ ☐ Reflectors
- ☐ ☐ Other_____

Tires
- ☐ ☐ Repair Tire
- ☐ ☐ Check Spare
- ☐ ☐ Check Wheels and Lug Bolts
- ☐ ☐ Other_____

Miscellaneous
- ☐ ☐ Drive Line
- ☐ ☐ 5th Wheel, Safety Chains and Pintle Hook
- ☐ ☐ Door Glass, Windshields and Mirrors
- ☐ ☐ Other_____

Refrigeration
- ☐ ☐ Will Not Cool
- ☐ ☐ Other_____

Emergency Equipment
- ☐ ☐ Fire Extinguishers
- ☐ ☐ Spare Fuses
- ☐ ☐ Tire Chains
- ☐ ☐ Three Reflective Triangles
- ☐ ☐ Other_____

DRIVER SPECIAL INSTRUCTIONS HERE:

MAINTENANCE ACTION: EXPLAIN BELOW	CORRECTIVE ACTION TAKEN ON ALL ITEMS	☐	CORRECTIVE ACTION TAKEN EXCEPT ITEMS LISTED BELOW	☐
	SIGNATURE DATE		SIGNATURE DATE	

DATE OUT	TIME OUT	MILEAGE OUT	DRIVER ACKNOWLEDGEMENT OUT

S4 09 (10/80)   ORIGINAL-LESSEE   PRINTED IN U.S.A.

OSHA requires daily inspections of any vehicle used by an employer to transport guests. (Courtesy of Ryder Truck Rental, Inc., Miami, Florida)

The Act established several new agencies, the most prominent being **OSHA, NIOSH,** and **OSHRC.** OSHA (the Occupational Safety and Health Administration) was created under the Department of Labor to enforce the Act by setting standards and regulations, conducting inspections of work sites, and issuing citations and penalties for violations. NIOSH (the National Institute for Occupational Safety and Health) was created under the Department of Health, Education, and Welfare (now Health and Human Services). Its primary purpose is to carry out research and recommend new safety and health standards. OSHRC (the Occupational Safety and Health Review

Commission) is an independent federal agency that hears appeals when employers choose to contest a citation or penalty.

Many thousands of occupational safety and health standards must now be complied with. For example, hotels that have an airport transportation van used by the public must have the van inspected daily according to an OSHA checklist, and adequate maintenance records must be kept. Standards are outlined for exits, ladders, railing heights, aisles, storage areas, carbon dioxide cylinders, and many other aspects of the workplace. For a complete list of the OSHA standards and requirements, refer to your local OSHA or U.S. Department of Labor office.

Employers must furnish employees with information and training on any known hazards in their work area. They must also provide personal protection equipment such as safety goggles or hard hats as required and maintain them in a sanitary and reliable condition. The employer is also responsible for ensuring that the safety equipment is used, even to the extent of invoking disciplinary procedures.

One very important aspect of the standards issued by OSHA has been the gradual strengthening of the requirements with respect to hazardous substances—those which represent a danger to workers through exposure or because they have the potential to cause fires, explosions, or other serious accidents. Manufacturers or importers of such materials must label their containers with information on each substance and how to handle it. They must also furnish the information to users on **material safety data sheets (MSDS)**.

Employers who use these hazardous materials must, in turn, make this information immediately available to workers who may be exposed to the chemicals. Because the manufacturer's labeled container is likely to be quite large, the substance is often transferred into smaller containers for use in the workplace. These containers must then be labeled, and employees must have ready access to the MSDS. Copies may be handed out to workers or posted in the immediate work area. The employer must furnish any necessary protective equipment or clothing. Workers must receive training in the use and handling of the hazardous material and the safety equipment.

For example, perchloroethylene (called PERK), which is commonly found in dry cleaning and laundry facilities, must be handled and disposed of as a hazardous material. Thus, employees in work areas where it's used must be informed of its presence as a hazard, trained in how to use it, and provided with the MSDS. In addition, special masks must be available in the area in case of leakage.

In a revision effective in 1988, OSHA modified its rule on **hazard communication** to extend its coverage beyond the manufacturing sector to all employers. Under this rule, the employer must have a written hazard communication program that includes provisions for the dissemination of information, including labeling, MSDSs, and employee training. This written program must be maintained on-site and must be readily available to employees, their representatives, the Assistant Secretary of Labor for Occupational Safety and Health, and the Director of NIOSH.

After an employee has received hazard communication training and information, the employer usually obtains a signed acknowledgment, which is kept in the personnel file.

The employer must ensure that medical and first aid services are available. If a hospital or clinic isn't within seven minutes' travel time, the company must have someone on staff with adequate training. Contents of the

HEALTH HAZARD RATING CHART

0	**MINIMAL HAZARD**	no significant risk to health
1	**SLIGHT HAZARD**	irritation or minor reversible injury possible
2	**MODERATE HAZARD**	temporary or minor injury may occur
3	**SERIOUS HAZARD**	major injury likely unless prompt action is taken and medical treatment is given
4	**SEVERE HAZARD**	life threatening major or permanent damage may result from single or repeated exposures

FLAMMABILITY HAZARD RATING CHART

0	**MINIMAL HAZARD**	materials which are normally stable and will not burn unless heated
1	**SLIGHT HAZARD**	materials that must be preheated before ignition will occur. Flammable liquids in this category will have flash points (the lowest temperature at which ignition will occur) at or above 200°F **(NFPA Class IIIB)**
2	**MODERATE HAZARD**	material which must be moderately heated before ignition will occur, including flammable liquids with flash points at or above 100°F and below 200°F. **(NFPA Class II & Class IIIA)**
3	**SERIOUS HAZARD**	materials capable of ignition under almost all normal temperature conditions, including flammable liquids with flash points below 73°F and boiling points above 100°F as well as liquids with flash points between 73°F and 100°F (NFPA Classes IB and IC)
4	**SEVERE HAZARD**	very flammable gases or very volatile flammable liquids with flash points below 73°F and boiling points below 100°F (NFPA Class IA)

REACTIVITY HAZARD RATING CHART

0	**MINIMAL HAZARD**	materials which are normally stable, even under fire conditions, and which will not react with water.
1	**SLIGHT HAZARD**	materials which are normally stable, but can become unstable at high temperatures and pressures. These materials may react with water, but will not release energy violently.
2	**MODERATE HAZARD**	materials which in themselves are normally unstable and will readily undergo violent chemical change, but will not detonate. These materials may also react violently with water.
3	**SERIOUS HAZARD**	materials which are capable of detonation or explosive reaction, but require a strong initiating source, or must be heated under confinement before ignition, or materials which react explosively with water.
4	**SEVERE HAZARD**	these materials are readily capable of detonation or explosive decomposition at normal temperatures and pressures.

HEALTH　　　　3
FLAMMABILITY
REACTIVITY

PERSONAL PROTECTION

Style NC-L502　　　Printed by LABELMASTER, CHICAGO, IL 60646

Information on workplace hazards, such as the abov
product label and rating charts, should be easy to read an
quickly understood. (HRIS® materials are part of a to
system, copyrighted by the National Paint & Coating
Association and marketed exclusively through Labelmaster
Chicago.)

first aid kit must be approved by a consulting physician. (A letter from the company's workers' compensation physician would be sufficient if it lists the necessary items.)

Any employee or representative of an employee who believes a violation has occurred can request an inspection from the Labor Department. An OSHA inspector may enter a business at any reasonable time and inspect the premises, and question privately any employer representative or employee. Officers may request that a representative of the employer and an employee accompany them during the inspection. The employer must pay workers for time spent on such inspections. No employee may be discharged or discriminated against in any manner because of the exercise of any rights accorded by the Act.

In addition to interviewing employees and physically examining the workplace, including equipment and materials, inspectors may examine company safety standards, safety committee meeting minutes, medical records, plant flow charts and layouts, OSHA-required records, and other records. Failure to comply with OSHA regulations can bring severe penalties.

An inspection may legally be refused if the inspector does not have a court approved search warrant. However, the lodging industry has generally accepted inspections merely based upon proof of identity as OSHA inspectors. Resistance, intimidation, or refusal to admit an OSHA inspector who has a search warrant is treated as a criminal offense carrying a fine of up to $5,000 and imprisonment for up to three years. Failure to correct a violation within the allotted time can result in a fine of $1,000 a day until the violation is corrected. Falsifying records is punishable by fines of up to $10,000 and/or six months' imprisonment. Making false official statements or failing to post the prescribed information appropriately can also result in substantial penalties.

The strict requirements for maintaining records include entering each recordable occupational injury or illness on an OSHA Form No. 200 (Log and Summary of Occupational Illnesses and Injuries—see Exhibit 13.4) within two working days of receipt of notification of the injury or illness. (The instructions on the back of Form No. 200 define a "recordable" incident.) These logs must be kept for five years past the end of the relevant calendar year.

Form No. 200 is also an annual summary which must be posted prominently for 30 days each year and within 30 days of year's end. It's advisable to write on the form the dates during which it was posted.

An employer must also maintain a record of each recordable injury or illness. A workers' compensation, insurance, or other report is acceptable as long as it furnishes the necessary facts; otherwise, OSHA Form No. 101 must be used. Any accident or health hazard resulting in a death or in hospitalization of five or more employees must be reported within 48 hours.

Since keeping up with these recordkeeping requirements is a major undertaking with enormous ramifications for non-compliance, every manager must carefully report *every recordable accident* immediately and follow up promptly with other reports as needed.

Workers' Compensation

Workers' compensation legislation dates back to the early 1900s. It is similar to unemployment insurance in that it is federally mandated but administered by the individual states. However, it shouldn't be confused with

Exhibit 13.4 OSHA Form 200: Log and Summary of Occupational

Log and Summary of Occupational Injuries and Illnesses					
NOTE: This form is required by Public Law 91-596 and Act 154, P.A. 1974 and must be kept in the establishment for 5 years. Failure to maintain and post can result in the issuance of citations and assessment of penalties. (See posting requirements on the other side of form.)				RECORDABLE CASES: You are required to record information about every occupational death; every nonfatal occupational illness; and those nonfatal occupational injuries which involve one or more of the following: loss of consciousness, restriction of work or motion, transfer to another job, or medical treatment (other than first aid). (See definitions on the other side of form.)	
Case or File Number	Date of Injury or Onset of Illness	Employee's Name	Occupation	Department	Description of Injury or Illness
Enter a nondupli- cating number which will facilitate com- parisons with supple- mentary records.	Enter Mo./day.	Enter first name or initial, Middle initial, last name.	Enter regular job title, not activity employee was per- forming when injured or at onset of illness. In the absence of a formal title, enter a brief description of the employee's duties.	Enter department in which the employee is regularly employed or a description of normal workplace to which employee is assigned, even though temporarily working in another depart- ment at the time of injury or illness.	Enter a brief description of the injury or illness and indicate the part or parts of body affected. Typical entries for this column might be: amputation of 1st joint right forefinger; Strain of lower back; Contact dermatitis on both hands; Electrocution — body.
(A)	(B)	(C)	(D)	(E)	(F)
					PREVIOUS PAGE TOTALS →
					TOTALS (Instructions on other side of form.) →

MIOSHA #200

unemployment insurance, nor with group insurance for accidents, employer-provided hospitalization, or other health insurance coverage.

While laws vary from state to state, there is a great deal of similarity due to the federal mandate. Almost all employers except the federal government must cover their employees with workers' compensation. Medical and income benefits are provided to employees for work-related injury or illness without regard to who may be at fault.

Benefits are paid either directly by the employer or through an insurance carrier. They are not paid by the bureau of workers' compensation. Thus, the cost and administrative overhead resulting from each accident or illness is a direct expense to the company.

Illnesses and Injuries

| For Calendar Year 19_____ | Page _____ of _____ |

Company Name			Form Approved O M B No 44R 1453
Establishment Name			
Establishment Address			

Extent of and Outcome of INJURY						Type, Extent of, and Outcome of ILLNESS						

Extent of and Outcome of INJURY

Fatalities	Nonfatal Injuries						

Injury Related	Injuries With Lost Workdays				Injuries Without Lost Workdays

| Enter DATE of death. Mo/day/yr. (1) | Enter a CHECK if injury involves days away from work, or days of restricted work activity, or both. (2) | Enter a CHECK if injury involves days away from work. (3) | Enter number of DAYS away from work. (4) | Enter number of DAYS of restricted work activity. (5) | Enter a CHECK if no entry was made in columns 1 or 2 but the injury is recordable as defined above. (6) |

Type, Extent of, and Outcome of ILLNESS

Type of Illness — CHECK Only One Column for Each Illness (See other side of form for terminations or permanent transfers.)

(a) Occupational skin diseases or disorders	(b) Dust diseases of the lungs	(c) Respiratory conditions due to toxic agents	(d) Poisoning (systemic effects of toxic materials)	(e) Disorders due to physical agents	(f) Disorders associated with repeated trauma	(g) All other occupational illness

(7)

Fatalities	Nonfatal Illnesses				

Illness Related	Illnesses With Lost Workdays				Illnesses Without Lost Workdays

| Enter DATE of death. Mo./day/yr. (8) | Enter a CHECK if illness involves days away from work, or days of restricted work activity, or both. (9) | Enter a CHECK if illness involves days away from work (10) | Enter number of DAYS away from work. (11) | Enter number of DAYS of restricted work activity. (12) | Enter a CHECK if no entry was made in columns 8 or 9 (13) |

INJURIES   ILLNESSES

FOLD

Certification of Annual Summary Totals By _____ Title _____ Date _____

M I OSHA No 200   **POST ONLY THIS PORTION OF THE LAST PAGE NOT LATER THAN FEBRUARY 1.**

Businesses are responsible for determining whether independent contractors have their own workers' compensation coverage. If not, the company must absorb the liability for these additional workers when they're working on the premises, even if the contractor who hired them is violating the law by not providing coverage. A company should always obtain workers' compensation insurance certificates (see Exhibit 13.5) from any workers who enter its premises, such as temporary agency help, musicians, general contractors and sub-contractors, window washers, exterminators, and elevator technicians. Even though a copy of the certificate may be obtained by the purchasing agent, chief engineer, food and beverage director, controller, or others who hire such specialists, all the certificates should be kept in a central location, usually the human resources department.

Exhibit 13.5   Workers' Compensation Insurance Certificate

ACORD. **CERTIFICATE OF INSURANCE**		ISSUE DATE (MM/DD/YY)

PRODUCER

THIS CERTIFICATE IS ISSUED AS A MATTER OF INFORMATION ONLY AND CONFERS NO RIGHTS UPON THE CERTIFICATE HOLDER. THIS CERTIFICATE DOES NOT AMEND, EXTEND OR ALTER THE COVERAGE AFFORDED BY THE POLICIES BELOW

COMPANIES AFFORDING COVERAGE

COMPANY LETTER **A**

CODE   **SUB-CODE**

COMPANY LETTER **B**

INSURED

COMPANY LETTER **C**

COMPANY LETTER **D**

COMPANY LETTER **E**

COVERAGES

THIS IS TO CERTIFY THAT THE POLICIES OF INSURANCE LISTED BELOW HAVE BEEN ISSUED TO THE INSURED NAMED ABOVE FOR THE POLICY PERIOD INDICATED, NOTWITHSTANDING ANY REQUIREMENT, TERM OR CONDITION OF ANY CONTRACT OR OTHER DOCUMENT WITH RESPECT TO WHICH THIS CERTIFICATE MAY BE ISSUED OR MAY PERTAIN, THE INSURANCE AFFORDED BY THE POLICIES DESCRIBED HEREIN IS SUBJECT TO ALL THE TERMS, EXCLUSIONS AND CONDITIONS OF SUCH POLICIES. LIMITS SHOWN MAY HAVE BEEN REDUCED BY PAID CLAIMS.

CO LTR	TYPE OF INSURANCE	POLICY NUMBER	POLICY EFFECTIVE DATE (MM/DD/YY)	POLICY EXPIRATION DATE (MM/DD/YY)	ALL LIMITS IN THOUSANDS	
	GENERAL LIABILITY				GENERAL AGGREGATE	$
	COMMERCIAL GENERAL LIABILITY				PRODUCTS-COMP/OPS AGGREGATE	$
	☐ CLAIMS MADE ☐ OCCUR.				PERSONAL & ADVERTISING INJURY	$
	OWNER'S & CONTRACTOR'S PROT.				EACH OCCURRENCE	$
					FIRE DAMAGE (Any one fire)	$
					MEDICAL EXPENSE (Any one person)	$
	AUTOMOBILE LIABILITY				COMBINED SINGLE LIMIT	$
	ANY AUTO					
	ALL OWNED AUTOS				BODILY INJURY (Per person)	$
	SCHEDULED AUTOS					
	HIRED AUTOS				BODILY INJURY (Per accident)	$
	NON-OWNED AUTOS					
	GARAGE LIABILITY				PROPERTY DAMAGE	$
	EXCESS LIABILITY				EACH OCCURRENCE $	AGGREGATE $
	OTHER THAN UMBRELLA FORM					
	WORKER'S COMPENSATION AND **EMPLOYERS' LIABILITY**				STATUTORY	
					$	(EACH ACCIDENT)
					$	(DISEASE—POLICY LIMIT)
					$	(DISEASE—EACH EMPLOYEE)
	OTHER					

DESCRIPTION OF OPERATIONS/LOCATIONS/VEHICLES/RESTRICTIONS/SPECIAL ITEMS

CERTIFICATE HOLDER

CANCELLATION

SHOULD ANY OF THE ABOVE DESCRIBED POLICIES BE CANCELLED BEFORE THE EXPIRATION DATE THEREOF, THE ISSUING COMPANY WILL ENDEAVOR TO MAIL ____ DAYS WRITTEN NOTICE TO THE CERTIFICATE HOLDER NAMED TO THE LEFT, BUT FAILURE TO MAIL SUCH NOTICE SHALL IMPOSE NO OBLIGATION OR LIABILITY OF ANY KIND UPON THE COMPANY, ITS AGENTS OR REPRESENTATIVES.

AUTHORIZED REPRESENTATIVE

ACORD 25-S (3/88)   ©ACORD CORPORATION 1988

Courtesy of ACORD Corporation, White Plains, New York.

Because the employer pays regardless of fault, the employee's right to recover workers' compensation benefits as a result of an accident has traditionally been the only compensation to which the employee was legally entitled as the result of a work-related injury or illness. However, this provision has been challenged by recent court decisions permitting employees to seek additional damages from the employer. On the other hand, employees may sue a third party, such as an equipment manufacturer; as a result, the employer may be reimbursed for expenses as part of the settlement.

The employer usually must pay for all medical care and the cost of crutches, artificial appliances, eyeglasses, hearing aids, and the like. Medical costs also include the cost of prescriptions and transportation to and from the doctor.

Compensation must also be paid to the employee to offset the loss of wages. While the amount varies with the state, it usually ranges from 50 to 80% of the after-tax wages up to a percentage of the average weekly wage for the state. The definition of lost wages also generally includes the cost of meals, uniforms, overtime, and other fringe benefits which may be discontinued after the injury. The employee can collect this amount for as long as the disability continues. In some states, the employee may be eligible for partial unemployment compensation as well.

Minors involved in a work-related accident or illness while employed in violation of any child labor laws can collect double benefits.

In order to be compensable, the injury or illness must have happened during or as a result of employment. Determination isn't generally limited to incidents that occur on the premises. Accidents at social or recreational outings conducted by the company, in employee parking lots, and even during travel under certain circumstances (such as traveling on company business) may be included. The latter are often deemed work-related because the employee wouldn't have been in that situation if it weren't for the job. Again, each state has different laws and interpretations.

Generally speaking, if an employee has a pre-existing condition which is aggravated in the course of the current employment, the current employer must pay all the costs. Some states provide for a **second injury fund** to limit the current employer's liability.

An employee who disagrees with any decision made by an employer or the employer's carrier may file for a hearing with the state workers' compensation board. Since workers' compensation is perceived to be a benefit to employees, the board will make every attempt to ensure that the employee receives every consideration and protection prescribed by the law.

Lump sum settlements allow the employee to draw all the compensation at once in return for giving up the right to any future claims resulting from an incident. Disputed claims are often settled this way. Most companies have a lawyer to help represent them at settlement hearings.

While employees can be disciplined for horseplay, failure to follow safety procedures, and carelessness, they can't be discharged or discriminated against in any way because they exercise their legal rights. And, regardless of the extent of worker neglect or irresponsibility, the employer must pay.

Courts have become more liberal in determining both that the disability has been sustained and that it originated through the course of employment. Because of more broadly defined causes of disability, such as stress, cardiovascular disease, and alcoholism, the number of claims has escalated along with medical, legal, and rehabilitation costs.

Stress

Increasingly, workers suffering from job-induced stress are being awarded workers' compensation benefits. In 1987, stress-related disability claims represented 11% of all claims for occupational diseases, with stress-related claims the principal occupational injury of white-collar and service employees.[6] We usually think of job-related stress as coming from situations in which a person must work under intense pressure or meet very demanding specifications. However, some states are granting payment for many other sources of stress determined simply to be within the employer's control. These include inconsistent or unpredictable supervision, poor communications, unpleasant working conditions, and criticism of work performance.

Some estimates place stress-induced job health care costs to employers as high as $150 billion annually.[7] In addition to workers' compensation benefits, costs that have to be assessed include absenteeism, tardiness, lower morale and productivity, and increased rates of accidents and breakage.

Reducing Costs and Liabilities

Workers' compensation should not be regarded as a fixed expense. An effectively managed program can greatly reduce not only the expense, but also the potential liability.

If your state has a second injury fund and you knowingly hire employees with certain illnesses, a major portion of related disability claims may be paid by the state. The employer has to apply for this protection within a specified period of time after the date of hire.

Many companies now have their own doctor or clinic for the treatment of all of their workers' compensation cases. Larger operations may even have a nurse to handle first aid and routine follow-up visits, thus cutting the costs of outside medical services and transportation. The employer generally has the right to insist that the employee see the company's doctor for a prescribed period of time. This is always advisable, since the employee may find it easier to get a disability statement from a family doctor than from the company doctor. (Of course, the company doctor should *never* deny disability statements merely to lower the company's costs.) In addition, a company doctor or clinic is equipped to complete the sizable amount of required paperwork more quickly and efficiently.

Companies are also giving more attention to the psychological effects of an accident or illness. They are following up with workers by calling them, sending cards, and just providing them with someone to listen as they work through the various stages of denial, blame, and anger. All of these gestures help employees start taking positive steps toward helping themselves.

Having another worker, preferably a supervisor, accompany an injured employee to the hospital after a serious accident also has the positive psychological impact of showing the company's concern. As a side benefit, lawyers seeking accident victims as potential clients are less likely to approach an injured employee while a co-worker is around.

Employers should avoid terminating employees who are on workers' compensation. Since there's no time limit on benefits, job termination frequently leads to malingering. Offering the employee the opportunity to return to work for **light duty** will reduce the compensation costs and

---

[6]P. R. Voluck and Herbert Abramson, "The Work Environment: How To Avoid Stress-Related Disability Claims," *Personnel Journal*, May 1987, p. 95.

[7]Penelope Wang, Karen Springen, Tom Schmitz, and Mary Bruno, "A Cure For Stress?" *Newsweek*, October 12, 1987, p. 64.

OPRYLAND USA EMPLOYEE REFERRAL

Name: _____ Age: _____ Dob: _____ Sex: [M] [F]
    Last   First   MI

Address: _____
    Street   City   State   Zip

SSN: _____ Phone: _____ ☐ Park ☐ Hotel ☐ Opry ☐ General Jackson

Date: _____ Time: _____ ☐ TNN ☐ WSM Radio ☐ Acuff Rose

Referred To: _____ Injury: _____

Referred By: _____ Date: _____ ☐ Initial Visit ☐ Followup

PATIENT AFTERCARE INSTRUCTIONS

Check with Opryland First Aid immediately upon returning to the park for clearance to return to work. The examination and treatment you received in the hospital Emergency Department was rendered on an emergency basis. Followup care is important. Any new or continuing problems should be reported to First Aid, as it is sometimes impossible to recognize and treat all elements of an injury or illness in one visit. You are to follow the aftercare items checked below:

WOUND CARE (cuts, burns, abrasions)

_____ Keep bandage dry and clean

_____ If wound becomes red, swollen, has pus or red streaks; or feels increasingly sore, return to First Aid or Hospital.

_____ Return to First Aid for bandage change.

_____ Elevate wound to reduce soreness.

HEAD INJURY (If any of the following occur, immediately contact FA or the hospital.)

_____ Convulsions, unconsciousness or unusual restlessness.

_____ Persistent vomiting, stiff neck or fever.

_____ Unequal pupils (one larger than the other).

_____ Stumbling or problem using arms or legs; or areas of skin numbness.

_____ Bleeding from the ears or nose.

_____ Awaken patient hourly for first 8-12 hours to check for alertness.

FRACTURE, SPRAIN OR SEVERE BRUISE

_____ Elevate injury to lessen swelling.

_____ Ice packs first 48 hours to reduce swelling followed after that by soaking in hot water to reduce pain and bruising.

_____ Rewrap elastic bandage if too loose or tight.

_____ Return to FA at once if extremity becomes blue, cold, numb or painfully swollen.

_____ Keep cast dry at all times.

_____ Avoid pressure on cast for first 24 hours.

_____ Wriggle toes or fingers to aid circulation.

BACK OR NECK INJURY

_____ Apply either heat or cold in injury site.

_____ Rest or sleep lying on a firm surface.

_____ Avoid positions or movements that cause or increase pain.

_____ Relax, tense muscles are more painful.

_____ Massage firmly but gently to increase circulation and help reduce soreness.

PHYSICIANS ATTENTION: Please complete the information requested below. If the patient cannot return to unrestricted duty following this visit, we may be able to temporarily change the job assignment to meet the limitations based upon your comments and instructions.

☐ May return to work without restrictions
☐ Must adhere to following limitations:
☐ No lifting
☐ Light lifting (weight ?) _____
☐ Limited walking, may stand
☐ Limited use of injured part
☐ No walking or standing; may work sitting
☐ Avoid using injured part

☐ Other limitations or comments: _____

I HAVE READ AND UNDERSTAND THE ABOVE INSTRUCTIONS:

_____
Patients Signature

☐ May return to work on _____
    Date   Time
☐ No work until released by the physician
☐ To be referred to: (from USF&G approved list)
  Physician: _____
  Office location: _____
  Date: _____ Time: _____
  Phone number: _____
☐ Return to this location for followup care:
  Date: _____ Time: _____
☐ Other Instructions: _____

Physician: _____

_____
Type or Print Name   Signature

An employee who is injured on the job should be given written authorization to receive medical attention and sent to a company-approved medical treatment facility. (Courtesy of Opryland USA, Nashville, Tennessee)

encourage the person to return to the old job sooner. Often, if an employee refuses to accept a return to light duty, compensation may be cut off completely.

Although it's expensive, rehabilitation is proving to be cheaper in many cases than the alternatives of paying a lump sum settlement or letting an employee continue to stay home indefinitely. Many rehabilitation centers use principles developed through sports medicine which were designed to get athletes back into the game as soon as possible. Injured employees are happy to have the additional assistance, while malingerers quickly find that going back to work is preferable to going through therapy.

Accident Prevention

To determine the true cost of an accident, you must consider not only the direct costs, but also administrative expenses, overtime incurred, the cost of the disruption in the department, increased breakage, poor guest service, and other indirect expenses. These figures may prove to be as much as four times the direct costs. When the true cost is examined, it becomes apparent why so many companies are placing more emphasis on the prevention of accidents.

Prevention begins with hiring the right people, training them properly, and giving them a written list of safety rules which you enforce and review occasionally at departmental meetings. To increase managers' awareness and enlist their involvement, businesses often charge the direct costs of an employee accident to the department in which it occurred. Many employers also consider the accident rate of the department when the manager's salary review date comes up.

Companies are also emphasizing the importance of their safety committees and taking other measures to protect employees and guests, including major training efforts. Almost every hotel and restaurant today is providing some form of information about choking, CPR, sanitation training, and fire drills.

More employers today are requiring pre-employment physical exams or health questionnaires where permitted by state law. This practice helps spot any applicants who have pre-existing conditions, such as varicose veins, back problems, and the like, that might suggest they be placed in a different position from the one for which they applied.

Reducing Hazard Liability

OSHA requires that the company have a formal procedure for reporting safety hazards. Employees should be advised that the first thing they should do each day is to look over the work area and report any hazards. Such instructions to employees not only help prevent accidents. They also prove helpful in defending against lawsuits by helping to establish that the employer took reasonable care.

Should a serious incident occur, make the necessary improvements, change some procedure, or at least send a memo to document that something was done to prevent future injuries or problems in the same area. If such an incident leads to a lawsuit, it will be the employer who must prove that reasonable care has been taken.

The formal procedure for reporting accidents should include a central location to which all hazards are reported—usually the engineering depart-

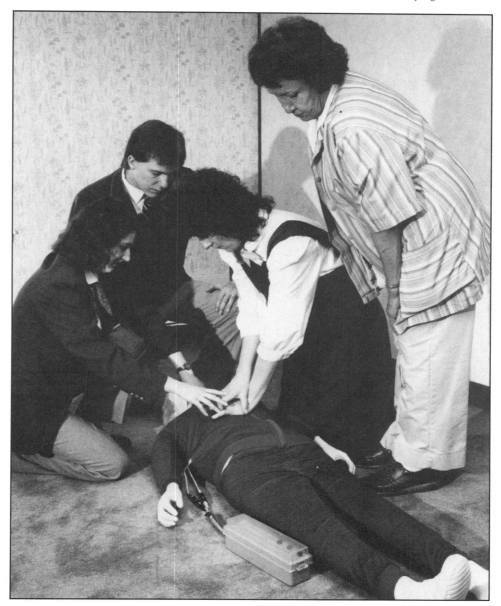

Employees receive on-the-job CPR training from a certified instructor as part of the Amway Grand Plaza Hotel's safety program to protect employees and guests.

ment. The company needs to respond promptly to these reports as part of the defense against possible charges of negligence. Safety hazards should be reported in writing on a distinctively marked form so that they'll be given priority. If the engineering department has a printed work order form, copies of it can be used if they're overprinted with the words, "SAFETY PRIORITY."

If the hazard represents imminent danger, it should be called in immediately, and the engineering department can complete the priority work order form. Items that represent a hazard should be removed immediately from operation or tagged with a "DANGER" or "LOCK-OUT" tag printed in red, black, and white (in accordance with OSHA requirements) until they can be repaired or removed.

The Safety Committee

While it doesn't relieve upper management of its ultimate responsibility, the safety committee can be a very effective tool in prevention and in conducting the inspections prescribed by law. Many safety committees have been expanded to include the safety of the guests as well as the employees.

Representatives of the human resources, engineering, and security departments should make up the core of the committee. However, its driving force should be the line employees. It's their committee, their responsibility, and, in the hospitality industry, they have the most expertise on how things can be done more safely. Representatives from different departments should be selected from among volunteers. The membership should be rotated once or twice a year to allow for new ideas and new enthusiasm.

Serving on the safety committee should be considered an honor, and recognizing and rewarding those employees who participate in the safety effort should be an important part of the program.

The major responsibilities of the safety committee include holding safety meetings, inspecting, reviewing accidents, making safety recommendations, training, and increasing safety awareness.

Meetings and Inspections. OSHA requires that safety committee meetings be held monthly and that minutes be kept of each meeting. Regular inspections to verify compliance with safety standards and report needed repairs are also now required by law.

Accident Review. Reports of employee accidents (see Exhibit 13.6) that have occurred since the last meeting should be reviewed by the safety committee.

All accidents should be reported and reviewed—not just those that are recordable on the OSHA Form No. 200. In terms of prevention, frequency is often more significant than severity. Several people can slip on a wet floor without having a recordable accident. However, the potential for a major injury is obviously quite high in that area, and preventive measures should be taken. Employees should be encouraged to report all injuries, including minor ones in which no one is hurt.

Reviewing the accident reports can also suggest areas in which additional training or education are needed because of the predominance of certain types of accidents. For example, if you're seeing reports for numerous back injuries or having claims related to back problems, perhaps a session on proper lifting techniques would be warranted.

An accident review may reveal that certain employees are having multiple accidents or that a small percentage of your work force is responsible for many of the accidents. Someone may need glasses, special training, or safety equipment. A safety committee recommendation for the use of such equipment as goggles and steel-toed shoes might prevent future accidents. Committee members might also notice that new employees are having more accidents than trained employees or that people suffering from fatigue—those who don't get their breaks, for example—are having more accidents toward the end of their shift. Even the time of day during which the majority of accidents are happening can suggest some appropriate action.

Many companies keep track of the accident rate to assess whether accidents are on the increase or decrease, or to see how they're faring against the

Exhibit 13.6   Sample Employee Accident Report Form

EMPLOYEE ACCIDENT REPORT FORM

Date of Accident _____ Time of Day _____ A.M. P.M.   When Reported _____

Who was the Accident Reported to?_____

Print Name of Injured _____   Department _____

How did the Accident Happen? What was the person doing at the time of the Accident? _____

_____

_____

Pin Point Exact Location _____

Describe the Nature of the Accident. (Which Finger on Which Hand) _____

_____

_____

Circle part of body injured

Treatment Given _____

Injured Sent: ☐ Home   ☐ Back to Work   ☐ Company Clinic   ☐ Hospital

Has the Employee returned to work? ☐ Yes   ☐ No   If yes, give date_____

Name of Witness _____   Employee? ☐ Yes ☐ No
If No, Give Address & Phone Number _____

right   left

What acts or conditions contributed most directly to this accident?_____

_____

_____

_____

What could be done to prevent a reoccurrence?_____

_____

_____

_____

_____

_____

Department Head Signature _____ Date _____

industry as whole. The rate is determined by dividing the number of recordable accidents (as defined by OSHA) by the total number of hours worked by all employees for the same period.

Safety committee members should be trained on how to use the different types of fire extinguishers.

Recommendations. The committee makes safety recommendations based on inspections and accident review. These recommendations are recorded and submitted to the proper departments. Their progress is followed at subsequent committee meetings.

It's these preventive steps which are the most important. Studying accidents that have already happened is only effective if it leads to the prevention of future accidents. You must follow up and implement the safety recommendations to achieve any gain in protection and savings.

Training. Time should be set aside at each meeting for training members on such topics as:

- The theory of accident prevention, including accident reporting systems and legal requirements

- Instructions and practice in using fire extinguishers

- A review of the company's fire and other emergency procedures

- Guest safety, including sanitation and health protection and observing and reporting suspicious activity

- First aid, including how to use the contents of the first aid cabinet and dealing with common accidental injuries such as burns and cuts

Committee members should also be involved in recommending, planning, and conducting training programs for all employees as needs are perceived, such as CPR or fire drills.

Safety Awareness. The safety committee should plan and conduct regular safety awareness programs for all employees. The content and presentation should vary from time to time. Any employee relations program has a short life. Any single statistic listed month after month will lose impact after a few months, since people will stop noticing it. More effective would be timely short-term programs. A fire drill or tips on how to keep a home safe from fires could be tied in with a review of fire procedures in the employee newsletter during National Fire Safety Week. A short time later, another subject could be presented using a different theme and vehicle of communication.

The Human Factor   Total hazard prevention can't be legislated, nor does the answer lie merely in the design and inspection of the mechanical aspects of the job. The psychological environment requires attention as well.

Most accidents are avoidable. They're caused by human error, resulting from carelessness, inattention, anger, frustration, or the worker's inability to cope with conflict, tension, and pressure. There's even some speculation that employees who find themselves in unbearable circumstances on the job may subconsciously provoke accidents as an acceptable way to take themselves out of such situations.

Managers with genuine concern for their people will address these human factors as carefully as the physical dangers. The challenge ahead for employers is to create a total working environment that encourages workers to share in the responsibilities for safety and make a commitment to accept responsibility for their own safe behavior.

Key Terms   comp-day program
employee assistance program (EAP)
ergonomics
hazard communication rule
Job Safety Act
light duty
material safety data sheets
National Institute for Occupational Safety and Health (NIOSH)
Occupational Safety and Health Act of 1970
Occupational Safety and Health Administration (OSHA)
Occupation Safety and Health Review Committee (OSHRC)
second injury fund
wellness program
workers' compensation

Discussion Questions   1. How can a manager improve employee attendance within the department?

2. What are some of the signs that an employee might have a personal problem serious enough for the manager to consider making a referral through the company's EAP?

3. Why should an employer consider setting up an EAP?

4. What should a company put in the employee handbook about the policy concerning searches?

5. What are some of the things a manager should do in a discussion with an employee who appears to have a drug or alcohol problem that is affecting work performance or workplace safety? What actions and statements should be avoided?

6. What can a company do to reduce its workers' compensation costs?

7. What are some of the indirect costs of an accident?

14 Discipline

Day after day, managers find themselves involved in so many disciplinary situations that it would seem they might become quite skillful at dealing with them. On the contrary, however, discipline is one of the tasks managers dread the most and often perform most poorly. Actually, few managers have ever been taught to use discipline properly. Most make some or all of the common errors associated with disciplinary procedures.

Dispelling the Myths

Most of the problems surrounding the use of discipline are directly related to a manager's misconceptions about its nature. If a manager bases his or her disciplinary acts on any of the following myths, discipline will not be an effective management tool. In fact, it will often be counterproductive. For this reason, we should begin by exposing misguided approaches to discipline.

Myth 1: Discipline Is a Form of Punishment. The identification of discipline with punishment is perhaps the biggest pitfall for the manager. Sometimes, the use of punishment is an outlet for anger, a release of tension, or an avenue for revenge; occasionally, it's an extension of the user's need for power; often, the manager is just frustrated and doesn't know how else to handle the situation.

Whatever the reason for its use, *punishment is not effective in the work environment*. At best, any improvement in behavior will only be short-term, while the long-term negative effects are devastating. Employees may react to punishment by covering up future mistakes or becoming more aggressive. To retaliate, they may even deliberately reduce productivity as soon as the boss's back is turned. In many cases, withdrawal and feelings of inferiority replace creativity and the willingness to take risks—the very qualities you want to encourage in your people. Finally—and perhaps most importantly—punishment doesn't really treat the original cause of the problem.

Myth 2: Being the Boss Means People Have to Do What You Say. Many managers feel that their position gives them power over people, and that others simply must do what they say. They often use threats and intimidation to motivate the employee behavior they want. The result of this approach is usually a win/lose power struggle, in which both sides feel they must prevail. Employees use their own power techniques, the manager responds with a greater show of power, and the struggle goes on until the manager eventually runs out of ways to threaten or intimidate. The final threat is termination, but a manager can't fire his or her whole crew. Once employees challenge that threat and don't get fired, they've won and the manager loses all power to manage.

The problems surrounding control by power are similar to those that result from punishment. The causes of problems aren't addressed, and employees respond negatively. They become defensive, defy authority, lie, and look for others to blame. Feelings of dissatisfaction, hostility, and stubbornness begin to surface.

An effective manager is expected to operate within a value system which includes high ethical standards, a belief in the dignity of people, and respect for their rights. Being the boss doesn't make you "better" than your employees. All other considerations aside, in a free society, the use of force is not condoned; furthermore, there are fewer and fewer people who are helpless or part of a captive work force. Employees who are unhappy working for an overly authoritarian manager will usually just quit and find a job elsewhere. If a manager continues to use power on employees who don't have other choices, their hostile feelings can develop into hatred and even violence.

Myth 3: If You're Nice to Your Employees, You Won't Need to Discipline Them. Fear of disciplining employees often motivates managers to become overly permissive. They seem to feel that by overlooking mistakes and infractions and by giving in to employee demands, they are winning friends and loyal followers who will then be happy and productive. In reality, the employees quite often accept these favors without developing any respect for the manager or loyalty to the department. Morale and productivity may actually go down. They frequently become demanding and self-centered, they begin to believe the rules don't apply to them, and they can seriously harm the morale of workers in other departments who don't have such indulgent managers.

Often, this type of manager stores up resentment toward employees who are taking advantage of the situation, until a breaking point is reached. The manager may then vent his or her hostilities on the next person who walks through the door or may punish the whole department. Other problems develop as employees become confused about what to expect from their supervisor. They may believe they have been unjustly treated, since the behaviors for which they're being disciplined aren't usually very different from the way they've behaved all along. It's actually the manager who's been inconsistent.

Myth 4: Every Disciplinary Situation Must Be Handled in Exactly the Same Way. One of the objectives of union contracts, labor laws, and government regulations has been to ensure that all people are treated fairly. However, many managers have overreacted in their interpretation of fair treatment. It's certainly true that you must be able to defend handling similar violations differently (especially if one of the violations involves a member of a minority group). Still, there's room for individual handling of different situations involving different circumstances and consequences. The choice of the best disciplinary approach to take in a given situation will depend on many factors.

For instance, it would be unfair to use the same disciplinary procedures for an employee who has had 20 years of perfect service and comes in late twice because of the serious illness of a spouse, and a second person—still in the probationary period—who's come in late twice because an alarm didn't go off.

You want to enforce the spirit, rather than the letter, of the law. Keep the overall purpose in mind. Be consistent, but flexible. The key is to handle each situation properly and effectively in the first place, keep complete records, and document every instance of disciplinary action (including the reasons for making an exception). As long as you apply the same set of goals and values to all, you may treat each person and each case individually.

Laying the Groundwork for Effective Discipline

Managers can eliminate many disciplinary problems from the outset through proper selection, hiring, training, and orientation; by obtaining employee commitment to the company's standards and goals; and by treating people as individuals, with respect and honesty.

Establish a Relationship of Mutual Respect

You can't stand over your employees and make every decision for them. They have to know what is expected of them and what the rules and limits are; they must be given the freedom and responsibility to do the job; and they need constant feedback about where they stand and how they're doing. Once these elements are in place, employees can begin to take responsibility for their own actions and to practice *self*-discipline.

An environment which promotes self-discipline is built on a relationship based on mutual respect. To create such an environment, you must be willing to be honest and open with your employees and let them know you care about them.

Pretending to be someone you're not, or even pretending to accept behavior you really don't like, is unnatural and will be perceived that way. It's unrealistic to expect to have all the answers, to make no mistakes, to like all employees equally, or to remain cool and unemotional at all times. Mature managers realize that they do have feelings and emotions, that they do make mistakes, and that it's all right to admit it. No relationship could survive if no one ever admitted a mistake or showed feelings.

You should also communicate with your employees. In disciplining someone, be willing first to listen and to consider the other person's side of the story. A great many cases of discipline wind up in court because the manager didn't listen or was too inflexible. As a result, the employee felt that his or her individual rights were denied.

Respecting the individual also means considering how background, needs, and environment contribute to behavior and perceptions. Feelings and attitudes about discipline are highly individual; and what's effective for one employee may not work for another. Always value and appreciate the good things about each employee when working to correct unwanted behavior.

If you can build a relationship based on mutual respect, you will be able to extract much higher standards from your people and subsequently correct even the smallest detail. As long as workers feel they're treated fairly, they'll accept a great deal of discipline and be less threatened by negative feedback. If they feel they're treated unfairly, no form of management will be effective.

Make Group Dynamics Work for You

Your most effective disciplinary tool may be your ability to sway peer pressure against undesirable behavior by controlling employee attitude in your department.

As discussed in Chapter 2, each work group has its own standards and rules of acceptable and unacceptable behavior. The need for a line employee to win group acceptance and follow the group's rules may be much stronger than the pressure to obey the manager's rules. Before you discipline, consider how the work group will react to it. The group's reaction won't change what has to be done, but it may influence how you approach the problem.

If you're going to control behavior and discipline effectively, you must be able to control the standards and goals of the groups within your department. Talking about your company's goals during the interviewing, hiring, orientation, and training processes will help keep the group members from developing their own objectives. If you set a good example by your own actions, continuously communicate and reinforce the desired goals, and recognize and reward employee commitment to them, you'll have no problem getting people to work for you. In fact, those employees who don't follow the rules will be rejected by the group.

Identifying all of the work groups is the first step. Then, you can identify the informal leaders and get them on your team. Every manager has some favorite people or work groups, but may be out of touch with or unaware of the rest. You have to control more than half of the groups in your department, not just the friendly one or two.

The next step in controlling group attitudes toward discipline is to explain changes and the reasons for them before they're implemented. Even if you're just tightening up an existing policy, explain first why violations are becoming a problem. Then, state that you'll have to begin to discipline all those who break the rule. Suddenly reviving and enforcing a dormant policy without notice won't be very acceptable with either employees or the court systems.

For example, take the new manager who makes a schedule change to reduce payroll. The surprised employees don't like it and make it their goal to see that the new policy doesn't work. One employee trying to win group acceptance chooses to take a day off based on the old schedule, and the upset manager writes a warning notice for absenteeism. The group rallies behind the employee, who suddenly becomes a hero and grows even more defiant to win more acceptance. Other employees soon join in, and every day someone else calls in sick. By the end of the week, the department is in chaos, the angry manager is trying to keep up with the warning notices, no one is sure who's coming to work that day, and guest service grows worse and worse. Meanwhile, members of the whole work group are feeling like winners—sitting back and saying, "We really showed him!" The confused and frustrated manager is wondering what went wrong: "I disciplined someone for absenteeism, and the whole department fell apart."

To head off such problems, of course, the first step should have been to inform the department of the planned changes and the reasons for them before they were implemented. The manager could then have solicited the employees' commitment and support. Immediately after the first instance of defiance, the manager should have spoken to the other employees who came in: "I'm sorry that Jack is sick today. It means you'll have to do his work as well as your own. I know you don't like extra work, and service is going to suffer, but guests have to be taken care of, and we have to do the best we can.

I really appreciate the fact that I can depend on the rest of you." This kind of communication would have helped to focus group disapproval on the offender instead of the manager.

Disciplinary Policy

A company should have one disciplinary policy and set of associated procedures. Policy and procedures should not differ from department to department, nor should they change with each new manager. Exhibit 14.1 presents an excerpt from a corporate-wide policy dealing with an employee appeals process.

Policies must also be applied consistently among all departments. Consider, for example, the controller who sets up a policy that cashiers who are over or short in their house bank by more than 5% will receive a written warning notice. Ten departments have cashiers, but only one manager writes up the offenders. If the cashier who was written up is ultimately fired as a result of this policy, the firing may be legally indefensible. Similarly, a company can't have some managers writing up employees for not wearing name tags unless every manager is supporting the requirement.

There should be handbooks and house rules for managers as well as hourly employees. When employees are promoted from hourly to salaried positions, the company should change their hiring agreements and have them sign for new handbooks and house rules.

A company should keep its disciplinary policy simple. Spelling out policies and procedures in complete detail isn't always the best approach. Trying to cover every possible procedure or exception in writing forces everyone to try to act like a lawyer and leaves people arguing over loopholes and interpretations. People who have to decide whether a three-inch blade or a six-inch blade constitutes a weapon before they can write a rule soon lose sight of the intent of the overall policy. It should only be specific enough to provide direction and intent. As long as you follow your disciplinary policy consistently and predictably, you'll find it much easier to defend your actions. A broad and simple policy gives you more flexibility in maintaining consistency and enforcing the spirit of the policy.

For example, you'd probably handle differently two cases of sleeping on the job if one is your only night telephone operator on duty and the other is one of 20 night housekeeping staff members who's just been transferred to the third shift and is trying to adjust to the new hours. Here, even though the mistake is the same, the cause and consequence of the error are not, and different disciplinary steps can be taken. While the rule must be enforced and the employee's behavior corrected in each case, the actions taken by the respective managers may not be the same. For a first offense, the night operator might be likelier to receive a written warning or even be fired for sleeping while on duty (which would probably be a violation of a house rule). On the other hand, a verbal warning might be adequate for the new housekeeper, particularly when accompanied by a review of the house rules and a caution that the next such violation could result in termination. In the latter case, of course, a memo should be written to document the reasons for the exception.

Exhibit 14.1   Sample Corporate Policy: An Excerpt from an Employee Appeals Process

![IF logo] STANDARD PRACTICE INSTRUCTIONS Radisson Hotel Corporation	Page 1 of 3	Classification No. VI - 608
By Order Of: Vice President Human Resources	Date: 3/25/X8	Sup. 5/14/X4
Forms Used in Connection with Instructions:	Distribution:	

R.E.A.P. - Radisson Employee Appeals Process

Subject:

OBJECTIVE: To provide employees with an opportunity to address employment related concerns and to seek resolution of conflicts within the company, to minimize cases of outside intervention.

POLICY STATEMENT:

1. Should differences arise concerning Radisson and any employee who has completed his/her trial period, as to the meaning and application of any Radisson personnel policies, practice and procedures, the employee shall be permitted to pursue their concerns by following the Radisson Employee Appeals Process.

2. Radisson has provided the REAP program for the benefit of both Radisson and employees. Both Radisson and employees agree to pursue problems and conflicts involving the employer/employee relationships through REAP before filing administrative claims, lawsuits, or any form of employee-related action. Radisson, in turn, agrees to waive any legal or administrative filing requirement in exchange for the employee's agreement to file a REAP first.

    The waiver of any statute of limitations or filing period will be for the period of processing of the REAP only. After the REAP has been processed and a final decision has been reached, employees shall, if desired, pursue any actions consistent with their rights under law.

    The purpose of this is to afford Radisson employees the ability to right wrongs by encouraging them to complain within the Radisson family. It is in Radisson's interest to encourage and nurture employee complaints before formal processes, administrative or judicial, are instituted.

3. There will be no reprisal for an individual for utilizing the REAP program.

PROCEDURE:

1. The following are the steps of the Radisson Employee Appeals Process:

    Step One: The employee shall take up the matter with his/her supervisor on an informal basis in order to settle the matter promptly.

Courtesy of Radisson Hotel Corporation, Minneapolis, Minnesota.

What the Disciplinary Policy Should Include

If management wants an environment that encourages employees to serve the guests—even if that means taking a risk at times by going beyond the job description—disciplinary policy should provide some sense of security for the employee. Although it's impossible to think of every offense that could result in termination, staff members should know what the **house rules** are, and that violation of one of the house rules—or any other infraction as serious as violating a house rule—can result in immediate discharge for cause. Exhibit 14.2 is a sample set of house rules.

Exhibit 14.2 Sample Set of House Rules

Strict enforcement of these policies will help protect our employees and ensure that our hotel runs in an efficient manner. Listed below are some of the violations which may result in immediate suspension or termination, at the option of the hotel.

- Being discourteous, rude, insubordinate, or using abusive language to a guest or fellow employee.
- Fighting, stealing, unauthorized possession of hotel property, or gambling on hotel premises.
- Unauthorized use of alcohol, possession, use, or appearance of being under the influence of alcohol, narcotics, intoxicants, or other substances prohibited by law, or the abuse of medication whether obtained legally or illegally, while on hotel premises.
- Possession of lethal weapons or other items prohibited by law while on hotel premises.
- Indecent, immoral, or disorderly conduct in the hotel, including willful destruction of property and failure to follow safety procedures.
- Falsification of work or time records, reports, or guest checks.
- Being in an unauthorized area of the hotel while working or in a non-public area of the building after hours without prior permission from your department head.
- Socializing with guests on hotel premises.
- Removing anything from the hotel without permission.
- Sleeping while on duty.

Assuming you have adopted a just-cause standard of dismissal, employees should also know that after they are out of the probationary period, they can only be terminated for an offense as serious as violating a house rule or after having received a final written warning. If the company has an employment-at-will philosophy (which inherently provides no more job security after probation), top managers need to draft carefully the language explaining that relationship in the employee handbook. The handbook should make clear that nothing in the policy prevents the employer from terminating any employee for economic or other reasons.

Policy should also indicate clearly who can discipline an employee. Usually, only the department head or immediate supervisor should discipline. If someone else observes an employee doing something wrong, it should be reported to the department head or immediate supervisor, who then takes the appropriate action. Having every manager discipline every employee results in too many bosses and too much confusion.

This doesn't mean that any manager who observes undesirable behavior should avoid commenting about it to the offender on the spot—if you were to observe employees from another department smoking in a "No Smoking" area, for instance. In fact, to overlook such actions would be to give tacit approval. This could make life more difficult for the manager who must later correct the offense. Problems most often arise when managers from outside a department start correcting operational procedures rather than enforcing general behavioral policies. In any case, only the department head should have the authority to fill out a written warning notice.

Of course, any upper level manager who observes behavior as serious as breaking a house rule can usually authorize a suspension if he or she is unable to locate the department head or supervisor. The employee should be told at the time of the suspension to report to the human resources department at a specific time during normal office hours. Enough time should be allowed for the department head and the human resources department to be advised.

Progressive Discipline

Even in companies that have adopted an at-will policy, employees need to have some sense of job security and know that they'll be treated fairly. They also need consistent rules and guidelines for which the consequences of deviation are predictable. Therefore, many companies use a management approach involving **progressive discipline**. In this approach, disciplinary procedures progress from milder to sterner measures for repeated infractions. The employer who wants to maintain an at-will relationship should probably avoid having a detailed written progressive disciplinary policy, since courts have ruled that clearly defining a progressive disciplinary policy can destroy the at-will relationship. Nonetheless, consistency and fairness are necessary components of the disciplinary process.

Progressive discipline starts by correcting behavior immediately with a positive tone and attitude, even in the training or coaching environment. Initial action takes place in an informal setting and manner. As undesirable behavior continues, the disciplinary approach becomes more structured and the techniques more specific.

Most forms of correction or feedback to the employee are spoken and are handled immediately when the inappropriate behavior is observed. If the infraction warrants, these **verbal warnings** should be documented in writing and kept in the departmental file for reference.

Written warnings should only be used for more serious offenses. If you issue written warnings for minor offenses, such as not wearing a name tag, employees won't take any written warnings seriously. The written notice should be completed and signed by the person who issued it. The employee is asked to sign it and it's placed in the personnel file. The manager should also keep a copy in the departmental file. If requested, a copy should be given to the employee. Exhibit 14.3 is a sample written warning notice.

If someone refuses to sign a warning notice, the issuer should write "refused to sign" on the form, along with the date and time. When a refusal is noted, it's a good idea for the human resources department to talk to the employee to find out why. The human resources representative can document that the warning meeting did take place, but that the employee refused to sign—thus serving as a third-party witness as well as giving the employee assurance of fair representation. In a union operation, the employee will probably contact the shop steward at once. In a non-union facility, the same appeal procedure should be provided or the employee may go outside the company to a lawyer or the Labor Department, which is the last thing you want.

The written warning must contain all the detailed actions and be specific. Writing "Insubordinate" isn't enough. You should record the manner in which the person was insubordinate. Include any important details or facts, such as, "The employee flipped a lit cigarette at the supervisor before walking away." It should also indicate date, time, and place of the incident. When the written warning has been preceded by verbal warnings, indicate that this is the case to help document the prior discussions and show clearly that discipline has been progressive.

Exhibit 14.3 Sample Employee Warning Notice

EMPLOYEE WARNING NOTICE

EMPLOYEE NAME_____ DEPARTMENT_____

DATE OF PROBLEM_____ TIME OF PROBLEM_____

NATURE OF PROBLEM
(Please Check)

[ ] Absence / Lateness   [ ] Carelessness   [ ] Work Performance

[ ] Violation of Safety Rules   [ ] Conduct   [ ] Breaking Hotel Rules

[ ] Attitude   [ ] Insubordination   [ ] Other

EXPLANATION REGARDING THIS WARNING (BE SPECIFIC: STATE EXACTLY WHERE, WHEN, WHAT, INCLUDING DATES, ETC.)

_____

_____

_____

_____

_____

ACTION TAKEN:_____

_____

_____

PREVIOUS WARNING? [ ]No [ ]Yes   If Yes, Date_____

[ ] FINAL WARNING: The employee has been told that any further violation of this type, or any other infractions of company policy may result in termination.

NOTE TO EMPLOYEE: Employees who have a problem affecting job performance are encouraged to seek help on a confidential basis by contacting the Employee Assistance Center at_____, or the Personnel Office at_____, for additional information about the program.

I HAVE DISCUSSED THIS MATTER WITH THE ABOVE EMPLOYEE ON

_____ at _____ Signature:_____
Date   Time   Supervisor

YOUR SIGNATURE ON THIS FORM INDICATES ONLY THAT YOU HAVE BEEN ADVISED OF THIS WARNING NOTICE. IF YOU FEEL THAT THE WARNING IS UNFAIR, YOU ARE ENCOURAGED TO TALK TO THE PERSONNEL OFFICE.

_____
Employee Signature

The final step before termination in progressive discipline is always a **final warning**. This is a written notice marked "Final." An employee should probably receive no more than two or three written warnings before a final warning is issued. Because of the final warning's nature and significance, we will discuss it in more detail at the end of this chapter.

Suspensions

In the past, disciplinary suspensions were used as a form of punishment. Today, the only time a suspension is used effectively is when an employee has committed a violation serious enough to result in termination. At that point, circumstances justify sending the employee home without pay, pending an investigation.

Using disciplinary suspension as a punishment only works against the manager. As with other forms of punishment, it doesn't solve the problem. It also creates additional problems, such as financial hardships and embarrassment for the employee, who has to explain what has happened to family members and fellow employees. Such explanations to peers are usually designed to rally support by stressing how unfair the manager has been. Furthermore, in these busy times and with so many working spouses, many employees actually welcome additional time off because there are so many things they need to do at home. Here, a suspension can be a reward, particularly for a tipped employee when business is slow. In either case, disciplinary suspension hasn't achieved its intended purpose. Instead, it results in poorer guest service and possible increases in payroll costs if another employee has to work overtime.

Grievance Procedure

The disciplinary policy and the employee handbook should include a **grievance procedure** spelling out what employees can do when they feel that any disciplinary action is unjust. (Many non-union companies dislike using the union term "grievance" and call their policy "guaranteed fair treatment.") Whether an employee actually was treated unfairly or only thinks so, the steps of the grievance procedure are the same.

Basically, workers should be encouraged to go to anyone in the company they think can help them. If satisfactory avenues aren't provided, they may look for help outside the company.

The employee who has a grievance should first discuss it with the supervisor. Unfortunately, most of the time the problem is with the supervisor. Therefore, insisting on this as the first step really eliminates the grievance process. Of course, part of the role of the human resources department is to see that employees get fair treatment. People who aren't comfortable going to their supervisors, or who have done so without satisfaction, should feel free to go to the human resources department. Anyone who doesn't receive satisfaction there should be encouraged to go to the general manager.

In some cases, it may be helpful to suggest that the employee submit a written description of the problem before talking to the general manager. Often, this helps clarify the concerns and put them into perspective, and may even eliminate the need to pursue the grievance further. However, the whole process should operate quickly. An employee who has a problem isn't going to give 100% on the job until it's resolved. If having to write a grievance slows down the process unnecessarily or prevents someone from using this avenue, it isn't appropriate.

In any case, employees should be guaranteed that they won't endanger their jobs in any way by bringing problems to management's attention or using the grievance procedure. Some managers will demand to know the names of people who have complained, insisting that they have the right to know their accusers. Usually, the motive behind such a demand is a desire for retaliation. One instance of retaliation will mean the end of all employees' use of the grievance procedure. To be effective, the grievance procedure must operate within an atmosphere of trust. Managers must understand that confidentiality should be an important part of the process.

Exhibit 14.4 Some General Guidelines for Disciplinary Action

1. Be consistent and predictable. The certainty of discipline is a stronger deterrent than the severity.

2. Don't overreact. Use only enough discipline to get the job done. There must be some equity between the violation and the amount of discipline taken. If you threaten to fire someone for a first offense or mistake, you have no back-up position as a further step in your progressive discipline approach. In addition, if the offense later recurs and you don't fire the person, but rather have to back down from your threat, you'll lose much of your effectiveness as a manager.

3. Discipline should take place immediately. Don't delay with statements such as, "We'll talk later," or "Next week, we're going to make some adjustments." If you aren't going to deal with it right away, don't even bring it up at this time. The exceptions to taking immediate action include providing a very short cooling-off period, allowing time to arrange for a private location, or giving the employee an opportunity to practice self-discipline. Remember, however, that some employees are much harder on themselves than you would be or than the situation dictates when they make a mistake, and you may have to *un*-discipline them by saying, "Yes, it was a mistake, but it wasn't that bad. Don't get discouraged."

4. Don't compare one person to someone else in the department. It won't help the employee come to grips with the problem, and can open the door for responses such as, "Yes, but there are others in the department who do it worse." These types of comparisons can also cause a more difficult working relationship between the two employees by creating unwelcome competition or resentment.

5. Don't pre-judge. Making premature judgments is one of the biggest mistakes inexperienced managers make; then, after hearing what the employees have to say, they're often forced to back down. Listen to all sides of the story, collect all the facts, and then decide.

6. By all means, never back down when you're right, even if the employee disagrees with your actions or the outcome. If necessary, repeat the same message after each objection: "I understand how you feel; however, the results of your action are still the same, and that's what we're talking about. It can't happen again or further action will have to be taken." You don't have to specify the action, since doubt is sometimes a stronger deterrent and you can't always predict what the circumstances of the next offense will be.

7. When the discipline is over, put it behind you. Don't harbor a grudge. Don't use the incident against the employee again later unless it figures in discipline for a subsequent offense.

Administering Discipline

Discipline is not a science that can be spelled out in a detailed manual or handbook. It's a management skill that can only be learned by practice and by following guidelines. Exhibit 14.4 presents several general guidelines for disciplinary action.

To a large extent, how you discipline will depend on four factors: your relationship with the individual; the nature of the mistake or violation; the determination of what is reasonable; and the definition of common knowledge. The last two elements call for some definition.

In determining what is reasonable, it's customary to define what a reasonable person would be expected to do in a given situation. Being late eight to twelve times a year and having up to six separate absences might well be considered reasonable in the hospitality industry. However, if a person were absent one day a week for six weeks in a row, it would probably be considered unreasonable.

Common knowledge is considered to be what the average employee in a given position can be expected to know. It's acceptable to have different expectations for different groups. You'd expect one level of common knowledge from managers and a different level from workers in entry-level positions.

As long as you're consistent in your definitions of reasonableness and common knowledge, you'll have few problems defending your position.

Positive Reinforcement

Praise can be one of your best disciplinary techniques. It's a powerful reward, and behavior that's rewarded tends to be repeated. Don't wait until employees have improved 100%. Praise them for trying. Just don't overdo it to the extent that it seems insincere. A simple phrase can be very effective:

- "Now you've got it."
- "You're getting better each time."
- "I admire the way you stick to it."
- "I'm proud of the effort you're putting into this."
- "Keep it up, you're doing fine."
- "You learn fast."

You can't build a relationship with your employees if you only talk to them when they do something wrong. If you have plenty of goodwill and respect invested, discipline won't bankrupt a relationship.

Minor Corrections

Training, performance discussions, and discipline frequently overlap in the management process. The chef who sees that a new cook isn't following the recipe may step in, take charge temporarily, and tell the employee what's going wrong, using correction as part of the training process.

Progressive discipline usually begins with these kinds of cordial, casual contacts. It wouldn't be necessary to formally reprimand a busperson for missing a fork while setting up a table when all the other tables were done properly. It would probably be adequate to remark, "You missed a fork on table six, but everything else looks great." You've indicated that your standards are high, that you're checking the person's work, and that the work is progressing in accordance with your expectations.

If you see that the incorrect behavior is being repeated and must be addressed, let the other person save face: "I don't know if I mentioned it to you or not, but this is the way I'd like to see this done." Ask questions instead of giving orders: "Do you think this will work better?"

Make problems seem easy to correct, and express confidence: "You've already learned the first three steps; I'm sure that, with some practice, you'll be able to master this one, too. I think your overall progress is just fine." Let people know that they're appreciated: "I know you're anxious to do a good job—let me show you a better way that I've learned. I think you could be really good here." These techniques are really just an extension of the kind of feedback and correction you use during training.

Training, performance discussions, and discipline often overlap as the manager steps in immediately to take corrective action when incidents occur.

Don't criticize too much in areas in which the employee can only make minor improvement. While you will always have 100% standards compliance and error-free work as department goals, the reality is that not every person is going to be perfect. Continual criticism will lower morale and self-image, thus creating even bigger problems. A little discipline goes a long way, particularly with service-oriented people. When it's important to someone to please others, harsh criticisms can be devastating.

True disciplinary problems usually develop over a period of time. If a manager deals with minor problems early, major disciplinary problems will seldom happen. However, when they do, the manager must be able to deal with them effectively.

Performance Discussion or Discipline Meeting?

When do performance problems become a matter for discipline? If the problem involves behavior, attitude, or reliability, the correction is clearly disciplinary in nature. Often, intent is the key to the manager's approach. Willful or wanton disregard of company policies and intentional conduct not in the employer's best interest are matters for disciplinary action.

However, when work performance is the issue, the distinction isn't so clear. In general, the performance discussion becomes ineffective when the work is chronically poor, the employee isn't responding with any improvement, and you see no sign of improved productivity. If performance

Exhibit 14.5   Employee Incident File

INCIDENT FILE	
NAME_____	TELEPHONE_____
DATE OF EMPLOYMENT_____	
PERSONAL:	
Spouse's name_____	Spouse employed?_____
Name & Ages of Children_____	
Hobbies, special skills, etc._____	

DATE	INCIDENT AND ACTION TAKEN
	(CONTINUE ON BACK)

problems can't be resolved through performance discussions, then you must begin the steps of the disciplinary procedure.

By comparison to the performance discussion, a discipline meeting is much more of a one-way conversation. There's far less negotiation. At this level, you're no longer tempering criticism with praise, since you need to focus on the problem. In addition, a disciplinary discussion should be documented. You're putting the employee on notice that the only alternative to change is termination, and you may need to have a written record of the conversation. Creating a clear paper trail for the personnel file is one of your most important ways to protect yourself and your right to manage. The employee incident file (see Exhibit 14.5) is one way a manager can record any instance of performance discussion or minor discipline. Some managers also use this file to record some personal information and keep track of positive achievements like training and awards.

Verbal Warnings

Problems not easily corrected require more personal attention. If a relationship of mutual respect exists, correction can be approached in a friendly, straightforward, coaching manner. After all, most employees don't come to work planning to perform poorly. They really do want to know when they're doing something wrong.

Such disciplinary discussions should take place as soon as possible after the unwanted behavior is observed. Try to arrange for as much privacy as possible, given the constraints of time and operational demands. Considering the following points may help you decide exactly how you'll approach the discussion:

- Did the employee know the rule?
- Was the inappropriate behavior deliberate?
- What is the employee's past record?
- Does the employee have a temporary personal problem?
- Is the mistake or violation totally the employee's fault?
- Has the behavior been overlooked in the past?
- What were the consequences of the behavior?

After you have reviewed the situation, talk to the employee, following these steps:

1. Indicate what the problem is. Your objective is to provide information which the employee can use to improve. Be specific, and discuss the problem, not the person. Say, "Walking away from a guest who's talking to you is rude." Don't say, "You're rude."

2. Don't use a negative tone or raise your voice. Avoid personal attacks, such as, "You just don't care, do you?" or "How many times am I going to have to tell you this?"

3. Explain the proper procedure and why it's important. Be tactful. Say something like, "I've made that mistake, too. Let me show you a trick I've learned," or "I need your help to improve this situation."

4. Demonstrate the correct way.

5. Ask if there are any questions or problems.

6. Emphasize that the person is a valuable employee.

7. Check back later and give positive reinforcement.

Again, although the warning is verbal, written documentation should still be part of the process, even if it's only a short memo for future reference.

Written Warnings   When a problem is too severe or is repeated too often, you may have to delay correction until you can leave the floor and give the matter your complete attention. Changing your approach also conveys that this situation is more serious. One change that makes this point is progressing from verbal to written warnings.

When you meet with the employee, don't have the warning completely written up. During the meeting, you should establish the circumstances and a course of action. For instance, if you find out that an employee was late because of a sudden death in the immediate family, you'd probably decide to discard the warning. You'll also need to solicit the employee's recommitment to goals and standards previously accepted. At the end of the meeting, you can summarize in writing what has been agreed upon and add it to the details of the behavior being discussed. Both of you can then sign the warning notice.

These kinds of problems may involve some conflict, largely as a result of the other person's defensiveness. It's human nature for people under stress to hide behind defenses until they can regain control. Defensiveness is a normal form of ego protection. Employees who make excuses or blame others aren't necessarily trying to make trouble. They're just trying to protect themselves as well as they can. Since discipline is most successful in a "no-fault"

Discipline Example: The "Maverick"

Mary does an outstanding job and has a real feel for the business, but she's also a non-conformist and doesn't always follow the procedures. In fact, she sometimes goes around them in order to get attention and strengthen her "hotshot" image within the informal work group of which she is a member. She comes in late, and when you speak to her, she responds by saying, "What's the difference—I still get all the work done, and I get it done better than anyone else in the department."

A response to Mary's comment might go as follows:

> You did get the job done, and I always like the quality of your work. We're lucky it was a slow day and your lateness didn't cause any problems this time. However, if we'd been busy, it could have caused a problem.
>
> Rules are like traffic lights. No one really likes them; but everyone knows that, without them, during rush hour we'd have a major traffic jam. As you know, around here it seems like everything comes at once and we can't always predict what's going to happen. That's why we need rules. Since every team member must be able to count on the others to follow the same rules, I can't make different rules for each individual. If I were to let everyone come in when they felt like it, I'm sure you know a few would really take advantage of it. Then, when I talked to them about it, the first thing they'd want to know would be why I picked on them when I let other people—like you—get away with it.
>
> Can you see the problem your actions can cause? What would you do if you were the boss? You'd probably have the same feelings I do. In this case, Mary, I really need your help because you do good work and set an example, and people look up to you.
>
> If we're going to have this place running as we'd like, it's going to have to be done as a team. The next time you're late, I'll have to write you up, like everyone else.

In this case, you've explained the rule, the reason for it, and the consequences of future violations. You did it while allowing the employee to keep her self-respect, and you tied it in with your mutual goals.

How Mary does the job didn't have to be addressed in this instance. If employee nonconformity involves work habits, look at several concerns when deciding whether discipline is called for. Do the employee's work habits violate the rules? Does the work fall below standards? Does the approach create any safety hazards or other problems or interfere with team spirit? It may be possible to give employees some freedom. You need to emphasize your department's overall goals, not necessarily how an employee does things. With some employees, you may have to be more specific about expected results and let them find the techniques that will work for them.

environment, you need to get past these defenses before you can get your employee to understand the real problem and agree to do things differently. The following steps should be helpful.

Designate the time and place. Even if an upset employee wants to talk right away, delay the meeting until the person has had time to calm down and become more rational again. Of course, you must always control your temper. Meet as soon as possible after the employee has calmed down. Choose a time that is early enough in the day to allow you to talk with the person again before the work day is over. Disciplining at quitting time or just before a day off means the employee will go home and "stew" about the confrontation.

The written warning meeting should take place in a private setting so that both parties can give the situation their complete attention.

Go to a neutral spot or a private section of the work area. If you must use your office, make sure you choose a time when you won't be interrupted, or have someone else answer your calls and pager. Don't fidget or look for things like files, pencils, or paper. Your employee should believe that this discussion is the most important thing on your mind at this moment.

Indicate your purpose at once. Small talk before a written warning only leads to more anxiety. Don't apologize or try to sandwich discipline in between servings of praise. At this stage, it can be confusing and will probably be perceived as insincere anyway.

Both of you should sit down and you should sit next to the person—not behind a desk. Be aware of the messages you're sending with body language and appearance. Instead of folding your arms or putting your hands on your hips, hold your palms up when you talk. Unbutton your suit coat, or even take it off. Loosen your collar and roll up your sleeves.

State clearly what the problem behavior is. It should neither be treated lightly nor exaggerated. Deal with one problem at a time. Be very specific, giving the time and place of the incident. Instead of saying, "You have an attitude problem," say, "Your remarks at lunch today to the guests at table six were rude. That kind of behavior is unacceptable." Stick to the facts and don't worry about finding out who's to blame. Talk about the act or behavior, not the person or the personality.

Explain how you feel about what has happened. Statements like, "When I saw all the broken dishes, I was disappointed, because I know it cost the company a lot of money," are more effective than saying, "When *you* broke those dishes, *you* cost the company a lot of money." Telling someone how you feel encourages that person to express his or her feelings. It also gives the problem back to its owner.

Listen to the employee's response and reasoning. You have to get defenses out of the way before the person can think clearly and be open-minded. Disagreement or arguments only provoke more defensive reactions from the employee. Never try to practice psychology to analyze someone else's motivation: "The real reason you did that was . . . ." Just listen attentively. This will communicate your acceptance of the person without condemning or condoning the defensive arguments.

Help the person relax by using active listening responses such as "Uh-huh," "I see," "I understand," comments like, "It must have been discouraging for you when that happened," or just nodding your head.

Once you have heard the employee's point of view, bring the discussion back to the facts by using a response like one of the following:

- "Well, I thought otherwise, but I may be wrong; let's look at the facts."

- "In certain circumstances, your actions might be correct, but it appears to me . . . ."

- "Let's not lose sight of the fact that the job wasn't done correctly."

Agree on the cause of the problem. This may happen during the employee's explanation of the incident. If not, additional questions like, "What do you think would have happened if this had been done?" or "What do you think the real problem is?" may be helpful. Then ask the person to summarize what went wrong.

Explain the consequences of the problem behavior. If an employee was late, for example, you could say, "I understand that you were late because the alarm didn't go off, but your work wasn't done and guest service suffered. We can't run a successful business if this continues."

Agree on the solution. Keep in mind that this is the employee's problem. The employee must take responsibility for his or her own actions. You might ask, "What do you think you can do to prevent the problem from happening again? Is there anything I can do to help?" Offer a choice of acceptable options: "Do you think you'd be better off on a different shift, or do you want to try getting a new alarm clock?" Giving choices heads off the win/lose power struggle that ensues when you present your solution as the only acceptable one. Involving people in the solution of a problem also helps elicit their commitment to making solutions work, and places responsibility for personal behavior—including solving future problems—back in their hands.

Be specific about the consequences the employee can expect if the situation arises again.

End on a positive note. Express confidence that the employee can improve. Indicate that it would make you happy to see the improvement because of the person's importance to the company. Make it easy for the person to come back to you with any other problems: "Things aren't as easy to correct sometimes as we first think. If you start to have any problems with this solution, let's get back together and discuss it. I really want to make it work." Shake hands or touch the employee on the shoulder as he or she is leaving.

Make contact again. It's important to check back with the employee before the day is over, even if it's just to talk about something else, so that it's clear that the reprimand is over.

Discipline Example:
A Conflict Between Two Employees

You can't solve a problem two employees have with each other, but you can bring them together and help them solve their own problem.

You'll still use disciplinary techniques, but with a few modifications. Separate them and provide a cooling-off period. Schedule them for different shifts, different hours, or different days off. Meanwhile, meet with each employee separately so that both have an opportunity to air their feelings and defenses and get emotions out of the way. After this step, and only then, have each agree to meet with the other.

Open the meeting by stating its purpose and outlining the rules. Let them know the consequences of not solving their problem by saying, for example:

> I'm giving you both a written warning for this last incident. I can't have employees arguing in front of guests. You two have a problem, and it's interfering with the operation of my department. If you can't solve it, I'm going to have to take action against both of you, because I can't let your problems hurt the department. What I want to do is to hear from each of you about what the problem is, and then together we can see what can be done. While one of you is talking, I want the other to extend the courtesy of listening without any interruptions. Now, John, let's begin with you. What seems to be the problem?

During the explanations, you can help by using active listening responses, such as asking the speaker how he felt about the situation. Help interpret or clarify what the person is saying: "If I understand you correctly, you feel that if Ed would tell you where he's going when he leaves the department, these problems wouldn't occur. What else?"

Help each person get all feelings out, and be sure each has equal time. When one is finished, let the other speak. Discourage them from repeating points. Try to get each to say something positive about the other.

To help decide what can be done, use direct questions, such as asking each person what he or she thinks the solution is. Keep them talking until they arrive at a solution. Encourage discussion but keep it under control, using the guidelines that you set up initially. Keep them focused on the issue and not on the person.

The solution has to be theirs, and both must agree to try it. Don't allow a win/lose situation to arise or let one person compromise too much and give in when he or she shouldn't. This type of arrangement doesn't obtain the necessary commitment from both parties. Furthermore, a great deal of resentment can be generated. Not only does the party giving in the most feel shortchanged, but the person who gives little or nothing also tends to harbor resentment because of the sense of obligation he or she feels toward the one who did all the giving.

Don't expect to solve every problem on the first try. If the meeting starts to drag on, bring it to a close. Reschedule another meeting after they have more time to think about everything.

This approach helps them realize how their actions affect each other, and gives them the procedures to deal with their own problems in the future.

The setting for the final warning meeting should convey the seriousness of the discussion and the company's support for the manager's concerns.

Follow up. Provide plenty of positive feedback. If needed, follow up to verify that the behavior has indeed been eliminated and that the job is being handled correctly.

Final Warnings

The final warning should be handled like any other written warning, but with a few modifications. It should be given in a location outside the department (usually an office in the human resources department) and a third party should be present as a witness. These steps help to convey the seriousness of the discussion and the fact that any further violation may lead to termination. They also demonstrate the company's support for the manager's concerns. You may now want to sit behind a desk in order to send a message of authority, particularly if you're a new manager and your control may be in question.

A final warning should be concluded something like this:

I can understand the problems you've had in trying to get to work on time, but guest service is still suffering. It's hurting the whole department and I can't have that. If you were in my shoes, I'm sure you'd have the same feelings, wouldn't you? (Nod your own head as you say this.) The next time you're late or absent, I'm going to have to replace you with someone who can get here on time more regularly. I don't want to do that, because I really want you to stay.

When I hired you, I thought you had something special to offer to help this department meet its goals, and I saw how you made a commitment and tried extra hard at times to make things work. Besides, we've got

Preventive Discipline Rules

- Knowledge of Employees
- Performance Standards
- Progressive Discipline

- Grievance Procedure
- Documentation

- Suspension Pending Investigation
- Total Investigation
- Employee's Notice & Hearing
- Consistency & Fairness
- Just Cause Discharges

©Copyright 1986
by Stokes, Lazarus & Carmichael
Atlanta
(404) 352-1465

A law firm specializing in employment law can help prevent legal problems by giving advice and assisting the employer in setting up a disciplinary program that is consistent and fair. (Courtesy of Stokes, Lazarus & Carmichael, Attorneys At Law, Atlanta, Georgia)

a lot of time and money invested in your training, and you know the procedures. I certainly don't want to start interviewing and training all over again; so your leaving is the last thing I want.

However, if you've changed your mind and really don't feel strongly about your job anymore, I can understand that, too. You're still a good person. I just need to know what you want to do.

I'd like for you to think about it for the rest of the day. Come back before you go home and let me know whether or not you can give me your commitment that you'll try to make this work and that you really do want your job here.

At this point, some companies actually send the employee home for the rest of the day—with pay—to emphasize the importance placed on the recommitment. Again, throughout the final warning process, you are treating the employee with respect, pointing out the options and letting the employee make the choice, and giving the individual responsibility for his or her own actions. A good manager doesn't fire people—they fire themselves.

How Long Is a Final Warning Final?

If a person who was given a final warning for habitual lateness wasn't late again for a year, would an immediate firing be in order? In cases like this, you have to rely on your definition of what is reasonable and on your sense of fairness and honesty. Warning notices do age and employees do correct problems. After a reasonable length of time, you may simply choose to ignore old warning notices. The length of time would probably vary with the offense. A final warning for more serious problems, such as fighting, might stay in effect longer than one for a problem such as lateness.

Since you may need the documentation to defend your actions some time in the future, it's advisable to retain the records as long as possible. Simply note on them that they're no longer being counted against the employee. Take the case of an employee who has been with a company for 20 years and has had warning notices every year. Each notice was thrown out after six months. Habitual lateness suddenly becomes a problem within a short period of time, and you fire the person. At the unemployment hearing, the referee is going to say, "He's been with you 20 years with no problem, and suddenly you want to fire him for lateness during the last six months? It's unreasonable."

On the other hand, some states require you to dispose of these records after a period of time. In these cases, of course, you must comply.

Key Terms

final warning
grievance procedure
house rules

progressive discipline
verbal warning
written warning

Discussion Questions

1. What do you think are some of the most commonly used forms of punishment for work-related discipline problems? Why aren't they effective?

2. What problems are created by a management style that is overly permissive?

3. How can a manager treat each disciplinary situation individually and still ensure that all employees will be treated fairly and that policies will remain consistent?

4. As department head, what should you do to ensure the success of your implementation of a change in a departmental procedure?

5. Why does the company need to have a strong grievance procedure system which is well-publicized and supported by managers?

6. When is disciplinary action more appropriate than a performance discussion?

7. Why shouldn't the manager complete the written warning notice before meeting with the employee about it?

15 Terminations

Firing an employee is probably the hardest thing a manager will ever have to do. If it is done poorly, it can also become the most expensive. One wrongful dismissal lawsuit can lead to a settlement of many hundreds of thousands of dollars. Exhibit 15.1 lists some of the ways a fired employee can currently claim the discharge was illegal. In addition, new laws and regulations governing the termination process appear so rapidly that most employers can hardly keep up.

While other types of termination are generally less traumatic, they can become equally complex. The manner in which terminations are handled can significantly affect the success and reputation of your company.

Termination Policy

Your company should have a comprehensive written policy that covers all areas of termination. It should be thought out before it's needed, when there is adequate time and everyone is calm. These termination policies should be publicized to employees and followed without exception. The policy should address several topics including giving notice, involuntary terminations, rehire, references, final pay, out-processing, exit interviews, benefits, severance pay, the exit package, outplacement, and employee review boards.

Notice
Your policy should spell out that you require notice when your employees leave. Two weeks' notice for hourly employees and up to one month for management employees is customary, unless other mutually agreeable arrangements are made. Employees should be informed that the failure to give proper notice may be mentioned in references and may affect their eligibility for rehire and certain benefits.

When employees resign, you can either allow them to work out the notice or pay them off in lieu of working out the notice. You should never fire an employee simply because he or she has given notice. If you do, no other employee will ever want to give you any notice again. They will all fear being fired on the spot and left without an income until the new job starts. It will also increase your potential for liability, because the employee is likelier to be able to collect full unemployment compensation benefits.

Exhibit 15.1 Possible Wrongful Dismissal Lawsuits

- **Discrimination** (statute) — race, color, creed, sex, sexual harassment, marital status, pregnancy, sexual preference, national origin, age, religion, handicap, union preference, welfare status, political affiliation, hemoglobin C trait, personal appearance, family relationship, etc.
- **Defamation** (slander or libel) (tort)
- **Wrongful or Abusive Discharge** (tort)
- **Intentional Infliction of Emotional Distress** (tort)
- **Intentional Interference with Performance of Contract or Contractual Relationship** (tort)
- **Sexual Harassment for Extortion of Sexual Favors** (tort)
- **Breach of Contract** (contract)
- **Breach of Duty of Fair Dealing/Promissory Estoppel/Implied Covenant of Fair Dealing & Good Faith** (tort)
- **Wage & Hour Suits** (statute)
- **Job Safety and Health Charges** (statute)
- **Violation of Polygraph Laws** (statute)
- **Unfair Labor Practice Charges** (statute)
- **Workers' Compensation** (statute)
- **Unemployment Compensation** (statute)
- **In-House or Union Grievance & Arbitration Procedure** (contract)
- **Retaliation & Violation of State, Provincial or Federal Laws & Rights** (statute, tort, contract)
- **Employment Protection Act of Great Britain** (statute)
- **Canada Labour Code 61.5** (statute)

Source: *The Preventive Program*™, "Firing Employees" © 1986 Stokes, Lazarus & Carmichael, Attorneys At Law, Atlanta, Georgia. Used by permission.

Employees who give you a long advance notice—sometimes even months ahead—provide you with a special challenge to keep them and the rest of your staff motivated while they stay on. When you receive a lengthy advance notice, thank the employee for the warning, ask to be notified of any changes in plans, and request that written notice be submitted two weeks before departure. You can also ensure greater productivity by giving your assurance that you're going to do everything possible to make the final weeks among the person's best time with the company. Point out that you'd like to be able to furnish the best possible reference and you're sure that the person would like to leave fellow employees on a good note. If performance slips, treat it as a discipline problem.

Involuntary Terminations

Company policy should forbid on-the-spot firing. It should clarify that only the department head can terminate an employee. It should also require the department head to obtain approval from the director of human resources and in many instances even the general manager, particularly in the case of management or long-term employees.

When an employee is fired, the following steps should take place:

Exhibit 15.2 Sample No-Rehire Statement

> Before deciding to quit, you should know that the hotel has a **no-rehire policy.** If you are unhappy with your job, talk to your department head or someone in the human resources department to try to resolve the matter.

1. The department head should suspend the employee without pay. If the employee is hourly, pull the timecard so that no more work time is logged.

2. The department head should advise the human resources department so that an investigation can begin at once.

3. If the investigation justifies the firing, the hours worked should be calculated so that the payroll department can have the final paycheck ready at the time the employee is called back in for dismissal.

4. Someone from the human resources department should be present at the time the employee is discharged to act as a witness and to give assistance with the steps of the separation processing.

5. The department head should see that all necessary paperwork and documentation are completed promptly and put in the employee's personnel file.

Rehire   A decision should be made at the time of the termination about whether the employee is eligible for rehire and, if so, under what conditions. This should be recorded on the termination form.

While rehiring good employees to fill part-time and on-call positions can be a good idea, many employers feel strongly that they don't wish to rehire employees into full-time positions. Some companies have a written no-rehire policy (see Exhibit 15.2), and any exceptions must go through a rigorous review board. The experience of many employers has been that rehires don't normally work out. Because looking for a job is so difficult, an employee has to develop a negative attitude about the company in order to quit. Once that happens, he or she never seems to obtain the same level of commitment when rehired. What led the person to quit the first time may very well cause him or her to quit again. Many rehired employees cause additional disciplinary problems; and most don't stay very long when they're rehired, anyway.

Having a casual rehire policy also encourages employees to quit without giving the idea serious thought or trying to work out their problems in a more effective manner. Unhappy employees may even leave a job with the intention of returning when the current manager is replaced, rather than trying to improve the existing situation. Others may leave just to find out if they can do better somewhere else or to take advantage of a temporary, higher-paying opportunity. If your employees think they can always fall back on you, you'll have difficulties maintaining the consistency and commitment needed to give your guests quality in service.

Of course, there are exceptions. These may be based on such factors as seasonal fluctuations, illness, obvious career advancement (such as the person who leaves as a busperson and comes back five years later as a manager),

WALT DISNEY WORLD CO.   COLLEGE PROGRAM   FINAL PERFORMANCE REVIEW

NAME   DEPARTMENT   REVIEW DATE

CLASSIFICATION   LOCATION   SCHOOL

SOCIAL SECURITY NUMBER   MAJOR

Please Complete This Evaluation By Checking The Response That Best Describes The Student's Job Performance. If An Item Does Not Apply, Do Not Check It.

	Excellent	Good	Satisfactory	Below Average	Unsatisfactory
Relations with Guests					
Relations with Fellow Employees					
Job Knowledge					
Cash Handling Ability					

	Excellent	Good	Satisfactory	Below Average	Unsatisfactory
Attitude					
Maintains Neat/Orderly Work Area					
Judgement					
Accepting Constructive Criticism					

	Excellent	Good	Satisfactory	Below Average	Unsatisfactory
Following Orders/Directions					
Initiative					
Attendance					
Personal Appearance					

OVERALL WORK PERFORMANCE: Outstanding   Very Good   Average   Marginal   Unsatisfactory

BUSINESS SEMINARS ATTENDED:_____

Comment on above performance factors and recommend plans for improvement:_____
_____
_____
_____

Based on his/her performance during this work period, would you be willing to hire him/her in your department as a full-time employee under your supervision, providing there was an opening: _____Yes _____No
Have you discussed this evaluation with the student?   _____Yes _____No

Prepared & Interviewed by   Date Approved by   Date Employee Signature   Date
WDW 2939 R4

Some companies that encourage rehiring—particularly those with seasonal business fluctuations or a high rate of student employment—find it helpful to complete a final performance review. (Courtesy of Walt Disney World, Lake Buena Vista, Florida)

or the rehiring of students each summer. Even so, all exceptions should be considered in light of the negative ramifications of rehiring. For example, you might rule out rehiring the untruthful employee who accepted a permanent job with you in June while having every intention of quitting to go back to school in September.

References

All inquiries regarding employment references should be handled exclusively by one source for the entire company, usually the human resources department. An off-the-record personal opinion uttered while trying to help out a counterpart in another organization can result in an expensive slander suit. Even when you have proof of the reasons for termination backed up by performance discussions and warning notices, providing the information to a third party may provoke a former employee to sue you for libel or slander out of frustration or resentment. Even if you win, the process will be costly.

Usually, a company will only provide the dates of employment and the position held, and will, by either a "yes" or "no" response, verify salary if the caller specifies the figure. A company shouldn't provide any additional information unless the former employee has signed a statement releasing the company from any liability for providing additional information. This release might have been obtained on the original application for employment, when the employee was being processed, or as part of separation processing. Sometimes the employer seeking the reference information will provide a copy of such a release obtained when the employee applied to that company for a job.

The policy should also restrict the issuance of letters of reference. If you issue occasional letters upon request, you may be required by law to issue such letters upon demand. Then, when an employee who's been discharged demands a letter specifying the exact reasons for dismissal and evaluating work performance, you may be required to provide one. Ultimately, the former employee could conceivably use that letter as an instance of libel. Some states have laws requiring the company to furnish a terminating employee with a written explanation of the termination, so each employer should be aware of state requirements before drafting a policy on reference letters.

Another hazard involves giving an employee a complimentary letter of reference following a dismissal for poor performance. The manager giving such a reference may sincerely want to help the person get a job somewhere else. Unfortunately, that manager may wind up in court accused of wrongful dismissal by the worker, who has written "proof" that his or her work was satisfactory.

Because of these problems, and because reference letters are so easily falsified, prospective employers really don't place much faith in the letter of reference, anyway. You may want to point this out when declining to provide one for an employee.

Final Pay

Most states require that employees who are fired be given their final pay at that time or within a certain number of hours. If an employee quits without notice, the final paycheck is usually issued according to the normal payroll cycle.

If an employee gives proper notice, it's customary to pay all money due to the person on the last day of work. All final checks should be issued in the human resources department, usually during the time of the out-processing.

Exhibit 15.3   Employee Separation Statement

I, _____, terminate my employment from the
    (Print Name)

_____ Hotel as of _____ for
    (Hotel Name)   (Date)

the following reasons:

_____

_____

_____

_____

_____(Use back for more space.)

My last date of employment with the Hotel is_____.

I understand that my group insurance will be cancelled effective that date, unless I complete the necessary forms within 30 days to convert to a private plan.

I have reported all industrial injuries to the company.

I release the Hotel from any responsibility for personal items that I have left in my department or locker.

Mail my W-2 form and/or final paycheck to (if different from your employee records):

_____
Number/Street   City   Zip

NOTE: Checks cannot be picked up by anyone other than the employee, unless there is written permission from the employee.

Date Final Check Picked Up:_____

Date Final Check Mailed:_____

Signature of
Employee_____   Personnel_____

Returned: ☐ ID Card   ☐ Uniform Card   ☐ Nametag   ☐ Meal Card
             Locker #_____ ☐ Parking Card   ☐ Housebank   ☐ Keys

Out-Processing   On the final day, the manager or department head is responsible for ensuring that the employee returns all departmental items that were issued, such as banks, keys, and manuals. The employee then goes to the human resources department and turns in all general items issued to all employees, such as uniforms and ID cards.

During the **out-processing**, the human resources department usually asks the employee to fill out a form stating the reason for leaving (see Exhibit 15.3). This form may contain other out-processing information, but its main objective is to ensure that both the company and the employee know the official reason for the termination. This is particularly true in the case of management employees, since there's not always a single, simple reason a manager leaves. Having details puts you in a better position to defend yourself later or to consider eligibility for rehire.

At this time, the human resources department must by law also advise employees of their legal rights regarding various benefits and complete any other necessary paperwork.

Exit Interviews

Your policy should also address whether you require exit interviews. Many companies have stopped conducting exit interviews except when they're trying to smooth over sensitive issues or looking for certain facts in problem areas. You already know why most people are leaving. Also, with the advent of more employee involvement programs, attitude surveys, and the like, much more reliable information is gathered from other sources.

Employees who are leaving often either moderate their comments in order to get a good reference or try to get even with someone through malicious remarks. If you have an organizational culture that encourages employees to express their opinions, the person who really had the company's best interests in mind would have said anything worthwhile before resigning.

Another consideration is how the information will be used. Obviously, it's not worth the time and effort to hold exit interviews and write up the comments if nothing is going to be done with the information.

On those occasions when the exit interview seems desirable, appointments are normally scheduled before the employee's final day. Many companies have also found that sending a survey to the employee's home two or three months after termination provides more reliable information.

During the exit interview, the interviewer usually probes to find out the real reason the person is leaving. The interviewer has a chance to pursue what the employee liked the most and the least about the company, the job, and the supervisor. Questions might focus on whether adequate training was provided and might solicit constructive suggestions or recommendations. When the exit interview ends, the employee's comments should be written up and placed in the personnel file or distributed according to the nature of the information and how it will be used. Some companies ask employees to fill out an exit statement such as that in Exhibit 15.4. (Exit interviews are also discussed in Chapter 9.)

Benefits

Since benefit packages today represent a major portion of the employee's earnings, the number of regulations protecting the departing employee's rights to certain benefits is growing. These rights vary from state to state. However, the company still has many options and must be guided by its philosophy with respect to many elements of the benefit package. In addition to the laws, companies usually consider why an employee is leaving, length of service, and how high up in the organization the person was.

Companies generally take the posture that benefits are designed to help attract and keep employees. Providing excessive coverage, such as paying accrued but unearned vacation, to those who are leaving doesn't achieve these objectives. They'd prefer to invest in those people who are still loyal to the company.

Medical Insurance. Employees' rights under the Consolidated Omnibus Budget Reconciliation Act (COBRA—see Chapter 10) and the conversion privileges built into existing medical and life insurance plans must be explained to employees at the time of termination (see Exhibit 15.5). A signed acknowledgment of notification should be obtained.

Exhibit 15.4   Sample Exit Statement Form

FourSeasons Olympic Hotel
SEATTLE

EXIT STATEMENT

The Four Seasons Olympic is interested in knowing your feelings and opinions regarding your employment at this hotel. Please take a few moments to answer the following questions.

1. What is your reason for leaving the Four Seasons Olympic?

    _____

    _____

    _____

2. What did you like most about your job? _____

    _____

3. What did you like least about your job?_____

    _____

4. Do you feel you received enough training for your job?

    ☐ Yes   ☐ No   How could training have been improved?

    _____

    _____

5. How did you feel about the following?

	excellent	good	average	poor
wages	☐	☐	☐	☐
benefits	☐	☐	☐	☐
working conditions	☐	☐	☐	☐

    What improvements would you suggest for any of the above?

    _____

    _____

Please answer if applicable:

6. If you were discharged, do you fully understand the reasons why?   ☐ Yes   ☐ No

    If no, please comment._____

    _____

    _____

Thank you for your time.

Courtesy of Four Seasons Olympic Hotel, Seattle, Washington.

Exhibit 15.5 COBRA Notification

OPRYLAND USA

```
                                        Current Date:
                                            Company:
                                                 SSN:
                               Qualifying Event Date:
                             Election Expiration Date:


Under Federal Law, the option to continue employer sponsored
group health coverage is extended to individuals who
otherwise lose this coverage due to one of the following qualifying
events:  (1) termination of employment, (2) reduction of hours worked,
(3) death of a covered employee, (4) eligibility for Medicare benefits,
(5) divorce or legal separation from a covered employee, and (6) loss
of eligible dependent status.

Continuation coverage for terminated or reduced hour
employees may last for a maximum of 18 months.  For other
qualifying events, the maximum continuation period is 36
months.  If you wish to exercise your option, you must do so
within 60 days of this letter or 60 days from the date your
coverage will cease, whichever is later.  If you do not
exercise your option within this time period, you will not
have another opportunity to do so.

An individual must be covered by the plan on the day before
the qualifying event to be eligible for continuation of
coverage.  If you were covered by family coverage you may
purchase either family or single coverage.  Your first
payment will be due within 45 days after the date you accept
coverage.  All subsequent payments are due on the first day
of each month.  Premiums are established annually.  The
current monthly premiums applicable to your situation are:




STEPS TO ELECT CONTINUATION OF YOUR GROUP HEALTH COVERAGE:

  1.  COMPLETE IN FULL THE ELIGIBILITY/ENROLLMENT FORM
  2.  ENCLOSE THE YELLOW COPY OF THIS NOTIFICATION LETTER
      ALONG WITH YOUR ENROLLMENT FORM AND RETURN IN THE
      ENVELOPE PROVIDED.
```

Courtesy of Opryland USA, Nashville, Tennessee.

Retirement Programs. Retirement programs and how they are vested and paid are also heavily controlled by legislation. Employers need to acquaint themselves with the current regulations and requirements before they design and implement programs and policies. Any rights the employee may have must be explained.

Vacations. Many states have stricter laws than the federal government concerning the payment of vacation time. Generally, all employees must be paid for all earned vacation at the time of leaving unless specified differently under contract. Vacation time most recently accrued for less than a full year of service may not have to be paid at all. Vacation pay doesn't generally continue to accrue during severance pay.

Severance Pay

Severance pay is pay over and above what the employee has earned. If a company has a severance pay policy, it must be clearly spelled out and consistently followed. You might choose, for example, to provide two weeks' severance pay to an employee with one or more years of service who was fired because of lack of ability. However, you might choose not to provide any severance pay to an employee who has been fired for willful misconduct.

Severance pay policy might also cover employees who lose their jobs through no fault of their own, such as in a cutback, layoff, or merger. In such situations, it is not uncommon for companies to provide salary for a certain time. Hourly employees might receive two weeks' pay plus one week for each year of service up to ten. Salaried employees might receive one to three months' pay plus one week for each year up to ten.

Companies may make such severance pay in a lump sum or allow the employee to draw the compensation through the normal payroll cycle. This latter option enables the employee to maintain an active status, which permits the extension of insurance coverage while on severance pay, if the company wishes.

Spelling Out the Exit Package

The more complex the exit package becomes, the more important it is that it be spelled out in writing to the employee. This is particularly true for management employees, for whom terms and conditions can become quite complex. Providing everything in writing gives additional security to both the exiting manager and the company by eliminating confusion and misunderstandings. When negotiating an exit package, particularly at the management level, the employer often has the terminating employee sign a statement agreeing not to sue the company later (see Exhibit 15.6) as part of the terms and conditions of the exit package.

Outplacement

Outplacement firms are becoming extremely popular in helping upper-level managers to find new positions. The services provided include self-assessments, career-counseling, counseling for the spouse, professional resume preparation, assistance in the development of a network of resources for finding new jobs, assistance in improving interview skills, psychological assessments, physical fitness programs, office space, telephones, secretaries, and mailing services.

Even though the cost is paid by the former employer, such services can be quite cost-effective, since they're designed to help the employee through the stress and depression of changing jobs. A company's cost to use a good outplacement program can be recouped quickly if it prevents a lawsuit that might otherwise result from the disgruntled ex-employee looking for someone to blame.

Employee Review Boards

If a manager has stepped through the progressive discipline of an employee correctly, much of the corrective action was handled in private. This means co-workers may not be aware of the extent of discipline already taken or the length of time involved. Consequently, when the person is fired, other employees may be surprised and often see the termination as arbitrary or unfair. This kind of perception is difficult to avoid under the circumstances, but it's certainly detrimental to another employee's willingness to

Exhibit 15.6 Sample Separation Agreement

SEPARATION AGREEMENT AND GENERAL RELEASE OF CLAIMS

As a material inducement to XYZ Hotel Corporation to enter into this Separation Agreement, and in consideration for the separation compensation to be paid to me by XYZ Hotel Corporation as described herein, I hereby forever release and discharge XYZ Hotel Corporation, its owners, officers, directors, employees, agents, representatives, successors, and assigns, from causes of action, and damages of any nature whatsoever, directly or indirectly arising out of, resulting from or associated with, my employment at XYZ Hotel Corporation and the separation of that employment.

I understand the XYZ Hotel Corporation will pay to me an additional amount of $_____.

I further state that I am signing this document of my own free will, fully aware of the fact that if I do not sign this document, I will not be entitled to the compensation listed above.

_____ (Employee Signature) _____ (Date) _____ (Witness) _____ (Date)

take risks and do something extra for a guest.

One way an employer can give employees more assurance that they will be treated fairly in the termination process is the use of the **employee review board**. This board is a group of peer employees who conduct their own independent investigation of a termination at the dismissed employee's request. The board members listen to both manager and employee, review personnel records and other documents as needed, and decide whether the termination was appropriate. Their decision is treated only as a recommendation to the top official, who would also be reviewing the facts surrounding the case.

In general, the terminated individual chooses board members to review the case from a rotating list of qualified employee volunteers who have received special training. Only two to four members are needed on the board. Some companies also have management representation on the board. Policy normally dictates that the discharged employee request the review within 30 days of termination, and that no one from the former employee's work unit serve on the board because of possible personal conflicts and the subsequent loss of objectivity.

As the push for greater employee involvement increases, many employers are establishing **alternative dispute resolution committees**, whose decisions are legally binding on both management and employees. They also often deal with disputes over other employment issues as well, such as discipline, layoffs, severance pay, and promotions. The company has to be prepared to accept the committee's decision in every instance, to make the appeal available to every employee, and to make employee acceptance of board decisions a condition of employment. These committees usually comprise five line employees and two disinterested managers. An important distinction to establish is that, while it can set penalties and determine settlements, the committee doesn't make rules or create policies.

Since the National Labor Relations Board's definition of a union specifies only that it be a group of employees of any number set up to represent

A manager should be able to spot the early warning signs of job dissatisfaction before the employee's commitment to the company is lost.

employee interests in dealing with management on any issue (see Chapter 16), careful attention must be given to the structure, composition, purpose, and authority of any review board. While the benefits of such boards certainly make them worthy of consideration, an employer needs expert guidance on these matters and should probably seek the advice of an employment law attorney before establishing an employee review board.

Voluntary Termination

All managers should know how to spot and head off voluntary terminations. Some of the early warning signs include loss of commitment and enthusiasm, an increase in lateness and absenteeism, and lower productivity. The employee may become pessimistic, irritable, or prefer to spend more time alone. Generally, you can spot changes in behavior, attitude, body language, sense of humor, tone of voice, facial expression, or eye contact.

When you notice these tell-tale signs, move in immediately and try to solve the problem before it goes too far. Ask what the problem is and what can be done. This doesn't involve making any promises, but does open the door to conversation.

You can also use peer pressure to help stop a voluntary termination. Have friends or informal leaders talk to such employees to encourage them to stay or to discuss their future. Help build a bridge back to the company.

If the employee has already accepted another job, it's generally too late to do any good. Looking for a job is very hard to do. To justify it, employees often convince themselves that things are bad and will never change. Once they reach the point of going out on interviews, perhaps even covering up by calling in sick, they have already begun to modify their attitudes. By the time someone accepts a new position, the original commitment to your company is lost, and the moral and emotional commitment to the new company has begun.

Counter-offers have a very low rate of long-term success. They cause internal resentment and suggest to other employees that the way to get ahead is to quit. Furthermore, in a tight labor market, almost everyone can get a job offer for more money. If employees know the company will make counter-offers, they'll use the negotiating leverage as a means for getting raises. Counter-offers can't make up for mismanagement. If employees are that valuable, the company should do something before they quit.

It's generally inadvisable to permit employee parties during work time, on company property, or at company expense for people who are leaving, except in the case of retirement. Turnover is expensive and, from the manager's point of view, not a cause for celebration.

Death and Retirement

The family and other employees expect a significant gesture from the company when an employee dies. This is a sensitive and emotional situation. An employer can ill-afford the reputation that, "You work your heart out for years, and the company doesn't even care when you die!"

Companies should have policies that operate very smoothly upon the death of a worker—advising the spouse of the benefits available, assisting in the completion of the various life insurance forms, and knowing what procedures to follow. You shouldn't wait until the spouse asks for the final check before deciding whether it should be paid to the employee's estate.

There should be policies on collections within the department, who should send flowers, and who should attend the service. Some companies also have policies under which the employee's pay continues for as much as three months, and medical insurance coverage is extended up to six months without additional premiums being paid.

With the aging of the population, retirement is becoming another major area of employee loss. This turnover represents a sizable expense. The procedures for handling retiring employees should be thought out well in advance.

What benefits an employer will provide and how they'll relate to length of service must be considered. If the company is providing any kind of continuing health coverage, the human resources department should tell all employees that this coverage is what current retirees get, but it could be changed or discontinued.

A retirement program might include retirement gifts, making arrangements to have the employee receive regular copies of in-house publications, invitations to annual picnics, furnishing financial and medical counseling, supplying information on available services for senior citizens, discounts, and retirement organizations, and advising employees about benefits under Social Security, Medicare, and Medicaid. Many companies today are even doing pre-retirement counseling several years before the employee actually retires.

Another consideration is that the traditional employee who works 30 years and retires isn't so traditional anymore. People work at many different places during their careers, and the benefits sometimes have to be coordinated or adjusted. If an employee joins you at the age of 55 and retires at 65, do you do the same thing for 10 years of service as you do for 30? Many people who have already retired once are also returning to the labor market, further complicating the planning and administration of a retirement program.

Involuntary Termination

Work is a central force in shaping a person's sense of identity and self-esteem. Being fired from a job can cause loss of self-confidence, a sense of helplessness, resentment, hostility, isolation, stress, and health problems, and can lead to long-term feelings of worthlessness and even permanent psychological damage.

Staff Reductions

The flexibility required in the hospitality business means advance thought must be given to the fluctuations in the number of employees needed. Automation, irregular or declining business, and even company closings are now common occurrences. Whether a company is going through a small cutback, which has no promise of recall, or going through a layoff, which implies certain recall rights, policies must address how staff reductions will be handled and what benefits the employees will have under these conditions.

Within a company, reductions are usually made by position, based first on skill and ability and then on seniority unless specified differently (as under a union contract). After the decision of who is being cut is made by position, it's then considered by department, and then for the entire company. The policy should state whether people will be allowed to bid on other jobs or "bump" other employees in different positions with less seniority.

Depending on the number of cutbacks and layoffs, or if a plant is closing, additional federal regulations may specify how much notice must be provided, as well as other obligations.

In a large cutback or layoff, the company should consider the impact on the community and the public relations aspect of the action. Many companies set up temporary assistance programs to help employees locate new positions. They provide additional counseling, send out letters of introduction, help employees prepare resumes, provide telephone and secretarial support, and furnish reference manuals, copies of newspapers, trade journals, and the like.

Buyouts, Mergers, and Takeovers

With the constant threat of buyouts, mergers, and hostile takeovers, employees are thinking more about getting what they can now because they have no job security for the long term. Companies are developing separation packages and programs to protect their employees in the event of a hostile takeover. This kind of gesture tends to evoke more commitment from employees and can also serve as a recruiting tool.

The complexities of buyouts, mergers, and takeovers can generate many concerns for top management, several of which are listed in Exhibit 15.7. In such a climate, it sometimes seems that protecting the company's most important asset—its people—is just an afterthought. However, the complicated legislation regarding the terminated or transferred employees' rights to benefits may create bigger problems for the company than the merger itself: How much liability does the new company have for the continuing medical coverage of retirees? Who will be liable for ongoing labor lawsuits or other employment litigation, and for existing workers' compensation and unemployment claims? Who will be responsible for future liabilities for claims not filed yet? Does the new management have to accept the union contract currently in effect? Will employees be terminated and rehired, and how will that affect the new employer's contribution to the state's unemployment compensation fund (discussed later in this chapter)? What about vacations, length of service dates, waiting periods for eligibility, seniority, and a host of other issues? Finally, and perhaps most significantly, how will employees adapt to a different organizational philosophy and culture?

Employees will wonder and worry about these issues, especially if they don't know what's happening. Communication programs should be directed at their concerns to prevent key people from quitting and guest service from suffering while employees worry. How an employer chooses to handle all of these factors will affect the futures of entire families.

Discharges

There are two types of discharges. The first involves the employee who doesn't have the ability to do the job but is trying. If the person is still in the probationary period, a simple termination is possible. After the probationary period, two weeks' notice is standard for hourly workers and up to a month for salaried. Whether the notice is worked or paid off is the manager's decision and depends on the situation. Most companies choose to pay off the employee in lieu of notice, to prevent the person's attitude from lowering the morale of the rest of the department, and to avoid a compromise in service and standards or possible problems of pilferage.

The second type of discharge is the **just cause termination**. It involves an employee who behaves willfully and wantonly in a manner which conflicts with the best interests of the company. If the problem concerns attitude or unwillingness to perform, termination usually follows progressive discipline. If the problem concerns misconduct, the infraction is usually serious enough to merit an immediate suspension followed by prompt investigation and termination.

Guidelines for Determining Just Cause. There's no guaranteed method for handling every firing that will always keep you out of court. The facts you'll need to disqualify someone for unemployment compensation, for example, are different from the facts you'll need to win a discrimination case. By the same token, evidence that may stand up with the Equal Employment Opportunity Commission may not win in a civil action. Since laws change so rapidly and vary from state to state, the best policy is to consult an employment law attorney when you're faced with a difficult situation that may lead to expensive litigation. This is particularly true when you lack adequate documentation or when you're terminating management employees.

Exhibit 15.7 Management Concerns during Takeovers

The Preventive Program®

TAKEOVERS
Copyright © 1986

Stokes, Lazarus & Carmichael

SUCCESSOR EMPLOYER

An employer who takes over a business with a union contract many times, succeeds to the bargaining relationship with the union, although the employer may not be obligated to the terms of the existing collective bargaining agreement. This employer is known as a "successor employer."

An employer can take over a business and not be classified as a "successor employer" or the obligation to bargain with the union. The main criterion is for the new employer to have fewer than fifty percent (50%) of the predecessor's employees in the departments comprising the predecessor's bargaining unit.

Negotiations

- If seller is currently in contract negotiations with union, seller should avoid inclusion of a successorship provision in the contract.
- Whether negotiations are in process or not, seller should notify union of intention to sell.

Sales Contract

- Seller must terminate all employees.
- Seller should pay severance:
  - Previously agreed upon
  - Arrive at an amount
  - Pay whether or not buyer employs person.
- Seller's representations and indemnities:
  - No outstanding NLRB proceedings
  - No outstanding arbitration proceedings
  - No lawsuits pending or threatened
  - Indemnify for wrongful discharge claims or breach of contract claims
  - No unfunded pension liability
  - Investigate funds, check for junk bonds, etc.
  - No post-retirement medical benefits liability
  - No ERISA violations for severance pay or other benefits
  - No COBRA violations (Consolidated Omnibus Budget Reconciliation Act).
- Buyer clearly doesn't assume union contract obligations of the Seller.
- Buyer purchases assets only.
- Orderly transfer of alcoholic beverage licenses (if applicable)

Sale of Union Property

Interim

- Publicity Campaign
  - Stress different philosophy of operations.
  - Hiatus in operations.
- Advertise for employment.
- Seller notifies each employee in writing of date of termination and amount of severance pay.

Hiring Employees

- Task Force
  - People unfamiliar with seller's employees, to avoid union bias
  - Charged with hiring best people for job based on Buyer's philosophy of operating
  - Interviewers should not have access to seller's employee records
  - Each applicant should complete a new application
  - Hire best person for the job.
- Location
  - If possible, interviews should be on another property if interviews begin before sale is consummated.

Is the Buyer a successor to union contract?

- Generally no — if fewer than 50% of the employees in the prior bargaining unit are hired.
- Other criteria the NLRB and case law have indicated may be relevant to a holding of no successorship:
  - Non-bargaining unit hourly employees comprise less than 50% of the prior employer's non-bargaining unit employees
  - Supervisors and managers of the prior employer comprise less than 50% of the total supervisors and managers of the new business
  - Of those employees in the prior bargaining unit, some on union check-off were hired (this is only relevant in right-to-work states)
  - There was a hiatus in operation when the ownership changed
  - Workers with new and/or different skills were needed
  - Different market sought — mix in dollar volume between conventions and individual bookings substantially different — mix in food and beverage and rooms sales different
  - Management criteria are different
  - Philosophy of operations is distinct from the prior employer
  - Name of hotel is changed to present new image
  - Wage scales different from prior employer — for example, banquet waiters and waitresses placed on hourly wage rate instead of commission
  - Elimination of departments by subcontracting, such as laundry
  - Prior employer had no contract in effect
  - Prior contract had no successorship provision
  - No evidence that the new employer attempted to discover from its predecessor, union sympathies of various employees; such evidence to be avoided could be in form of letters, over-heard telephone conversations and discussions, and loose comments
  - New employer interviewed at-large, with former employees making application, as well as applicants who had never worked at the particular hospitality enterprise
  - No individual employment decisions, were shown to be part of an overall scheme designed to insure that fewer than a majority of the new employer's employees worked for the predecessor; new employer hired best person for job, with no anti-union bias or scheme to defeat union
  - Comparison of hiring procedures when prior employees and new applicants are interviewed does not show anti-union bias.

Source: The Preventive Program®, "Takeovers" © 1986 Stokes, Lazarus & Carmichael, Attorneys At Law, Atlanta, Georgia. Used by permission.

In addition to following your progressive discipline procedures and maintaining good documentation, however, some common elements do exist that can help support just cause terminations:

- Did the employee know the rule? If the employee is surprised at being discharged, you did something wrong. You should be able to prove that the person knew the rule, such as by having employees sign for house rules or providing procedures in writing.

    Sometimes common knowledge can be assumed. Employees shouldn't have to be told, for example, that stealing company property can result in termination before you can ever fire someone for it. (Of course, prohibiting such theft would certainly be listed as one of your house rules.)

- Did the employee know the consequences of violating the rule? If the employee is being terminated and hasn't violated a house rule, was progressive discipline used? Did the employee have a final warning— preferably in writing and with a witness?

- Was the employee's action beyond personal control? The term "misconduct" is limited to willful and wanton conduct that deliberately disregards what the company has a reasonable right to expect as being in its own best interests. Coming in late because of an "act of God" wouldn't be considered within a person's control and thus not cause for dismissal. Furthermore, inexperience, lack of information about procedures, and good-faith errors in judgment are usually not considered willful misconduct.

- Was the rule reasonable? Your policies should indicate that, even if the employee feels a rule is unreasonable, it must be followed while the objector pursues the grievance procedure. The exception is that the employee can't be asked to do something that would jeopardize his or her safety or integrity. In that case, the employee might have grounds for refusing to follow your order.

- Did you investigate before the disciplinary decision was made? The employee has the right to be heard, regardless of the nature of the violation.

- Was the company's investigation conducted thoroughly and objectively? Did the investigation uncover substantial proof that the employee was guilty? What were the dates of the lateness or absenteeism, for instance, and what were the reasons for them?

    If discharging an employee is going to lead to litigation in civil court, you may have a heightened burden of proof. Labor disputes, unemployment claims, and other arbitration may not require such extensive proof, but you'll still be expected to have adequate substantiation.

- Was the decision fair and objective? A minimum of two people should be involved in the investigation and subsequent decision to fire someone. In fact, the investigation is better left in the hands of the human resources department, rather than the manager, since the same party shouldn't act as accuser, judge, and juror.

In cases of involuntary termination, the employee review board helps to ensure that a thorough and objective investigation is conducted.

- Was the disciplinary action timely? Any action serious enough to warrant discharge should result in suspension immediately. You can't let the offender work three or four days until business slows down and expect to win in court with the argument that the offense was serious enough to require termination. When an infraction isn't discovered for several weeks, the manager should still take immediate action upon discovery.

- Did the company consistently enforce the rule and disciplinary procedures? If not, you may have to reduce the degree of your contemplated disciplinary action from dismissal to a final warning. Remember from Chapter 14 that telling employees beforehand is the necessary first step when reviving a dormant policy.

- Was the dismissal reasonable, given the nature of the offense? Overreacting by firing an employee merely to make an example to others will usually lead to a reversal.

- Was the dismissal in keeping with the employee's work record and length of service? The number of prior offenses should help determine the severity of the discipline, as would the fact that the person had been with the company for a long time.

The need to act promptly when firing an employee for just cause must be weighed against the necessity of having proper documentation and evidence. If you lack adequate evidence, consider waiting to get additional support for citing misconduct. Acting prematurely can cost your company thousands of dollars if the person collects unemployment compensation.

How to Fire Someone

Many people fail as managers because they won't accept the responsibility of firing people. The simple truth is, there is no easy way. You'll probably lose sleep over it, but you can't put it off. Get it out of the way because it will affect your own job until you deal with it, and you have many other things to worry about.

New managers will often procrastinate by saying, "It's too busy, I'll wait until things slow down or until I get a full staff." In reality, letting the person go may increase the productivity of the rest of the staff. Managers may also shy away from terminating an employee because they are reluctant to offend someone, when in effect they're giving enormous offense to many others who have to work with the person.

Discipline can't be expected to correct all the problems of deviant behavior, so managers have to get the counterproductive influence out of the department. Some good employees may not continue to work at a high-production level when one person's poor conduct seems to generate no apparent repercussions.

Managers should pay particular attention to employees during the probationary period and deal decisively with behavior such as poor performance, attitude, lateness, and accidents. If someone performs only marginally during the probationary period—a time when a person is most concerned with putting the best foot forward—it's almost certain performance levels will slip later. If you're not sure the employee is going to make it through the probationary period, extend it in writing.

Keep in mind that most employees know when dismissal is forthcoming and also feel uncomfortable waiting for it to happen. In reality, many are relieved when it's over. Most people will agree later that they're far happier in new jobs than they were working in the old environment. Your company is not their last hope.

Who Should Do It?

The employee's manager should conduct the termination. A representative from the human resources department should be present to provide support and act as a witness.

When Should It Be Done?

You can make things easier by considering your timing carefully. Don't terminate people around holidays, birthdays, and other major events. Monday morning is the best time; Friday afternoon is the worst. Arrange the time so the person can gather up personal belongings when others aren't around.

Where Should It Be Done?

The termination should be conducted in a private setting. Because some employees won't leave without creating a disturbance, the manager's office or any other location near the work site or guest areas may not be a good choice. In most instances, an office in the human resources department is probably the best site. In a small property with no human resources department, the general manager's office or a meeting room could be used.

What Should Be Said?

Do it quickly, spending only five to ten minutes at the most. Sitting around discussing the past would be agonizing for both of you and should be unnecessary at this point. The employee just wants to leave, so don't drag the process out.

Come right to the point, but don't be blunt. You should be firm and direct. This is no time for indecision or beating around the bush. Be certain the employee knows you have the authority to conduct the dismissal. You might begin by saying, "I've discussed this with the director of human resources and the general manager, and we all agree."

Specify the real reason for the dismissal, but be cautious in your wording. Don't state that you're firing someone for drinking on the job, for instance, unless you have absolute proof, with witnesses who saw the person actually drinking. It's better to say that the person violated a house rule, as spelled out in the employee handbook, by appearing to be under the influence of any substance while on company premises.

Follow up the reason by saying something encouraging or that puts the firing in the most optimistic perspective. Such a statement gives the person something to say to family and friends later, which at this point is a major concern. You might say something like:

> Everyone recognizes and appreciates the fact that you cared a lot about this company and you worked hard and made some contributions. Perhaps at another time and in another situation, things could have been different. I've seen many instances in which someone didn't work out in one area, and at the next job in the right environment became a top employee.

After you state what's happening and why, move quickly to a review of the terms and conditions of the termination, covering areas such as insurance and severance pay. Ask if there are any questions about the exit package, but make it clear that the only discussion at this stage is the package.

Get the person to shift thinking at once toward the future and away from what has just happened. Cover how references are handled and what will be said.

Be optimistic. For instance, if appropriate, you might mention that the labor market is improving, there are lots of jobs, and people are often surprised when they actually see what's available. In a few cases, you may be able to help in locating another position for which the individual would be qualified. If you can, do so. The quicker new employment is found, the less likely the company is to be sued or to pay unemployment benefits.

Try to part on friendly terms. Be sincere. Don't be afraid to say that this is the last thing you wanted to do. Help the person maintain some self-respect. It doesn't do any good to attack someone's character or personal shortcomings which can't be changed. Getting even should be the furthest thing from your mind. Creating animosity at this time will only generate more problems for you later, when the employee goes to work for a competitor or gets angry enough to take you to court or even sabotage your operation. Remember, firing people puts them in one of life's most stressful situations. Making it harder on them for your own personal satisfaction is unacceptable.

When you've finished, stand up, shake hands, and move toward the door.

Treat all the information regarding a dismissal as confidential. Only those with a need to know should be informed of the details. Telling unaffected employees what happened just because they ask, or to show that you're important enough to be privy to confidential information, can leave you and your company vulnerable to a slander suit. If the information is written on a termination notification form (which should be completed immediately for every terminating employee to facilitate out-processing—see Exhibit 15.8) and sent to the human resources department, be certain the information doesn't appear on a copy of the form that may be left lying around or sent on to payroll. The payroll department has no reason to know the cause or details of a termination, only that there was one.

Unemployment Compensation

The most frequently asked questions concerning terminations deal with the eligibility for unemployment compensation, also known as unemployment insurance. Every manager should have a basic understanding of how it works.

Most employers have to provide unemployment insurance for their employees. (The exceptions are the civil service, the military, the railroads, and the self-employed.) The federal government charges everyone an unemployment tax (FUTA), which is a percentage of payroll. This money is used chiefly to administer national unemployment programs and assist states having difficulties because of high unemployment or other financial problems. FUTA is a fixed business expense.

The state unemployment tax (SUTA) is not a fixed cost. In fact, the term "unemployment insurance" is misleading if it makes you think that a company pays the same insurance premium whether the company uses the insurance or not. The amount a company pays is the amount of claims paid by the state on its behalf. In other words, the state has a company's open checkbook to make payments to the company's former employees. The more claims paid on a company's behalf, the higher its SUTA tax will be.

While each state has to comply with the federal guidelines regarding unemployment compensation, they can vary the applications of those guidelines. Since this is a large and controllable expense, you should know and understand the laws in your state at least as well as your employees do.

A company usually must submit to the state a quarterly payment determined as a percentage of payroll. The percentage used is based on the company's total unemployment charges over the previous two or three years. This percentage is paid on all wages up to a certain level of income for each employee. The level of income is set by each state. For instance, the level in some states is the first $4,800 of each employee's earnings. If a position has turned over several times during a year, the earnings of each employee in that position (up to $4,800 for each) would be added into the year's total. Thus, the more turnover you have, the more you'll pay in unemployment tax.

How much a claimant can collect is based on how much the person earned during a base period defined by the state. The federal standards require that the total amount collected be at least one half the take-home pay during the base period. A state can allow for a higher total amount to be collected, but can't set a maximum that's lower than the federal standards.

The ceiling on the maximum collected each week is based on a percentage of the state's average wage. The claimant can collect this weekly amount for up to 26 weeks. Federal law provides for an extension of up to 13 additional weeks in areas of high unemployment.

The intent of unemployment compensation is to provide income while people look for a job when they are unemployed through no fault of their

Exhibit 15.8   Sample Termination Notification Form

```
_____ The Breakers                                    
_____ Breakers West                           [logo]
_____ Breakers Row                                    
_____ Flagler Computer              FLAGLER SYSTEM, INC.
_____ Flagler System            EMPLOYMENT TERMINATION FORM
_____ Other _____

                        COMPLETE #'s 1-5

   1.  Today's Date:_____

   2.  Employee Name:_____

   3.  Employee #:_____

   4.  Department: _____

   5.  Effective Date of Termination:_____
                                        (last scheduled work day)

   TERMINATION REASON: ("✔" ONLY ONE)

   _____ No Show          _____ School          _____ Unsatisfactory Performance

   _____ Better Job       _____ Dissatisfied    _____ Violation of Policy

   _____ Relocation       _____ Medical         _____ Lay Off

   _____ Personal         _____ Retired

   TERMINATION TYPE: (Complete all 3 Columns)
       ( ✔ ONE )                ( ✔ One )                 ( ✔ One )
   _____ Left With Notice    _____ Voluntary        _____ Before 90 Day Prob.

   _____ Left Without Notice _____ *Involuntary     _____ After 90 Day Prob.


   REMARKS, REASONS, COMMENTS: _____

   _____

   _____

   _____


   *NOTE:  This section must be completed for all involuntary terminations.


   REHIRE ELIGIBILITY:        _____ Eligible       _____ Not Eligible


   APPROVED:  Supervisor: _____  Date:_____

              Division  Head:_____  Date:_____

              Director of Human Resources: _____  Date:_____

                (FOR HUMAN RESOURCES DEPARTMENT USE ONLY)
   PRO RATA VACATION PAY:       _____ Eligible      _____ Not Eligible
              Pro Rata Vacation Pay Determined:_____ Days

   22103 L-4/3
   5C 12/88                          Supervisor/Division
```

Courtesy of The Breakers, Palm Beach, Florida.

own. This is a very important and needed program. Unfortunately, like many programs, it must be tightly controlled to prevent abuse.

In many states, low-income employees can make enough money in unemployment compensation that—without such additional expenses as baby-sitting and transportation to the job, and supplemented with programs such as food stamps and Aid for Dependent Children—they can make more by staying home than they can by working.

In addition, if weekly job earnings fall below certain levels, an employee can collect partial unemployment payments while holding a job. This means that an employee who requests to go home early one day could reduce his or her earnings to just below the qualifying level. The employee may then file and collect up to half a week's unemployment compensation in addition to what is earned on the job. The total income for the week could be higher than working all week. Many employees are aware of these possibilities. Managers must be just as aware in order to deal with abuses.

Eligibility

Anyone who has enough credit weeks (weeks in which earnings meet or exceed a specified amount as determined by the state) is eligible to collect, as long as certain requirements are met. Usually, the person must:

1. Be available for work

2. Be able to work

3. Be actively seeking work (unless temporarily laid off)

4. File with the state unemployment office

People can lose their eligibility if they're out of work owing to a labor dispute in which they're directly involved, or if they earn wages in excess of the weekly benefit amount. Employees may also be ineligible if they receive pension amounts greater than the weekly benefit amount.

Protesting Unemployment Compensation Claims

When someone files a claim for unemployment compensation, any employer whose account may be charged will be notified. If a company receives such a notice, it will have a short time, usually about 10 days, in which to protest that claim as it affects the company's account. After that time, the state rules on the claim and advises the interested parties. Either the claimant or the employer can then appeal the state's ruling and a hearing will be held. In general, a company can protest claims against its account if it can be established that the former employee:

• Was suspended or discharged for misconduct

• Left without good cause attributable to the employer

• Failed to accept suitable work when offered

If a company appeals a ruling, at the hearing the manager involved will be expected to testify about the reasons for the protest and to provide evidence in support of the testimony. To prove misconduct, for instance, you'd have to establish that the employee willfully behaved in a manner inconsistent with the company's best interests or violated a house rule. You'd be expected to furnish witnesses and any relevant documentation, such as copies of written warnings, house rules, or lateness and attendance records.

An employer would also receive notice of a hearing if a former employee disputes the state's decision on a claim. It's a good idea for the company to be represented at this kind of hearing as well. Otherwise, only the claimant's version will be heard, and any allegations the person makes about your organization will be placed into the hearing's written records.

Most employers have one person—usually from the human resources department—who routinely reviews and verifies the validity and correctness of all claims for which the company receives notices. This person also follows up on protests, hearings, and appeals. In addition, many companies retain a lawyer or service company whose specialty is unemployment compensation to assist in protests and preparations for hearings.

Still, as the claimant's former supervisor or department head, *you* will represent the company in a protest hearing. You must be prepared to provide first-hand knowledge and written records of the circumstances under which the employee left the company. The human resources officer and the company's attorney can only advise and assist you. The significance of good recordkeeping and the documentation of all disciplinary incidents becomes apparent when one realizes that thousands of dollars in charges could be involved, even for a single claimant.[1]

Exhibit 15.9 lists some suggestions to help an employer prepare for an unemployment compensation hearing. While the company will probably be represented by a lawyer and a member of the human resources department, other managers also have to attend from time to time and should know what the company representative's responsibilities are.

Protesting Quarterly Charges

Along with notifying your company of claims, the state will provide a list of unemployment benefits paid for your company to former employees, usually in a quarterly report. This listing of your account should be examined by the human resources department, and any protest of charges filed within a short time.

Once again, the keys are proper procedures and recordkeeping within your own company. Understanding credit weeks, base periods, and other elements of the unemployment compensation program and keeping track of changing laws and rightful claims can become a complicated and time-consuming task. It should be handled by an experienced company representative or by an unemployment service company.

Key Terms

alternative dispute resolution
   committee
employee review board
just cause termination

outplacement firm
out-processing
severance pay
unemployment compensation

Discussion Questions

1. What are the proper steps to take when firing an employee?

2. What problems may result from rehiring an employee who once left your company voluntarily and now wants to come back to work for you?

3. Why is out-processing such an important step in the termination of any employee?

4. What are some warning signs a manager should watch for in order to head off voluntary terminations?

5. What are the elements for determining whether just cause exists before terminating an employee?

---

[1]Joe Holman, "Are You Prepared for Your Unemployment Hearing?" *Michigan Forward,* November/December 1987, p. 7.

Exhibit 15.9 Preparing for an Unemployment Hearing

The manager or supervisor who was directly involved in the employee's termination should attend the hearing with the representative from the human resources department. Any other witnesses who can corroborate the manager's testimony as to the circumstances of and reasons for the termination should also attend. Any information that isn't presented firsthand will only be considered hearsay. Witnesses should appear calm, relaxed, and objective, and should stick to the facts. Personalities shouldn't become an issue.

The human resources representative has several responsibilities. He or she should:

- take the employee's personnel file—as well as copies of any records from the file that will be introduced as exhibits—and be prepared to testify that these are company records kept in the normal course of business.

- meet with all witnesses beforehand and review their testimony. They should understand the issues and how your defense will be presented. For example, if you're going to maintain that the former employee had the ability to do the job but wasn't working to the best of his or her ability, the witnesses should be prepared to present what they know about the person's ability and job performance.

- not take so many company representatives or prepare such a polished defense that the result is "overkill." The former employee may look so helpless that the referee's sympathy swings toward the claimant.

- dress conservatively and look businesslike, but shouldn't overdress. A "power" image, expensive clothing and jewelry, or three-piece suits can suggest that your side can easily afford to pay this claim.

- arrive early for the hearing and ask to review the unemployment commission's file on the former employee's claim before the hearing begins. It will specify the issues the claimant is raising.

- ask—when questioning the former employee or his or her witnesses—only direct questions that can be answered in a few words.

This initial hearing is the only chance you'll have to introduce evidence. If a key witness can't make it on the date that has been set for the hearing, either ask for a postponement as soon as notice is received of the date or get a notarized statement. If a key witness doesn't show up at the last minute for the hearing, ask for an adjournment.

6. What are some of the points that should be covered during the discussion in which a manager tells an employee that he or she is fired?

7. Why is it important for managers to understand something about how unemployment compensation works?

16 Unions

Unions have made significant contributions to the advancement of the American worker. Unions originated to protect employees against cruel and inhumane treatment at the hands of powerful and unscrupulous industrial giants. Even today, they serve a necessary function by keeping alive a system of economic checks and balances.

However, greater social awareness, advances in human relations techniques in business, and more governmental involvement in the issues of human rights have eroded the union cause somewhat. The need to crusade for higher wages and improved working conditions and against unfair discharges has almost been eliminated by minimum wage, occupational safety and health, equal employment opportunity, and other social legislation.

In addition, traditional union membership has derived its numbers and strength from the ranks of the blue-collar jobs of the manufacturing sector. As the number of these positions has declined because of foreign competition and automation, membership has dropped.

The labor movement is not over, however. Just as management has adjusted to changing times, the union has also adapted. The old issues have been replaced with new approaches to improve the quality of life for workers. Also, substantial inroads have been made in organizing many people not traditionally unionized, such as white-collar workers and public employees.

In fact, as the economy shifts to a service base, organized labor is shifting more attention to service industries as well. The labor movement hasn't really made concerted efforts to organize the service sector in general because of high turnover, low wages, and the high percentages of part-time and temporary employees, many of them students. But, as traditional membership declines, the stronger, more effective unions are re-evaluating the potential of the hospitality and other service industries. Powerful groups like the International Brotherhood of Teamsters and the United Food and Commercial Workers International Union, who have previously shown little interest in hotel and restaurant workers, are beginning to bring their experience, professionalism, and skill to the organization of the hospitality industry.

Why Do People Join Unions?

Today, people join a union because of poor supervision. They don't vote *for* a union so much as they vote *against* the boss. They don't want to work for managers who are insensitive, authoritarian, inconsistent, or who show favoritism, don't listen, or use other poor management practices.

Workers often feel that, by grouping together, they'll be able to get the company to respond to their needs for improved wages, job satisfaction, and working conditions. Sometimes, they're reluctant to speak for themselves out of fear of retaliation or because they feel the manager won't listen. They like the idea of having a union representative to speak for them.

Employees want fair treatment as reflected in pay, promotion, and other company practices. They view with suspicion the management team that gives itself separate dining facilities, different bonus programs, better medical coverage, or other exclusive benefits.

In addition, seniority rights continue to be important, increasingly so as our population ages. With all the corporate turmoil, such as buyouts, plant closings, management turnover, and automation, job security is still a major factor. Workers often feel the union will fight harder than their managers to achieve it for them.

Some categories of workers consistently show more support for the union effort than other workers. Older employees, women, and minority groups tend to favor unions. So do employees who have credit problems or unstable family backgrounds, those who may be dissatisfied because they've recently been disciplined or passed over, and habitual gripers, loafers, or job-hoppers.

Why Doesn't Management Want a Union?

When hospitality managers are asked to list their objections to unionization, the following points (summarized in Exhibit 16.1) are usually among their complaints.

Increased Payroll Although most non-union hotels pay at rates equal to or higher than unionized facilities, unions still create additional payroll costs. In fact, indications are that a union operation will run a 25% higher payroll than a non-union company because of restrictive policies and job definitions, slow-downs, and strikes.[1]

With their roots planted firmly in the 1930s and '40s and a history of success in manufacturing traditions, many unions are still trying to operate with the "one man, one job" philosophy. This idea doesn't transplant successfully to the seasonal, unpredictable hospitality environment. In some cases, for instance, a housekeeper can't change a light bulb; an engineer must be called. A bartender can't serve a drink to a customer; only the cocktail server can do it. Such restrictive descriptions also promote the deadly "It's not my job" attitude that never fails to irritate the customer.

Inflexibility Managers feel that union policies tie their hands by stressing seniority and across-the-board pay demands at the expense of reward and recognition based on merit and ability.

---

[1]Charles L. Hughes, *Making Unions Unnecessary* (New York: Executive Enterprises Publications Co., 1976), p. 2.

Exhibit 16.1 Why Managers Don't Like Unions

- Increased payroll because of restrictive policies and job definitions, strikes, and slowdowns
- Inflexibility in reward and recognition systems
- Inefficiency and lack of responsiveness to change
- "Molehills" unnecessarily becoming "mountains"
- Increased conflicts and ill will among employees
- Reduced employee commitment to the organization's goals
- Interruption of business
- Loss of personal communication between employee and manager and loss of the employee's individuality

Inefficiency and Lack of Responsiveness

Managers find the union structure inefficient and slow to respond to the need for change. Both problems are devastating in an industry where efficiency is the difference between profit and loss, and rapid change is a way of life.

"Mountains Out of Molehills"

Managers feel that they waste much valuable time dealing with unnecessary grievances. To justify the collection of dues, they say, unions raise many unnecessary issues so employees can see that their union is fighting for them. This practice seems to escalate when the union is having an election of officers or a union position opens up. Most managers feel that conflicts are minimized when legitimate complaints are handled on a one-to-one basis.

Increased Conflicts and Ill Will

Many people have very strong feelings either for or against unions. Conflicting employee attitudes toward having a union result in controversy, hard feelings, and even open disputes. Such conflicts can make it difficult to develop or maintain group cohesiveness and build an effective team.

Reduced Employee Commitment

Managers also feel that it's hard to get the employees' commitment to the company when the union is fighting for the same loyalties. The traditional union approach has been to break down the relationship between management and employees in order to control their members. Without the strong support of the membership, officials wouldn't be successful in calling for a strike vote, for example. Hence, in addition to their job requirements, union workers have a set of union rules and regulations which they must follow to avoid fines.

Interruption of Business

Work stoppages, strikes, slowdowns, and picket lines pose a threat to the normal operation of business. Many managers feel that in these situations the employees, the company, and the guests all lose.

Loss of Personal Communication and Individuality

In unionized properties, managers feel that they can't deal directly with their people. Rather, they must go through a third party, a much slower and more impersonal process. This is also a chief reason employees object to joining unions: the relationship with the employer becomes impersonal, and they lose their individuality.

The NLRA and the NLRB

The **National Labor Relations Act** (**NLRA**) of 1935 was designed to accomplish three things:

1. To provide workers the right to self-organize, to form and join a labor organization, and to participate in the collective bargaining effort

2. To define unfair labor practices by management

3. To establish the **National Labor Relations Board** (**NLRB**) to administer the Act

The NLRA was followed in 1947 by the **Labor-Management Relations Act**, better known as the **Taft-Hartley Act**. This Act amended the NLRA and expanded its coverage, largely to eliminate what was perceived by many as a pro-union bias in the 1935 Act.

The NLRB enforces the provisions of the NLRA on businesses that engage in interstate commerce with sales in excess of half a million dollars per year. (There are additional, varying parameters for different industries.) Its primary activities are:

- To ensure that the employee's rights to organize are protected, and to ensure that employees are not coerced either by management or by the unions when they're exercising their rights

- To assist the company and the union in developing an agreeable formula for determining the bargaining unit

- To conduct secret ballot elections

- To investigate unfair labor practice complaints, which can be filed by the employer, employee, union, or other interested parties

- To seek injunctions on unfair labor practices

What Is a Union?

A union exists to protect and promote the interests of its members. According to the NLRA, a union is defined as:

Any organization of any kind, or any agency or employee representation committee or plan, in which employees participate and which exists for the purpose, in whole or in part, of dealing with employers concerning grievances, labor disputes, wages, rates of pay, hours of employment, or conditions of work.

This means that if just two employees band together for the purposes indicated above, they could be construed as a union and protected by the NLRA. Thus, a company must be cautious in developing programs in which there's employee involvement, such as an employee review board or employee task force. Three key elements can help keep an employee body from being considered a union:

The grievance procedure for employees in a non-union property usually appears in the employee handbook.

1. The employer selects the members.
2. The membership is rotated.
3. It is clear that the group's purpose is to provide information and not to negotiate on any issue.

It's important that an employer select employee group members with care. If management makes poor choices, the result may be exactly opposite to the one intended—that is, it may convince employees that they need an independent union to represent them.

The Shop Steward

A key person in the union structure is the **shop steward**, an employee designated by the union officials. Strong consideration is given by union officials to human relations skills such as negotiating and persuasiveness. Although paid by the company and not by the union, a shop steward isn't selected based on the quality or amount of work done. At times, the people chosen may be the company's most militant, dissatisfied, and vocal employees.

It's the duty of the shop steward to advise all new employees of what the union has done for them and of their rights under the contract. They ensure compliance with the contract by watching for violations and complaining to management as soon as a violation is observed. They also act as counselors and advocates for the employees. Most of the union business they conduct is handled during their work day on company time.

When shop stewards are initially selected, they go through extensive training in identifying grievances, using the grievance procedures, and negotiating. They're given a copy of the contract and a shop steward's training manual and instructed on the importance of their job's authority and its responsibilities. They also attend regular meetings to stay on top of problems, trends, and current affairs.

A company's main line of defense against unions is the supervisor or department head. However, contrast the training that the unions give their shop stewards with the much less detailed training management gives to their counterparts in your company. You can quickly see why management loses so often when dealing with the union. Even contrasting the selection

Article 8
GRIEVANCE & ARBITRATION PROCEDURE

§25. Grievance Procedure for Employees. Should differences arise concerning HYATT, the UNION and/or any employee who has completed his/her probationary period, as to the meaning and application of this Agreement, the following procedure shall be followed by an employee and the UNION.

STEP 1. The employee may take up the matter with his/her supervisor on an informal basis in order to settle the matter promptly. An aggrieved employee may have the UNION Steward assist him/her with STEP 1, if he/she so desires.

STEP 2. If the grievance is not satisfactorily settled in STEP 1, the aggrieved employee or the UNION shall, within seven (7) days from the date on which the incident which gave rise to the grievance occurred, file a written grievance with the Personnel Director; provided, however, the seven-day requirement and the written-grievance requirement may be waived by mutual written agreement.

The written grievance shall set forth the facts giving rise to the grievance, including the date and persons involved, and designate the provisions of the Agreement which allegedly have been violated. Failure to file such written grievance within seven (7) days shall result in such grievance being presumed to be without merit, and it shall be barred from further consideration.

STEP 3. The representative or representatives of HYATT will confer with the UNION Steward and/or UNION Business Agent within ten (10) days after receipt of such written grievance in an effort to settle the grievance, unless the time limit is extended by mutual written agreement of the parties. If not settled at this conference, HYATT shall issue a decision in writing on any such written grievance within seven (7) days from the time such grievance meeting is adjourned.

§26. Grievance Procedure for HYATT. Should differences arise concerning HYATT, the UNION or an employee as to the meaning and application of this agreement, the following procedure shall be followed by HYATT:

STEP 1. HYATT may take the matter up with the authorized UNION Representative on an informal basis, in order to settle the matter promptly.

STEP 2. If the grievance is not satisfactorily settled in STEP 1, HYATT shall, within seven (7) days from the date on which the incident which gave rise to the grievance occurred, file a written grievance with the UNION, provided, however, the seven-day requirement and the written-grievance requirement may be waived by mutual agreement.

The written grievance shall set forth the facts giving rise to the grievance, including the date and person involved, and designate the provisions of the Agreement which allegedly have been violated. Failure to file such written grievance within seven (7) days shall result in such grievance being presumed to be without merit, and it shall be barred from further consideration.

STEP 3. The representative or representatives of HYATT will confer with the UNION Business Agent within ten (10) days after such written grievance in an effort to settle the grievance, unless the time limit is extended by mutual written agreement of the parties. If not settled at this conference, the UNION shall issue a decision in writing on any such written grievance with seven (7) days from the time such grievance meeting is adjourned.

§27. Arbitration Procedure. If the grievance cannot be satisfactorily settled by the above steps of the grievance procedure, either of the parties may request arbitration by giving the other party written notice of its desire to arbitrate within seven (7) days after HYATT or the UNION has made its final written answer as provided in STEP 3 (unless HYATT and the UNION mutually agree in writing to extend the time limit), in which event the grievance shall be arbitrated according to the following procedure:

The party desiring to arbitrate shall request the Federal Mediation and Conciliation Service or the American Arbitration Association (with a copy of such request to the opposite party) to furnish the parties with a panel of five (5) names of impartial Arbitrators. From this panel a representative of HYATT and the UNION shall select the Arbitrator. The Arbitrator shall be selected by each party striking in turn one strike at a time, two (2) names from the list of five (5) persons, the complaining party having the first strike. The person remaining on the list after each party has exercised his/her strike shall become the Arbitrator. The parties may select an Arbitrator by other means, if such other method of selection is confirmed by a written stipulation.

The selection of the Arbitrator and the hearing shall be within thirty (30) days of the request for Arbitration, whenever practicable.

The expenses of the Arbitrator shall be borne equally by the UNION and HYATT, each party bearing its own preparation and presentation expenses.

(continued)

> **§28. Final and Binding.** Any decision reached at any stage of these grievance proceedings or by the arbitration procedure shall be final and binding upon the parties as to the matter in dispute. HYATT, the UNION and the aggrieved employee shall comply in all respects with the result of such decision reached. The parties agree that such decision shall be enforceable in a court of law.
>
> **§29. Arbitrator Limited to Terms of Agreement.** The Arbitrator shall not have the power to add to, ignore, or modify any of the terms, conditions, or Sections of this Agreement. His/her decision shall not go beyond what is necessary for the interpretation and application of this Agreement in the case of the specific grievance at issue. The Arbitrator shall not substitute his/her judgment for that of the parties in the exercise of rights granted or retained by this Agreement.
>
> **§30. Award of Arbitrator.** Where an employee has been discharged in violation of this Agreement, the Arbitrator may order him/her reinstated, either with or without back pay for loss of income resulting from such discharge. An award of the Arbitrator shall not in any case be made retroactive to a date prior to the date on which the subject of the grievance occurred, and in no event more than thirty (30) calendar days prior to the filing of the grievance. The Arbitrator's written decision shall be issued within sixty (60) days of hearing, unless otherwise mutually agreed in writing.
>
> **§31. Chart of Grievance & Arbitration Procedure.** The illustrative chronology and chart of the Grievance & Arbitration Procedure is set forth in the Appendix with a view towards avoiding timeliness questions.

In unionized companies, the union's role in the employees' grievance procedure is clearly defined in the union contract.
Source: Arch Y. Stokes, *The Collective Bargaining Handbook for Hotels, Restaurants, and Institutions* (Boston: CBI, 1981), pp. 319–324.

processes reveals how unions often gain an advantage. Shop stewards are selected for their ability to communicate, motivate, and negotiate, and for their demonstrated loyalty. Management often selects supervisors solely on the basis of their technical skills.

Union Officials and Organization

Union representatives are full-time officials appointed by national officers to act as go-betweens for the national and local unions. Business agents are full-time elected officials who visit company sites to conduct union business with members and give support and assistance to the shop stewards. The business agents are paid by the union local and report to the union local president. They can visit union workers on the job at any time as long as it doesn't interrupt business.

The union president, who is the head of the local union, is also an elected official and may or may not be paid by the local. Depending on its number of members, the local may also have additional staff and its own offices and meeting halls.

There are two types of local unions. The **craft union** restricts its membership to workers utilizing a particular skill, such as meat cutters or maintenance engineers. The **industrial union** is made up of people working in a particular industry. The Hotel and Restaurant Employees and Bartenders Union is an example of an industrial union. The distinction between the types of unions is diminishing in terms of the kinds of professions represented.

Local unions are controlled by the national or international union of which they are a part. The offices at the national level are usually staffed with attorneys, trainers, organizers, and other support specialists.

A federation of unions, such as the American Federation of Labor and Congress of Industrial Organizations (AFL-CIO), comprises many unrelated unions which come together to coordinate the union movement on a broader scale. A federation works toward obtaining laws favorable to the unions and settles disputes between unions.

All union expenses are supported by union members' initiation fees and monthly dues, supplemented by the various assessments and fines that the unions levy upon members.

Terminology   When a company and a union agree to require all employees to join the union in order to retain their jobs, they've agreed to have a **union shop**. An applicant doesn't have to be a union member in order to be hired (this arrangement is known as a **closed shop**, which is illegal), but he or she must become a union member within a certain period of time, usually 30 days. Having a union shop is a very important issue to the union. It will usually do whatever it takes to get this clause into the contract.

Some states have passed **right-to-work laws** to outlaw the union shop provision from labor contracts in unionized companies. Such laws allow each newly-hired employee to choose to join the union or not. However, the union must still represent all employees in the bargaining unit, regardless of whether they're union members. Also, union employees can't receive preferential treatment over non-union employees working at the same facility.

Under the **dues checkoff** arrangement, a company automatically deducts union dues from the employee's paycheck and forwards them directly to the union. Like the union shop, dues checkoff is almost non-negotiable as far as the union is concerned.

A **strike** may be defined as an employee work stoppage. It's really a test of strength between the union and the company. There are many types of strikes. Some do not violate the NLRA, while others do. Strikes that are generally permissible under the NLRA include the following:

- An **organizational strike** tries to compel the company to recognize the union.

- An **unfair labor practice strike** protests an unfair labor practice the company has allegedly committed.

- An **economic strike** exerts economic pressure on the company during bargaining.

- A **sympathy strike** results not because the union has a problem with the employer, but because the employees refuse to cross the picket line of a striking group who does have a grievance with the company.

- A **jurisdictional strike** occurs as a result of a dispute between unions to determine which will represent which employees, or what work is to be done by which union's members. Members of the disputing unions stop work at the company, even though the company isn't involved and has no control over the issues in question. In some states, jurisdictional strikes are illegal.

If strikers employ methods prohibited by the NLRA, the NLRB can obtain an injunction to stop the strike. Unfortunately for the employer, obtaining such an injunction can be a time-consuming and difficult process. Strikes generally impermissible under the NLRA include:

- **Secondary boycott:** the union has no grievance against the company, but strikes it because it's doing business with another company with whom they do have a disagreement.

- **Wildcat strike:** the union members strike without the approval of their local union.

- **Slowdown or sitdown strike:** the employees intentionally slow down or stop working, but don't walk off the job.

The **lockout** is the employer's form of a strike. It occurs when the company refuses to let employees come to work until the dispute has been settled.

Picketing is the posting by the union of its members at the company site to notify the public that a labor dispute exists. By picketing, union members hope to gain sympathy for their cause, discourage potential customers from using the facility, stop other employees from crossing the picket line, and prevent deliveries. As long as pickets are on public property and aren't creating a disturbance, most of them are protected under the First Amendment covering freedom of expression. Employees who are off-duty, sympathetic non-employees, and even total strangers are protected and allowed to picket. If the picketing is illegal, the employer can attempt to get an injunction from the NLRB. Laws vary from state to state, but among the commonest forms of illegal picketing are blocking the entrance to the company, use of violence or verbal abuse, secondary picketing, and picketing on private property.

Injunctions are court orders used to compel a person to perform or refrain from performing a particular act. The NLRB obtains such court orders to stop unfair labor practices or the illegal use of strikes or pickets. If the offender(s) ignore an injunction, federal officers may be brought to the scene to enforce it.

If the union and the company can't agree on the interpretation of the contract language, they may turn it over to a third party (called an arbitrator) and accept the third party's ruling. This third party review and subsequent ruling is known as **arbitration**. Most union contracts have a **binding arbitration** clause, which means that both parties agree to abide by the arbitrator's decision.

In **mediation**, a mediator assists in negotiations by bringing a fresh and objective viewpoint to the problem. Unlike an arbitrator, he or she makes no final ruling or binding decision. Mediators are normally called in when the union and the company have reached a stalemate. They try to get the parties to arrive at an acceptable compromise.

Union members may choose to **decertify** or remove the union as their representative. In no way may the company suggest decertification; nor may it abet or assist employees in this effort. If asked, the employer may furnish the name and address of the nearest office of the NLRB.

The Organizational Process

Times are changing and so are the ways in which unions organize companies. In the past, an outside organizer would come into town and start the labor movement. While this occasionally still happens, most organizational attempts now begin from within the company.

Disgruntled employees usually go to the local union and ask for help. Usually, the local union then brings in organizers from regional or national offices to direct the subsequent drive. The employees are asked to start

Employees have a legal right to organize and campaign for a union within the limitations set by the employer's no solicitation rule. Trying to find an excuse to fire them would be a violation of the NLRA.

collecting information on the company, such as financial data, payroll records, employee listings, and the names of people fired. The organizers look for inequities in pay and poor supervisory practices within the company, and analyze the personalities of the managers. They talk with employees who have been fired and contact current employees in parking lots, at home, or at local hangouts. They try to identify and recruit dissatisfied employees—the people who are willing to speak out against the company. They also look for the natural leaders. These employees are asked to help circulate printed materials and to solicit the cooperation of other employees who would be sympathetic to the union movement.

The longer the organizers' activities can be kept from the company, the more information they can collect, and the more effective the entire drive will be. Early indications of union activity include:

- Unfamiliar people near the employee entrance during shift changes, usually seated in a parked vehicle

- Former employees coming back into the employer's place of business

- Employees regularly out of their work area, talking to employees in unrelated departments

Exhibit 16.2 Sample Pro-Employee Statement

There are no unions in the MMI organization of affiliated hotels. We believe that our relations with our staff members, our policies and the joint attitudes of employees and management made unions unnecessary. We intend to make every effort to keep it that way. In each of our obligations we seek a good working environment, with customer and employee relations free of artificially created tensions that could be brought on by outside parties such as a union.

We were built from the ground up by hardworking, dedicated employees and managers working together. Policies and programs were designed in a sincere effort to assure open and easy communications. We don't need a third party between us. That would discourage easy access to one another. A union, after all, can guarantee nothing without the hotel's agreement, except regular payment of union dues by the employee.

We are pledged to maintain high standards of individual treatment and personal respect for you. We do not need a union to assure the maintenance of this philosophy.

Courtesy of MMI Hotel Group, Jackson, Mississippi.

- Employees who come in earlier, start taking longer lunches, or leave later
- Employees hanging around the locker room during their work shift, talking to other workers
- An increase in employee get-togethers off company property
- Employees' writing down the names of other workers from timecards
- Unusual questions about policies, benefits, or pay; or unusual comments using union terms, such as, "What does seniority count for around here?"
- Employees becoming more distant to you, or acting nervous or ceasing to talk when you come near

At the first sign of any union activity, top management should contact a labor attorney immediately. Progressive companies have on retainer a labor attorney who makes regular audits, advises, and recommends a preventive course of action.

Companies that don't want a union can tell their employees that they don't feel a union will help the employees. A company might do this by placing a **pro-employee statement** in its employee handbook (see Exhibit 16.2).

Companies may also publish **no solicitation statements** to prevent anyone from soliciting their employees (see Exhibit 16.3). Such rules, however, have to exclude *all* soliciting in the workplace. This includes taking up collections and selling such products as Avon or Tupperware. The no solicitation rule can't be invoked just when the union shows up. (To date, the United Way campaign is the only exception to the no solicitation rule allowed by the NLRB.)

After the union organizers have their information, they begin a more active solicitation and attempt to get employees to sign **authorization cards** (see Exhibit 16.4). Obtaining signatures is generally easy, since employees

Exhibit 16.3   Sample No Solicitation Statement

> The hotel encourages participation in charitable and worthwhile causes outside of the hotel. However, limitations are necessary within the hotel in order to ensure a smooth operation. Work time is for work. The hotel, on behalf of all employees, will send flowers, cards, etc., depending on the occasion (illness, death, etc.). Please notify the Human Resources Department.
>
> Oral and written solicitations on behalf of any organization, individual, or cause are allowed only during non-work time, in non-work areas, and when the person being solicited is on non-work time. Distribution of pamphlets or any other written materials must first be approved by the Human Resources Department.

often don't know what they're signing or fail to realize the extent of their commitment. They may sign just to get the person to go away, or they may succumb to peer pressure thinking they'll have a chance later to cast a vote, if the movement goes that far.

Unfortunately, such employees usually don't realize that it only takes 30% of the employees' signatures on cards in order for the union to petition for an election. By signing the authorization card, the employee is, in fact, casting a vote for the union and authorizing the union to negotiate on his or her behalf. If a union comes to you with 50% of your employees' signatures *and you bargain with them*, it is *de facto* recognition of the union which removes the requirement that there even be an election. However, if you refuse to bargain with them until there's an election, you can force the election to be held.

When the organizers have enough signed authorization cards, they'll attempt to obtain recognition for the union. They usually approach a manager and assert that they have signed authorization cards for more than 50% of the employees. Often, they'll then try to show the cards to the manager to verify this statement.

Generally speaking, you should not see the union representatives at this stage. Treat them as you would any other unannounced visitor, stating that you don't have time to see anyone—there's too much work to do. If they ask for an appointment, suggest that they go to the NLRB. If you do see them momentarily before you realize they're from the union, *do not look at the authorization cards*. If they're placed on your desk, leave your desk immediately and call in a witness to verify that you didn't look at them. If you do look at these cards, the union will later raise many issues before the NLRB, including:

- You've recognized the union.

- You've agreed with their bargaining unit determination.

- You know the names of the employees who favor a union, and a fair election is no longer possible.

If you lose on these issues, you may be forced to negotiate without an election.

Never make any comments to the union organizers that might be construed by anyone as negotiation. Simply state that you doubt whether they

Exhibit 16.4   Union Authorization Card

AUTHORIZATION FOR REPRESENTATION BY
HOTEL, MOTEL, RESTURANT EMPLOYEES AND BARTENDERS UNION, LOCAL

I desire to be represented by _____ which is part of the AFL-CIO and I hereby designate the AFL-CIO and/or its appropriate affiliates as my Bargaining Agent in matters of wages, hours and other conditions of employment.

Signature (Do not print.)

Date

Home Address—Street and Number

City   State   Phone

I am employed by_____

Name of Company

Job Title   Shift   Witness

ALLIED PRINTING TRADES UNION LABEL COUNCIL ATLANTA, GA.

represent a majority of your employees. Suggest that if they would like to pursue the matter further, they should go to the NLRB. Even requests for your assistance in some situation, such as helping to calm down a few employees or to defuse a potential crisis, might lead to actions or comments on your part that could later be interpreted as negotiation.

The organizers usually then go to the NLRB and file a petition for an election. At this point, the supporting employees and the union organizers begin an active and open solicitation. An organizer may come into your facility, sit down at the bar as a paying customer, and talk to the bartenders about unions. In this case, there is little that you can do, other than perhaps being present in the hope that they'll eventually get discouraged and leave, since it's unlikely that an employee will talk with you there.

Employees who start soliciting within the plant have the right to do so on their free time, which is generally before and after work and during lunch, coffee, and smoking breaks. If they're on an authorized break in an authorized break area, they're free to talk about whatever they like. If, however, employees are paid for breaks and meal periods, you can prevent them from soliciting others at those times. If the employees they're talking to aren't on authorized breaks, you can also intervene, stating something like, "Stop. Work time is for work. We don't allow solicitation of employees by anyone during work time or in work areas." They can be told that if they're caught soliciting again, they could be subject to disciplinary action. However, it must be the same disciplinary action that you normally take for anyone soliciting for contributions, selling products, and so forth.

During a union campaign, it's especially important that company decisions be based on business as usual. Granting unusually high or unscheduled wage increases, suddenly having parties or picnics, or making other unusual changes that would influence employees' opinions could be considered unfair labor practices. If the NLRB decides that the company's interference was very severe, it could order management to bargain with the union in spite of the election results.

The same is true for the enforcement of your discipline and termination policies. You have to be particularly careful in dealing with employees who have been active in the union drive. It's better to know who they are than to fire them and risk facing charges of unfair practices. At times like these, top management should definitely contact the property's labor counsel before the department head makes any decision on a termination.

The NLRB will arrange for a hearing on the petition filed by the union. The primary purpose of the hearing is to determine the **bargaining unit**—the workers whom the union will represent. These are the people who will vote in the union election. The union will try to designate those departments it feels will be likeliest to vote for it. In the hospitality industry, these traditionally include engineering, housekeeping, and banquet services. Management, depending on its strategy, may wish either to keep the unit very small in case it loses or to expand the unit to include many departments that probably wouldn't vote for the union.

The main test to determine the bargaining unit is that the group have a **community of interest**. That is, they depend on one another, but operate sufficiently independently of other departments. If management wishes to expand the unit, it will have to prove that employees work across departmental lines on a regular basis, a process known as **functional integration**.

To establish a case for expanding the bargaining unit, managers should previously have:

1. replaced many of the specialized job titles with fewer and more general titles—general maintenance instead of carpenter or plumber, for example.

2. established as few different starting rates of pay as possible.

3. kept records of transfers between departments.

4. cross-trained employees between departments, and used them during the peaks and valleys of the business cycle. If, for example, the food server covers the host/hostess or cashier station when that person is on a break, the bargaining unit would have to include host/hostesses and cashiers as well as servers. If the restaurant cashier is cross-trained and works occasionally as a garage cashier, isolating the restaurant unit may be more complicated. If the busperson, steward, and cook exchange duties regularly, the bargaining unit would have to include the kitchen and stewarding as well as the restaurant.

The NLRB hearing will also determine which employees within the designated bargaining unit will be eligible to vote in the election. The decision is based on which employees have an "interest" in the company. Determinations must be made concerning seasonal employees, part-time employees, employees in the probationary period, and the cut-off period for new-hires. In most cases, regular full-time and part-time employees and employees hired up until three weeks before the election are normally eligible to vote.

The NLRB also determines who is a supervisor in the bargaining unit and who isn't. The definition of a supervisor is quite clear in the Labor-Management Relations Act:

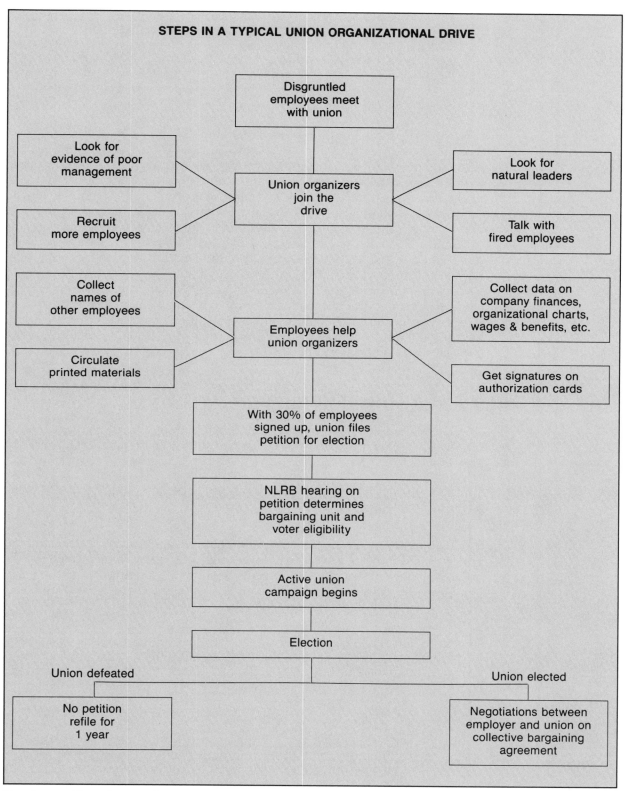

The above outlines the steps in a typical union organizational drive.

The term "supervisor" means any individual having authority, in the interest of the employer, to hire, transfer, suspend, lay off, recall, promote, discharge, assign, reward, or discipline other employees, or responsibly to direct them, or to adjust their grievances, or effectively to recommend such action, if in connection with the foregoing the exercise of such authority is not of a merely routine or clerical nature, but requires the use of independent judgment.

After the bargaining unit and voter eligibility have been established, if the union can present signed, verifiable authorization cards for more than 50% of the employees, the employer may have to recognize and negotiate with the union without an election. If the union has cards for more than 30% of the employees but less than 50%, the Board will call for an election. If they have less than 30%, time (usually 60 days) will be allotted for them to obtain more signature cards. At that point, management must turn over to the NLRB the names and addresses of all current employees in the bargaining unit, whether the employees want this information released or not. The NLRB will forward this information to the union.

During this time, the union will try to get as many signed authorization cards as possible. Management will campaign equally aggressively to present its side of the story. The law requires that all campaigning cease 24 hours before the election. Therefore, both campaigns are usually timed to climax two days before the election.

Dos and Don'ts of a Union Campaign

During a union campaign, there are a few things which managers must not do, since they may result in charges of unfair labor practices. There are also many things they can do.

Things You Can't Do

The things you can't do are indicated by the acronym STOP—that is, you can't spy, threaten, omit, or promise.

Spy. You can't spy on employees attending meetings. You can't act in a way which would indicate to your employees that you're watching them to determine whether they're participating in any union activities. You can't ask employees to express their feelings or thoughts about the union, and you can't ask loyal employees to spy for you.

Threaten. You can't threaten employees with loss of job, reduction of wages, or discontinuance of privileges, nor can you discipline or discharge employees because of their feelings about the union. You can't threaten, even jokingly, such actions as moving the company, closing down, or refusing to bargain.

Omit. You can't omit employees from work schedules, change their days off, reduce their hours, or in any other way omit them from the normal or customary working conditions. It's business as usual for everyone regardless of union affiliation.

★ NOTICE TO EMPLOYEES

FROM THE

National Labor Relations Board

A PETITION has been filed with this Federal agency seeking an election to determine whether certain employees want to be represented by a union.

The case is being investigated and NO DETERMINATION HAS BEEN MADE AT THIS TIME by the National Labor Relations Board. IF an election is held Notices of Election will be posted giving complete details for voting.

It was suggested that your employer post this notice so the National Labor Relations Board could inform you of your basic rights under the National Labor Relations Act.

YOU HAVE THE RIGHT under Federal Law

- To self-organization
- To form, join, or assist labor organizations
- To bargain collectively through representatives of your own choosing
- To act together for the purposes of collective bargaining or other mutual aid or protection
- To refuse to do any or all of these things unless the union and employer, in a state where such agreements are permitted, enter into a lawful union security clause requiring employees to join the union.

It is possible that some of you will be voting in an employee representation election as a result of the request for an election having been filed. While NO DETERMINATION HAS BEEN MADE AT THIS TIME, in the event an election is held, the NATIONAL LABOR RELATIONS BOARD wants all eligible voters to be familiar with their rights under the law IF it holds an election.

The Board applies rules which are intended to keep its elections fair and honest and which result in a free choice. If agents of either Unions or Employers act in such a way as to interfere with your right to a free election, the election can be set aside by the Board. Where appropriate the Board provides other remedies, such as reinstatement for employees fired for exercising their rights, including backpay from the party responsible for their discharge.

NOTE:
The following are examples of conduct which interfere with the rights of employees and may result in the setting aside of the election.

- Threatening loss of jobs or benefits by an Employer or a Union
- Misstating important facts by a Union or an Employer where the other party does not have a fair chance to reply
- Promising or granting promotions, pay raises, or other benefits, to influence an employee's vote by a party capable of carrying out such promises
- An Employer firing employees to discourage or encourage union activity or a Union causing them to be fired to encourage union activity
- Making campaign speeches to assembled groups of employees on company time within the 24-hour period before the election
- Incitement by either an Employer or a Union of racial or religious prejudice by inflammatory appeals
- Threatening physical force or violence to employees by a Union or an Employer to influence their votes

Please be assured that IF AN ELECTION IS HELD every effort will be made to protect your right to a free choice under the law. Improper conduct will not be permitted. All parties are expected to cooperate fully with this agency in maintaining basic principles of a fair election as required by law. The National Labor Relations Board as an agency of the United States Government does not endorse any choice in the election.

NATIONAL LABOR RELATIONS BOARD
an agency of the
UNITED STATES GOVERNMENT

U.S. GOVERNMENT PRINTING OFFICE: 1972 O—472-989

THIS IS AN OFFICIAL GOVERNMENT NOTICE AND MUST NOT BE DEFACED BY ANYONE

When the union files a petition for an election, the NLRB recommends that the employer post notices like this one in prominent locations so that all employees can be notified.

Promise. You can't promise employees a pay increase, promotions, better working conditions, additional benefits, or special favors if they vote down the union.

Things You Can Do

You can encourage employees who support the company's position to talk to fellow employees and voice their concerns to them. (Remember, however, that they're subject to the same restrictions on solicitation as any employee who's speaking for the union.) You can also talk about a personal experience you've had with unions as long as you're factual. If employees ask your opinion, you may express your personal feelings. If they inquire about authorization cards or how unions operate, you're free to explain.

You can tell employees that if a union were to come in, they wouldn't automatically get everything that they now have plus more. Bargaining on a union contract doesn't start with the existing package. All wages and benefits are subject to negotiation, just as any other union demand. During contract negotiations, the union will often trade away some of the employees' previously provided benefits in exchange for getting the employer to yield on issues significant to the union, such as dues checkoff.

While much of the company's campaign to its employees will be orchestrated by the labor attorney, managers shouldn't be afraid to speak. The NLRA provides that:

> The expression of any views, argument, or opinion, or the dissemination thereof, whether in written, printed, graphic, or visual form, shall not constitute or be evidence of an unfair labor practice under any of the provisions of this Act, if such expression contains no threat of reprisal or force or promise of benefit.

The Election

The NLRB handles the election. It sets the date, hours, and place. On the day of the election, an NLRB agent will be in charge. The union and the employer will each have a representative officially designated as "observer" to oversee the proceedings. Each employee marks an unsigned ballot with one X only, and places it into the ballot box.

Questions sometimes arise about the eligibility of certain voters. Either observer or the NLRB agent can challenge an individual's right to vote. The challenged ballot is marked with the voter's name and set aside in a special envelope. These ballots won't be counted unless their number would affect the outcome of the election. If the challenged ballots must be counted, they have to be verified. The challenge will only be upheld for a good cause—not for personal reasons or clerical error. However, there's no penalty for challenging any number of voters, even if the challenges are later determined to be unjustified.

Collective Bargaining Agreement

If the union wins the election, the employer must bargain with the union over all issues regarding wages, benefits, and working conditions. Exhibit 16.5 presents a list of typical items that may be negotiated. The results of these negotiations are outlined in the **collective bargaining agreement**—the union contract.

Exhibit 16.5   Typically Negotiated Topics

Term	Grievance procedure for employer (name)
Purpose	Arbitration procedure
Coverage	Final and binding
Complete agreement	Arbitrator limited to terms of agreement
No vested interest acquired by employees	Award of arbitrator
Union recognition and individual agreements	Chronology and chart of grievance and arbitration procedure
Union cooperation	Right to discipline
Union recognition	Just causes for discharge
Continuous service	Leaves of absence
Recognition of applicable laws	Military leave
Equal opportunity	Maternity leave
Union representative	Holidays observed
Union stewards	Holiday pay
Bulletin boards	Eligibility for holiday pay
Management rights	Disqualification of holiday pay
No strikes or lockouts	Amount of vacation
Regular rate of pay	Bonus vacation
Definition	Computation of vacation pay
Probationary employee rates	Scheduling vacation periods
Meals	Blue Cross Blue Shield
Uniforms and costumes	Sick leave disability program
Job safety and health	Retirement
Medical examinations	Banquet compensation
No guarantee	Successorship
Standard workweek and workday	Remaining agreement valid
Overtime work	Change of business conditions
Overtime pay	Governmental legislation coordinated
Premium pay	Grievance prior to administrative agency or judicial action
Twelve-hour day	
No duplication of overtime pay	
Report-in pay	Posting
Call-in pay	Seniority
Exceptions to report-in pay	Probationary employees
Definitions and application	Qualifications
Departmental job classifications seniority	Unit work
Probationary period	Continuation of benefits
Work opportunities	Checkoff
Layoffs and recalls	Maintenance of standards
Notice of recall	Construction of contract
Loss of seniority	"Most favored nation" clause
Continuation of seniority	Merit increase
Grievance procedure for employees and union (name)	Combination jobs
	Craft rules

Source: Arch Y. Stokes, *The Collective Bargaining Handbook for Hotels, Restaurants, and Institutions* (Boston: CBI, 1981), pp. 113–116.

The negotiation of such agreements and their renewals is often unnecessarily theatrical. A novice negotiator, whether on a contract or a grievance, should be aware that neither side begins by asking for what it really wants. One side may state that it wants a two-dollar increase or it will strike. The other side responds that it can only pay 20 cents more and that's its final offer. Later, when they agree on a dollar an hour, neither side feels that its statements were made in bad faith. Although it seems that negotiations would be more efficient if both sides were more straightforward, they seldom are.

Working with the Union

If the unit is unionized, every manager should obtain a copy of the union contract, become well-acquainted with it, and show good faith in complying with all of its provisions. Before managers can make changes in any area covered by the contract, the company must first clear it with the union.

In most instances, an employee who has a grievance will take it to the shop steward, who discusses it with the manager. If it can't be resolved, the shop steward then turns to the union, and the union files a written grievance with the company. Representatives of the union and the employer meet and try to settle the issue. If it remains unresolved at that level, the contract usually provides for binding arbitration.

The adversarial relationship that has traditionally existed between most employers and their employees' unions can restrict the levels of quality and productivity an organization is able to provide. However, in more and more companies, both sides are beginning to realize that the only way to achieve their own objectives is to eliminate the adversarial roles and to work toward common goals.

Key Terms

arbitration
authorization card
bargaining unit
binding arbitration
closed shop
collective bargaining agreement
community of interest
craft union
decertification
dues checkoff
economic strike
functional integration
industrial union
injunction
jurisdictional strike
Labor-Management Relations Act
lockout
mediation
National Labor Relations Act
   (NLRA)

National Labor Relations Board
   (NLRB)
no solicitation statement
organizational strike
picketing
pro-employee statement
right-to-work law
secondary boycott
shop steward
sitdown strike
slowdown strike
strike
sympathy strike
Taft-Hartley Act
unfair labor practice strike
union shop
Wagner Act
wildcat strike

Discussion Questions

1. Why do people join unions?

2. What are some of managers' chief objections to having a union?

3. Why is the shop steward often more effective in dealing with co-workers than their supervisor?

4. What are some signs a manager should watch for that indicate a union campaign may be under way?

5. Why is functional integration so important in determining the bargaining unit?

6. What are some of the things a manager is prohibited from doing during a union campaign?

7. What can a manager do during a union campaign?

17 The Human Resources Function

Chief executive officers and other top managers in hospitality organizations are spending much more of their time making human resources decisions than ever before. They are actively involved in, and must stay informed about, such key areas as employee productivity and motivation, labor costs, staffing, succession planning, and the growing and ever-changing body of employment legislation. Their background in and understanding of these areas will markedly affect the levels of productivity and service their organizations can achieve, as well as their bottom line figures.

Upper management is also demanding more of the human resources department than ever before. Planning for the growth of a service company means integrating plans for the development of its chief resource—its people—with the business and marketing plans. Because of these demands, it's now common for the director of the human resources department to report to the president or general manager, rather than to another division head. Human resources executives should have strong business and operations backgrounds in addition to their knowledge and experience in areas of human resources management. It's not uncommon for top managers to direct their best managers into the human resources area.

The demands are growing not only on the human resources director, but also on the support staff. This staff may include specialists in such areas as employment, training, employee relations, wage and salary, benefits, policy administration, labor relations, and safety. These growing demands have contributed to the emergence of this area of management as one of the fastest growing and best compensated in the hospitality industry.

The need for top managers to be skilled in all areas of human resources management and the contribution of the human resources staff to the company's growth are leading employers to conclude that the human resources department is an excellent training ground for upper management positions. In addition, the values and qualities that make someone successful in human resources management are the same ones that enable the person to succeed in upper management. These values and qualities include being effective without relying on power or authority, being a good educator, and being able to serve as the conscience of the company.

Despite the growing importance of human resources departments, however, this department is still a staff function. Its purpose is to serve as a resource to help managers manage more effectively. Some of the ways in which this support is provided is discussed in the next section.

Responsibilities of the Human Resources Function

Whether you're at the smallest unit or part of a large corporation, the basic human resources functions remain the same. They include:

- **Employment:** internal job posting, transfers, and promotions; external recruiting through the development of outside sources and advertising programs, interviewing, and extending offers; checking references, testing, and following up with new hires

- **Training:** processing and orienting new managers and line employees; conducting "train the trainer" programs and assisting managers in developing programs for their departments; administering tuition reimbursement programs, supervisory development programs, internship programs, and assessment centers; organizational development, including staff planning, career pathing, and succession planning

- **Employee relations:** monitoring the overall working environment, including lockers, cafeterias, vending machines, uniforms, parking, lighting, and noise; developing, implementing, and administering programs to maintain and improve morale and employee motivation, as well as other employee programs such as length of service awards, recognition, United Way, employee meetings, and retirement; employee counseling and management of employee assistance programs and other employee services such as a credit union; recreational activities such as sports teams and clubs; employee communications, including in-house newsletters, suggestion programs, and attitude surveys; quality circle programs and overall concern with job enrichment and job design

- **Compensation:** developing and administering the wage and salary programs of the facility, including participation in wage surveys, using job evaluations to establish starting salaries and staffing guides, and ensuring compliance with wage and hour, equal pay, and other regulations; administering the pay and performance review programs to ensure that policies regarding pay for performance are implemented and administered

- **Benefits:** administering all insurance programs, including choosing from the options, setting them up, and handling claims; developing and maintaining a wellness program; compliance with ERISA, COBRA, the Tax Reform Act, and other legislative requirements; administering the other benefits, such as holiday pay, vacation pay, jury duty, flextime, day care, and flexible benefit plans; administering workers' compensation and maintaining the records

- **Administration:** developing policies and ensuring the uniform interpretation of those policies; handling various personnel reports and statistics, such as turnover reports and EEO logs; maintaining records and files, handling and developing management information systems, and developing employee handbooks; ensuring that the facility is in compliance with all local, state, and federal record-keeping requirements; administering the affirmative action program

Because of the impact the human resources department now has on an organization's bottom line, companies are demanding more from the function and its managers than ever before. Now more than ever, personnel is not an appropriate "dumping ground" for employees who haven't worked out elsewhere in the company.

- **Labor relations:** defending the company against suits brought by the Equal Employment Opportunity Commission and the Labor Department, and against civil suits alleging employment practices such as wrongful discharge; in union facilities, negotiating and administering the union contract and ensuring compliance with the contract; in non-union facilities, maintaining the non-union environment; coordinating in-house discipline, final warning and termination procedures, employee review boards, grievance procedure, and exit interviews; handling unemployment compensation

- **Safety:** managing the accident and loss prevention safety programs; coordinating the safety committees; complying with related OSHA requirements; company medical safety, including first aid kits and medical nurse or medical facilities; conducting safety training programs, such as CPR

In smaller units, one person may be responsible for several or even all of these functions. In large corporations, each of the areas may be handled by one or more specialists.

Operating Requirements for the Human Resources Department

As the responsibility, accountability, and influence of human resources departments have increased, so has the size of their staffs and budgets. This expanded role is reflected in the growing preference of businesses for the broader term *human resources* over *personnel*.

Clearly, the hospitality industry comprises establishments of all types and sizes. Many are not large enough to justify the creation of a separate office or position. In these operations, the general manager usually handles many of the human resources functions. Increasingly, however, companies of all sizes are finding they can't operate or manage effectively without a human resources department—even many smaller units where such departments were thought to be unnecessary just a few years ago. Where a separate office is justified, some elements of its operating requirements are fairly consistent.

Staff Size

The number of staff members needed in the human resources department is based primarily on the company's total number of employees. For a long time, the standard ratio has been one employee in the human resources department for every 100 workers in the company. This means a company with 1,000 employees would have ten people in the human resources department. Six of them would probably be technical or specialist staff, and four would be clerical or support. However, because of the increasing responsibilities of the human resources department, the ratio is moving toward one person for every 75 employees. The actual number needed varies with the type of operation and the demands placed on the department.

Staff requirements may be lower when the human resources function is centralized at a corporate office, which reduces the local demands, or when outside consultants are used. Factors that could increase the size of the human resources staff include: high turnover; diversification of positions; the higher personal service standards usually associated with luxury hotels, affecting training responsibilities in particular; and a large percentage of food and beverage employees, who are harder to recruit and keep.

Physical Requirements

A human resources department has a number of physical requirements. For a new property, these aspects are best addressed in the planning stages. For example, many departments need a training room, a company library, and space for computer equipment. In addition, consideration should be given to how the human resources office affects the company's image, since this office has the most contact with the community. For every one person hired, five to ten people apply. They're still customers, as are their friends, with whom they'll discuss their impressions.

The office also influences the first impressions that each newly-hired employee has of the company. First impressions are as important to an employee as they are to a guest arriving at the front desk. If cleanliness is important to your operation, entrances and offices should be immaculate and well-maintained, including the applications area, the pencils and telephone books, interviewing offices, public restrooms, and hallways. Similarly, if employees will be expected to acknowledge guests immediately, to establish eye contact, to call them by name, and to smile, the human resources staff should greet and treat applicants and employees in this manner.

Although the location of the office must meet the property's individual needs, direct public access, as well as easy access for all employees, should be included. The public entrance is generally at street level, next to or combined with the employee entrance. Both must be barrier-free.

Ideally, the human resources department should be located nearer to the

Many people in the community receive their first impressions of a company when they apply for a job.

public entrance than the security office is, so that security only has to screen the people who go beyond the human resources department. Being challenged by a security officer is discouraging and intimidating to applicants who may already be nervous about being there.

If the security checkpoint is between the entrance and the human resources department and redesign is impossible, the same first-impression considerations apply to security as to human resources. Attention should be given to the area's appearance, and to how officers greet and assist applicants.

The human resources office should be as attractive as any other office that the public sees, without being overly luxurious. Conducting an interview in a plush office with walnut paneling conveys the wrong impression to the employee who's going to work in a dish room.

The office environment should be friendly, comfortable, and inviting. It should communicate that people are important. Display photographs of people at work in the facility. A booklet of complimentary letters to the company can make excellent reading material for applicants waiting to be interviewed.

Staff Image   The physical environment of the human resources department is clearly important. Equally important is the attitude and image conveyed by the staff. Personal appearance should be appropriate for professionals with a high amount of public contact, although clothing should suggest that the staff members are approachable and friendly. Severe styles and three-piece suits may be too intimidating and authoritarian.

Applicants are already apprehensive and can sense whether they're welcome. Therefore, the human resources staff should exhibit genuine warmth and concern for people. This is especially true of the receptionist, who must handle a huge volume of business rapidly. This person should be chosen with care and the position should be managed conscientiously. The same attention should be given to motivation and service attitude that would be given to a desk clerk or any other guest-contact position in a high-stress environment.

Regardless of how hectic the moment, each visitor should be treated with courtesy and sensitivity. For example, when employees who are visibly upset come in for help, they shouldn't be told, "I'll have someone call you." Someone should see them right away. Workers must know their needs will be taken seriously and treated with dignity.

Since the human resources department is perceived, correctly or incorrectly, as the maker and enforcer of all policies, employees expect staff members to set an example. They can't operate contrary to policy and expect to be able to enforce policies. If people from the human resources department are late coming to work or opening the office, the company can hardly expect other employees to arrive on time. The human resources manager who isn't wearing a name tag is in no position to admonish other employees when they're not wearing theirs.

Employees also have high expectations of the human resources department when it comes to the personnel records. Every piece of paper affects someone's life, and none can be allowed to become unimportant. Even though thousands of forms and requests are processed each year, mishandling one may have a major impact on someone. For example, a bank request for job and salary verification may be a prerequisite for a home mortgage. If it's shuffled to the bottom of a stack or routinely stamped "employment verified," the loan could be delayed or denied.

Confidentiality is also very important. Employee records shouldn't be allowed to leave the human resources department, nor should managers be given general access to the files. If a manager wishes to see one of his or her employees' files, a member of the human resources staff should obtain it.

The people who work in the human resources department can help to foster employee confidence by getting out of the office, becoming visible on all shifts, and establishing ongoing relationships. The person responsible for hiring should visit newly-hired employees to express an interest in their progress and offer encouragement. The employee relations coordinator should walk around the property checking that the employee areas—locker rooms, restrooms, bulletin boards, and the cafeteria and other break areas—are clean and well-maintained. They should be pleasant and attractive, well-lit, and relaxing, with no bad odors or loud noises. All of these actions help express the company's values and standards to employees.

While staff members should be open and friendly to everyone, close relationships with co-workers can create problems. If someone from human resources has a close friendship with an employee from outside the department, it may influence the department's ability to operate fairly. Even giving the appearance that the human resources staff can't be trusted because they're partial to someone must be avoided. If the labor relations manager goes to lunch every day with the executive housekeeper, the housekeeping employees may feel too threatened to go to human resources with a grievance or may assume that they won't get fair treatment during disciplinary procedures.

Conversely, suppose a manager wants to start building a file to document a pending termination. If someone in human resources is a close friend

Many human resources departments have turned to computerization for their personnel files. This helps them keep up with the massive recordkeeping requirements imposed by current employment laws. It also helps maintain the confidentiality of their employee records.

of that employee, the manager will probably be reluctant to turn to human resources for the proper information and guidance.

The need for reliability and integrity has other ramifications. The things that happen to people are interesting enough, but the hospitality environment seems to add to the interest. People want to know what's going on, and those in the human resources area are often aware of events before others are. However, talking about work or co-workers can be damaging to the company. Even idle conversation at home or in social situations could complicate someone else's job or lead to a slander suit.

The staff of the human resources department represent the values, beliefs, and culture of the organization. As role models, particularly for line employees, they should be team players, motivated more by a desire to help people than by ambition for status or power. Those who see themselves as more important than others aren't cut out for the human resources department, and probably not for a service industry.

The Personnel Policy and Procedure Manual

Every manager looks to the human resources department for valuable assistance. One of the most valuable ways the department helps its company's managers is by developing personnel policies and procedures. The personnel policy and procedure manual, generally referred to simply as the policy manual, is one of the most critical documents in an organization. It reflects the values and philosophy of the company and directs how its people are managed.

An effective policy manual sets guidelines for managers to follow as they make countless human resources decisions each day, saving them time and ensuring fairness and consistency. This consistency is a crucial element. Different departments shouldn't have different policies with respect to the same problems. Managers should know that, by staying within this framework of established policies, no decision they make will conflict with decisions made by other department heads.

Policies can't be copied from a book or borrowed from other companies. They should be written based on each company's own needs and requirements. Policies should reflect not only the company's values, but also its size and location and whether it's centralized or decentralized, union or non-union, and bound by area practice or corporate controls.

The policy manual should be comprehensive enough to cover most situations that arise in the normal course of business. It should give managers the direction they need in handling day-to-day situations. Its purpose is not to limit managers, but to help them solve problems.

Turning Philosophy into Practice

As we discussed in Chapter 2, an organization's philosophy is a collection of principles and values which are used to define objectives and goals. **Policies** are the practical application of these values and goals to the everyday operation of the company. They should also provide the framework within which intelligent exceptions can be made with consistency. **Procedures** are the detailed instructions for carrying out the policies and are intended to cover the commonest situations and questions. It isn't appropriate to have a policy, or even a procedure, on every minute item or covering every exception.

Policy Development

When a policy is developed, three things should be considered:

1. **The philosophy and values of the company:** The statement of philosophy is the company's guiding force. Without it, policies will vary depending on the interests and values of the people using them. It will be difficult for anyone to understand the rationale or intent behind a policy.

2. **The support of senior managers:** If they don't believe in a policy, they'll make exceptions. It only takes a few exceptions to erode the policy.

3. **The participation of line management:** The policy manual is designed to help line managers effectively use their human resources, so they must see it as helpful. They should be involved in its development, and it should be written in language they understand.

Introducing a new policy represents change. Getting a representative group of line managers involved increases the chances for acceptance and commitment by all the managers. It also helps counteract the rumors and reduce the apprehension any anticipated change can bring.

The timing of the implementation will also influence its acceptance. For example, a company wouldn't introduce a policy improving the benefit plan for salaried employees when laying off hourly employees.

The company planning to implement an entire policy manual for the first time in an existing organization shouldn't attempt to do too much all at once. Trying to introduce a policy manual and also change policies at the same time increases the probability of resistance to the whole idea. Instead, the company should use the manual at first merely to document all current procedures. The primary goal is to gain acceptance of the manual itself and the idea of having one. Later, policies and procedures can gradually be changed. It's easier to deal with managers' disagreement with one policy than to overcome their rejection of the whole manual.

Although policies do change with the times, they shouldn't change each time a manager changes. They provide uniformity and continuity over the years and should plot a stable course. The manual must be realistic, relevant, and responsive if it's to help rather than hinder. The last thing people should hear is that they can't do something constructive and innovative because of a policy.

Manual Format

The policy manual should be held in a loose-leaf binder to facilitate modifications (usually procedural) and updates. Some companies may have a separate manual for personnel policies and procedures. In other places, personnel policies and procedures are combined with other company policies and procedures in what is usually called the company policy and procedure manual. In either case, it should be divided into sections, with the policies numbered within each section. While the number of divisions and policies needed will depend on a variety of factors, a standard medium-sized hotel will probably have a division and a listing of policies similar to the one shown in Exhibit 17.1.

A policy should be a brief one- or two-paragraph statement. Each policy should be on its own page. If procedures are needed in following the policy, they should be added on the same page. Certain other information should be included with each policy:

- The policy number

- The number of pages for the policy

- The effective date and whether or not it supersedes any existing policy

- The area affected, such as salaried, non-union, full-time, or part-time employees

- The name and title of the person who initiated the policy (including the title provides a cross-reference in case the person changes positions or leaves)

- Any approvals that are required

Issuance

The person responsible for policy administration, usually the director of human resources, is also responsible for issuing the policy manual. This manual is a confidential reference guide to aid managers only. Control should be exercised over who gets a copy. A list, by title, of each person who is issued a copy should be included in the master copy. This list can be used later when policies are changed or added.

Receiving a manual is sometimes perceived as a status symbol. Many people would like a copy. To simplify maintenance and control, however, it's

Exhibit 17.1   Suggested Divisions of Policy Manual

EMPLOYMENT
Equal Opportunity Statement
Recruiting
Employment Requisitions
Candidate Interview Expense
Extending Offers
Reference Checks
Employment of Aliens
Employment of Minors
Testing
Employment Agencies
Pre-Employment Physicals
Employment of Relatives
Rehires
Relocation
Job Posting
Probationary Period
Entering and Leaving the Building
Moonlighting

TRAINING
Orientation
Career Counseling
Succession Planning
Assessment Center
Cross Training
Management Interns and Trainees
Supervisory Development
Management Development
Tuition Reimbursement
Membership in Professional Organizations

EMPLOYEE RELATIONS
Retirement Program
Length of Service Program
Special Recognition Programs
Quality Circle
Attitude Surveys
Suggestion Program
Newsletters
Employee Meetings
Bulletin Boards
Employee Cafeteria
Lockers
Uniforms
Employee Assistance Program
Community Relations

WAGE AND BENEFIT ADMINISTRATION
Company Organizational Chart
Departmental Organizational Charts
List of Hourly Positions (Including Grade, Actual
   Titles, Number Required, and Starting Rates)
List of Salaried/Exempt Positions
Wage and Hour Practices
Equal Pay
Pay for Performance
Salary Increase Program
Performance Appraisal Programs
Budgetary Guidelines for Increases
Promotions
Transfers
Lead Pay
Tip Reporting
Tip Credit/Tip Pooling
Other Credits (Meals, Lodging, Uniforms)

Donated Time
Pay During Training
Issuing Paychecks
Payday
Time Recordkeeping
Payroll Procedures
Scheduling
Overtime
Absenteeism
Sick Leave
Leaves of Absence
Jury Duty
Funeral Leave
Retirement
Holidays
Vacation
Meals and Other Breaks
Parking
Life Insurance
Health Insurance (Medical, Dental, Optical)
Day-care Center
Flextime
Company Discounts
Eligibility for Full-time Status (Who Gets What
   Benefits: Full-time, Part-time, and On-Call)

LABOR RELATIONS
House Rules/Standards of Conduct
Discipline
Warning Notices
Terminations—Voluntary and Involuntary
Final Paycheck Distribution
Cutbacks and Layoffs
Exit Interviews
Giving Notice
Dealing With the Union or Non-Union Philosophy
   (Pro-Employee Statement)
At-Will Employment
Sexual Harassment Policy
Age Discrimination Policy
Handicap Discrimination Policy
Employee Review Board
Grievance Procedure
Privacy and Protection
EEOC and Affirmative Action
Employee Personnel Files

MISCELLANEOUS
Personnel Action Form (for status changes)
Reporting Accidents
Safety Committee
Life Threatening Illnesses
No Smoking Areas
Workers' Compensation
Unemployment Compensation
Employee Recordkeeping
Files and File Retention
Package Passes
Name Tags
ID Cards
Use of Facilities
Emergency Procedures
No Solicitation
Check Cashing
Dress Code

generally best if only the manager of each department is issued a copy. He or she is then responsible for disseminating the policy information. The manual should be available within the manager's office as a reference for other supervisors within the department.

The policy manual should be written in a general style for easy reading. It isn't generally written to be a legal document. Careless handling, indiscriminate lending, or copying pages from it and handing them out to anyone not authorized to receive the manual could lead to misinterpretation or distortion of the company's original intent, and legal problems could result.

The employee handbook is usually a short version of the company policy manual. The handbook covers the commoner practices for employees and is normally written in general terms with the policies stated briefly.

New department managers should receive the manual as part of their orientation, and it should be reviewed with them by a representative from the human resources department. The first page of the manual should spell out clearly to everyone that the policy manual is issued to a position and not to an individual. People shouldn't take the manuals when they leave or get transferred.

Administration and Maintenance

The policy manual must be kept current or it will lose credibility and impact. One person in the human resources department should be assigned to ensure that manual content keeps up with changing times. This person distributes copies of new policies, oversees the updating of every copy of the manual, and keeps a record of old policies so that there's a history of what policies were in effect during any given period.

Personnel Forms

Personnel policies are supported by many forms (for a suggested list, see Exhibit 17.2). The person who develops the policy usually develops associated forms and should keep in mind the need for continuity, simplicity, and professional appearance.

Continuity. The forms should have continuity of size, layout, and appearance, including the typeface. Each department should coordinate its forms as closely as possible with those of other departments. If the first line on one form is "Employee Name" and the second is "Department," this should be the case on all forms where possible. The same is true of space allowed for other standard required information, like signatures, approvals, and dates.

Color-coding by subject is helpful in organizing and keeping track of forms. All forms for salary and performance reviews could be one color, those for disciplinary procedures another color, and hiring procedures could be a third.

Simplicity. The number of forms should be kept to an absolute minimum. They should be as simple and as easy to read as possible. They should ask for the least amount of information possible. Most are only used occasionally and should be self-explanatory. If a manager has to go back to a reference manual to complete a form, it has been poorly designed. If the request for information isn't self-explanatory, a brief instruction note should be added to the form.

Exhibit 17.2   Suggested List of Personnel Forms

1. Application for employment
2. Interview evaluation
3. Employment requisition
4. EEO identification
5. Form I-9
6. Tax forms (local, state, and federal W-4)
7. Add to payroll authorization
8. Hiring form
9. Transfer/status change form
10. Termination notification
11. Exit interview form/outplacement
12. Personnel record change form
13. Leave of absence form
14. Payroll deduction authorization
15. Telephone reference check
16. Mail reference check
17. Performance review form
18. Pay review form
19. Warning notice
20. Probationary notice
21. Suggestion form
22. Accident report form
23. Hiring agreement
24. Tuition reimbursement application
25. Insurance forms (applications, waivers, claim forms)
26. Employee handbook
27. Employee ID card/badge
28. Employee ID card/badge receipt
29. Employee name tag
30. Employee name tag receipt
31. Lock/locker control/receipt/instructions
32. Uniform control card
33. House bank receipt
34. Master key receipt
35. Vacation request form
36. Meal authorization card
37. Tip reporting form
38. Notification of tip credit taken
39. Authorization for treatment of workers' compensation injury
40. Package pass
41. Acknowledgement of receipt of handbook/house rules
42. Employee attendance record
43. Personnel jacket/file folder
44. Networking source log
45. Employee incident file
46. Recognition/achievement certificate
47. Hazard communication receipt
48. EEO.1 Report
49. OSHA Form 200
50. OSHA Form 101
51. Government required posters
52. Union forms (if applicable)

Professional Appearance. Frequently used and highly visible forms— particularly those used during the hiring process—should be well organized, attractive, and professionally typeset. They should be clean and neat, not

PERSONNEL ACTION FORM

Employee's Name _____ Department (36X) _____

☐ **HIRE**

Position (36Y) _____ Shift: from _____ to _____

Employment Status (36E): ☐ regular ☐ part time ☐ on call Rate _____ Date of Hire (391): _____

TO BE COMPLETED BY PERSONNEL

Address		City	State	Zip

Social Security Number	Sex	Marital Status	EXEMPTIONS			EEOC 574
	☐M ☐F	☐Married ☐Single	Federal	State	City	

Birthdate 393	Review Date 39A	Language 22	Grade	Minor

☐ **STATUS CHANGE**

Effective Date _____

From	To
Department _____	_____
Position _____ Grade _____	_____ Grade _____
Rate _____	
Status: ☐ Regular ☐ Part Time ☐ On Call	Status: ☐ Regular ☐ Part Time ☐ On Call

☐ **VACATION** from _____ to _____ Needs Check By _____
(Hourly Only)

☐ **PERFORMANCE REVIEW** *(Appraisal form must be attached.)*

Rate: from _____ to _____ Effective Date _____

Date of Last Increase _____ Amount of Last Increase _____

☐ **TERMINATION**

Last Day Worked _____ Date of Termination (392) _____

Reason for Separation *(Check one and explain in comments.)*

Resignation
(36R-V)
1. ☐ Job Abandonment
2. ☐ Another Position
3. ☐ Leaving Locality
4. ☐ Return to School
5. ☐ Other
(36Q)

Discharge
(36R-I)
1. ☐ Broke House Rules
2. ☐ Absenteeism
3. ☐ Insubordination
4. ☐ Other
(36Q)

Miscellaneous
1. ☐ Cut-Back
2. ☐ Position Eliminated
3. ☐ Temporary Employment
4. ☐ Retired
5. ☐ Other

Rehire: ☐ Yes ☐ No ☐ Conditional *(Explain in comments)*

Comments: _____
_____
_____
_____
_____

The above action does not become effective until all signatures are affixed.

Dept. Head _____ Date _____ Div. Head _____ Date _____

Personnel _____ Date _____ Gen. Mgr. _____ Date _____

Form 5-6 Rev. 9/84   PERSONNEL COPY

Many companies have one form to serve a number of purposes. (Courtesy of Amway Grand Plaza Hotel, Grand Rapids, Michigan)

The staff of the human resources department represents the values, beliefs, and culture of the organization.

photocopied, dog-eared, or wrinkled. Forms that are seldom used, those that change regularly, and those with a lower visibility, such as in-house transmittals, can be handled in a less expensive manner.

A Resource for Everyone

Whose side is human resources department on? Clearly, the government and courts view it as part of management. Anything a human resources representative says to an employee may be legally interpreted as reflecting the position of the employer. In addition, managers see the department as the place to get help when dealing with problem employees.

However, the employees also perceive the human resources department as their representative, particularly in non-union properties. It's where they go when they have a complaint about management.

Each group has its own set of expectations, personal interests, and concerns. It's the job of the human resources department to get each to realize that the company's best interests embody the best interests of all. In that capacity, the human resources department is on everybody's side.

A human resources strategy is built around people. It conveys a feeling that reflects the company's personality. Even subtle differences between companies can become tremendous differences when they're the reason people choose to work for one company or another, to produce or not, to frown or to smile.

Developing the strategy that provides the right environment for people to grow in is the key to productivity. Remember the parable about the farmer who sows his seed, some falling on rock and some on the ground. Regardless of how good the farmer or the seed is, if the seed falls on rock, it won't grow. But in the right environment, even a fragile seed will take root and flower.

Key Terms

policy
procedure

Discussion Questions

1. If you were a general manager, what would you expect from your human resources department?

2. Why is the human resources department a good training ground for upper management positions?

3. What are some criteria that should be considered when designing the offices of a human resources department?

4. Why is it so important for the members of the human resources staff to be good role models?

5. What background and skills would you look for when hiring a director of human resources?

6. Why is the personnel policy and procedure manual considered one of the most important documents a hospitality company can have?

7. How can the human resources department be effective as a representative for both management and employees?

Glossary

A

AD HOC COMMITTEE

A committee set up for one specific purpose and disbanded when the purpose is carried out.

ADVISORY AUTHORITY

The type of authority exercised by a department that provides support and advice in an organization without becoming directly involved in operating procedures.

AFFIRMATIVE ACTION

A determination by an employer of the areas in which the ratio of employed workers in protected categories does not correspond to the ratios in the labor force in which recruiting is conducted, and the plan of action developed to correct the under-utilization.

AGE DISCRIMINATION IN EMPLOYMENT ACT

Federal law passed in 1967 to prohibit employment discrimination against people over the age of 40 (as amended in 1987).

ALIEN REGISTRATION RECEIPT CARD

A card issued by the Immigration and Naturalization Service that must be carried by any person who is not a citizen of the United States so that the person can reside in the United States. More commonly known as a green card (although it's no longer green).

ALTERNATIVE DISPUTE RESOLUTION COMMITTEE

A group of line and management employees who review disputes over employment issues (such as discipline, terminations, severance pay, and promotions) and arrive at a decision that's legally binding on both management and employees. In order for the committee's decisions to be legally binding, the agreement to abide by the committee's decisions must be a condition of employment.

ANNUAL PLANNING SESSION

A yearly meeting between manager and employee that involves an exchange of information about the company, the department, the job, and the work unit's goals for the coming year, but doesn't include a pay review.

ARBITRATION

A process used to settle a labor dispute between employer and union through the use of a third party (known as an arbitrator), whose decision may be binding if both employer and union have previously agreed to be bound by it.

AREA COST ALLOWANCE

A special wage adjustment made to compensate an employee while he or she lives and works in an area with a high cost of living.

ASSESSMENT CENTER PROGRAM

A method of selection, usually for supervisory and managerial candidates, in which participants demonstrate in realistic settings or simulations their ability to perform major managerial tasks.

AUTHORIZATION CARD

A card that, when signed by an employee, authorizes a union to represent the employee in any negotiations with the employer.

AUTOCRATIC MANAGEMENT

A management style in which the manager has unlimited and exclusive authority over all of his or her subordinates.

B

BARGAINING UNIT

A group of employees represented by a union, as determined by the National Labor Relations Board.

BEHAVIORAL INTERVIEW

An interviewing format based on identifying behavioral traits that contribute to success in a specific job and then tailoring questions to reveal those particular traits.

BENCHMARK JOB

A job that can be used for wage or other comparisons among different companies because it's a common job, its title and duties are acknowledged as being easily defined, stable, and similar in the surveyed companies, and a significant number of people work in that job. A wage survey usually uses only one benchmark job from each pay grade or skill level.

BFOQ

See **Bona Fide Occupational Qualification.**

BINDING ARBITRATION

A process used to settle a labor dispute between employer and union through the use of a third party whose decision must be accepted by both parties.

BLIND AD

Help-wanted advertising in which the name of the employer is not identified.

BONA FIDE OCCUPATIONAL QUALIFICATION (BFOQ)

A provision of the Civil Rights Act that allows an employer to hire people based on the need for a specific age, sex, religion, or national origin for the performance of the job.

BRAINSTORMING

A group approach to problem solving that encourages participants to think freely and creatively by placing more emphasis on quantity and variety of solutions than on quality or practicality.

BREACH OF CONTRACT

A violation of any of the terms of a spoken or written agreement between parties.

BREAK-OUT ROOMS

Small meeting rooms used in conjunction with a larger meeting room to allow participants to form smaller groups that can practice or confer simultaneously.

BUSINESS PLAN

An organizational plan that outlines how the company's marketing objectives will be achieved in terms of resources such as financing, materials, timetables, and measurement systems.

C

CAFETERIA BENEFIT PLAN

See **Flexible Benefit Plan.**

CALL-BACK LIST

A reference list kept by a manager that contains the names of potential employees, compiled from internal and external sources and former employees eligible for rehire.

CAREER PATHING

A program in which the manager assists the employee in planning the latter's career progress within the company, including a consideration of relevant strengths, weaknesses, and interests. Also called career planning.

CASE STUDY

A training technique that presents participants with a situation based on real life and allows them to consider possible solutions to the problems posed.

CENTRAL TENDENCY

In evaluations or appraisals, the tendency of the evaluator to rate all subjects as average.

CHILD LABOR LAWS

Federal and state legislation that deals with the employment of people under 18, outlining the jobs that are prohibited for them and the hours and conditions under which they may work.

CIVIL RIGHTS ACT

Federal legislation passed in an effort to deal with racial and sexual discrimination in the United States—most commonly, the landmark legislation enacted in 1964 and amended numerous times. Often used just to refer to the section of the Act known as Title VII, which prohibits discrimination in employment.

CLASS ACTION SUIT

A lawsuit brought on behalf of a group of people with a common interest or concern.

CLASSIFICATION SYSTEM

A system of establishing the relative value to the company of all of its jobs by placing them into pre-assigned pay grades.

CLOSED SHOP

The illegal arrangement that would exist if a candidate for employment had to be a member of a union before he or she could be hired.

COLLECTIVE BARGAINING AGREEMENT

The contract between the union and the employer that determines all work-related issues.

COMMUNICATION BOX

A communication program designed to encourage employees to submit their ideas, questions, and concerns to management for response and possible action. Sometimes called a hot-line or suggestion box.

COMMUNITY OF INTEREST

A test to determine which employees should be in a bargaining unit, based on whether they depend on each other and operate sufficiently independently of any other group of employees.

COMP-DAY PROGRAM

A program which gives an employee one day off for achieving a specified number of days of perfect attendance.

COMPRESSED WORK SCHEDULE

An adaptation of full-time work hours that enables an employee to work the equivalent of a standard workweek in less than the traditional five days.

COMPUTER INTERACTIVE INTERVIEW

A computerized interviewing technique in which the applicant reads a question on the monitor and responds on the keyboard. The computer program develops an applicant profile based on answers, response time, and other factors.

COMPUTER INTERACTIVE TRAINING PROGRAM

A form of self training in which the trainee reads information, questions, and feedback from the monitor and responds on the keyboard.

CONSTRUCTIVE DISCHARGE

The illegal termination of an employee by an employer who constructs, or arranges, a situation that forces the person to resign or be fired.

CONTINGENCY SEARCH

A recruiting search conducted by a private employment agency in which no fee is paid unless one of that firm's referrals is hired.

CORPORATE CULTURE

See **Organizational Culture.**

COST PARITY

A company's practice of keeping its labor costs approximately in line with industry standards.

COUNTER-OFFER

An offer to improve the existing terms of employment, extended to a worker by his or her current employer after the person gives notice of intent to accept a job with another employer.

CRAFT UNION

A union that restricts its membership to workers utilizing a particular skill or craft.

CREDIT REPORTING ACT

Federal legislation (1971) restricting the collection and dissemination of information about individuals, and giving individuals access to credit information about themselves once it has been made available to others.

CROSS-TRAINING

Teaching employees to fill the requirements of more than one position.

D

DECENTRALIZATION

The delegation of decision-making authority to the lowest possible level in an organization.

DECERTIFICATION

The process by which union members elect to remove a union as their representative.

DEPARTMENT TRAINER

Any employee in the department who conducts training activities that focus on operational procedures and skills.

DIRECT QUESTION

A question used to elicit a specific answer.

DOWNTIME

The period of time that begins when a position becomes vacant and lasts until the person hired to fill the opening attains the minimum expected performance level for the job.

DUES CHECKOFF

An arrangement in which the employer automatically deducts union dues from employees' pay and forwards them directly to the union.

E

EAP

See **Employee Assistance Program.**

ECONOMIC STRIKE

A strike used to exert economic pressure on a company during bargaining with the union.

EEO.1 REPORT

A report required of every employer who employs more than 100 people (or federal contractors with 50 or more employees and federal contracts of $50,000 or more) and which summarizes the number of people employed according to job categories, sex, and minority status.

EMPLOYEE ANNUAL REPORT

A yearly report prepared by the management of an organization to inform employees on areas of interest and concern to them, such as accomplishments of the past year, a financial review, and current company status.

EMPLOYEE ASSISTANCE PROGRAM (EAP)

A program set up to assist employees with any kind of personal problem, largely through referrals to the appropriate internal or external counseling or other support services. Costs of external services may be paid by the employee, paid by the company, shared, or covered under the company medical insurance plan.

EMPLOYEE POLYGRAPH PROTECTION ACT

Federal legislation enacted in 1988 to prohibit pre- and post-employment polygraph and lie detector testing, with limited exceptions.

EMPLOYEE REVIEW BOARD

A group of line and management employees who conduct their own independent investigation of a termination at the dismissed employee's request, then make a recommendation to top management.

EMPLOYMENT AT WILL

Originally, the philosophy that either the employer or the employee can terminate the employment arrangement at any time for any reason. Now more commonly used to refer to the idea that the employer can terminate the employee at any time for any reason.

EMPLOYMENT CONTRACT

An agreement, usually in writing, between the employer and employee, spelling out the terms and conditions of employment.

EMPLOYMENT LITIGATION

Legal action taken by a past or present employee in a civil court against an employer because of an event arising out of the employment relationship.

EMPLOYMENT REQUISITION

A standard form used to notify the company's recruiting coordinator that a position is or will soon be open and containing key information about the job, such as hours, compensation, duties, and skill requirements.

ENTITLEMENT

The philosophy that workers have certain work-related rights to which they are automatically entitled, regardless of performance, such as the right to keep a job, to be promoted, or to receive certain wage increases.

EQUAL EMPLOYMENT OPPORTUNITY COMMISSION (EEOC)

Federal agency established by the Civil Rights Act to administer and enforce the Act.

EQUAL PAY ACT

1963 federal legislation requiring that pay differentials for substantially similar jobs in the same establishment shall not be based on the sex of the employee.

ERGONOMICS

An approach to the design of work environment and equipment that recognizes the mental and physical needs of the worker to perform productively in comfort and security. Sometimes known as human factors engineering.

EXIT INTERVIEW

A meeting between a terminating employee and a company representative (usually someone other than the employee's immediate supervisor) to discuss any aspect of the termination, the job, and the company.

EXTERNSHIP PROGRAM

See **Internship Program.**

F

FAIR LABOR STANDARDS ACT

Federal legislation (1938) to regulate pay and hours worked, including overtime, deductions, and the employment of minors. More commonly known as the Wage and Hour Law.

FAST TRACK PROGRAM

A special management training program designed to move high-potential trainees more quickly.

FEDERAL WAGE GARNISHMENT LAW

Part of the federal Consumer Credit Protection Act passed in 1968 to limit the amount of an employee's disposable earnings that may be garnished in any one week and to prohibit the dismissal of an employee because of a garnishment for any one indebtedness.

FEEDER JOBS

Positions from which workers can be promoted or transferred into key positions.

FINAL WARNING

The final step in a system of progressive discipline; the last written warning notice issued to an employee before termination, to put the person on notice that any further infraction will result in termination.

FIXED RATE

A system of paying wages under which every worker doing the same job gets the same rate and the same increase, regardless of skill, effort, or length of service.

FLEXIBLE BENEFIT PLAN

A benefit plan which offers a number of options from which employees may choose. Also known as a cafeteria benefit plan.

FLEXTIME

A system of scheduling work hours that permits employees to vary their times of starting and ending work while still working certain core hours during which all workers for that shift must be on the job. Also called flexible work hours.

FORECASTING

See **Labor Forecasting.**

FUNCTIONAL AUTHORITY

A restricted form of operational authority given to a staff department over a specific function.

FUNCTIONAL INTEGRATION

Employees working across departmental lines on a regular basis.

G

GENERAL COMPANY ORIENTATION

A formal program presented by an employer to introduce the organization's mission and values to employees, usually conducted two to four weeks after hiring.

GOOD FAITH

Honesty and genuineness in dealing with others or in the effort to comply with the intent of a law.

GREEN CARD

See **Alien Registration Receipt Card.**

GREEN-CIRCLED EMPLOYEES

Employees who are below the pay range for their jobs and will thus usually require accelerated salary reviews and increases.

GRIEVANCE PROCEDURE

A published company procedure that spells out the course of action for employees who feel that they've been treated unjustly by the employer.

GUARANTEE PERIOD

A specified length of time negotiated by an employer and a private employment agency, during which the agency will provide a free replacement or fee refund if a referred hired employee leaves the employer.

H

HALO EFFECT

The incorrect assumption on the part of an evaluator that, because an individual has one or two outstanding traits, all of the factors being rated are good.

HAZARD COMMUNICATION RULE

Identification and information standards set by OSHA and required of every employer to ensure that workers are aware of any hazardous materials to which they may be exposed in the workplace and that they're trained in handling and precautionary procedures.

HIGH-COMMISSION EMPLOYEES

Workers who earn more than one-and-a-half times the current minimum wage and more than half of their total income from commissions. Such employees are exempt by federal Wage and Hour Law from eligibility for overtime pay.

HIRING PERIOD

The period of time which starts when a job offer is extended and lasts until the new employee has acquired most of the basic skills and knowledge needed to do the job.

HOT-LINE

See **Communication Box.**

HOUSE RULE

Any published, company-wide rule for which violation can result in immediate discharge.

HUMAN FACTORS ENGINEERING

See **Ergonomics.**

HUMAN RESOURCES STRATEGY

The long-term, systematic approach to the development and maintenance of all the elements that affect the organizational culture of the workplace, so that all the elements support each other and the goals of the company.

I

IMMIGRATION REFORM AND CONTROL ACT

Federal legislation (1986) requiring employers to confirm each employee's citizenship status and right to work in the United States.

INDUSTRIAL UNION

A union that restricts its membership to workers from a particular industry.

INJUNCTION

A court order used to compel a person or organization to perform or refrain from performing a particular act.

INTERNSHIP PROGRAM

An arrangement between a school and an employer in which students are given time off from school to work and obtain actual job experience, often while they earn school credit. Sometimes called externship program.

INTERVIEW EVALUATION FORM

A form used by an interviewer/evaluator to determine whether a job applicant's qualifications meet the requirements of the job.

J

JOB AID

A brief, at-hand reminder of the key steps of a job procedure.

JOB ANALYSIS

A system of breaking a job down into various elements—including the job's title, department, purpose, specific duties and responsibilities, working conditions, supervision received and exercised, and minimum skill and experience requirements—for the purpose of evaluating and ranking the job to set a pay rate for it.

JOB ENRICHMENT

Changing a job by adding motivational factors—such as responsibility, decision-making, variety, and challenge—to the job itself.

JOB EVALUATION

A system of ranking all of the jobs in an organization according to their relative value or contribution to the company, for the purpose of establishing pay grades and rates within the company.

JOB ORIENTATION

The period of time devoted to teaching a new employee the basic elements of the job, including the skills and information required to perform the job.

JOB OUTLINE

A set of written guidelines, prepared by a trainer as a training aid, containing information about the purpose and accountability of the job being taught and a breakdown of the elements and standards of the job.

JOB POSTING

A program for advertising job openings within the company.

JOB PROFILE

A brief description of a job, specifying the job's hours, compensation, duties, requirements, and any other key information.

JOB SAFETY ACT

See **Occupational Safety and Health Act.**

JOB SHARING

An arrangement in which two or more part-time employees share the responsibilities of one full-time job. Also called job pairing and job splitting.

JOB TASK LIST

A list identifying all of the key duties of a job in the order of their importance.

JURISDICTIONAL STRIKE

A work stoppage by members of disputing unions that are trying to determine which union will represent which employees, or what work is to be done by which union's members. Illegal in some states.

JUST CAUSE TERMINATION

Discharge of an employee as the result of willful and wanton misconduct that conflicts with the company's best interests.

L

LABOR FORECASTING

Using business trends and volume as well as turnover and other labor statistics to anticipate job vacancies.

LABOR-MANAGEMENT RELATIONS ACT

Federal legislation passed in 1947 to amend and modify the National Labor Relations Act of 1935, including an intent to modify what was perceived as a pro-union bias in the earlier Act. Also known as the Taft-Hartley Act.

LEAD TIME

The amount of time required to hire the best available employee for a position.

LEARNER CONTROLLED INSTRUCTION

Any training program that is used to teach a single trainee working largely without an instructor and setting his or her own pace. The training is usually broken down into steps with feedback given as to the learner's progress. Also called self instruction.

LIGHT DUTY

Work that has been modified from the worker's normal job description to allow for the person's reduced capacity owing to illness or injury.

LINE DEPARTMENT

A department directly involved in providing the service or product for which the company is in business. Also called operating department.

LOCKOUT

An employer's refusal to let employees come to work until a labor dispute is settled.

M

MANAGEMENT TRAINEE PROGRAM

A training program designed to provide a specific set of management experiences in order to help bridge the gap between participants' schooling or other job experiences and the new work environment.

MARKETING PLAN

An organizational plan to identify the company's customers and define marketing objectives.

MARKET SATURATION POINT

The point at which supply of a product or service meets or exceeds consumer demand.

MARKET SEGMENTATION

Identifying and targeting a small and individualized group of customers to whom a highly specialized service or product is offered, thus isolating one segment of the market.

MATERIAL SAFETY DATA SHEET (MSDS)

A sheet (or sheets) of paper containing information about a hazardous substance used by employees to tell them how to handle and use it safely. Sometimes called a safety data sheet.

MEDIATION

A process used to resolve a stalemate between union and management negotiators, in which a third party (known as a mediator) assists by getting the parties to arrive at a voluntary compromise.

MENTOR

A manager within the company who serves as friend, advisor, confidant, and advocate for a new managerial trainee or promotee; preferably not the new manager's immediate supervisor.

MINIMUM WAGE

Set by federal and state law, the lowest rate which a worker can be paid unless specifically exempt by law.

N

NATIONAL INSTITUTE FOR OCCUPATIONAL SAFETY AND HEALTH (NIOSH)

A federal agency whose primary purpose is to carry out research and recommend occupational safety and health standards.

NATIONAL LABOR RELATIONS ACT (NLRA)

Landmark federal legislation passed in 1935 to establish and protect the rights of employees to form labor unions and participate in collective bargaining efforts with employers. The Act also established the National Labor Relations Board. Also known as the Wagner Act.

NATIONAL LABOR RELATIONS BOARD (NLRB)

Independent federal agency created by the National Labor Relations Act in 1935 to administer and enforce the provisions of the Act, and subsequently the provisions of the Labor-Management Relations Act of 1947.

NEEDS ANALYSIS

A systematic consideration by a manager of a work unit's training needs and their order of priority.

NEGLIGENT EVALUATION

The failure of an employer to express dissatisfaction with an employee's work prior to the employee's dismissal for poor job performance.

NETWORKING

A manager's use of personal contacts, such as friends, business associates, school officials, purveyors, and trade associations, to assist in developing potential applicants for a job opening.

NEW MANAGEMENT PREPARATION CHECKLIST

A form used to list all of the steps necessary to prepare adequately for the arrival of a newly hired manager.

NEW MANAGER'S JOB ORIENTATION PROCEDURE

A checklist of the responsibilities each manager has during a new manager's orientation, shown by job title.

NORMS

The common attitudes, opinions, and feelings that determine the actions of a group of people.

NO SOLICITATION STATEMENT

A company's published policy to prohibit anyone from soliciting its employees in the workplace.

O

OCCUPATIONAL SAFETY AND HEALTH ACT

Federal legislation enacted in 1970 to provide safe and healthful working conditions for all workers by establishing standards, requiring regular inspections and recordkeeping, and creating policing agencies, including the Occupational Safety and Health Administration. Also known as the Williams-Steiger Act and the Job Safety Act.

OCCUPATIONAL SAFETY AND HEALTH ADMINISTRATION (OSHA)

An agency within the U.S. Department of Labor to establish occupational safety and health standards, set up regulations, conduct inspections, issue citations, and propose penalties for noncompliance.

OCCUPATIONAL SAFETY AND HEALTH REVIEW COMMISSION (OSHRC)

Independent federal agency that holds hearings on employer appeals of citations and penalties issued by OSHA.

ON-THE-JOB TRAINING (OJT)

Training that takes place at the job site during working hours.

OPEN-DOOR POLICY

A management practice of ready accessibility to any employee who wishes to speak to the manager.

OPERATING DEPARTMENT

See **Line Department.**

ORGANIZATIONAL CULTURE

The learned attitudes, behaviors, and traditions that make up the human environment of the workplace and determine how work is done. Also called corporate culture.

ORGANIZATIONAL STRIKE

A strike to try to compel the company to recognize a union.

ORIENTATION

See **General Company Orientation** and **Job Orientation.**

OUTPLACEMENT FIRM

A firm hired by an employer to assist a former upper-level manager in finding a new position after an involuntary termination.

OUT-PROCESSING

The steps conducted by an employer on an employee's last working day to satisfy all company and legal requirements with respect to the termination.

OVERHEAD QUESTION

A question directed to a group of people to initiate a discussion.

OVERTIME

A pay rate defined by federal law as being one-and-a-half times the regular pay rate, and which must be paid after 40 hours of work in one week, unless the employee is exempt by law.

P

PAPER TRAIL

The written documentation kept to justify any employment-related decision.

PARITY

The equivalence in ratio of the composition of a company's work force and the labor market from which the company recruits, with respect to workers in protected categories.

PARTICIPATIVE MANAGEMENT

A management style which involves employees in setting objectives and making decisions.

PATTERNED INTERVIEW

An interviewing format that involves asking the same questions in the same order to every applicant.

PAY FOR PERFORMANCE

A system of paying wages based on individual work performance, usually within established guidelines.

PAY GRADE

The range of pay rates, from minimum to maximum for a job or class of jobs; all jobs with the same starting rate of pay will fall into the same pay grade.

PAY REVIEW

A meeting held between manager and employee solely for the purpose of advising the employee of the amount of his or her pay increase, if any, and the justification for the decision.

PERFORMANCE DISCUSSION

A meeting held between manager and employee solely for the purpose of addressing a work performance problem.

PERFORMANCE STANDARD

An observable, measurable benchmark work standard that can be used in determining whether a job is well done.

PERK

See **Perquisite.**

PERQUISITE

A privilege or benefit provided to an employee in addition to the regular compensation package provided to all full-time employees. Commonly called a perk.

PERSONAL INTERVIEW

An unstructured, face-to-face conversation between the job applicant and the interviewer.

PERSONNEL FILE

Any records concerning a worker used in making employment-related decisions, usually kept for all workers in a central location such as the human resources department.

PERSONNEL PROCESSING CHECKLIST

A form used by the human resources department listing all of the key employment areas common to workers in every department. It helps ensure that these common areas are covered with every new employee.

PICKETING

The posting by a union of its members at the company site to notify the public that a labor dispute exists.

POINT FACTOR ANALYSIS

A system of establishing the relative value to a company of all of its jobs by assigning point values to elements that can be standardized and objectively analyzed—such as skill, effort, responsibility, and working conditions—based on the extent to which each element is required.

POLICY

A guiding principle used to apply a value or goal to a practical course of action in a company's everyday operations.

PRIMARY JOB REQUIREMENT

A job requirement that must be met in order for the job to be performed successfully.

PROBATIONARY PERIOD

A trial period, usually one to three months, during which employees are observed to determine whether they meet job requirements.

PROCEDURE

A company's detailed instructions for carrying out a specific company policy in everyday operations through a practical course of action.

PRO-EMPLOYEE STATEMENT

A company's published policy that it is a non-union facility and doesn't feel that a union is needed.

PROGRAMMED INSTRUCTION MANUAL

A self-training manual that is broken down into steps, each of which must be completed before the next is undertaken.

PROGRESSIVE DISCIPLINE

A system of discipline that progresses to sterner measures with repeated infractions.

PROJECT TEAM

A temporary team, or committee, created for a special purpose and dissolved when the project is completed.

PUNITIVE DAMAGES

In employment litigation, an amount of money awarded to a plaintiff in excess of or addition to actual damages, where the plaintiff is a past or present employee who has shown that the employer's conduct was extreme and outrageous beyond the bounds of all decency.

R

RANKING PROCESS

A system of establishing the relative value to a company of all of its jobs by simply having managers compare the jobs within their respective departments.

RECRUITING COORDINATOR

The person responsible for coordinating all aspects of employment recruiting for the company.

RED-CIRCLED EMPLOYEES

Employees who will require some separate attention from the company because they've reached the top of the pay range for their jobs.

RELAY QUESTION

A group discussion technique used to pass along a participant's question and involve more group members in its consideration.

RETAINED SEARCH

A recruiting search conducted by a private employment agency in which a fee is paid regardless of whether the job opening is filled.

RHETORICAL QUESTION

A question used to provoke thought rather than a specific reply.

RIGHT-TO-WORK LAW

Legislation passed by some states to allow each employee of a unionized company to choose to join the union or not.

ROLE-PLAYING

A group training technique that allows participants to assume roles and act out parts in a realistic situation away from the job site.

ROUND-TABLE DISCUSSION

See **Speak-Up Meeting.**

S

SCIENTIFIC MANAGEMENT

A management philosophy developed by Frederick Winslow Taylor in the late 1800s to increase worker productivity by reducing each job to its simplest skill level and having each worker perform one task repeatedly. Sometimes called Taylorism.

SECONDARY BOYCOTT

A strike of a company by union members who have no grievance with the company, but strike because the company is doing business with an employer with whom they do have a grievance; not generally permitted under the NLRA.

SECONDARY JOB REQUIREMENTS

A list of desirable job requirements preferred in an applicant, but not necessarily needed in order for the job to be performed adequately.

SECOND INJURY FUND

A fund provided by some states to limit a current employer's workers' compensation liability if an employee suffers aggravation of a pre-existing condition in the course of the current employment.

SELF-ANALYSIS FORM

A form designed to assist an employee in taking stock of his or her own work-related strengths, weaknesses, interests, and goals.

SELF INSTRUCTION

See **Learner Controlled Instruction.**

SEVERANCE PAY

Pay over and above what the employee has earned, given at the time of termination.

SHOP STEWARD

A company employee and union member who represents the interests of other employees in grievances with management.

SIMULATION

A group training technique that allows participants to assume roles and work through a situation in a more realistic environment than that of the role-playing exercise, usually at the actual worksite.

SITDOWN STRIKE

A strike in which employees stop working but don't walk off the job; not generally permitted under the NLRA.

SLOWDOWN STRIKE

A strike in which employees intentionally slow down their work but don't walk off the job; not generally permitted under the NLRA.

SPAN OF CONTROL

The number of people that one person can manage effectively.

SPEAK-UP MEETING

A meeting between top management and a group of line employees to discuss any topic the participants wish without the employees' supervisors being present. Also called a round-table discussion.

STAFF DEPARTMENT

A department that exists to provide support and advice to line or operating departments, and which is not directly involved in providing the service or product for which the company is in business.

STAFFING GUIDE

A system used to establish the number of workers needed.

STATEMENT OF PHILOSOPHY

A company's formal statement of its purpose and the values with which it will operate.

STORYTELLING

A process of collecting and recounting a company's traditions and legends to reinforce values and the organizational culture.

STRIKE

Refusal of employees to work because of a labor dispute.

STRUCTURAL UNEMPLOYMENT

The situation that exists when the skills of the worker don't match the skills required by available jobs.

SUCCESSION PLANNING

The identification by the employer of key positions within the company and of employees who might eventually be able to fill those positions, and the subsequent planning for training, promotions, and replacements to keep the succession process moving.

SUGGESTION BOX

A communication program set up by a company to solicit employees' work-related suggestions.

SUSPENSE FILE

A manager's trace or reminder file for keeping track of pending activities, containing two sets of folders—one set numbered 1 through 31 for the days of the month, and the other labeled with the 12 months. Each day and at the beginning of each month, the appropriate folders are checked for previously placed reminder notices of any items that are due to be followed up.

SYMPATHY STRIKE

A strike by union members who don't have a grievance with the employer, but refuse to cross the picket lines of striking employees who do have a grievance with the employer.

T

TAFT-HARTLEY ACT

See **Labor-Management Relations Act.**

TAYLORISM

See **Scientific Management.**

TIP CREDIT

The amount earned by an employee in tips and included in the calculation of the employee's wages to establish a minimum wage base that meets or exceeds the legal requirement.

TITLE VII

The section of the Civil Rights Act that prohibits employment discrimination on the basis of race, sex, religion, or national origin.

TRAINING DIRECTOR

An employee working in the human resources department who is responsible for the administration and control of the company's training function and budget.

TRAINING PLAN

An outline prepared by a group trainer for his or her own use in planning and conducting a training session or any other informational group meeting.

TUITION REIMBURSEMENT PROGRAM

Employer-provided financial assistance toward an employee's further education.

TURNOVER

A method of measuring the rate at which a work unit loses workers.

2 × 6 RULE

A rule of thumb for deciding how large a viewing screen to use for slides or films, based on the size of the audience and meeting room: the width should be half the distance from the first row of seats to the screen, and the height should be one-sixth of the distance from the last row of seats to the screen.

TYPE 1 RECORDS

Employee documents containing information that could identify the employee and that has been or could be used in connection with the employee's qualifications for employment, promotion, transfer, raises, or disciplinary action. Generally kept in a centrally located personnel file.

TYPE 2 RECORDS

Employee documents containing information that should not be used in evaluating the employee—such as medical records or I-9 forms—and that should not be kept in the employee's personnel file.

TYPE 3 RECORDS

Documents pertaining solely to investigations of employees' criminal misconduct perceived to be harmful to the employer.

U

UNEMPLOYMENT COMPENSATION

A program administered by each state to provide income to people who aren't currently working but who are eligible and able to work.

UNFAIR LABOR PRACTICE STRIKE

A strike used to protest alleged violations of the NLRA.

UNION SHOP

An arrangement between the employer and union requiring all employees to join the union.

UNITY OF COMMAND

The commonly-accepted organizational principle that each employee should be accountable to only one boss.

V

VALIDATION

A process used to establish that a test measures the essential elements required for job success, that it won't screen out a disproportionately high number of minority or female job applicants, and that the test results are free from distortion by personal bias as they're used by the evaluator.

VERBAL WARNING

The first step in a system of progressive discipline. A correction or reprimand that is spoken rather than administered in writing, although keeping a written record of the discussion in the departmental file is usually advisable.

VETERANS REEMPLOYMENT ACT

Federal legislation passed in 1942 and subsequently amended to ensure that veterans and current members of the military services don't lose their civilian jobs or seniority because of their military service obligations.

W

WAGE AND HOUR DIVISION

The division of the United States Department of Labor that administers and enforces the regulations of the Fair Labor Standards Act of 1938.

WAGE AND HOUR LAW

See **Fair Labor Standards Act.**

WAGE SURVEY

A poll taken by an employer to obtain information about the pay rates and practices of other (usually similar) companies in the area in which recruiting is conducted.

WAGNER ACT

See **National Labor Relations Act.**

WEIGHTED EVALUATION FORM

A rating form on which certain factors are given more importance (or weight) than others. The higher values assigned to some factors may be consistent on every form, or value assignment may be controlled by the evaluator.

WELLNESS PROGRAM

A company-sponsored program aimed at illness prevention through such activities as regular physicals for employees, health education, and exercise classes.

WILDCAT STRIKE

A strike conducted by union members without the approval of their local union; not generally permitted under the NLRA.

WORKER ELASTICITY

The ability of a worker to move among different jobs or among different work areas, units, or facilities.

WORKERS' COMPENSATION

Payment of an employee's medical bills and some portion of income by the employer because of a work-related injury or illness, as provided by state law.

WRITTEN WARNING

An intermediate step in a system of progressive discipline; the written documentation that accompanies a formal disciplinary meeting, and which should be signed by both manager and employee. A copy is placed in the employee's personnel file.

Bibliography

Albrecht, Karl, and Zemke, Ron. *Service America! Doing Business in the New Economy.* Homewood, Ill.: Dow Jones-Irwin, 1985.

Blake, Robert R., and Mouton, Jane Srygley. *The New Managerial Grid.* Houston, Tex.: Gulf Publishing, 1978.

Blake, Robert R., Mouton, Jane Srygley, and Allen, Robert L. *Spectacular Teamwork: How to Develop the Leadership Skills for Team Success.* New York: Wiley, 1987.

Bolles, Richard Nelson. *What Color Is Your Parachute?* Berkeley, Calif.: Ten Speed Press, 1984.

Convention Liaison Manual. 3rd ed. Washington, D.C.: Convention Liaison Council, 1980.

Coulson, Robert. *The Termination Handbook.* New York: The Free Press, 1981.

Deal, Terrence E., and Kennedy, Allan A. *Corporate Cultures: The Rites and Rituals of Corporate Life.* Reading, Mass.: Addison-Wesley, 1982.

Eisen, Jerry M. *Reducing Employee Turnover.* East Lansing, Mich.: Educational Institute of the American Hotel & Motel Association, 1982.

Ellis, Raymond C., Jr., and the Security Committee of AH&MA. *Security and Loss Prevention Management.* East Lansing, Mich.: Educational Institute of the American Hotel & Motel Association, 1986.

Famularo, Joseph J., Ed. *Handbook of Human Resources Administration.* 2nd ed. New York: McGraw-Hill, 1986.

Ferry, T. S. *Readings in Accident Investigation: Examples of the Scope, Depth and Sources.* Springfield, Ill.: Thomas, 1984.

Forrest, Lewis C., Jr. *Training for the Hospitality Industry.* 2nd ed. East Lansing, Mich.: Educational Institute of the American Hotel & Motel Association, 1989.

Gordon, Thomas. *T.E.T.—Teacher Effectiveness Training.* New York: McKay, 1974.

Handbook for Employers: Instructions for Completing Form I-9 (Employment Eligibility Verification Form). Chicago, Ill.: Commerce Clearing House, 1987.

Harris, Philip R. *New World, New Ways, New Management.* New York: AMACOM, 1983.

Henderson, Richard I. *Compensation Management: Rewarding Performance.* 4th ed. Reston, Va.: Reston, 1985.

Herzberg, Frederick. *The Managerial Choice: To Be Efficient and To Be Human.* 2nd ed., revised. Salt Lake City, Utah: Olympus, 1982.

Hocker, Joyce L., and Wilmot, William W. *Interpersonal Conflict.* Dubuque, Iowa: Brown, 1978.

Hughes, Charles L. *Making Unions Unnecessary.* New York: Executive Enterprises, 1976.

Hughes, Charles L., and Flowers, Vincent S. *Value System Analysis*. Dallas, Tex.: Center for Values Research, 1982.

——. "Why Employees Stay Is More Critical Than Why They Leave." *Personnel Journal*. Oct. 1987.

Johnson, Robert G. *The Appraisal Interview Guide*. New York: Warner Books, 1985.

Josefowitz, Natasha. *You're the Boss! A Guide to Managing People with Understanding and Effectiveness*. New York: Warner Books, 1985.

Kellogg, Marion S. *What to Do about Performance Appraisal*. New York: American Management Association, 1965.

King, Patricia. *Performance Planning and Appraisal: A How-to Book for Managers*. New York: McGraw-Hill, 1984.

Lipset, Seymour Martin, Ed. *Unions in Transition: Entering the Second Century*. San Francisco: Institute for Contemporary Studies, 1986.

Lopez, Felix M. *Personnel Interviewing, Theory and Practice*. 2nd ed. New York: McGraw-Hill, 1975.

Mager, Robert F., and Pipe, Peter. *Analyzing Performance Problems or "You Really Oughta Wanna."* Belmont, Calif.: Fearon Publishers/Lear Siegler, 1970.

Mandell, Milton M. *The Selection Process: Choosing the Right Man for the Right Job*. New York: AMACOM, 1964.

Marcus, Stanley. *Quest for the Best*. New York: Viking Press, 1979.

Marting, Elizabeth, Finley, Robert E., and Ward, Ann, Eds. *Effective Communication on the Job*. Rev. ed. New York: American Management Association, 1963.

Maslow, Abraham H. *Motivation and Personality*. 2nd ed. New York: Harper & Row, 1970.

McCaffery, Robert M. *Managing the Employee Benefits Program*. Rev. ed. New York: AMACOM, 1983.

McDermott, Albert L., and Glasgow, Fredrick J. *Federal Wage and Hour Standards for the Hotel-Motel and Restaurant Industries*. Washington, D.C.: American Hotel & Motel Association, 1983.

McGill, Michael E. *Organization Development for Operating Managers*. New York: AMACOM, 1977.

McGregor, Douglas. *The Human Side of Enterprise*. New York: McGraw-Hill, 1960.

Mills, Daniel Quinn. *Labor-Management Relations*. 3rd ed. New York: McGraw-Hill, 1986.

Miner, John B. *People Problems: The Executive Answer Book*. New York: Random House, 1985.

Morgan, Henry H., and Cogger, John W. *The Interviewer's Manual*. New York: Psychological Corporation, 1975.

Naisbitt, John, and Aburdene, Patricia. *Re-Inventing the Corporation: Transforming Your Job and Your Company for the New Information Society*. New York: Warner Books, 1985.

National Restaurant Association. "Food Service and the Labor Shortage." *NRA Current Issues Report*. Jan. 1986.

——. *A Primer on How to Recruit, Hire, and Retain Employees*. Washington, D.C.: National Restaurant Association, 1987.

——. *Safety Operations Manual*. Washington, D.C.: National Restaurant Association, 1981.

Ouchi, William. *Theory Z: How American Business Can Meet the Japanese Challenge*. Reading, Mass.: Addison-Wesley, 1981.

Peskin, Dean B. *The Doomsday Job: The Behavioral Anatomy of Turnover*. New York: AMACOM, 1973.

Peters, Thomas, and Austin, Nancy. *A Passion for Excellence: The Leadership Difference*. New York: Random House, 1985.

Potter, Beverly A. *Changing Performance on the Job: Behavioral Techniques for Managers*. New York: AMACOM, 1980.

Stokes, Arch. *The Collective Bargaining Handbook for Hotels, Restaurants and Institutions.* Boston: CBI, 1981.

——. *The Equal Opportunity Handbook for Hotels, Restaurants and Institutions.* Boston: CBI, 1981.

——. *The Wage and Hour Handbook for Hotels, Restaurants and Institutions.* Boston: CBI, 1981.

U.S. Department of Labor. Bureau of Labor Statistics. *Recordkeeping Guidelines for Occupational Injuries and Illness.* Washington, D.C.: Government Printing Office, 1986.

——. Employment Standards Administration. Wage and Hour Division. WH Publication 1209, *Equal Pay for Equal Work under the Fair Labor Standards Act.*

——. WH Publication 1223, *Employment of Full-Time Students at Submininum Wage.*

——. WH Publication 1261, *Records to be Kept by Employers under the Fair Labor Standards Act of 1938, as Amended.*

——. WH Publication 1262, *Regulations, Part 778: Interpretive Bulletin on Overtime Compensation.*

——. WH Publication 1281, *Regulations, Part 541: Defining the Terms 'Executive,' 'Administrative,' 'Professional,' and 'Outside Salesman.'*

——. WH Publication 1306, *Hotels and Motels under the Fair Labor Standards Act.*

——. WH Publication 1312, *Interpretive Bulletin, Part 785: Hours Worked under the Fair Labor Standards Act of 1938, as Amended.*

——. WH Publication 1330, *Child Labor Requirements in Nonagricultural Occupations.*

——. Occupational Safety and Health Administration. OSHA 3084 (revised), *Chemical Hazard Communication.*

U.S. Department of the Treasury. Internal Revenue Service. Publication 572, *General Business Credits.*

——. Publication 906, *Jobs and Research Credits.*

Work in America: Report of a Special Task Force to the Secretary of Health, Education, and Welfare. Cambridge, Mass.: MIT Press, 1978.

Yate, Martin John. *Hiring the Best: A Manager's Guide to Effective Interviewing.* Boston: Bob Adams, 1987.

Index